D1528990

The Unity of Christ

The Unity of Christ

Continuity and Conflict in Patristic Tradition

Christopher A. Beeley

Yale

UNIVERSITY PRESS

NEW HAVEN AND LONDON

Published with assistance from the foundation established in memory of Philip Hamilton McMillan of the Class of 1894, Yale College.

Yale University Press books may be purchased in quantity for educational, business, or promotional use. For information, please e-mail sales.press@yale.edu (U.S. office) or sales@yaleup.co.uk (U.K. office).

Set in Fournier MT type by IDS Infotech Ltd., Chandigarh, India.
Printed in the United States of America.

Library of Congress Cataloging-in-Publication Data

Beeley, Christopher A.
The unity of Christ : continuity and conflict in patristic tradition / Christopher A. Beeley.
p. cm.
Includes bibliographical references and index.
ISBN 978–0–300–17862–3 (cloth : alk. paper)   1. Fathers of the church.
2. Theology, Doctrinal—History—Early church, ca. 30–600.
3. Church history—Primitive and early church, ca. 30–600.   I. Title.
BR67.B377 2012
273'.1—dc23
2011046032

A catalogue record for this book is available from the British Library.

This paper meets the requirements of ANSI/NISO Z39.48–1992 (Permanence of Paper).
10 9 8 7 6 5 4 3 2 1

There are some authors who departed this life as catholics . . . ; yet they either have not been understood, or, weak as human beings are, they lacked the ability to penetrate obscure matters with a sharp mind. By mistaking a semblance of truth for the truth itself, they have given presumptuous and rash people the opportunity to spawn some heresy and set it loose. But that isn't surprising, since even from the canonical scriptures . . . many have produced harmful teachings that have severed the unity of communion.

—St. Augustine, *De catechizandis rudibus* 8.12.6–7

Contents

Preface

No time in history was at once more foundational, and yet so deeply divisive, for the development of Christianity than late antiquity (200–800 CE). During the patristic era—so named for the great fathers and mothers of the early church, the *patres*—church leaders, theologians, monks, and laity set in place the basic elements of Eastern and Western Christianity and many features of the wider culture as well. By the end of the period, the catholic or orthodox faith was solidly rooted in the Roman empire and its successors, and it was prominent in many places beyond the imperial borders, as Christian faithful began to face the pressure of Muslim invasions. Yet what may appear to be the golden age of the early church was also a time of conflict and division, marked by heated debates, excommunications, and the fragmentation of Christianity into rival churches—Nicene and Arian; Chalcedonian (Byzantine, Slavic, and Russian), Non-Chalcedonian (Oriental Orthodox), and Nestorian; Donatist and Catholic—and eventually the Great Schism between Eastern and Western Christendom.

At the heart of this formative process was the drive to identify the central beliefs, practices, and authorities of the faith. Long before the reign of Constantine—beginning, in fact, in the New Testament period— apostles and other church leaders found it necessary to articulate the true faith, both to provide guidance and strength for the faithful and to define Christian truth against its various rivals. This constructive and polemical enterprise involved more than substantive teaching alone. As they defined the faith, church leaders had to determine which theological and ecclesiastical authorities should serve as a basis for their beliefs, and how those authorities were to be interpreted. In other words, they had to define what constitutes authentic Christian tradition.

The nature of Christian tradition has been contested for centuries, beginning in the patristic period itself. The authority of particular theologians and church councils, such as the Council of Nicaea in 325, took decades, and in some cases centuries, to establish, through a process of further doctrinal debate and definition. In addition to the work of theological reception and interpretation, and the competing ecclesiastical and political agendas that often came into play, scholars in the modern period have only gradually secured access to key sources. A critical Greek edition of the great Byzantine theologian Maximus Confessor, for example, did not appear until the 1980s; the set of orations by Gregory of Nazianzus, one of the three pillars of Eastern Orthodoxy, appeared in English translation only in 2003; and scholars have been systematically studying the full range of Augustine's work for just a few decades. Even so, patristic sources have continued to hold great authority in many churches and in seminal works of modern theology, from the Trinitarian revival fostered by Karl Barth and Karl Rahner and the *ressourcement* of early sources that led to the Second Vatican Council to a surge of new interest in early and medieval church history across denominational lines.

The aim of this book is to present a new account of the unity and complexity of patristic tradition. It offers a new "map" of what proved to be the most central concern of the period, namely, the definition and confession of who Jesus Christ is and what he accomplished—or, in technical terms, the development of orthodox Christology. Scholars in recent decades have given a great deal of attention to recovering the authentic teaching of "heretics," and in some cases the heretics have turned out to be at least as "orthodox" as the historical winners were. I will be doing some of that here—with Origen, Apollinarius, and especially Eusebius of Caesarea—but my chief interest lies in the other direction. I am especially concerned to bring out the complexities, and at times the the unrecognized conflicts, that exist within the orthodox fold. Only by critically reassessing both the winners and losers of church history is it possible to identify where the real theological continuities lie, and so to tell an accurate story of the church's life.

I have organized the book around three key subjects: one theological, one procedural, and one personal. Theologically, it focuses on the unity of Jesus Christ, or the way in which patristic theologians understood Christ to be a single, divine-human figure. By concentrating on a central tenet of the faith, we will be able to make detailed comparisons with some accuracy, and to make sense of an otherwise bewildering complexity of material. In terms of ecclesiastical procedure, the book describes how theologians and church councils constructed the notion of authoritative theological tradition, by choosing which earlier theologians to follow and deciding how to interpret them. Along the way, we will gain insight as well into the pervasive influence that certain outstanding teachers came to have over later developments: Origen of Alexandria above all, and in the later centuries Gregory of Nazianzus, Augustine of Hippo, and Cyril of Alexandria.

Given the prominent role that patristic tradition has played in the Christian churches, it goes without saying that the figures and events treated here are (for the most part) well known and much studied. Beginning students of early Christianity often wonder, what more could possibly be discovered about this familiar territory? Quite a lot, in fact, if we look closely with fresh eyes. In order to draw a clearer map of patristic theological tradition, I have given lengthy treatments of those theologians whom I reinterpret in significant ways: especially Origen, Eusebius of Caesarea, and Athanasius. A handful of others receive a moderate amount of attention, including the Cappadocians, Augustine, and Cyril of Alexandria; while still others are dealt with in briefer scope, such as Marcellus of Ancyra, Hilary of Poitiers, Ambrose of Milan, Leo of Rome, and the post-Chalcedonian theologians and councils. Readers interested in current scholarship on these matters will find plenty of references in the notes, and I have registered my agreements and disagreements there. However, since my primary concern is to clarify the patristic materials themselves, I have endeavored to keep such discussions to a minimum in the main text.

I am grateful to several colleagues who shared with me their unpublished work on related topics: John Behr, Elizabeth Clark, Brian Daley, Mark DelCogliano, Brian Duvic, Mark Edwards, Ronald Heine, Stephen Hildebrand, Rebecca Lyman, Robin Orton, Ilaria Ramelli, William Rusch, Thomas Sheck, Warren Smith, Kelley Spoerl, and Markus Vinzent; to those who graciously read and offered comments on portions of the work in progress: David Brakke, Mark Edwards, Joseph Lienhard, Rebecca Lyman, Frederick Norris, Andrew Radde-Gallwitz, Ilaria Ramelli, Kelly Spoerl, and Peter Widdicombe; to my colleagues at Yale University who read the original proposal and sample chapter: Stephen Davis, Carlos Eire, Bruce Gordon, and Denys Turner; and my editors at Yale University Press, Jennifer Banks and Ann-Marie Imbornoni. Portions of chapter 6 first appeared in the *Journal of Early Christian Studies*.

A book of this scope may be of interest to readers in multiple fields of study. Patristic tradition bears directly on Western European, Byzantine, Eastern European, and Russian history; Middle Eastern studies; church history and systematic theology, among others. As in ages past, it also stands to contribute to the ongoing life of the Christian church and the important work of ecumenical relations. To all of these audiences this book is respectfully addressed.

Part I
The Great Master

1. Origen of Alexandria

Christianity was born in Jerusalem, the temple city of ancient Israel where Jesus was crucified and his disciples first witnessed the risen Lord. Yet the great flowering of Christian theology began farther south, in the cosmopolitan port city of Alexandria on the northern coast of Egypt. A century and a half after Jesus's death, Alexandria produced the most prolific theologian of the early Christian period and the person who had the greatest influence on the church's understanding of Christ for over five hundred years—Origen of Alexandria (c. 185–c. 254).

Well before the time of Christ, Alexandria had become the most important commercial, educational, and cultural center of the eastern Mediterranean. It was the second-largest city in the Roman empire[1] and the leading center of Greek culture and learning for much of late antiquity. By the time of Origen, the city had long been the site of pioneering work in textual and literary criticism, such as the critical edition of Homer produced by Zenodotus, the first curator of the city's famous Museum. When the Romans sacked Athens in the first century CE, Alexandria became the unquestioned center of Platonic and Aristotelian philosophy as well. Greek philosophy, literary criticism, rhetorical studies, and science dominated the intellectual culture of the city in Origen's time. In recognition of its cultural importance in the early second century, the philosopher Dio Chrysostom referred to Alexandria as the crossroads of the world (*Or.* 32.35–36).

Late antique Alexandria also proved to be a fertile seedbed for Judaism and Christianity. By the first century CE, the Jewish population of Alexandria was the largest outside Palestine, occupying a sizeable sector of two of the city's five quarters. Alexandrian Jews developed a distinctly Greek, or Hellenistic, form of Judaism, which is reflected in such major works as the Septuagint, the Greek translation of the Jewish Scriptures that remains the definitive text of the Old Testament for most of the Greek-speaking church; the Book of Wisdom; and the many works of the biblical commentator and Platonist philosopher Philo (c. 20 BCE–c. 50 CE). However, in a violent backlash against Jewish revolts between 115 and 117, the Roman authorities of Alexandria, with support from the Greek citizenry, crushed the Jewish community, destroying the synagogue and obliterating most of the population.[2] As a result, there remains precious little record of Alexandrian Judaism between the second and the fourth centuries.

The origins of Christianity in Alexandria are notoriously murky. Most scholars now believe that Christianity first appeared there in the first century through the mission of Jewish Christians from Palestine, and that the earliest Alexandrian Christians lived in fairly close contact with the Jewish population. The popular idea that Mark the Evangelist founded the Alexandrian church and served as its first bishop, first attested in Eusebius's *Ecclesiastical History* in the early fourth century (*H.E.* 2.16), is unlikely. Following the destruction of the Jewish community in 117, Christians preserved several priceless works of Hellenistic Judaism, including the Septuagint and Philo's writings. Like the city's Jews, second- and third-century Alexandrian Christians were strongly influenced by the surrounding Greek cultural environment. By the mid-second century we know of Christian teachers of widely different views, from proto-orthodox writers such as Clement of Alexandria to Gnostic Christians Basilides, Valentinus, and Carpocrates. The interrelations among these figures is unclear; while there were certainly major differences among them, which one can see, for example, in the anti-Gnostic remarks in Clement, the divisions were not as fixed as they would later be, as indicated by Clement's positive use of certain Gnostic ideas.[3]

Clement appears to have worked as an independent teacher, possibly as an ordained presbyter of a Christian congregation, but probably not as the head of an official school under episcopal sponsorship, as Eusebius portrays him; nor does he appear to have been Origen's teacher, although Origen later read his works. From what little evidence we have, second-century Alexandrian Christianity appears to have been rather diverse, possibly including Jewish Christians oriented toward the Jerusalem church, Greek-speaking Christians of a more ascetical bent, an apocalyptically oriented variety, and a form of Marcionite Christianity—or some combination of these. As far as we can tell, more Christian literature of the second and third centuries was produced in Alexandria than in any other location, although much of it is either lost or exists in fragmentary quotations or later Coptic translations, such as the texts found in the Nag Hammadi library. Particular Christian communities were led by presbyter-teachers, who may have elected one of their own to serve as bishop; however, the city does not appear to have been supervised by a single bishop until Origen's bishop, Demetrius (189–232).[4]

The greatest fruit of Christian Alexandria was the indefatigable teacher, scholar, and near-martyr Origen. Many other writers from the second and third centuries influenced later Christian traditions, from the apologists and Irenaeus to the teachers of the Roman church, while the Scriptures remained at the heart of the church's theological musings and liturgical life. Yet Origen towered above all earlier theologians of record as the great master—or, in some cases, the persistent nemesis—of those who undertook to do serious theology for several centuries to come. Even when his legacy was tarnished with accusations of heresy, it was usually an Origenist theological program that governed the discussion. Origen synthesized much of the theology that others had produced before him, and by the end of his life he had become the most highly regarded Christian authority of international scope since the apostles.

LIFE AND WORKS

Throughout his adult life Origen combined a passionate dedication to the work of biblical interpretation with a broad knowledge of Greek culture, particularly philosophy. Born around 186, Origen came from a Christian family of middle-class means or better. His father, Leonides, was a teacher of Greek literature, a known Christian, and a Roman citizen, while his mother may or may not have been a Roman citizen. By all accounts, Origen's parents raised him in the Christian faith. Eusebius writes of Leonides's teaching his son from the Bible (*H.E.* 6.2.7–11), and Jerome tells us that Origen's mother taught him to recite the Psalms at a young age (*Ep.* 39.22). In addition, Origen received a thorough training in "the Greek subjects," namely, literature, philosophy, science, and medicine, first from his father and later from others (Eusebius, *H.E.* 6.2–3). However legendary these accounts may be, Origen's written works show the depth and rigor of his engagement with Christian Scripture and his extensive study of pagan Greek culture.[5]

When Origen was sixteen, his family suffered the horror of Leonides's imprisonment and beheading during the persecution of Emperor Septimius Severus. As part of their reprisals, the Roman authorities confiscated the family's savings, which meant that, as the eldest of seven sons, Origen was forced to go to work as a *grammaticus*, or a teacher of Greek literature (Eusebius, *H.E.* 6.2.15–31), as his father had, in order to support the family. By the time Origen was eighteen, Bishop Demetrius put him in charge of the instruction of catechumens, making him possibly the first person to serve as official catechist for the Alexandrian church as a whole. Over the next several years, Origen developed himself as a Christian teacher with legendary zeal and discipline, concentrating on biblical interpretation while continuing to study Greek subjects.[6] His skilled teaching attracted a solid following of students, including the wealthy government official Ambrose, whom Origen converted from Valentinian Christianity and who later became Origen's major financial supporter (*H.E.* 6.23.2). According to Eusebius, Origen studied philosophy under a Christian philosopher named Ammonius (*H.E.* 6.19.4–16), who may or may not have been Ammonius Saccas, the teacher of Plotinus. Like most intellectuals of the day, Origen's philosophical learning was eclectic, yet the predominant framework was Platonic.[7] He also studied the Hebrew language with a person he calls his "Hebrew teacher," who seems to have been a Jewish Christian (*Princ.* 1.3.5; 4.3.14; Eusebius, *H.E.* 6.16.1). Eventually Origen gave charge of the elementary catechumens to Heraclas, the brother of one of his students who had been martyred; Heraclas eventually became the next bishop of Alexandria (*H.E.* 6.3.2; 6.15).

Origen's intellectual approach can best be described as devotion to the Word above all. The Greek term *logos* can refer to the written word of texts, the exercise of human reason, and the Word of God present both in the Christian Scriptures and in Jesus, the Word made flesh. For Origen, it meant all of these. Although he disagreed with certain points of Greek philosophy when he thought them incompatible with Christian doctrine, he saw no conflict in principle between biblical Christianity, Greek philosophy, and devotion to Christ, and he regularly made use of philosophy for the analysis of the Scriptures and the exposition of the faith. We catch an invaluable glimpse into Origen's intellectual profile and pedagogical method in the report of a student's first encounter with the master. A certain

Theodore—Origen's most famous student, who was later called Gregory Thaumaturgus (the Wonder-Worker), the great missionary to Cappadocia—describes the first time he heard Origen teach, when he and his brother were passing through Palestine on their way to study law in Beirut. Theodore was instantly enthralled by Origen's "love for the holy Word, the most beautiful object of all which, by its ineffable beauty, attracts all things to itself," and by the man himself, who was its "friend and spokesperson." Then and there the brothers abandoned their plans to study law and remained with Origen to pursue the only goal that mattered: "philosophy—and that divine man, my guide in philosophy!" (*Adr.* 6.83–84). Theodore reports that Origen's curriculum proceeded according to the following order: Socratic dialectic; followed by physics, geometry, astronomy, and natural history; after which came ethics; and finally the study of theology, which is the summit of philosophical wisdom (*Adr.* 7–13). Christian philosophy, as Origen conceived it, thus proceeded from learning basic habits of reasoning and thought, to the contemplation of the natural order, to the study of the virtuous life, and finally to the contemplation of God and the divine economy of salvation. A similar progress from natural to divine contemplation would later be inscribed in monastic spirituality by Origenists such as Evagrius of Pontus.

Origen's reputation as a Christian teacher quickly spread beyond Alexandria. Starting around the 210s, he began to travel abroad to teach and conduct research. He visited Palestine, Athens, and Nicopolis of Actium, and at some point he went to Rome, where he heard the Christian teacher Hippolytus and was reportedly greeted with honor (Jerome, *Vir.Ill.* 61). Soon bishops invited Origen to teach and to participate in theological disputes and local church synods in places as far ranging as Arabia, Palestine, and Antioch. At one point, Julia Mammaea, the mother of Emperor Alexander Severus, brought Origen to the imperial court in Antioch to participate in theological debates, which may have included Valentinians from Alexandria (*H.E.* 6.21.3–4).

Origen's career was divided into two major phases. After working for two decades in Alexandria, he moved to Caesarea in Palestine, probably in the year 231. The main cause of this move was a falling-out with his bishop. Although we have little evidence to go on, it appears that some jealousy on Demetrius's part, or a mutual rivalry between the two men, was a major factor in the demise of their relations.[8] That their differences were at least theological is suggested by the letter that Origen wrote to his friends in Alexandria, in which he defends his orthodoxy but not his ecclesiastical status.[9] At one point Bishop Theoctistus of Caesarea ordained Origen a priest, a gesture that seems to have been intended to formalize Origen's permanent association with the Caesarean church, and possibly to establish him as the head of a new Christian library and school in Caesarea, which would help to raise the profile of Christianity in a city that already boasted active philosophical and Rabbinic Jewish intellectual activity. Demetrius protested the act to the Palestinian hierarchs and sought the intervention of a Roman synod; Origen was forced to defend himself to Fabian of Rome and others. Origen took refuge in the Caesarean church and made it the base of his activities from then on. In his first work written in Palestine, he describes himself as an Israelite who has just escaped the persecution of the Egyptians (*Com.Jn.* 6.pref.).[10]

Origen's time in Caesarea was the most productive period of his life. He devoted himself to the creation of what would become the first Christian university, a resource that Pamphilus and Eusebius further developed in the early fourth century and which contributed to the theological training of Gregory of Nazianzus. As an ordained priest, Origen preached extensively through the Scriptures, often extemporaneously.[11] His congregation in Caesarea was mixed, including both advanced students and relatively illiterate catechumens and church members. From Caesarea Origen also continued to make research trips and to serve as a theological expert at synods and debates in the surrounding regions.

The last two decades of Origen's life were scarred by further violence. When anti-Christian persecution broke out after the murder of Alexander Severus in 235, Origen went into hiding. Roman authorities arrested Origen's patron Ambrose in Nicomedia as well as a Caesarean priest named Protoctetus. To support his friends, Origen wrote an *Exhortation to Martyrdom*, which became a classic statement of the rationale of Christian martyrdom. In 250 Palestinian Christians suffered heavily from new persecutions under Emperor Decius. Bishop Fabian of Rome was martyred, and Alexander of Jerusalem and Babylas of Antioch were imprisoned and eventually died as confessors of the faith. Origen too was arrested, imprisoned, and severely tortured; according to Eusebius, he was "stretched four spaces" on the rack (*H.E.* 6.39.6). During his imprisonment Origen received a letter of encouragement from Dionysius, the new bishop of Alexandria and a great admirer, who later helped to rehabilitate Origen's reputation and enabled Origenian theological tradition to carry forward in Alexandria (*H.E.* 6.46.2). During his painful final years Origen wrote letters to encourage others who were suffering for the faith (*H.E.* 6.39.5). He died in 254 or 255 as a result of the injuries he had incurred.[12] Ever since the murder of his father, Origen had deeply honored the spirit of Christian martyrdom. In the end, he too perished at the hands of the Roman state and died as a confessor of the faith.

Origen was a theologian of massive industry. In the course of his studies he memorized much of the Greek Scriptures, and he wrote between one thousand and two thousand total volumes,[13] making him the most prolific author in the early church. Only a small fraction of Origen's corpus survives, and much of what remains exists only in Latin or other translations. Fortunately, we still possess several major works that give us a reliable sense of his theological outlook. The main focus of Origen's labors was biblical interpretation; most of his works are commentaries, notes, and homilies on the Scriptures. Yet, while Origen was a meticulous reader of the sacred text, his commentaries on Scripture also served a contemporary purpose. Unlike modern commentaries, which seek to give a comprehensive and historically informed account of the meaning of a biblical book, Origen believed that the true interpretation of Scripture reflects a distinct theological position, which itself derives from Scripture (and so on). He often advanced his views in direct competition with rival interpreters whose doctrine he thought posed a threat to the church's received rule of faith, and he tends to comment on passages that his opponents had used. He never wrote a commentary on an entire book of the Bible.[14]

The most important of Origen's biblical works, and the first of three major texts that form the basis of our study of his Christology, is his lengthy though incomplete *Commentary on John*. Begun in Alexandria as early as 216 and completed in Caesarea in the 240s, the commentary spans Origen's entire career. The immediate aim of the work is particularly important for its interpretation. The *Commentary on John* is a direct rebuttal to a similar work on John's gospel written by the Valentinian teacher Heracleon. Among the many subjects that Origen takes up in the long commentary, the most pressing of all is the doctrine of Christ. As he interprets passages from John's gospel and responds to Heracleon's theories, Origen advances his own Christology against several heretical positions and other types of error. In addition to the *Commentary on John*, we will draw on other passages from Origen's many exegetical works.[15]

Our second major source is *First Principles*, a summary of the faith and the first extant work of systematic theology in Christian tradition. After teaching in Alexandria for several years, sometime between 220 and

230 Origen gave formal expression to his theological position. Like the *Commentary on John*, this work too is antiheretical, as Origen positions himself against (and sometimes with) Gnostics and Marcionites in particular, as well as monarchians (those who deny the existence of the Father, Son, and Holy Spirit as three distinct beings) and radical subordinationists (those who deny the full divinity of Christ), even as he aims to lay out his own theological vision in positive terms. *First Principles* is thus both didactic and antiheretical in character. As its title indicates, the work is an account of the basic principles of the Christian faith, "ἀρχαί" in the title meaning both "fundamental principles of being" and "elementary principles" of the Christian faith, as Origen explains elsewhere (*Com.Jn.* 1). These key principles derive from Scripture as it was interpreted by the consensus of the churches—a deposit of teaching known as "apostolic tradition" (*Princ.* 1.pref.2)[16]—and articulated in the church's "rule of faith." The rule of faith gave a summary of the basic tenets of the faith, such as a new believer would profess at his or her baptism, and served as a guiding norm for biblical interpretation and theology. Origen distinguishes this basic deposit of Christian truth, which is accessible to all believers and is sufficient for salvation, from the deeper sense of that truth, which is accessible only to those who are spiritually gifted with wisdom and who progress in sacred knowledge. In *First Principles* Origen aims to present Christianity in what he calls "a connected body of doctrine" (*Princ.* 1.pref.10), a science in the Aristotelian sense of a demonstrative, logically coherent system of knowledge. He does so by basing himself on the rule of faith, while also extending the reach of his treatment into the level of more advanced teaching. The work is thus both normative and, in certain places, exploratory—a hybrid character that caused many difficulties for later interpreters when it was not clear which sort of teaching was being offered.[17]

Origen gives an important summary of the rule of faith in the preface to *First Principles*.[18] The basic principles of the faith include the oneness of God, who is the creator of the universe, the God of Israel, and the Father of the Lord Jesus Christ; that Jesus Christ was generated from God the Father before cosmic time and was the instrument and minister of creation, and that he emptied himself to become human (while remaining God), took on a body like ours, truly suffered, died, rose from the dead, and ascended into heaven; and that the Holy Spirit, who shares in the honor of the Father and Son, inspired the saints in both the Old and New Testaments, although other aspects of its identity are unclear in the Scriptures. The Father, Son, and Holy Spirit are the cardinal principles of Christianity in Origen's view, much as the three-part form of other second-century rules of faith seems to convey. To these three chief principles Origen adds the reality of the soul and God's moral judgment of it, the existence and work of angelic and demonic beings, the creation and future destruction of the world, the inspiration and the dual sense of the Scriptures, and the incorporeality of God. Based on the teaching of Scripture, these tenets are the basic elements on which a whole body of Christian doctrine can be built through further reasoning. Origen offers such a body of teaching in two major cycles, followed by a concluding summary. The importance of *First Principles* can hardly be overstated: Origen's presentation of his doctrinal system here is arguably the most influential single theological project in all of Christian tradition outside of the canonical Scriptures.

Together with *First Principles* and the *Commentary on John*, Origen's third major theological work is *Against Celsus*, a text that we are fortunate to possess entirely in the original Greek. Written near the end of his career (after 246), *Against Celsus* is a piecemeal reply to the attack on Christianity published by the Platonizing pagan rhetorician Celsus in 178. It is Origen's only work directed entirely against an opponent outside of the faith, and it is one of the two most important apologetic works of the early church, together with Augustine's *City of God*. For his own part, Origen was inclined to ignore Celsus's work, at least in print, but Ambrose persuaded him to publish a response, believing that such a virulent attack must not go unanswered. Here again, the purpose and the nature of the work are crucial for our interpretation of it. More balanced in tone than many other ancient apologies, *Against Celsus* defends Christianity in two contrasting ways: (1) by countering Celsus's often harsh criticisms, when Origen thinks that Celsus has misconstrued the faith or his pagan views are wrong to begin with, and (2) by explaining how the Christian gospel does *not* in fact violate the principles that Celsus is advocating, when Origen agrees with Celsus's views. Origen's replies to Celsus are extremely important for assessing his Christology because the main target of Celsus's ridicule was a set of claims that Christians make about who Jesus is. Most importantly, Origen answers Celsus's accusation that Christ's incarnation violates the purity and transcendence of the Divinity, as traditional Greeks had understood it.

Several of Origen's shorter works are important for our study. The *Dialog with Heraclides*, which was discovered in 1941, contains the record of a meeting of Arabian bishops at which Origen had served as a theological expert. In the first part of the dialog Origen examines the doctrine of Bishop Heraclides concerning the unity and plurality of the Trinity, followed by two questions on the soul and the resurrection—all three of which were controversial topics in Origen's legacy over the next century. Origen's treatises *On Prayer* and the *Exhortation to Martyrdom*, also requested by Ambrose and Tatiana, contain important passages on Christ as well.

Even apart from the fragmentary nature of his surviving corpus, Origen has been difficult to interpret since his own time, on account of the depth and subtlety of his thought, the sheer volume of his writings, and the fact that he often gave expression to both sides of a question and occasionally changed his mind. Yet he also ran afoul of certain readers because he drew on the Greek intellectual heritage, and especially Platonist philosophy, in order to understand matters that were not clearly stated in the Scriptures, such as the nature of the soul, the resurrected body, the beginning and end of the cosmos, and even the person of Christ. The fact that Origen announced his intention to remain subject to the authority of Scripture and the catholic ecclesiastical tradition has not deterred his critics. It will be one of our tasks in this chapter to determine the extent to which that heritage affected his Christology. As we shall see, Origen's multiple resources and his vast learning came at a cost, even if it also gave his work a lasting brilliance. His work was at once a treasure chest of riches for those who could gain access to them, and at the same time a Pandora's box of troubles that theologians in later generations were obligated to contain. Origen's legacy definitively shaped later theological traditions, in both the Christian East and West, even as it was often clouded with controversy, false accusations, and sheer misunderstanding. The controversial teaching of some of his followers eventually led to his condemnation and an order proscribing his books by Emperor Justinian in 543. However, by that time Origen's program had long established itself as the basic template of most patristic theology.

CHRIST AND COSMOLOGY

In Origen's view, the center of Christian teaching and the focus of all existence is Jesus Christ. Christ's priority is the first point that Origen establishes in the preface to *First Principles*: the most basic belief of all Christians is that Jesus Christ is the source of all divine grace and truth, and indeed Christ *is* the truth, according to John's gospel (John 1:17; 14:6). The Christian faith and life are therefore based on "no other source but the very words and teaching of Christ." For Origen, as for most early Christians, the words of Christ include not only the sayings of Jesus reported in the four canonical gospels, but the whole of Scripture: the law, the prophets, and the apostles (*Princ.* 1.pref.1). All human knowledge of God occurs through Christ, who is the mediator, the high priest, and the door, as Origen explains in the *Commentary on John* (1.221; 2.209). His entire theological project, in other words, is focused on Christ as he is presented in the Gospels and other parts of the New Testament, and, by extension, in the Old Testament as well. Christ is the meaning of the church's present life in this world, and he is the rationale of the cosmos, from its creation to its final consummation.

Yet here already a puzzle arises for Origen's reader. Who exactly does Origen mean when he argues that "Jesus Christ" is the center of the Christian life? If we assume that he means the incarnate Lord, the Word made flesh in human form, we will in fact have overlooked the most crucial part of Origen's teaching. Throughout his works, Origen urges his readers to move *beyond* the human Christ and the historical economy of salvation to a knowledge of the divine Word in its pure, eternal existence. He argues that the aim of true religion is to come to know the divine Son of God, and while this knowledge begins with the earthly career of Jesus and the literal meaning of Scripture, it must ultimately move through them to a deeper, spiritual knowledge of the Son, through whom alone we can come to know God the Father. But even this way of putting it is a gross oversimplification. How Origen imagines Christians achieving this act of faith, and particularly the nature of the relationship between Jesus's divinity and his humanity, is a matter of no little difficulty.

In order to understand Origen's Christology, beyond the simple rule of faith that he gives in the preface of *First Principles*, we must appreciate that Origen understands Christ in terms of a predominantly dualist view of God and the cosmos, which he derived from the Hellenized Jewish and Christian traditions of Alexandria and his own philosophical study. Although Origen's theology differs from Plato's in several important ways, he nevertheless retained a predominantly Platonist worldview, which he coupled with certain Pythagorean elements and a large measure of Stoic ethics. In this view, the physical and sensible world is seen as radically impermanent compared with the reality of the intellectual sphere and God above all.[19] The question here is not whether Origen's thought is biblical *or* philosophical; it very plainly is both. Nor should we expect his system to be recognizable as "Platonic" per se by any roughly contemporary Platonist, such as Plotinus or Porphyry. For Porphyry especially, Christianity was profoundly insufficient and even corrupt, as it was for the earlier Platonizing critic Celsus. Rather than adjudicating between Origen's Christianity and Platonism, our task must be to evaluate *how* his eclectic Platonism contributed to his overall Christian theology.

An influential precedent in this regard was the Platonizing Jewish theologian Philo, whose allegorical exegesis of Scripture sought to bring the Bible into harmony with a Platonist cosmology, a synthesis that influenced Clement as well.[20] In many ways, the overarching goal of Origen's work was to show the compatibility of the best of Greek culture with catholic Christianity—or better, to reorganize Greek culture under the chief principle of Christ. The extent to which Origen succeeded in making Greek philosophy serviceable to the Christian gospel, or whether he was, in effect, pursuing a quixotic quest to harmonize irreconcilable systems, depends on one's analysis of his work. Even though Origen was painfully aware of the violent and demonic aspects of contemporary Greco-Roman culture, in his own view, the relationship between the Greek and biblical heritages was not fundamentally conflicted at all, as long as one had a proper appreciation for the centrality of Christ. Within these parameters, the mystery of Christ poses the question of how the infinite and all-transcendent God can be said to relate with finite, created existence.

The effect of Origen's dualist cosmology on his Christology can be seen from the early *Commentary on John* through the late *Against Celsus*. For example, Origen writes the following to explain the biblical images of the Son of God's mouth as a sharp sword (see Isa 49:2) and the Word of God as a "two-edged sword" (Heb 4:12). The Word is like a sword "because he came not to cast peace on the earth, that is on the things that are corporeal and perceived by the senses, but a sword, and because he cuts through the harmful friendship of soul and body, so to speak. In this way the soul, by devoting herself to the spirit, can fight against the flesh and so be made a friend of God" (*Com.Jn.* 1.229). Elsewhere Origen calls the purifying effect of the Holy Spirit "a more divine fire that removes everything material, and utterly destroys everything earthly" (*Com.Jn.* 6.162). Here we see Origen identifying the Pauline language of spirit versus flesh with the difference between intelligible and sensory things, including the human soul and body.

For Origen, God, and eventually the saints, exist in a spiritual world that stands in contrast to the physical world, and our redeemed state will exclude the physical body and its desires as we know them. Although our material bodies reflect the mercy of God, thus avoiding the Gnostic view of a defective creator and evil materiality, they do so as a punishment and chiefly through bodily sufferings such as hunger, pain, and illness; and they must perish and become spiritualized in the resurrection.[21]

The dualist tendency of Origen's cosmology is again evident in the way he responds to one of Celsus's objections. Celsus makes a standard Platonist argument that it is possible to see God only if one "closes off the senses and gazes with the mind, if one abandons the flesh and awakens the eyes of the soul" (*C.Cels.* 7.39),[22] against what he takes to be the Christian belief that God can be known by the senses. In reply, Origen accepts Celsus's basic distinction, and he denies that even simple Christians believe that God can be grasped or known by the senses in any way, for example in defense of the resurrection of Jesus: "Even though human beings in this life have to begin from the senses and from sensible things when they intend to ascend to the nature of intelligible things, they must on no account remain content with sensible things. Nor would they say that it is impossible to have any knowledge of intelligible things except by sense-perception." John's statement that "our hands have touched the Word of life" (1 John 1:1) must therefore be interpreted figuratively, Origen says.[23] Moreover, he argues that Celsus's Platonist principle was anticipated by the teaching of Scripture anyway (*C.Cels.* 7.34, 37, 39).[24]

Origen's understanding of the human being is likewise an amalgam of biblical and philosophical ideas. In his view, human beings are essentially souls, which are currently placed in physical bodies (*Princ.* 4.2.7), and our ultimate destiny is to be something like angels, who possess a sort of ethereal body (*Com.Jn.* 2.140, 148).[25] In his commentary on Genesis 1:27 (God made man "according to the image of God"), Origen denies that the human body in any way contains the image of God, such as Irenaeus had argued before him. Rather, "it is our inner man, invisible, incorporeal, incorruptible, and immortal which is made 'according to the image of God'" (*Com.Jn.* 1.13). Our current embodied condition therefore represents a kind of problem for the growth of the soul toward God. Commenting on Jesus's statement in John 8:23 ("You are from below, I am from above; you are of this world, I am not of this world"), Origen writes that those whom Jesus calls "from below" are embodied human beings, who take their origin from material substance and are of the earth, and who cannot speak of anything higher; they do the works of the flesh (Gal 5:19), and they love this world. Our attention to earthly materiality, which Origen associates with the biblical language of flesh and the world, represents our opposition toward God, for "it is impossible for love for the world to coexist with love for God" (*Com.Jn.* 19.130, 139).

By contrast, there is another, spiritual realm beyond the perceptible world of the heavens and earth, an invisible world that the saints must be trained to behold instead of the present, physical one. The contrast between the two is stark: "That world has nothing below, even as this world has nothing above." The genuine disciples of Jesus are chosen out of this perceptible world, so that by bearing their own crosses they might come to be no longer of the perceptible world, but outside of the perceptible world entirely (*Com.Jn.* 19.146–50). Origen frames the spiritual life in cosmological terms, again linking them with Paul's language of flesh and spirit. To please God and to be present with God, one must be not in the flesh or the body but in the spirit (*Com.Jn.* 13.85, 109; Rom 8:8; 2 Cor 5:6). Similarly, those who are devoted to the bodily, literal meaning of Scripture and walk by faith but do not perceive its spiritual meaning, Origen says, are present in the body but still absent from the Lord. But when one does perceive the spiritual meaning of Scripture and becomes a spiritual person, he or she comes to be absent from the body and present with the Lord (*Com.Jn.* 13.359–61). Even though Origen maintains that corporeality is a necessary and permanent condition of individual existence (*Princ.* 1.6.4; *C.Cels.* 5.18–21),[26] our human bodies and the physical world as we now know them nonetheless represent distractions from God and a kind of false reality compared with the true reality of the intelligible heavens. Growth in faith, then, means to pass beyond the physical realm, so that one can contemplate and participate in the Son and thereby come to the knowledge of God the Father.

To be sure, Origen is not a radical cosmic dualist, as he has sometimes been accused of being. Against the Gnostics, he firmly defends the goodness of the body and the material world. He argues that the origin of evil lies not in materiality per se, but in the soul's turning away from God; and in its return to God the human body is not lost, but is spiritualized, as Paul teaches (see 1 Cor 15:44). In order to be recognizably catholic in the early third century, it would be impossible not to defend the goodness of the body and material creation, as Irenaeus had done previously. Yet it is a radically different body compared with the physical life that we now experience. Consequently, Origen leaves considerably less room for the body in the Christian life than Irenaeus did. Despite his repudiation of Manichean and Gnostic dualism, Origen upholds in his own way a strongly dualistic structure of spiritual ascent, according to which the material world and the body pose as a kind of hindrance and distraction to the soul's ascent, even though they are not evil in themselves and the struggle is ordained by God. Under these conditions, the soul must turn away from the body and the material world in order to return to God, from whom it has fallen.[27]

By analyzing Origen's cosmology in this way, my purpose is not to suggest that what I have called Origen's dualism is faulty or illegitimate in every way, nor even that it is fundamentally incompatible with biblical concerns. One could make a convincing case that such a cosmology in fact succeeds as an interpretation of certain passages of Scripture. Rather, I am arguing that Origen's dualizing cosmology and anthropology, however they might otherwise succeed, also come at certain costs, particularly in reference to his understanding of the person of Christ. When he begins his treatment of Christ in *First Principles*, Origen defines Christ's identity in a parallel, dual sense: "The first thing we have to know is this: that in Christ there is one [*alia*] nature, his Divinity, because he is the only-begotten Son of the Father, and another [*alia*], human nature, which in recent times he took on for the economy" (*Princ.* 1.2.1).[28] This combination of two natures or realities serves as the organizing pattern for much of Origen's treatment of Christ throughout his career. The fact that he approaches the identity and work of Christ from the standpoint of two very different realities, calling them two "natures," within a wider dualist cosmology and anthropology, holds enormous implications not only for our understanding of Origen's work, but also for the course of later patristic Christology.

THE DIVINITY AND DISTINCTNESS OF CHRIST

The single most important fact about Christ, in Origen's view, is his divinity, or divine nature, and this is the first subject he treats in the main chapter on Christ in *First Principles*. Origen argues throughout his major works that Moses, the prophets, the apostles, and Christ himself all declare that Christ is the eternal, divine Son of God. Although he has been accused for centuries of subordinationism (or making Christ to be less divine than God the Father), Origen asserted the divinity of Christ in stronger terms than any Christian theologian to date.[29] Origen argues that Christ is equal to God the Father in both divinity and eternity, and that he possesses the same divine nature and a power fully equal to that of the Father. Even during the incarnation, when the Son emptied himself to become human, Origen specifies that "he still remained what he was, namely God" (*Princ.* 1.pref.4).[30] In *Against Celsus* Origen explains that just as "God is light" (1 John 1:5), so too Christ the Son of God is "the true light," as Jesus himself said (John 1:9; 8:12). "The divinity of God . . . and also that of his only-begotten Son" is thus superior to all things and entirely beyond description (*C.Cels.* 5.11), and Christians worship only "one God [εἷς θεός], the Father and the Son" (*C.Cels.* 8.12).

The source of our knowledge of Christ's divinity is Scripture, and yet, as Origen notes, Scripture calls Christ by many different names or conceptions (*epinoiai*). Origen's extensive reflection on the *epinoiai* of Christ is one of his most original and influential ideas, and each of the major theologians of the fourth century will take it up in various ways. Yet among the many titles for Christ, "Son of God" stands above the rest; all of the other *epinoiai* are "titles of the Son" (*Com.Jn.* 1.123, 153). While there are many different titles or conceptions, there is in reality only one Son. Christ is divine above all "because he is the only-begotten Son of the Father" (*Princ.* 1.2.1).

After noting Christ's divinity as the Son of God, Origen makes it his next task "to see what the only-begotten Son of God is" (*Princ.* 1.2.1), that is, to get a clearer idea of the character of the Son's divine nature, or *how* Christ is divine, in light of his many biblical titles. Origen identifies four main titles that designate Christ's divinity: Wisdom, Word, Truth, and Life. The chief of these four titles is Wisdom, a designation that reflects the wisdom literature of the Old Testament, especially Proverbs 8 and the Hellenistic Jewish Book of Wisdom, and which is echoed in more oblique ways in John and Paul in the New Testament. In his *Commentary on John*, Origen writes that among the multitude of things and goods that the Son is, Wisdom is the premier designation of his nature (*Com.Jn.* 1.119, 289). As Wisdom, the Son is the principle of all of God's ways and especially of created existence, as Wisdom herself says in Proverbs: "The Lord created me as the beginning of [God's] ways, for the sake of his works" (Prov 8:22), a verse that proved to be explosively controversial in the Christological debates of the fourth century. As Wisdom the Son is the "beginning," "source," or "principle" (ἀρχή) of God (*Com.Jn.* 1.118).

Moreover, as divine Wisdom, the Son contains in himself all of God's thoughts, as it were, and particularly the forms and the possibilities of creation. "[Wisdom] fashions beforehand and contains within herself the species and causes of the entire creation" (*Princ.* 1.2.2–3).[31]

As John 1:1 states, the Son is also the Word of God. Just as Wisdom contains in herself all the thoughts and plans of God, so too the Son is God's Word, in the sense that the divine Wisdom communicates her thoughts outward toward creatures. The Word is "in" Wisdom, a fact that Origen discerns in the statement that the Word is "in the beginning with God" (John 1:1; *Com.Jn.* 1.118). As the Word, the Son is, "as it were, an interpreter of the secrets of the mind" that is the Father (*Princ.* 1.2.3), or the communicative principle of God. The Word (*Logos*) is also the principle of all rational (*logikos*) existence, and we are created in the image of God by virtue of our rationality (*Princ.* 1.3.6; 4.4.10). Similarly, the Son is also divine Truth and Life (see John 11:25), by which other beings truly exist and receive life again after they have fallen away from God and brought death upon themselves (*Princ.* 1.2.4). In addition to arguing from biblical titles, Origen frequently opposes what he takes to be the heretical denial of the Son's divinity. In order to adhere to the received rule of faith, he writes in the concluding sections of *First Principles*, two views of Christ must be avoided: that Christ lacked "any quality of the Divinity" or that he was in any way separated from the divine being of God the Father. Rather, the Son's divinity is an incorporeal and invisible substance, which cannot be divided into parts or separated from God the Father (*Princ.* 4.4.3–4).[32]

Yet no sooner does Origen assert Christ's divinity than he immediately cautions his readers against another sort of misunderstanding, namely, collapsing the distinct existence of Christ the Son into that of God the Father. Orthodox belief requires that the Son be conceived as a distinctly existing being. Origen's technical term for this is "hypostasis," a word that will later become central to orthodox theology through Origen's disciples Basil of Caesarea and Gregory of Nazianzus. For Origen a hypostasis is a distinctly existing thing, a concrete entity or being (though not necessarily possessing a body), and also something that exists in reality and not only in thought (*Com.Jn.* 10.212). In his discussion of the Son's divinity in *First Principles*, Origen is simultaneously concerned to avoid any suggestion that the Son does not exist distinctly, that is, hypostatically (*Princ.* 1.2.2). Similarly, in the *Commentary on John*, he interrupts his discussion of the title "Word" to criticize those who make too much of Christ's identity as Word, "as if the Christ of God is Word alone" (*Com.Jn.* 1.125). Specifically, Origen is critical of those who imagine the Son of God too much in terms of a human word, which is merely a sound that proceeds from a single speaker, rather than appreciating that the Son of God is a divine being with his own particular manner of existence (ὅπως ποτὲ οὐσίαν, *Com.Jn.* 1.151), and a being with life in himself, which a spoken word does not possess, when compared with the person who spoke it (*Com.Jn.* 1.152). Indeed, despite the predominance of the Logos idea—taken, we must remember, from the first verse of the gospel on which he is commenting—Origen normally speaks throughout his commentary of Christ as the "Son of God." To be sure, his Christology is a type of Logos doctrine, but what exactly that entails must be borne out with careful scrutiny. As we shall see, divergences over how to characterize Christ as Word were the cause of major divergences in the following century. As divine Wisdom, then, the Son is more like a wise, living being than he is like an impersonal reality that makes people wise by imparting itself into their minds (*Princ.* 1.2.2). Wisdom should be conceived as "an incorporeal hypostasis that is made up of various ideas that embrace the principles of the universe, and which is living and, as it were, animate" (*Com.Jn.* 1.244). The Father, Son, and Holy Spirit, then, are three distinct things or hypostases in this sense (*C.Cels.* 8.12).[33]

Origen's confession of three distinct divine beings arises from the biblical account of different characters or figures: God (the Father), who raised Christ from the dead, for example (1 Cor 15:15), must be different from Christ who was raised, or else Paul's statement makes no sense. In this regard, "Father" and "Son" are not different *epinoiai* for the same divine being, but they refer to distinctly existing hypostases, since a father must have a child and a son must have a father for them to be truly a father and son (*Com.Jn.* 10.246). Christian prayer is likewise structured according to the distinctness of the Father, Son, and Spirit: prayer always proceeds to the Father through the Son and the Holy Spirit (*Prayer* 15).

In such passages Origen is opposing the view that scholars term monarchianism. One sort of monarchian position holds that the Father, Son, and Holy Spirit are merely different versions or manifestations of God, but not distinct beings in themselves, a view also known as modalism. One implication of this view can be that Jesus is the incarnation of God the Father, which holds the scandalous implication that God the Father suffered in the incarnation (or patripassianism). The second type of monarchian view is that God the Father adopted the human Jesus as his son, which tends to imply that Christ is otherwise merely human, since he is not seen as the incarnation of a preexisting divine entity (*Com.Jn.* 2.16). Both monarchian positions seek to maintain the oneness of God by denying that the Son of God is a distinct, divine being who became incarnate as Jesus of Nazareth. Origen would have encountered such views during his visit to Rome, and he once comments that the majority of believers in fact hold some such view (*Com.Jn.* 2.27–29). Origen seems to be talking about this sort of mono-theism when he refers to people who are afraid to confess two gods, so that they deny that the distinct individuality (ἰδιότης) of the Son is other than (ἕτερος) that of the Father (by saying that the Son is merely the Father by another name), or else they acknowledge that the Father and Son are different individuals but deny that the Son is divine (*Com.Jn.* 1.152; 2.16). In this connection Origen may also have in mind a Valentinian notion that Wisdom lacked individual subsistence before her emanation from God.[34] The true confession, in Origen's view, is that the Son is both divine and also other than the Father as a distinct individual or hypostasis. John's gospel expresses this similarity and distinction in the two terms "the God" (*ho theos*) for the Father and "God" (*theos*) for the Son (John 1:1; *Com. Jn.* 2.17).[35]

One of the most characteristic ways in which Origen defines Christ's identity brings together these two concerns about his divinity and distinct-ness. The Son of God is divine, Origen says, because he exists and possesses all the qualities of divinity "essentially," that is, in his very being or nature, rather than by receiving these qualities from without, as all other creatures must. "The only-begotten Son of God is Wisdom existing essentially" (*Princ.* 1.2.2).[36] Similarly, Christ is the Son of God "by nature" and the only being who is a natural child of God (*Princ.* 1.2.5).[37] By contrast, Christians can become sons and daughters of God only by grace, or accidentally (*Princ.* 4.4.10). A related aspect of the Son's essential divinity is the simplicity of the divine nature that he possesses (*Princ.* 1.5.3),[38] by contrast with the complexity of all other natures. It is the very definition of the Son of God, his inner rationale, as it were, to be divine intrinsically, a fact that he shares with only the Father and the Holy Spirit. Every divine quality resides in the Son essentially, not accidentally as in creatures, which makes the Son unchanging and unchangeable (*Princ.* 1.2.10). Origen stresses that essential goodness is found only in Christ as in the Father and the Holy Spirit (*Princ.* 1.5.3). By contrast, all rational beings created by the divine

Father and Son participate in goodness, holiness, and so on accidentally; they achieve and maintain these qualities by free will and merit, and they are therefore capable of change in either direction. This distinction between essential and accidental divinity is Origen's chief metaphysical expression of the Son's divinity and of the common divinity among the Trinity as a whole.[39]

In his *Dialog with Heraclides* Origen gives a succinct summary of Christ's identity as the Son of God. It is crucial for the Christian faith—and specifically for Christian prayer—to maintain two central beliefs: first, that Christ is a distinct being whom Christians know and to whom they pray (against monarchian modalism), and second, that Christ is divine and must be included in the one God of Scripture (against subordinationism), which is the main sense of Jesus's statement "I and the Father are one" (John 10:30; *Heracl.* 3). The Son is both distinct (ἕτερος) from the Father—he is a son, not also a father—and also God, but only in such a way that these two Gods are one thing.[40] Thus, even if this means that the Father and Son are in one sense "two Gods" (an obviously shocking assertion), they are two only in such a way that they are also "one God" (*Heracl.* 2). Christ's divine nature is the summit of theological knowledge, and the main purpose of his coming in the flesh was to enable believers to know that he is the Son of God (*Princ.* 2.6.1).

CHRIST AND THE TRINITY

The full significance of Christ's divinity in Origen's work is not simply the fact that Christ is divine, but *how* he is so. Indeed, Origen's thought on the manner of Christ's divinity—its origin, basis, and broader significance—lies at the heart of much later patristic reflection on the divine mystery. For Origen, Christ is not only divine, or God, pure and simple; Christ's divinity is based on and reflective of his relationship to God the Father. Likewise, God the Father must have an offspring in order to be what he is as father (*Princ.* 1.1.9). Christ is therefore divine because he is the *Son* of God, and in no other sense. The divinity of Christ, in other words, is tied up with the mystery of the Trinity as a whole.

Christ's relationship to God the Father is the first thing that Origen mentions in the section on Christ in the rule of faith given at the beginning of *First Principles*. Jesus Christ was sent by God the Father to call people to faith; he is the Son of the Father, "begotten of the Father before every creature"; and he aided the Father in the creation of all things (*Princ.* 1.pref.4).[41]

God the Father is the source both of Christ's eternal existence and of his mission in the created order. The same principle is at work at the start of Origen's first extended treatment of Christ in the body of the work: Christ is divine *"because* he is the only-begotten Son of the Father" (*Princ.* 1.2.1, emphasis added). Similarly, Christ's derivation from the Father is reflected in the first four biblical titles that Origen lists next: Christ is the Son of God, the Wisdom of God, the Word of God, and the Power of God (*Princ.* 1.2.1–3), each signifying a distinct relationship to the Father. It is the Son's source and origin in the Father that explain his divine nature (*Com.Jn.* 6.190). In the terms of John 1:1, it is "by being 'with *the* God [ὁ θεός]'" that the Son "always continues to be 'God' [θεός]" (*Com.Jn.* 2.18, 10). As Origen writes against Celsus, the Father "gave a share of himself and his greatness" to the Son, making him to be great like the Father (*C.Cels.* 6.69). Everything else there is to say about Christ follows from this most basic fact of his identity.

One of Origen's favorite metaphors for the Son's generation from the Father is the image of brightness shining from a source of light, or light coming from light (*Princ.* 1.2.4–5), which appears in several biblical texts.[42] Yet Origen interprets the image of light in a particular way, so as to preserve the Son's divine identity as he understands it. On Origen's reading, the Son possesses the same quality of light as the Father, namely, the divine nature; the Son shines forth from the Father immediately (the ancients considered light to be instantaneous), so there is no temporal interval dividing the Father and Son; the Son shines only from the Father, so there remains only one divine source and first principle (*Princ.* 1.2.11); and whenever the light source exists, its rays will always be shining, so that the Son's generation from the Father is eternal, or timeless (*Princ.* 1.2.4).[43] With these qualifications, God the Father is to the Son as the "Light of the true Light" (*C.Cels.* 5.11).

For multiple reasons, Origen is concerned to maintain that, even though the Son exists as a distinct hypostasis from the Father, he is nevertheless inseparably united with the Father, and his generation is incorporeal and eternal. On the positive side, Origen's view of the divine generation is reinforced by his Platonist cosmology, according to which the incorporeality of the Trinity is radically differentiated from the corporeality of all other beings (*Princ.* 2.2.2; 2.4.3). Yet he is also concerned to oppose Gnostic conceptions of the emanation of Wisdom from God, which involves an extension or prolation of the Godhead that catholics took to be a division of the divine substance, with strong connotations of material division. Against this view, Origen illustrates the incorporeality, inseparability, and persistent unity of the divine generation by comparing it to human mental activity, much as St. Augustine would do later. A person's will comes from his or her mind and expresses the mind, somewhat like a ray of light shines from a light source. Yet, on the other hand, the will is not separated or divided from the mind like a physical object might be: the will isn't a "piece" of the mind that the mind no longer possesses once a choice has been made. (The choice of the will also comes only from one's own mind, not from any other source, thus preserving monotheism.) Similarly, the Father generates the Son in a way that does not divide the Son from the Father. So too, Origen famously asserts that the Father's generation of the Son is eternal as well (*Princ.* 1.2.2–4, 6, 9; 4.4.1).[44] The Father is always Father of the Son, and there was never a time when the Son did not exist with and in the Father (*Princ.* 1.2.9).[45]

Yet these are only illustrative comparisons: Origen does not believe that the Father *is* the mind of the Son or the Son the will of the Father any more than God is a light like the physical sun. With each concept and image, there is also a sense in which God is *unlike* what is being compared. This applies as well to the language of creaturely fatherhood and sonship: the Father's generation of the Son is different from human procreation in that it does not involve passion, a division of substance, or the separation of the parent and child, as we have seen. Consequently, the divine generation is ultimately beyond our understanding (*Princ.* 1.2.4, 6).

As will already be evident, each of these qualities expresses and qualifies the unity of the Father and the Son. Even though it is a distinct hypostasis, Wisdom continues to exist "in God," from whom it came (*Princ.* 1.2.5). Origen highlights the unity of the Father and the Son by contrast with lesser kinds of unity described in the Scriptures. When human beings are joined together in marriage, they are called "one flesh" (Gen 2:24). When the righteous are united with Christ, they are called "one spirit" with him (1 Cor 6:17). But when Christ is united with God the Father, they are "one God"—as Jesus says, "I and the Father are one" (John 10:30)—which is a union far greater than the first two kinds (*Princ.* 2.6.3).[46] Similarly, Origen contrasts the way in which the Word is "with God" (John 1:1) with the way in which it is with the prophets and the saints: whereas the Word must "come to be" with the prophets and saints, the Word simply "was" and "is" with God (*Com.Jn.* 1.187).

Aside from the simple assertion of their unity and inseparability, Origen further understands the unity of the Father and the Son in terms of knowledge and willing. The Son knows "everything that is known by the Father in the depth of his wealth and wisdom and knowledge" (see Rom 11:33), and he is ignorant of nothing whatsoever, since he is himself the Truth (*Com.Jn.* 1.187). The Son also perfectly knows the Father in endless, intimate contemplation of the depth of God. The Son's knowledge of the Father, moreover, is constitutive of what it means for the Son to be God (*Com.Jn.* 2.18).[47] Similarly, the Son is united with the Father by sharing or "participating in the divinity" of the Father (*Com.Jn.* 2.17). Again, the Son's unity with the Father is indicated by the fact that he perfectly cooperates with the will of the Father, so that in effect they have the same will. Only the Son (and possibly the Spirit) has "comprehended the complete will of God and does it" (*Com.Jn.* 13.231). Even when Origen or Scripture speaks of the Son doing the Father's will *instead of* his own (as in Mark 14:36 and par.; *Com.Jn.* 6.295), it amounts to the same thing, since they have the same will precisely because it is the Father's will, not any other, that the Son follows: "the will that is in [the Son] is an image of the first will, and the divinity that is in him is an image of the true Divinity" (*Com.Jn.* 13.234). Origen comments further on John 4:34 ("My food is to do the will of the one who sent me and to perfect his work"): "It is proper food for the Son of God when he becomes a doer of the Father's will, that is, when he wills in himself what was also the Father's will, so that the will of God is in the will of the Son, and the will of the Son has become indistinguishable from the will of the Father, and there are no longer two wills but one. It was because of this one will that the Son said, 'I and the Father are one'" (*Com.Jn.* 13.228). Because of his generation from the Father, the Son perfectly reflects the will, activity, and operation of God the Father. He works everything that the Father works, as Jesus says of himself in John 5:19 (*Princ.* 2.12). Even though the Son is a distinctly existing entity in his own right (which the Father caused him to be), there is no difference or separation between the works of the Father and the Son.

In order to express the incorporeality, inseparability, and unity of the divine generation, Origen argues that the Father generates the Son by his will alone, as opposed to generating him in being (which would indicate monarchian modalism) or through begetting (which in Valentinian parlance connotes a division of substance, as in the procreation of animals). Although Origen does believe that the Father begets the Son, as the parental language obviously suggests, he is keen to avoid the notion of material division that is connoted by the literal act of procreation. Origen thus describes the divine generation in terms of willing in order to preserve the unity, inseparability, eternity, *and* commonality of nature involved in the Father's generation of the Son. Whether the Son is generated by the will or the being of the Father will be a central matter in Athanasius's dispute with Arius in the following century. However, in Origen's scheme we may note that generation by will in no way undermines the Son's true derivation from the Father, their commonality of nature, or their equality; rather, in consideration of the Gnostic and modalist alternatives, it preserves it.

Several other expressions in Origen's work may likewise seem to threaten the Son's equality with the Father, when in reality they do not. The fact that Origen describes the Father as greater than the Son does not refer to any difference of divinity, power, wisdom, or truth. Such expressions refer instead to the Father's unique role and character within the Trinity, which we will discuss further below.[48] Nor does the language of participation, already mentioned, signal any lessening of divinity in the Son merely because Origen also uses it to refer to the relationship between the saints and God. Elsewhere, Origen writes that the Son is divine not by participation but in substance (κατ' οὐσίαν, *Frag.Ps.* 134.19–20) and that the Son is what he is not by participation only (*Schol.Apoc.* 20).[49] Again, the fact that Origen speaks of the Son's generation in terms of both creation and begetting likewise does not indicate any inferiority on the Son's part, even if it appears to violate the later Nicene distinction between the two categories. Origen himself sees no crucial difference between begetting and creating or coming to be (apart from the worry about the material division of begetting, already mentioned); in the case of the Son, they all serve to indicate his origin from God the Father, by contrast with the creation of all other things through the Son and out of nothing. Origen's usage derives quite naturally from the plain sense of Scripture, which speaks of the Son's generation both as creation (Prov 8:22) and as begetting (John 1:14).[50]

A final point of confusion is Origen's use of the language of being (*ousia*), particularly in light of the Nicene confession that the Son is "of the same being with the Father" and was begotten "out of [or from: *ek*] the Father's being." As we might expect, the idea that the Son was begotten from the Father's essence in Origen's milieu suggests a diminishment, material division, or corporeal passion like a human birth (*Com.Jn.* 20.157–58). While Origen holds that the Son is divine in nature like God the Father, he firmly denies that they share the same being. Similar to the term hypostasis, "being" denotes the actual existence of a thing as well as its nature. To say that two things have the same being or substance means either that they are the very same thing and not two things at all, or else that they share a common nature as members of a class (*Com.Jn.* 13.147–50) or by participating in the nature of a third, higher thing (*Princ.* 4.4.9). Origen vehemently opposes each of these ideas in reference to the Trinity. The Father, Son, and Holy Spirit certainly do not participate in a fourth, higher principle of divinity, nor are they three members of a generic class of Divinity; and, as we have seen, they are not exactly the same thing as each other, as the monarchian modalists held. The term *homoousios*, found in the Nicene Creed, may even have begun its theological life as a technical term among Origen's Valentinian opponents. Even if Origen did use the term in something like a Nicene sense, in a fragment of his *Commentary on Hebrews* quoted in Pamphilus's *Apology for Origen* (assuming its authenticity), it was a rare and uncharacteristic occurrence, and the term was avoided by many other theologians well into the fourth century for the reasons noted.[51] Origen's restriction of the term being/*ousia* to each of the three members of the Trinity as individuals thus preserves each one's unique existence, the Father's role as source of the other two (against the additional principle of a common divinity), and the incorporeality of their being and relations with one another. It does not serve to deny their common divinity or equality; nor does it indicate that Origen espoused a position that the Council of Nicaea, or later Athanasius, sought to oppose.

In sum, the Father's generation of the Son makes the Son divine, distinct from the Father, and yet also equal to the Father in divinity. It is because the Father has given the Son to possess everything that the Father has that "in the name of Jesus every knee shall bow" and "confess that he is Lord in the glory of God the Father" (Phil 2:10–11; *Princ.* 1.2.10). Or, as Origen writes against Celsus, Christians "worship only one God, the Father and the Son. . . . We worship the Father of the truth and the Son who is the truth; they are two distinct existences, but one in mental unity, agreement, and identity of will" (*C.Cels.* 8.12).[52]

THE IMAGE OF GOD

There is another sense in which the Father and the Son are distinguished from one another—a difference of the manner of their divinity, we might say—which takes us more deeply into the mystery of the Trinity. Origen points to the distinct character of the Son's divinity in his treatment of the image of light in John 1, which he takes up in the second book of the *Commentary on John*, a book devoted to the question of how the Son is divine (*Com.Jn.* 2.149–51).[53] Where John calls the Son the light that "shines in the darkness and is not overcome by it" (John 1:5), Origen remarks that the being of the Son is different from that of the Father, who is the light "in which there is no darkness at all" (1 John 1:5) and which has not "shined in the darkness" as the Son has. The two lights are not the same, Origen says, because the one came into the darkness of the world while the other did not; they are distinguished, in other words, by their economic activity. Yet, as Origen continues, the two divine lights are distinct in their permanent identities as well, apart from the Son's involvement in the divine economy. The light that is God the Father is greater than the light that is the Son because he is the source of the Son, just as the Father of Truth surpasses Truth and the Father of Wisdom surpasses Wisdom. Note that Origen does not say that the Father is a brighter light or wiser or truer than the Son. In fact, he argues the reverse several times: the Son is just as brilliant, wise, and true as the Father. But Origen does insist that the Father's role as source of the Son makes him in that sense greater than the Son. The two divine lights of Father and Son, then, are different beings or subsistent entities, and the Father is the greater of the two equally brilliant lights, both because of the manner of their divine being (the Father is source of the Son) and because of their different economic activities. The eternal and economic modes of existence are interconnected in a necessary way for Origen, to the point that he instinctively conflates the two and feels no need always to explain them as such. The Son's eternal divine nature as Wisdom, Word, Truth, and Life is, we might say, the character that enables him to mediate the life and knowledge of God to all creatures and ultimately to become incarnate in Jesus Christ. Conversely, the Son's economic activity indicates or reflects his eternal character as the divine Wisdom and Word of God (*Com. Jn.* 1.255).

At the same time that the Father and Son have a common divine nature, are equally divine, powerful, true, and wise, and share all the same qualities of the Divinity, they differ in the *manner* of their divine being. They are what we might call both equally divine and also "differently divine." Moreover, the difference of the Son's manner of being equally divine lies in the uniquely revelatory and communicative character *of his divine nature*, while the Father possesses (or is) the same divine nature in a way that is always the source and is not directly communicative. Origen describes the Son's special manner of being by means of the Son's many *epinoiai*, which stand in contrast with the pure simplicity of the Father. It is the Son's unique identity to be knowable and describable under the different conceptions contained in Scripture and to act in diverse ways toward creatures in their many different conditions; and yet at the same time there remains only one Son, and his different *epinoiai* and activities do not divide his singular divine being (*Com. Jn.* 1.200, 222).[54] On the other hand, the Father is purely and absolutely simple and is not directly describable by the same conceptions, nor does he adapt himself to people's different needs in the economy in the way that the Son does. It is only Christ, the divine Son, who "becomes many things, or perhaps even all these things, as the whole creation . . . needs him" (*Com. Jn.* 1.119).[55]

Origen captures this uniquely adaptive and revelatory manner of the Son's divine being chiefly through the idea of the image of God. Some have argued that Christ's identity as the image of God is the conceptual center of Origen's Christology.[56] His idea of Christ as image builds on his treatment of the titles Wisdom and Word. Although the Son is preeminently Wisdom, Origen says, he does not merely contain the thoughts and intentions of God in himself, apart from any act toward creation. It is an equally real aspect of the Son's divine identity—even apart from the incarnation—to be Word as well, the agent and means of creation and the communicator of God's mind and will to all those whom God has made. Considering the unity of all Christ's *epinoiai* in a single subject, we could say that the Word is simply Wisdom conveyed and communicated to others: "For Wisdom opens to all other beings, that is, to the whole creation, the meaning of the mysteries and secrets that are contained within the Wisdom of God, and so she is called the Word, because she is as it were an interpreter of the mind's secrets" (*Princ.* 1.2.3). It is in this sense that the Son is also the image of God.

As with the metaphors of light and human willing, Origen again qualifies the idea of image in a particular way. Christ is the image of God the Father more in the way that a human child is the image of its parent than in the sense of a painted or carved image: he is a distinctly existing being just like his parent, not a mere artifact made by a superior being. Christ is the image of God more like Seth is the image of his parent Adam (Gen 5:3); whereas a painted or carved image is a better metaphor for the creation of human beings after the image of God (Gen 1:26). The difference between the two types of imaging is that the Father and the Son are of the same nature, just as a human parent and child are both human beings; whereas an artist and an artifact are not of the same nature.[57] In other words, the Son is the exact image of God the Father. In *First Principles* Origen writes that if the Father is the original goodness, then the Son is an image of the Father "in every respect" (*per omnia*), including "an Image of his goodness." For this reason the Son possesses no other goodness than that of the Father, as indicated by Jesus's statement that no one is good but God the Father (Mark 10:18). It is not that the Son and the Holy Spirit are not also good; but their goodness comes only from the Father and is his goodness in them, and it is in this same sense that the Son is God's image (*Princ.* 1.2.13). Here again, there are certain passages in which Origen might seem to be saying that the Son as image is less than the Father in his divinity or goodness,[58] including further interpolations to that effect by his later detractors.[59] Yet, as before, other texts make Origen's meaning clear enough. In *Against Celsus* he argues that the Son is an image of equal magnitude as the Father, for "he gave a share of himself and his greatness to the only-begotten and firstborn of all creation, that being himself an 'image of the invisible God' [Col 1:15] he might preserve the image of the Father also in his greatness" (*C.Cels.* 6.69). The Son's nature as exact image of the Father can be seen most clearly in the way that the Son does everything that the Father does, as Jesus says of himself (John 5:19), and so the idea of the Son as image clearly expresses the nature of the Father-Son relationship: "from it we learn how God can rightly be called the Father of his Son" (*Princ.* 1.2.6).

The Savior is the "image of the invisible God" in the sense that he is the one through whom alone creatures are able to know God the Father, who is the source of divinity and all existence (see Matt 11:27). For Origen, the Christian knowledge of God as Father marks a new departure in the human relationship with God, although the Word did come spiritually to some in the Old Testament (*Prayer* 20). As image, the Son reveals the Father by being understood himself, as Jesus said of himself, "Whoever has seen me has seen the Father also" (John 14:9; *Princ.* 1.2.6).[60] In the same way that the Son is the radiance of the light of the Father, without any separation or diminution, so too is he the Way to the Father, the Word that interprets the hidden Wisdom, and the image of God. "For it is through its brightness that one knows and perceives what the light itself is" (*Princ.* 1.2.7). And yet, at the same time, the Son is the image of the Father and the brightness of his radiance, but not the Father himself nor the source of light, mainly because the Son attenuates the divine light "softly and gently on the tender and weak eyes of mortals," being "a kind of mediator between human beings and the light"; so he is "the express image of [God's] hypostasis" (Heb 1:3) because he makes God known and understood (*Princ.* 1.2.7–8). The Son is therefore the image of God both by shining with the same light and by doing so in a unique way that can be seen by finite creatures. He is the image of God eternally, with respect to the Father alone, and also in the economy, in his relations toward creation.

The Son's aspect as image is therefore rooted in his permanent, divine identity, and it expresses the way in which he is "communicatively divine," so to speak. The Son's characteristic manner of being God, his personal or hypostatic *idios*, is to be the Wisdom, Word, and image of God. The Son is the mediator between God and creation not because he is any less divine, but rather because of the *way* in which he is divine; the Son is hypostatically mediatory in such a way that characterizes the manner of his divine being itself. Apart from the incarnation, the Son too is invisible, just as the Father, yet he is the invisible *image* of the invisible God, which the Father is not (*Princ.* 1.2.6).[61] Moreover, the Son's nature as image is the basis of the supreme revelation of God accomplished in the incarnation: because it is the Son's eternal identity to be the revealer and communicator of the Father's divinity, he is uniquely suited to undertake the mission of the incarnation.

INCARNATION: THE IMAGE REVEALED

The Son's identity as the image of God includes more than his eternal existence with the Father apart from creaturely affairs. For Origen, we cannot understand even the Son's character as God's image without an account of his incarnation. If the Son is the invisible image of the invisible God, then the purpose of the incarnation is to make the invisible image of God finally visible in the life, death, and resurrection of Jesus Christ. Whereas the Word of God came to dwell in only a few individuals previously (Moses and the prophets), now through Christ the Son is revealed to all people, and the Word comes to dwell in all who have true faith in Christ. As the visible image of God, Christ is the Word made flesh and the "one mediator between God and human beings" (1 Tim 2:5; *Princ.* 1.2.8; 2.6.1).

Christ's identity as image of God is central to Origen's Christology because it serves as the linchpin between the eternal, divine life of God and the human life of Jesus and his disciples in the church. Origen indicates this close connection in his discussion of the Son as image in *First Principles* by moving seamlessly from the Son's identity as eternal Wisdom of God, who "outlines first in herself the things that she wishes to reveal to others," to the Son's incarnation as Jesus Christ (*Princ.* 1.2.8). He illustrates the connection with the metaphor of a statue. As the invisible image of God, the eternal Son is like a statue that is larger than the world, so large in fact that it cannot be seen.[62] In order to make the immense statue seen, another statue is made exactly like the invisibly large one, the same in every detail except that it is smaller and capable of fitting within the world and of being perceived—a visible image, in other words. This second statue is the incarnate Lord, who reveals God as an image just like the large, invisible image, except that it is smaller in magnitude. As a result, those who were unable to perceive the invisible statue can be confident that they nevertheless have seen it when they behold the visible one, because it preserves every line of the limbs and features and the very form and material with an absolutely indistinguishable similarity.[63] This illustration, Origen says, helps to give a more complete understanding of how the Son is the "identical imprint of God's substance" (Heb 1:3). The Son is ultimately the image of God, then, by becoming visible as Jesus. This is the whole purpose of his self-emptying to become incarnate: "to show us the fullness of the Divinity," to reveal the invisible God, to make God known and understood (*Princ.* 1.2.8).

At this point Origen's dualist cosmological framework makes itself felt in profound ways. If the purpose of the incarnation is to make the invisible image of God visible, and so to bring about the knowledge of God the Father, how does this happen? Indeed, how is it possible at all for an intelligible, divine nature to come into contact with our fleeting, sensible world? What sort of revelatory incarnation does Origen imagine? The answer is rather complicated, and not what one would expect if one already has in mind something like the orthodox Christology of the later patristic councils.

We have already noted that Origen introduces his treatment of Christ in *First Principles* by stating that Christ has "two natures": he understands Christ above all as a combination of these two very different realities. Similarly, when he turns from Christ's divinity to the incarnation later in the work, Origen frames the subject in the same dual terms, beginning with an expression of sheer amazement. How could God, the transcendent Son and image of God, possibly have become human in Jesus Christ? "How can the very Word of the Father and Wisdom of God . . . be thought to have existed within the compass of the man who appeared in Judaea? How could the Wisdom of God have entered into a woman's womb and been born as a little child?! . . . And how is it that he was troubled in the hour of death? . . .

How, finally, was he led to that death that is considered the most shameful of all, even though on the third day he rose again?" (*Princ.* 2.6.1–2). At the outset, Origen's consideration of the incarnation is characterized by the great difference between the intelligible and the sensory realms. He thus approaches the incarnation as a sort of metaphysical problem, or even a scandal. Origen may be the first Christian theologian of record to view the incarnation as a logical or ontological problem, and this approach befits his philosophically colored mind-set.[64]

Origen describes the problem specifically as one of biblical interpretation. As we read Scripture, we see certain things in Christ that are just as frail and human as all other mortals are, but we also see other things that are so divine that they could belong only to the divine nature. The combination of the two is so perplexing, Origen exclaims, that our narrow human understanding is halted with amazement and loses all sense of direction. "If it senses God, it sees a mortal; if it thinks of a human being, it perceives one who returns with spoils from the dead, having vanquished the kingdom of death!" (*Princ.* 2.6.2).[65] The resulting task of the theologian, then, is to "show how the truth of each nature exists in one and the same being [*in uno eodemque*]." But here Origen quickly issues a qualification, revealing the deeply embedded pattern of his thought: the way to make sense of the incarnation is to observe the two-sided rule that "nothing unworthy or unfitting should be thought to exist in that divine and ineffable substance," and "the things that [Christ] has done must not be judged to have been the illusions of deceptive imaginings." It is crucial, in other words, that one maintain the integrity of the divine and the human natures of Christ, in their own terms. Origen's rule thus reflects his dualist cosmic framework, and to observe it "with all fear and reverence" is a matter of sober piety. The explanation of such a mystery, Origen concludes, surpasses his powers, and even that of the apostles, the angels, and every heavenly being (*Princ.* 2.6.2). This is a striking introduction to Origen's discussion of the incarnation in his only systematic theological work. At this point in the work he has adopted a predominantly rational or philosophical mode to set up the problem of the incarnation, however much he may disavow it or state its limits.[66] Judging from the torturous debates that consumed much of the church during the next five hundred years, Origen's comments are somewhat prophetic; although we could also say that he is as responsible as anyone for the fact that those debates took place at all.

Given these disclaimers, Origen goes on to explain the union of divinity and humanity in Christ in the following way. We must bear in mind that this explanation serves to resolve the problem of how these two radically different natures can exist together. In Origen's account, the only-begotten Son, through whom all things were made, granted to all created rational beings a participation in himself proportionate to the love with which each one clung to him. Yet of all created souls, only the soul of Jesus clung to God permanently, "in an inseparable and indissoluble union" (*Princ.* 2.6.2), from the time of his creation.[67] On account of this union, Jesus's human soul received the divine Son, Wisdom, Word, and Light into itself completely, and, conversely, he entered into the divine light: Jesus is fully "in" the Word, and the Word is "in" Jesus, and Jesus was made one spirit with the Word from the very beginning of his existence.

The human soul of Jesus bridges the gap between Christ's divinity and humanity in two key respects. First, Jesus's soul, like all souls, bears some innate resemblance to the Word, having been created in the image of the image of God, as a rational (*logikos*) being through its participation in the Word (*Logos*). It is therefore able to bridge the divine-human gap on account of its rational constitution. In this respect Jesus's soul acts as "a medium between God and the flesh," since it was not otherwise possible for the divine nature to "mingle" with a human body. It is contrary to the divine nature, Origen says, for it to assume a human body, and vice versa, although it is not contradictory for a human soul to assume human flesh or to "receive God, into whom it had already completely entered." The incarnate Lord possesses a full and complete human nature, body and soul (*Princ.* 4.4.4), which suffered human things, was mortal during his earthly existence, and died a human death (*C.Cels.* 2.16, 42; 4.16; 7.17). A famous passage in Origen's *Dialog with Heraclides* expresses Jesus's humanity in terms that will become important later. Because Christ wanted to save the entire human being—body, soul, and spirit (see 1 Thess 5:23)—he assumed all three parts as an entire human being (ὅλον τὸν ἄνθρωπον, *Heracl.* 7).[68] Through the mediation of Jesus's human soul (*Princ.* 2.6.3), Christ is thus born as "a sort of composite being" (*C.Cels.* 1.66).[69]

The second way in which Jesus's soul mediates between divinity and humanity is the result of his righteousness and love for God. With apologies for how difficult it is to find suitable comparisons for God or Christ, Origen argues that Jesus's soul remained united with God as a reward for "the perfection of his love" for the Word. The Word took up, or assumed, this soul as "a privilege conferred upon it in reward for its virtues," as the psalmist testified (Ps 45:7), and Jesus was likewise filled with the Holy Spirit as a reward for his love (*Princ.* 2.6.3).[70] Moreover, Jesus's love of the Son, which brought about this intimate union, was achieved as a result of his free choice. Against docetist and Gnostic views, Origen is concerned to maintain that Jesus is fully human in every proper sense, and this means that he makes moral choices and is capable of both good and evil, at least in principle. At the same time, Origen is committed to the belief that Jesus was in fact sinless, as the New Testament reports (Heb 4:15). In order to maintain both, Origen explains that Jesus chose to love righteousness with such an immensity of love that his firmness of purpose caused his soul to transform from being morally mutable to being immutable. Having chosen to love righteousness so intensely, Jesus became incapable of sinning in actual fact, and "what formerly depended upon the will was, by the influence of long custom, changed into nature." Jesus therefore had a human soul that makes choices and was originally capable of evil in principle, yet he was also in a real sense unable to sin (*Princ.* 2.6.5).

Origen gives us a further sense of how his Christology works in the influential illustration that he offers next. The natural righteousness of Jesus's soul is like iron that is constantly held in the fire and so is consumed by the fire. Because it is totally engulfed in the fire's heat, the iron can no longer admit of cold, as it could have before it was placed in the fire. The fire has so entirely consumed the iron, Origen adds, that the iron has "completely changed into fire," since nothing other than fire can be perceived in it, as anyone who tries to touch it will quickly find out. In like manner, Jesus's soul has dwelled in the divine Son so constantly that he is "God in all his acts and feelings and thoughts," and he has acquired the divine quality of immutability. Origen couples the natural righteousness and stability of Jesus's soul with the idea of essential divinity already discussed. Unlike the saints, in whom the Word and Spirit of God dwell accidentally, in Jesus the divine fire of the Word rests essentially (*substantialiter*) (*Princ.* 1.5.3, 5; 1.6.2; 2.6.4).[71] Likewise, only in Jesus does the Spirit "remain," as John the Baptist witnessed (John 1:33–34; see Isa 11:1–2); whereas the Spirit came upon the prophets from time to time, since they were sinners (*Hom.Isa.* 3.2). The state of Jesus's soul is unique as well in that he is the source of the warmth of God that others must receive from him. Jesus's soul is like the vase that contains the ointment that the saints merely smell, or he is the substance of the ointment while the saints are its odor. While Jesus can never lose his beautiful smell, the saints can become more or less sweet smelling depending on their proximity to Jesus (*Princ.* 2.6.6).

On the face of it, Origen appears to have solved the exegetical problem he has set for himself. The reason why Scripture sometimes says human things about Christ's divine nature and divine things about his human nature is that the union between Jesus and the divine Word is so close. Yet when we examine Origen's treatment of specific biblical texts, he allows for less unity between Jesus's divinity and humanity than one might expect. Here we have a classic example of the way in which one's actual practice of biblical interpretation can reveal more about one's theological commitments than the technical terms and dogmatic formulas that one espouses more generally. In a key chapter of *First Principles*, Origen gives the following account of his Christological exegesis. The way to solve the exegetical dilemma of divine and human statements made about the same Christ is this. Because Jesus's soul intermingles with the divine Son in the way we have noted, it is appropriate to call the man Jesus "Son of God" and other divine titles, and also to call the divine Son of God "Jesus," "Son of Man," and other human titles—and even to say that the Son of God died on the cross—such as we find occurring throughout Scripture (*Princ.* 2.6.3). Again, in his *Commentary on Romans*, Origen gives this definition: "Because of the inseparable unity of the Word and flesh, everything that is of the flesh is attributed to the Word also, and the things that belong to the Word are foretold in the flesh. For we often find the designations 'Jesus' and 'Christ' and 'Lord' referred to both natures" (*Com.Rom.* 1.6.2). Thus Origen gives the first extant account in patristic literature of what will later be called the *communicatio idiomatum*, the "communication of idioms" or "attributes," whereby divine statements are cross-predicated of Christ's humanity and human statements of his divinity.

So far Origen appears to have given a strong account of Christ's unity. But in his actual treatment of the *communicatio idiomatum*, Origen is in fact more concerned to note the *limitations* of such expressions than he is to highlight any deep Christological unity that they might indicate. On the whole, Origen's account merely serves to explain a convention of verbal predication. Nowhere does he attempt to justify biblical cross-predication on the grounds that such human statements are *real and true* descriptions of the Son of God, or that divine statements are accurate descriptions of the human Jesus on account of the incarnation (apart from the sort of transformation already mentioned). On the contrary, Origen takes pains to deny that such statements are realistically true. His comments on John 8:19 make the situation quite plain: "At one time the Savior is speaking of himself as a human being, but at another time he speaks of himself as a nature that is divine and united with the uncreated nature of the Father. For when he says, 'But now you seek to kill me, a human being . . .' (John 8:40), he says this knowing that what they are attempting to destroy is *not* God but a human being. But if he says, 'I and the Father are one' [etc.], he is *not* teaching about the human being whom they are attempting to destroy" (*Com.Jn.* 19.6). In the following sections of the *Commentary on John*, Origen proceeds to distinguish which statements refer to the human Jesus and which ones refer to his divinity. He assumes, in other words, that there are two different subjects of action, and that a given biblical statement must refer to one or the other. The two types of expression are different because, as the divine Son, Christ is "a different being [ἕτερος], as it were," from the one who says things about his human nature (*Com.Jn.* 19.7–11).[72] Not surprisingly, Origen occasionally shows some pressure toward adopting a more realistic cross-predication, as in his statement that "the different forms of Jesus are to be applied to the nature of the Logos" (*C.Cels.* 6.77). Yet, as a rule, he enforces a strict separation of divine and human refer- ents, and he denies that the divine Son is the proper referent of Jesus's crea- turely titles and actions and the many *epinoiai* that Christ becomes toward creatures, excepting Wisdom, Word, Life, and Truth, which denote the Son eternally (*Com.Jn.* 1.200). When Jesus says that his soul is troubled or sorrowful unto death (Matt 26:38; John 12:27), it is the human Jesus who is speaking, *not* the divine Word, since he is speaking about his soul in a way that cannot refer to the Word in any appropriate sense (*Princ.* 4.4.4).[73] In passages such as these, Origen makes it clear that the *communicatio idiomatum* is merely a conventional practice of biblical language; it does not signify a real sharing of attributes, nor a singularity of subject to which both apply.

The separation that Origen maintains between Christ's divinity and humanity is nowhere more conspicuous than in his treatment of Christ's passion and crucifixion. Origen occasionally describes the crucifixion as the climax of Christ's saving work and the point at which we should expect to see his divinity most fully revealed. The idea undoubtedly comes from Jesus's statements in John's gospel that he will glorify the Father and the Father will glorify him in his death. Commenting on John 13:31 ("God is glorified in him"), Origen writes that Jesus will "rise up for the world" and be supremely glorified on the cross. In Jesus's crucifixion "the Son will reveal the Father by means of the economy, on account of which 'God has been glorified in him,'" and here it will be especially true that "whoever has seen me has seen the Father who sent me" (John 12:45) (*Com.Jn.* 32.359).[74] Earlier in the *Commentary on John*, Origen makes the point quite strongly: "We must dare to say that the goodness of Christ appeared greater and more divine and truly in accordance with the image of the Father when 'he humbled himself and became obedient unto death, even death on a cross,' than if he had 'considered being equal to God robbery' (Phil 2:8, 6) and had not been willing to become a servant for the salvation of the world" (*Com. Jn.* 1.231).[75] The greatest part of Christ's incarnation was therefore "the fact that he became an innocent little lamb . . . led to be slaughtered, that he might 'take away the sin of the world' [John 1:29] . . . and we might all be cleansed by his death" (*Com.Jn.* 1.233).[76] Here it is the crucifixion that shows God's divinity and goodness most of all, beyond any revelations of the divine status of the Son apart from the incarnation. Yet, despite the force of such claims, the "daring" quality of such a confession tends to win out in the bulk of Origen's reflections on Christ. Elsewhere in the *Commentary on John*, he carefully qualifies what the Lamb of God is and what it is not. The Lamb is Christ's humanity alone. The divine Son ("God in man") is *not* sacrificed on the cross, but is the great high priest who does the sacrificing. Indeed, Origen understands Jesus's statement in John 10:18—"I lay down [my life] of myself. I have power to lay it down, and power to take it up again"—as referring to Christ's divinity and humanity as two subjects (*Com.Jn.* 6.273–75).

Although Origen's mind-set is well established by the time he wrote the first books of his *Commentary on John* and *First Principles*, his late work *Against Celsus* shows the dualist framework of his Christology especially clearly. Here Origen seeks to answer Celsus's acute and ridiculing objections to the ignominy of Jesus's life and death, to the idea that the transcendent God mixes in creaturely affairs, and especially to the suggestion that God can suffer in any way. Several times Celsus registers a typically Greek complaint that the vulnerability and humiliations of Jesus, as presented in the New Testament and the church's rule of faith, are unbefitting of God, according to a respectable notion of the Divinity. Origen's answer is consistent throughout. In book 7, for example, he argues that, first of all, it was the image of God, not God the Father (ὁ θεός), who became human in Jesus; and second, it was Jesus's humanity that suffered and died, not his divinity. The "unseemly matters" of Jesus's death therefore do not

conflict with "the accepted notion of God," and Celsus's theological principles are in fact correct, even if he is mistaken about what Christians believe
in certain details (*C.Cels.* 7.17). Origen denies that there is even a popular
devotional sense in which one can speak of the death of God in Christ: not
even simple Christians would say that the Way, the Truth, and the Life
(John 11:15) died. If anyone were to say such a thing, it would be idiotic,
and Celsus would be further justified in his objections to Christianity.
Rather, Origen explains, "the rationale of [the divine Son] and his essence is
different from the rationale of the human being that is observed in Jesus"
(*C.Cels.* 7.16).[77] Although the one who "dwelt in" Jesus said such things
about himself (according to the *communicatio idiomatum*), it was strictly
speaking the human Jesus who died on the cross. Consequently, whatever
one refers to Jesus's divinity must be "pious, and not in conflict with the
[proper] notion of God." One can speak of the death of Jesus only under
the proviso that one keeps the divine and the human aspects of Christ clear
and distinct (*C.Cels.* 7.16–17).[78] It is simply wrong, Origen believes, to think
that "the tortured and punished body of Jesus, rather than the Divinity in
him, was God" (*C.Cels.* 7.42). In short, "it is not permitted to say that God
dies" (*Com.Jn.* 20.85) because "the Word suffers nothing" (*C.Cels.* 7.15).[79]
Throughout his work Origen denies that God, or the divine Son, suffers
anything in the divine economy. He is constantly concerned to preserve an
appropriate notion of God, which does not allow that creaturely passivities
can cross the sharp dividing line between the divinity and the sensible
creaturely realm. Even the statements of Scripture and the many *epinoiai* of
Christ can refer to the divine Son only as a linguistic convention. Jesus's
birth and human life, as well as his death, cannot be seen to pollute
God with the impurity of embodiment or human brokenness (*C.Cels.*
6.73; 7.13).[80]

Origen's denial of God's suffering in the incarnation and crucifixion
informs his understanding of Christ's atoning sacrifice as well. When he
interprets Christ's saving work on the cross, he further qualifies what it
means for God to glorify Christ and for Christ to glorify God. Especially in
his biblical commentaries and homilies, it is clear that Origen believes that
salvation comes directly from Christ's death on the cross. Indeed, he argues
in the *Commentary on John* that the greatest aspect of the incarnation, as
noted, is that Jesus became an innocent Lamb of God who was slaughtered
in order to take away the sin of the world (Isa 53:7; John 1:29; *Com.Jn.* 1.233;
28.163). Jesus's death is a propitiatory sacrifice, comparable with the Old

Testament sacrifices (*Com.Rom.* 3.8), and it is such a powerful remedy that it cleanses believers, and indeed the entire cosmos, from sin and the powers of evil (*Com.Jn.* 1.233; 28.163). Given the centrality of the crucifixion for salvation, it is all the more significant what Origen believes took place on the cross, and why Christ's death is a universally saving event. Jesus is the Lamb of God only as a human being, as we have noted; as the divine Word, Wisdom, peace, and justice of God, however, he is the Great High Priest who sacrifices the Lamb, again "because the Image of the invisible God . . . does not admit of death" (*Com.Jn.* 28.157–59). The chief "mechanism" that makes Jesus's death salvific is not his divine identity or even the proximity of God in his death, but Jesus's sinlessness and perfect obedience as a human being (*Com.Jn.* 28.160). Even though the Word and the Holy Spirit dwell in the soul of Jesus, and vice versa (*Com.Rom.* 3.8.5–6), they do not figure in the sacrifice in any discernable way; rather, as we have seen, Origen is more concerned to keep the Word safely distant from the corruption and disgrace of Christ's death. Indeed, Origen applies a variant of Hebrews 2:9 to say that Jesus died "apart from God" (*Com.Jn.* 28.163).[81] Like his initial union with the divine Son, Christ's atoning sacrifice is essentially an act of human heroism. Consequently, Origen stresses Jesus's bravery and virtue in the face of death (*C.Cels.* 2.24), to the point of resisting any suggestion of human weakness or vulnerability on Jesus's part. Those who think that Jesus had any fear in the face of death are wrong (*Com.Jn.* 32.295): when Jesus asked for "this cup to pass from me," he was actually seeking an even greater ordeal of suffering than what the Father had willed him to endure (*Ex.Mart.* 29)![82]

To be sure, Origen sometimes describes the unity of Christ in terms that appear quite strong. In one section of *Against Celsus*, he writes that since Jesus's soul was united to the Word by a supreme participation, we should make no further distinction between them: "For the sacred words of the divine Scriptures also mention other things that are two in their own nature, but which are reckoned to become *and really are* one [ἕν] with each other" (*C.Cels.* 6.47, emphasis added). There are other passages in which Origen speaks of the incarnation as primarily the act of God, and where God seems to be the unifying agent (*Com.Jn.* 32.46; *C.Cels.* 3.28). Yet in most of these texts Origen is merely echoing unitive statements found in Scripture, such as "the Word became flesh" (John 1:14) or Paul's statement that "Christ Jesus, . . . who was in the form of God, . . . emptied himself and took the form of a slave" (Phil 2:5–7). Occasionally, Origen uses terms that will later indicate a high degree of unity, such as "union," "communion," "intermingling," and "composition" (*C.Cels.* 1.66; 2.16; 3.28, 41).[83]

Here again, Origen's broader argumentation shows his real thinking on the matter. A good example can be found in book 2 of *Against Celsus*, where he answers Celsus's objection that Jesus does not seem much like a son of God by traditional Greek standards. Origen first states that Christians do not separate (*chorizontes*) the Son of God from Jesus, since after the incarnation the soul and body of Jesus became one with the Word of God, being united more closely than Christians are in spirit with the Lord. Yet he immediately qualifies himself against the suspicion that such a statement might violate the canons of Greek theology or Jewish monotheism: "Not even *we* suppose that the body of Jesus, which could then be seen and perceived by the senses, was God. . . . Not even his soul was God." Rather, "it was the divine Logos and Son of the God of the universe that spoke in Jesus, saying, 'I am the Way, the Truth, and the Life' " (John 14:6), and so on (*C.Cels.* 2.9). Even though he is committed to confessing the incarnation in some unitive sense for biblical and traditional reasons, Origen's main stance against Celsus, as it has been throughout his career, is to keep the divine and human elements of Christ neatly and safely distinct in their respective spheres.

We are now in a position to make a final assessment of Origen's account of the union of Jesus's humanity with the Word of God. As we have already seen, Origen's technical description of the union hinges on Jesus's soul. Jesus's soul provides a bridge between the irreconcilable spheres of divinity and humanity not only for ontological reasons, but especially as a result of Jesus's righteousness and love for the Word. Origen explains further in *Against Celsus*, "The perfect man cleaves to the Word itself by his virtue and so is united with him," and it is for this reason that Jesus is the Son of God (*C.Cels.* 6.47–48). Even when he speaks of the Word "assuming" a human body and soul, as if the Word were the active agent in the union (*Princ.* 1.2.2; *C.Cels.* 4.15), in fact the unifying activity comes from the side of Jesus's humanity. Origen gives no indication in his focused Christological discussions that the Word inspires or moves Jesus's soul to love him, and, as we have seen, he denies that Jesus's human experiences are also the Word's. From the beginning of Origen's account of the incarnation, the soul of Jesus is an independently existing creature who acts (either logically or ontologically) "prior" to his union with the Word.[84] Even if its effects are transformative of Jesus's human nature, the incarnation is fundamentally the product of a moral union between Jesus's soul and the Word, rather than a union achieved by the Son's divine nature or his distinct personhood in what later theologians would call a substantial or hypostatic union.[85] Despite some indications to the contrary, Origen's Christology is basically dualist, in a way that largely mirrors his Platonic cosmology and anthropology.

CHRIST THE EXEMPLAR

In his overall view of spiritual development, Origen distinguishes between simple faith, which is a mere beginning to the Christian life, and its proper end in the knowledge of God. He bases himself in part on Paul's distinction between faith and knowledge among the gifts of the Holy Spirit (1 Cor 12:8–9), with reinforcement from the language of knowing God in John's gospel. Accordingly, Abraham had faith, as the Scriptures say (Rom 4:3; Gen 15:6), but he did not "know" God. For Origen, knowledge comes only for those who "continue in [Jesus's] words" (see John 8:31–32), because to know something is to be united with it and participate in it, as the sexual connotations of biblical knowing suggest.[86] Knowing and being known by God mean that the Lord has been made one with his own, "has given them a share of his own divinity, and has taken them up . . . into his own hand" (*Com.Jn.* 19.18–19, 25). In this way basic faith leads to a fuller participation in the divine nature.

Here again we appear to be in the territory of union. In one sense Origen wants to say that faith perceives both divine and human in Jesus: the invisible image *in* the visible image and the Son of God in the face of the crucified and risen Jesus. This vision produces a transformation similar to that experienced by Jesus himself: "Christians see that from [Jesus] a divine and a human nature began to be woven together, so that by communion with what is more divine, human nature might become divine, not only in Jesus, but also in all who believe and go on to undertake the life that Jesus taught" (*Princ.* 3.28). Yet, again, there is more to the picture than these simple expressions suggest. Faith becomes knowledge through Christ by moving *beyond* Christ's humanity, which is the purview of the "simple," to the perception of his divinity, which can be had only by the advanced. To know God means to have proceeded from knowing "Christ crucified" (1 Cor 2:2; *Com.Jn.* 1.43, 58), "Christ according to the flesh" (2 Cor 5:16; *Com.Mt.* 11.17; 12.4; 15.3)—that is, the human Jesus—to knowing the only-begotten Son of God; and from there to knowing God the Father. Origen imagines believers, in other words, moving from seeing the visible image of God, to the invisible image, to the archetype itself (*C.Cels.* 1.66; 3.14).[87] In this scheme Origen envisions a shift from the human Jesus, who existed in the sensible realm, to the divine Son, who exists incorporeally in the intelligible realm. While the incarnation is necessary for this vision to take place, at least for heuristic purposes, the goal is to move beyond the incarnate Christ, just as the philosopher generally aims to move away from the sensible and toward the divine, heavenly realm.[88]

It is here that Origen's view of the resurrected body later came to haunt him. On the one hand, he solidly anchored himself in Paul's teaching of the necessary demise of the earthly body and the eschatological prospect of the resurrected, spiritual body (1 Cor 15). Yet in light of his broader Platonist cosmology (which Paul did not share), Origen's views on earthly versus heavenly existence often proved to be indistinguishable from a flat denial of the persistence of the human body and the physical world in the redeemed state. This idea is evident as well in Origen's suggestions that the final consummation (*apokatastasis*) involves a return to our original condition of existence as pure souls (even if we allow for a nontemporal sense of our origin), and in his notion that angels too have bodies, which would hardly be a sufficient constitution for a New Earth. The controversy over Origen's doctrine of the resurrection was misplaced at a technical level,[89] but it was not without foundation within the larger scope of his work.

Origen's focus on Christ's divinity beyond (rather than always through) his humanity reflects his general division of Christ into two independently existing natures. Consequently, the burden of the union—both for Christ and for his followers—inevitably falls on the human side, apart from what otherwise appears to be the primary, divinizing work of God.[90] As indicated in the above quotation, the union of divine and human natures for all Christians depends on the moral progress that makes one worthy of such union, and communion with Christ is achieved chiefly by imitation of his virtue (*Com.Jn.* 1.59). Faith will not be "reckoned as righteousness" (Rom 4:22), Origen warns, for those who continue in wicked deeds (*Com. Rom.* 4.7). In order to perceive Christ's divinity at all, one must be purified and so made worthy of the grace of being able to perceive God with eyes that are more divine than our mere physical sight (*Com.Jn.* 1.58–59, 189). Just as Jesus's soul merited union with the divine Son through his perfect virtue, and he effected atonement for sin through his heroic obedience on the cross, so too Jesus helps to bring about the redemption of his followers chiefly as an example for their imitation. At the most basic level, Origen's Christ is a moral exemplar, and it is in this sense that he is the pioneer of our salvation (Heb 2:10). Because Christ always chose the good and hence God anointed him, we too can become partakers of the divine nature by imitating Christ's life (*Princ.* 4.4.4).[91]

In both respects we see the moralizing tendency of Origen's soteriology. He likens the movement of Christ's soul in its union with the Word to "the shadow of Christ" (Lam 4:20). It is the task of Christians to live under Christ's shadow by imitating his soul through their way of life.[92] Through such imitation the lives of his followers will be "hidden with Christ in God" (Col 3:3), and it will be Christ who speaks in them (2 Cor 13:3; *Princ.* 2.6.7). In an important sense Christ *is* the virtues, all of which are *epinoiai* (*Com.Jn.* 32.127), so that formation in Christ is synonymous with formation in virtue (*Com.Rom.* 2.5; 9.34). What Jesus reveals most of all is human obedience to God,[93] and the promise of union with God thus depends on a Christic moralism. Origen's Christology is one of intense moral striving, and it is no wonder that he practiced and promoted such a rigorous form of asceticism. His defense of divine impassibility and his high regard for human self-determination (*autexousia*) helped to oppose Gnostic predestinarianism and disparagements of God and Egyptian astral fatalism, much as it did for other Platonists. Perhaps the shock of his father's murder—an unremittingly life-changing act on the part of a power unfriendly to Christianity—also contributed to Origen's reliance on human perseverance to bring about rectitude and union with God. Origen himself went on to become a scholar of unsurpassed industry and dedication, in defense of the true philosophy, in response to his family's great loss. Origen certainly believed that Jesus Christ, rather than Plato or Socrates, is the ultimate source of religious truth, and we must remember that he paid for this belief with great physical suffering, and ultimately with his life. At the same time, the way in which he understood Christ was undoubtedly framed by the philosophical and cosmological views that he adopted through years of study since his youth in Alexandria.

In the end, Origen's understanding of Jesus Christ is a strange paradox. On the one hand, he articulates Christ's divinity, distinctness, and eternal relation to God the Father, as well as Christ's full humanity, to an extent that was unprecedented in its time and in a way that would later be seen to be faithful to the biblical witness and the rule of faith. In this respect

Origen proved to be foundational for later thinking about Christ's divinity and humanity and the mystery of the Trinity. Yet, on the other hand, he manages to keep the two spheres of reality neatly separated, and he seems at a loss about how God might affect the created order of physical bodies and human wills, and particularly how the darkest and most threatening aspects of our existence could be taken up in the divine economy. In his Christological dualism and moralizing spirituality, we see the full effect of Origen's philosophical worldview on his theology, and it is here that the legacy of his Christology proved to be most unsettling in the succeeding centuries. Despite the tantalizing suggestion that Christ's nature as the invisible image of the invisible God inclines him toward the revelation of God to creatures, Origen generally works to keep the Son away from the dark abyss of Jesus's death, safely enclosed in the preserve of philosophical divinity.[94] Considering that in the broader sweep of patristic tradition, a pluralist Trinitarianism such as Origen's normally accompanies a highly unitive Christology, whereas a dualist Christology normally belongs with the sort of monistic view of the Trinity that Origen opposed,[95] this tension is arguably the most deeply contradictory aspect of Origen's work as a whole.

Origen believed that orthodoxy must be received and reconstructed anew in each generation by inspired interpreters of Scripture.[96] For the patristic theologians who came after him, this reception inevitably involved grappling with Origen's own teaching about Christ. As we shall see, the long-term difficulties with Origen's theology were not primarily Trinitarian, as is often supposed, but Christological. And yet he seems to have been aware of this at some level. In *First Principles* Origen voices his concern that the incarnation is a profound ontological and conceptual problem. Accordingly, he issues a disclaimer that is also a challenge: "If anyone can discover something better and prove what he says by clearer statements out of the holy Scriptures, let his opinion be accepted in preference to mine!" (*Princ.* 2.6.7). That is exactly what Christian theologians strove to do for the next five centuries.

Part II
Fourth-Century Authorities

2. Eusebius of Caesarea

The official accounts of church history and the standard textbooks of late antiquity tend to depict the great fourth century as being determined by the first "ecumenical" Council of Nicaea in 325 and the rise of the Christian Roman empire under Constantine. Even the most recent studies of fourth-century theology begin with some sort of prelude to the Arian crisis and the great council of 325, from which the narrative then takes shape.[1] Yet this momentous period of Christian history did not commence with any sense that conflict was about to erupt between the Alexandrian presbyter Arius and his bishop; nor were the issues that precipitated the crisis acutely controversial before the early 320s, when disputes over the legacy of Origen began anew. On the contrary, the fourth century began in the Christian East with a sizeable number of bishops basing their ministries on the sacred Scriptures and seeking guidance from notable pastors and theologians of the past—above all Origen.

The most influential church leader of the early fourth century was not Athanasius of Alexandria, as most accounts would have it, but the great scholar-bishop Eusebius of Caesarea in Palestine. Having become a Christian in Caesarea, where Origen had established his library and study center, Eusebius went on to become metropolitan bishop and the most accomplished Christian scholar of his generation—a great Origenist himself, and the most prolific extant writer of any kind from this period. As we shall see, Eusebius also became one of the major influences on the development of mainstream orthodox Christology in the remainder of the patristic centuries, although he is rarely recognized as such. Before we turn to Eusebius, however, we take note of the state of Origenist theology, and opposition to it, in the early fourth century.

EARLY-FOURTH-CENTURY ORIGENISM

During the several decades that followed his death, Origen's works were much studied and debated. We know little about theological developments in the latter half of the third century, but toward the beginning of the fourth some signs begin to emerge. Our clearest picture of early-fourth-century Origenism comes from what remains of the work of Pamphilus of Caesarea. Originally from an aristocratic family in Beirut, the priest Pamphilus (240?–310) studied in Alexandria under the Origenist teacher Pierius after a dramatic conversion to Christianity (*H.E.* 7.32).[2] In his Origenist phase, Jerome lauded both Pamphilus and Pierius. Pamphilus was an ardent disciple of Origen, "on fire with such love for the sacred library that he copied with his own hand the greatest part of the volumes of Origen which are contained to this very day in the library of Caesarea." Jerome himself boasted of owning twenty-five volumes of Origen's *Commentary on the Twelve Minor Prophets* copied by Pamphilus, which he regarded with such joy as if he possessed the riches of Croesus (*Vir.Ill.* 75.1–2). Pamphilus was responsible for enlarging the work and influence of Origen's school in Caesarea, and it was there that Eusebius acquired his formation in Christian theology and spirituality. The fruit of Pamphilus's work endured for three hundred years, until the library was destroyed during the Arab conquest in the seventh century. In 307, during the persecution of Diocletian, Pamphilus was arrested and condemned to hard labor in the mines. Eusebius frequently visited him there and later reported that the Romans had tortured Pamphilus by scraping the skin of his sides down to the bone (*Mart.Pal.* 7.6; 11.17). In 310, under the reign of Maximinus Daia, Pamphilus was finally beheaded.[3]

Pamphilus's only surviving work is his *Defense of Origen*, of which he wrote five books while in prison (Jerome, *Vir.Ill.* 4), Eusebius completing the sixth book after Pamphilus's death; only the first book survives, in the Latin translation of Rufinus. The first book of the *Defense* gives us valuable insight into the state of Origenist theology, and recent opposition to it, in early-fourth-century Caesarea and beyond. It presents a general account of Origen's intentions and method as a theologian and a basic summary of his doctrine, all in reply to contemporary criticisms of Origen's work.

Pamphilus's work consists mainly of excerpts from Origen's texts, introduced by Pamphilus's comments in response to particular criticisms. The collection concentrates on *First Principles*, which had apparently become the main text under dispute (*Apol.* 46). At a social level, Pamphilus speaks of popular devotion to Origen, among both the simple and the well educated, that is strong enough to be thought excessive (exceeding the authority of the apostles) by Origen's opponents (*Apol.* 1).[4] It is difficult to know to what extent this portrait reflects a real social situation or Pamphilus's rhetorical elaboration.

Pamphilus's description of Origen's doctrine and theological ethos is extremely interesting. In the introductory sections of the work, he takes pains to present Origen as a loyal man of the church. Origen's work focused mainly on the exposition of Scripture; he explicitly deferred to the authority of the apostles, and he qualifies all theological knowledge, including his own, as incomplete and tentative until the final, eschatological fulfillment. He is, moreover, a man of great humility and personal piety, and in sum, a giant teacher of the church, whose works are especially helpful in the central and ongoing task of interpreting Scripture (*Apol.* 3–15). This general picture is borne out in Pamphilus's more detailed account of Origen's doctrine, which contains three main points.

The first point is that Origen adheres to the church's rule of faith and seeks to represent it in all his work. As evidence of this, Pamphilus quotes most of the preface to *First Principles*, in which Origen gives his summary of the rule of faith. What is most notable about Pamphilus's account here is that he regards Origen as the authoritative teacher or transmitter of the rule of faith in the early fourth century. Second, Pamphilus depicts Origen as a fundamentally antiheretical, catholic theologian, whose own doctrinal position was clearly defined against the errors commonly opposed by the church at large. This point too (minus the term "catholic") follows Origen's statement of intent in the preface to *First Principles*, to adjudicate among the various disagreements and misunderstandings of the gospel that have arisen in the church. In order to depict Origen the heresiologist, Pamphilus quotes a lengthy excerpt from Origen's lost *Commentary on Titus* in which he gives a summary definition of heresy and lists the particular examples that stand in opposition to the true faith (*Apol.* 29–37).[5] Commenting on Titus 3:10–11, which speaks against causers of divisions, Origen defines his theological position against the following key heresies, which he believes oppose the church's rule of faith (*Apol.* 31–33).[6] In the third place,

Pamphilus summarizes Origen's teaching on the basic doctrinal areas under contention, giving extensive excerpts from the opening chapters of *First Principles* book 1. We can best appreciate Pamphilus's version of Origenism by placing the heretical views and Origen's views side by side on each topic.

Origen's key theological commitments, as Pamphilus characterizes them, concern the Trinity above all (*Apol.* 38–85). There are several heresies concerning God the Father: the followers of Marcion, Valentinus, and Basilides (often grouped together as "Gnostics"), and the Sethians and Apelles. Although they claim to believe in Christ, these groups have introduced a false notion of God. They allege that the Father of Christ is not the Old Testament God of the law and the prophets but a higher, unknown God, thus denying the God of creation and the Old Covenant and radically separating the Old Testament from the New Testament. Against these views, Origen maintains the oneness and singularity of God. Further excerpts stress the incorporeality, superiority, and unity of the divine nature and the fact that all knowledge of God comes from God's works (*Apol.* 40).

Origen also opposes heretical views of the Lord Jesus Christ. There are those who deny Jesus's divinity (either denying his miraculous birth, such as the Ebionites and Valentinians, or his nature as God's eternally generated Word and Wisdom); those who deny his humanity (which is defined as a soul and an earthly body) and say that he only "seemed" human and are thus called docetists; and finally those who say that although Jesus was human, his divinity is really only that of the Father, that is, he lacks distinct existence (modalism). In reply, the excerpts from Origen's works stress Christ's divinity—he is "God from God"—and his coeternity with God the Father (*Apol.* 45–52). Here again the distinct existence of each of the three persons arises: because they are each coeternal, God has always been the Father of the Son, and the Son and Holy Spirit have always existed with God the Father. Interestingly, the initial excerpt that Pamphilus supplies on the Son's divinity also emphasizes the Son's role as mediator and image and his derivation from God the Father, even though Pamphilus doesn't comment on this (*Princ.* 2.6.1). It is here that Pamphilus supplies an important quotation from Origen's lost *Commentary on Hebrews*: "there has never been a time when the Son did not exist." Having reported all this, Pamphilus is finally concerned to have Origen maintain that the Son's divinity and coeternity with God the Father mean that the Son is "not unborn." Origen denies that the Son's divinity makes him a second divine source or first principle; that is, the Father and Son are not two Gods, because the Son has his source in the Father, who is the only first principle (*Apol.* 48, 50). In addition, the Son is inseparable from the Father, which makes his generation unlike human generation (*Apol.* 61–66), and there is an extra disclaimer that Christ's preexistence applies to his spirit, but not his flesh, which was born of Mary. In these sections Pamphilus supplies numerous extracts to make his point (mostly from *Princ.* 1.2), showing that Origen considers the Son's divinity, coeternity, and distinct generation from the Father to be of paramount importance (*Apol.* 52–53).

On the Holy Spirit, Origen mentions those who say that there are two Holy Spirits, again, one in the Old Testament (the spirit of the prophets) and another in the New Testament (the Spirit of Christ and the apostles; possibly Marcionites). In reply, he argues that there is one Spirit in both Testaments and that the Holy Spirit is holy by nature, unchangeable, like the divine nature, and participated in only by the saints. Finally, Pamphilus reproduces Origen's statement in *First Principles* 1.3 that salvation occurs through the whole Trinity and that the Father, Son, and Holy Spirit all know the same things, unlike creatures (*Apol.* 81–85). Following these key points on the Trinity, Pamphilus appends Origen's views on the soul and the resurrection. He has Origen briefly state his belief in human free choice and the reality of divine punishment and reward for human actions, including the punishment of the devil, against the Valentinian idea that there are different types of human souls, those who deny that souls have free choice, and those who deny the resurrection of the dead or the devil and his army.

Rhetorically, Pamphilus's main point is that one who so clearly supports the church's rule of faith and who opposes what the catholic church recognizes as heresy surely cannot be a heretic himself, as Origen is accused of being (*Apol.* 36). "Let those declare what other ecclesiastical doctrines exist, besides these which [Origen] has summarized above" (*Apol.* 37). In this sense Pamphilus's argument professes to be based on a received, common understanding of what the typical heresies are, and he indicates that he (and possibly others) believe that the most viable catholic theological program he knows is that of Origen. Origen is, in other words, the chief catholic authority, both as measured by the common faith and also as a key determiner of what that faith is. Although these texts do come from Origen's own hand and his work was clearly defined against what he thought were heretical positions, Pamphilus has selectively heightened

Origen's Trinitarian profile and his antiheretical self-definition. This is an approach to Christian doctrine that we will see Eusebius repackage and carry forward, and Alexander and Athanasius do likewise in the Alexandrian milieu. In Pamphilus's *Defense of Origen*, Origen appears as the chief orthodox authority on the Trinity and the catholic opponent of all heresy.

In the second, main part of the first book, Pamphilus then gives a detailed reply to ten contemporary criticisms brought against Origen. These sections give us an important insight into anti-Origenism near the beginning of the fourth century. The identity of Origen's opponents is unclear, except for Methodius of Olympus, to whom Pamphilus refers several times directly, though anonymously. But there does seem to have been a self-conscious group of anti-Origenists that included Methodius, Eustathius of Antioch, and Eutropius of Adrianople.[7] The combination of things that Origen is accused of is interesting and quite varied. Some of them are mutually contradictory and thus indicate the widely different ways in which he was being interpreted. According to Pamphilus, Origen is accused of (1) making the Son *too* divine, that is, ditheism, or positing two first principles; (2) dividing the Godhead by positing Valentinian emission; (3) supporting psilanthropism or adoptionism; (4) teaching docetism and overly strong allegorization; (5) teaching two Christs; (6) denying the literal biblical history; (7) denying the resurrection of the dead; (8) denying the punishment of the wicked; (9) teaching the preexistence of the soul; and (10) teaching the transmigration of souls. The first two charges pertain to the divine generation, or intra-Trinitarian relations, and they both show that some perceived Origen as having confessed the divinity of Christ too strongly; he did not have a uniform reputation, as he came to have in later periods, for being a subordinationist. Numbers 3 and 5 bear an interesting resemblance to concerns that appear soon in the Arian controversy and may represent the grievances of someone like Arius. All of these charges are easy to disprove from Origen's works, except for number 9, where Origen's doctrine of the preexistence of souls may well have not differed considerably from other known catholic views such as that of Augustine.[8] Pamphilus accuses the anti-Origenists of dullness, lack of education, and malice—they "condemn ideas that they have not even succeeded in first learning" (*Apol.* 13); of ignoring the vast amount of good in Origen's theology in preference for certain contestable elements (*Apol.* 2, 14); of ignoring Origen's humility and tentativeness about what he knows and does not know (*Apol.* 3); and of being disingenuous, since they typically admire Origen's teaching until they find out whose it is (*Apol.* 12).

EUSEBIUS OF CAESAREA

Eusebius of Caesarea is one of a small group of early Christian leaders who are well known in several fields of humanistic study. Like St. Augustine of Hippo, he is an important source for students of ancient history, classics, philosophy, geography, politics, and, of course, church history and theology. Yet, although there is no doubt as to his importance as the first church historian, Eusebius has been either ignored as a theologian or grossly misunderstood. One of the great ironies of early church history is that the real heart of Eusebius's scholarship and episcopal leadership is as neglected as his work of church history is famous. His most important theological work, the *Ecclesiastical Theology*, for example, has yet to appear in a published English translation. While Eusebius has had a few defenders among ancient and modern interpreters, he is normally thought to be an Arian subordinationist, or at best doctrinally confused and insufficient. Consequently, his influence on later patristic theology is almost universally overlooked. Such a misrepresentation of early Christian history holds enormous consequences for our understanding of Trinitarian and Christological orthodoxy both in the patristic period and in the contemporary church. By excluding Eusebius from the Athanasian-centered picture of the fourth century, scholars and theologians have routinely failed to make sense of the later Christological controversies, as well as the use of religious images and the development of church-state relations.[9]

The misunderstanding of Eusebius began during his own lifetime, as a result of attacks on his work by the anti-Origenist Marcellus of Ancyra, and, after Eusebius's death around 339, through the polemics of Athanasius of Alexandria, both of whom we will examine in the next chapter. Following the lead of Marcellus and Athanasius, Eusebius's reputation was further tarnished when he was cited, again mistakenly, in support of the iconoclasts at the Second Council of Nicaea in 787. If we hope to understand the high patristic period, both theologically and culturally, it is imperative that we break through the heresiological barrier erected by Marcellus and Athanasius and view Eusebius's theological achievement on more objective terms. Like his great teacher, Origen, Eusebius was primarily a scholar of the Christian Scriptures, as well as a bishop (which Origen was not), and he soon became the most authoritative theologian for large parts of the Greek-speaking church, and in parts of Syria, for at least fifty years. Eusebius developed as a Christian intellectual under his adoptive father, Pamphilus, in the library that Origen had started and Pamphilus had augmented, while traveling occasionally to use the library in Jerusalem, and he went on to become the greatest Origenist theologian of the early fourth century. One of the benefits of studying Eusebius afresh within the context of a larger work such as this is that we will discover the solid and crucial link between later patristic orthodoxy and the theology of the first three centuries—a link that has often been regarded as tenuous on account of the way that much pre-Nicene theology appears substandard from the Athanasian-Nicene perspective.

Eusebius knew a fair amount of just about everything. Yet the overriding quality of his work is the way in which he views God, human history, contemporary society, and the entire cosmos through a deeply traditional picture of Christ, rooted in the careful study of Scripture. Eusebius's literary corpus is somewhat difficult to interpret, thanks to his ongoing revision of certain works and the major historical developments that occurred during his career, including the Great Persecution of 303–313; Porphyry's attack on Christianity, which reached the East sometime after 303; the outbreak of the Arian controversy in the 320s; and the later struggle against Marcellus of Ancyra, which lasted until Eusebius's death. It is therefore important to keep track of the time, motives, and assumed audience of Eusebius's works.

We will examine Eusebius's works in two distinct periods. The first includes all editions of the *Ecclesiastical History* as well as his three apologetic works, the *Preparation for the Gospel*, the *Proof of the Gospel*, and the *Theophany*, culminating in the oration he delivered for the dedication of the Church of the Holy Sepulcher in 335, which repeats large portions of the *Theophany*;[10] it also includes the Caesarean creed that Eusebius presented at the Council of Nicaea (c. 311–335). The second period begins after the depositions of Athanasius and Marcellus and comprises Eusebius's late works against Marcellus of Ancyra and the unfinished *Life of Constantine* (c. 337–339). His works on Constantine's support of the church, *In Praise of Constantine* (containing Eusebius's panegyric to Constantine from 336 and the Holy Sepulcher oration of 335) and the *Life of Constantine*, are treated together in the final section. The reason for dividing his work between these two periods is that Eusebius's early views remain substantially unchanged, even during the Arian crisis and through the Council of Nicaea; it is in his late works against Marcellus that we find a noticeable shift of emphasis.

Eusebius's theological and ecclesiastical position is poorly represented by the terms of the Arian controversy. He found himself aligned with Eusebius of Nicomedia and others who supported Arius, against the network established by Arius's bishop, Alexander, in which the young deacon Athanasius also belonged. The two decades from approximately 325 to 345 were an extremely polarizing time for many Eastern bishops, some of whom found themselves allied with others with whom they had little in common.[11] This can be said for Eusebius of Caesarea and Alexander of Alexandria, who arguably had more in common with one another theologically than Eusebius did with Arius or Alexander did with Marcellus of Ancyra, with whom he was associated throughout the conflict. But such is often the case in times of severe conflict. Here we examine Eusebius's work in what I take to be its real connections and oppositions, which are not those of the Arian controversy, except for his debate with Marcellus.[12]

EARLY CHRISTOLOGY (310–337):
ECCLESIASTICAL HISTORY AND APOLOGETIC WORKS

Eusebius has justly earned the title "father of church history" for his pioneering work in the field. His *Ecclesiastical History* is the only work of its kind, providing a narrative and documentary account of the first three centuries of Christian history. Because he often writes like an archivist, providing extensive quotations of multiple sources, the book is our only source for many documents and much information that have otherwise been lost. It is no surprise that the *Ecclesiastical History* is usually regarded as a purely historical work. Yet what many readers do not realize is that it is also the most important theological work of the first part of Eusebius's career, for reasons that have to do with his view of history itself. Eusebius believes that the history of the church, in its most particular and mundane aspects, is fundamentally determined and characterized by Jesus Christ, the Son of God through whom all things were made and through whom alone God is truly known. Consequently, at the outset of the work, Eusebius gives an important account of the identity of Christ and the power of God made manifest through him, from which the rest of the story flows. In the main body of the work come accounts of selected second- and third-century heresies, followed by a final theological statement in the oration that

Eusebius delivered for the dedication of the new church in Tyre in 315, which he reproduces in book 10. In the intervening books Eusebius describes the presence and the power of Christ in the church's life from apostolic times to the Great Persecution and its termination by Constantine in Eusebius's own lifetime.

The theological, ecclesiastical, and cultural vision that Eusebius presents in the *Ecclesiastical History* is especially important because it represents the original and lasting views that he held as a scholar between the ages of forty and sixty, in the middle of which he became bishop of the metropolitan see of Caesarea around the age of fifty (in 313). This material is also important because much of it predates the Arian controversy of the 320s,[13] and at least the earliest editions predate Porphyry's attack on Christianity and Eusebius's subsequent reply in the dual apologetic work, even as his apologetic work in turn seems to have affected the later editions of the *Ecclesiastical History*. None of Eusebius's work in this period contains the political theology that he later develops in connection with the person of Constantine. Compared with other histories written in antiquity, the *Ecclesiastical History* is a wholly new kind of work, since it chronicles the development of a community or institution that transcends all national and geographical boundaries.[14] The work focuses especially on the course of Christian literature and the channels of correct doctrine, and once we get beyond book 3, this seems to be, in effect, what Eusebius means by "the succession of the apostles," which he lists as the first purpose of the work (*H.E.* 1.pref.1).

As a history of Christianity and its apostolic doctrine, the *Ecclesiastical History* is admittedly selective (*H.E.* 1.1.3); not surprisingly, it is also sometimes inaccurate, though not for reasons of deliberate obfuscation.[15] The work as a whole focuses on the Greek-speaking churches of the eastern Mediterranean; Eusebius briefly mentions but knows relatively little about events and people in Rome, Gaul, and North Africa. The bishops and theologians whom he takes to be normative sources of Christian doctrine include, primarily, Justin, Irenaeus, Clement of Alexandria, Dionysius of Alexandria, and Origen, together with Hegesippus for second-century history; he cites Tertullian several times, though he appears to know his *Apology* only in Greek translation; and he read a considerable amount of episcopal correspondence. Eusebius had access to the works of these authors through the finest Christian libraries of the day, in Caesarea and Jerusalem. He cites many other teachers more briefly and with apparently less acquaintance. From 260 on, he is writing about his own lifetime. As Eusebius presents it, orthodox Christian doctrine is often defined against erroneous or heretical views; accordingly, he quotes from Irenaeus's great work *Against Heresies* in the first sentence of the *Ecclesiastical History* (1.pref.1). As in Irenaeus, a crucial part of opposing heresy is the task of identifying the true succession of Christian teachers and the history of the passing down of orthodox doctrine—which, for Eusebius, constitutes a large part of the task of writing church history itself.[16]

Modern assessments of Eusebius's theology tend to concentrate on his long, dual apologetic work, the *Preparation for the Gospel* and the *Proof of the Gospel*, which Eusebius wrote sometime between 314 and 323 and which amplifies, with only slight modification, the theological and historical views that he had already expressed in the *Ecclesiastical History*.[17] The major event that precipitated this work was the publication of Porphyry's *Against the Christians*. Porphyry's work was not an armchair exercise; he argued with force and conviction that Christianity was essentially incompatible with Roman civilization and must be wiped out. He denounced Christians as apostates from their own ancestral religion, Judaism, and atheists who deserved to be put to death. He attacked the Christian God, the Christian interpretation of the Scriptures, particular teachers such as Origen, the Christian understanding of history, contemporary behavior, and the claim that the Christian faith stands above reason and rational proof. The intended aim of Porphyry's polemical efforts was the violent suppression of Christianity.[18] Eusebius felt compelled to respond decisively and quickly; he prepared an initial reply to Porphyry's work, as did Methodius of Olympus, these two now being lost. Over nearly a decade, Eusebius then presented a full-scale engagement with Greco-Roman culture in his lengthy dual apology. While the work is much broader than simply a response to Porphyry, Porphyry's attack on Christianity remained the chief motivator, and Eusebius refers to Porphyry directly and indirectly many times.

In order to interpret the *Preparation for the Gospel* and *Proof of the Gospel* well, it is necessary to appreciate its genre and intended audience and the nature of the attack that gave rise to it. Eusebius addressed the dual work to pagan readers whom he believed he could persuade that Christianity was a viable religion and new cultural institution, or who at least would come to regard it with more respect. He also may have intended it as a catechetical guide for serious inquirers, written during the Eastern reign of Licinius, when public Christian teaching was illegal. He took the task very seriously. In the dual work Eusebius presents Christianity as being superior to pagan culture, containing and superseding the best of Greco-Roman philosophy and religion. Historically speaking, his argument, as in the *Ecclesiastical History*, is to say that Christianity, which was inaugurated by Jesus Christ only three centuries ago, is in fact the full and final manifestation of the original true religion of humankind, the religion of the biblical patriarchs before Moses and the Jewish law, from which all other religious practices derive and eventually deviate. On more purely conceptual grounds, Eusebius also responds to the charge that the Christian faith is without reason, by trying to show the reasons, or the "proof," of Christianity, which for the most part amounts to identifying its existence and precedents in the Old Testament Scriptures. Contrary to how these works have appeared to some readers,[19] Eusebius does not see himself as a philosopher, nor does he imagine Christianity as a philosophically based religion. He does not even keep up with the philosophical currents of his own day, such as the work of Plotinus, but merely repeats expeditiously what he has gleaned from his second- and third-century Christian sources, which in turn guides what reading he does in Plato and other ancient philosophers for apologetic purposes.

Eusebius's understanding of Christ forms the basis of the *Ecclesiastical History*. He begins the work with a doctrinal preface that provides the foundation of the narrative that is to follow. This preface (*H.E.* 1.2–4) is the most important doctrinal statement in the first half of Eusebius's career, to be surpassed only by certain passages in the *Ecclesiastical Theology*, written near the end of his life. The Christology represented in the preface, as we currently have it, most likely belongs to the final stages of revision, which Eusebius undertook as late as 325 or 326. To discover the earliest strata of his doctrinal and cultural vision we must therefore look to the oldest part of the work, books 2–7.[20] In these books, which cover the reigns from Tiberius to Gallienus (from 14 to Eusebius's lifetime, around 268), Eusebius shows what he takes to be the orthodox faith of the church through brief direct statements, reports of doctrinal controversies, and theological commentary, which he frequently intersperses in the general narrative—all of which is of course selective on his part and shows a particular view of second- and third-century norms.

There are three main passages in books 2–7 in which Eusebius discusses Christology at any length. In the first, and briefest, he refers to the letter written by Pliny the Younger, governor of Bithynia, to Emperor Trajan in the year 112, expressing concern about the large number of

Christians who are "being put to death for their faith," as Eusebius describes it. According to Pliny's letter, the Christians have done nothing to violate the law. They merely rise at dawn to "sing hymns to Christ as to God [θεοῦ δίκην]"; they avoid adultery, murder, and other nefarious crimes; and they are otherwise law-abiding citizens (*H.E.* 3.33.1, 3).[21] Eusebius thus observes that, in the early second century, Christians worship Christ as God and are being persecuted for it.

In the second passage, in book 5, Eusebius presents excerpts from a work that combats the Christological heresy of Artemon, together with Eusebius's own commentary. He believes that the work was written during the reign of Severus and the Roman episcopacy of Zephyrinus (c. 198–211); although Eusebius does not give the title, the work is known from Theodoret as the *Little Labyrinth* (*Comp.Haer.* 2.5).[22] As Eusebius reports it, the error of Artemon is the belief that Christ is not divine but a "mere human being" (ψιλὸς ἄνθρωπος), known still from the Greek as psilanthropism. According to the *Little Labyrinth*, these heretics allege that their belief has the authority of apostolicity and the claim of antiquity in Rome through the episcopacy of Bishop Victor until it was suppressed during the time of Bishop Zephyrinus. The first section of the work that Eusebius quotes argues that (1) the divine Scriptures oppose the heretics, and (2) many Christian writers before Victor's time, including Justin, Miltiades, Tatian, and Clement, defended the truth against both pagans and Christian heresies by "theologizing" Christ, that is, confessing his divinity. Writers such as Irenaeus and Melito, moreover, "proclaim that Christ is God and a human being [θεὸν καὶ ἄνθρωπον]," and many songs written by faithful brethren "theologize" Christ, the Word of God. Not only do such views represent the long-standing mind of the church, the *Labyrinth* continues, but Victor himself excommunicated Theodotus the Cobbler, who was the "father of this God-denying [ἀρνησίθεος] apostasy" and the first to say that Christ was merely human. In addition to the heretics' insulting "the standard of the primitive faith" and not knowing Christ, the work reports that they "corrupted the word" and do not believe in the inspiration of Scripture by the Holy Spirit (*H.E.* 5.28.13–19). In this passage and again in book 7, Eusebius twice notes that Artemon's heresy of psilanthropism has been revived more recently by Paul of Samosata (c. 268, *H.E.* 5.28.1; 7.30.16). On the basis of several earlier patristic authorities, Eusebius thus shows his opposition to psilanthropism, which is a "denial of God," and his support of the church's true doctrine of Christ, which is, on the contrary, "theology," or the confession that Christ is God. The church's true theology, moreover, stands in opposition to Paul of Samosata, who will later come to be known as a paradigmatic modalist.

Third, in book 6, Eusebius reports Origen's opposition to Beryllus of Bostra (*H.E.* 6.33). In Eusebius's view, Beryllus has perverted the church's traditional standard by holding what appears to be a form of modalism. Following Origen, Eusebius faults Beryllus for denying that the Savior preexisted the incarnation as a distinct figure "in his own proper circumscription of being" who is divine in his own right, as opposed to being merely an aspect or manifestation of the Father's divinity. Eusebius presents Beryllus's condemnation as an act of the wider church leadership on behalf of its normative tradition: many bishops argued against him, after which the theological expert Origen succeeded in persuading him of his error.

Eusebius's early Christology stands out fairly clearly from these texts, together with briefer statements scattered throughout books 2–7. The dominant theme is the divinity of Christ: the church confesses, or "theologizes," that Christ is God, against various denials of the same. This focus on Christ's divinity is also represented in Eusebius's brief references to the "confession" of Christ by church leaders and the witness of Christian martyrs during times of persecution, beginning with the martyrdom of James the brother of Jesus (*H.E.* 2.22.5). To confess Christ is to affirm, either in word or deed, that Christ is the divine Son of God; the martyr's confession of Blandina (*H.E.* 5.1) thus stands in contrast with the denial of Paul of Samosata (*H.E.* 7.30). For Eusebius, the confession of Christ's divinity lies at the heart of the Christian faith and is literally what it means to "theologize" Jesus (*H.E.* 4.22; 6.1). Closely related to the confession of Christ's divinity, as a necessary precondition or corollary, is the belief that Christ is a distinct figure prior to his incarnation in the flesh. This is clearest in the third passage on Beryllus. Here, Eusebius gives us a brief glimpse of the logic of the antimodalist doctrine that he takes from Origen and other second- and third-century theologians: if Christ is not a distinct figure, he cannot be divine, but is merely a manifestation of the divinity of God the Father, which must inevitably be a lesser thing, since—as most theologians in the first four centuries agreed—the Father himself (as a complete divine figure) cannot possibly become incarnate. Yet, although Eusebius speaks of Christ as a preexistent or precosmic figure, he is equally clear that Christ is not limited to the realm of creation and its temporal scheme.[23]

At this point it is especially interesting to note that Eusebius does not fault Artemon or Paul of Samosata for modalism, but for psilanthropism.

He does not seem to be aware of this charge against Paul yet, nor does he know of the modalism of Sabellius in Rome, because of his relative ignorance of Western Christian sources and events. This indicates that Eusebius's antimodalist views derive not from more recent (and soon to be famous) problems in this area, but from the earlier, second- and third-century antimodalist sources, above all Origen. Eusebius's initial insistence on Christ's distinctness is aimed not against "Sabellians" (as he will later call Marcellus of Ancyra), but chiefly against Gnosticism, as in Origen and Irenaeus. Nor, we should emphasize, does this point stem from a desire on Eusebius's part to present a middle Platonic scheme of cosmological mediation, such as he later employs for apologetic purposes.

Being divine, Christ is thus the object of Christian faith and worship, together with God the Father. Even the crucified Lord (*H.E.* 4.15) is worshipped as the Creator-God, the immortal one, to whom Christian hymns are offered (*H.E.* 3.36; 4.13; 7.30). For Eusebius, the confession of the divinity of Christ is in large measure a recognition of his power, both as the power of God spoken of in 1 Corinthians 1:24 and as God's power made manifest in the world through the church's teaching and the lives of Christians. The power of God, which was confessed by the apostles, is the water of life that stems from Christ's own being (*H.E.* 5.1; 3.24.1). This is, again, shown clearly in and by the martyrs, as in Christ's own divinity and miracles (*H.E.* 5.3; 5.7). Eusebius's early views about Christ include, finally, the belief that the one God is the Father of Jesus Christ (*H.E.* 4.11, 15, 22). Since this is not an apologetic work aimed at pagan readers, Eusebius generally assumes the singleness of God, although he does argue for one divine principle against Marcion (*H.E.* 5.12).[24] Along with belief in the Holy Spirit, who is chiefly noted for inspiring Scripture, belief in God the Father and Christ the divine and distinct Son of God is the heart of the Christian faith in the *Ecclesiastical History* books 2–7. This is the Christology with which Eusebius begins his career; it is selectively traditional and forms the basis of the whole work. His use of early Christian tradition is not merely for the sake of acknowledging his sources; his extensive appeals to prior sources reinforce the argument of the entire work, that Christ, the Son of God, himself brought the knowledge of God the Father and instituted the church, which has proclaimed that knowledge ever since the apostles.

The preface to the *Ecclesiastical History* (1.1–4) provides the essential principles and the main rationale of the story that Eusebius is about to unfold (*H.E.* 1.5.1; 2.pref.1). Occupying the first half of book 1, the preface is essentially a summary account of Christian doctrine—specifically, the doctrine of Christ—and, as we have noted, it is the most important and succinct doctrinal statement in the first half of Eusebius's career (*H.E.* 1.1–1.2.27), before his late works against Marcellus.[25] In just a few pages, with echoes in the late books 8–10, Eusebius lays out the Christology and cultural vision on which he bases his theological teaching; his pastoral ministry; and his views on history, Roman and Christian culture, and indeed the entire cosmos. Throughout the first major phase of his career, Eusebius deviates little from the theological, historical, and cosmic scheme expressed in the first few sections of the *Ecclesiastical History*. According to Eusebius, the story of the church begins with the divinity of the saving Word, the early history of its teaching (the Old Testament witness), the antiquity of the Christian evangelical way of life, and especially Christ's recent advent, events before his passion, and his choice of the apostles (*H.E.* 2.pref.1).

After outlining the overall plan of the work and noting the difficulties involved, Eusebius defines for the reader his basic approach to the task, or what we might call his theological method. He calls the introduction "the economy and theology of Christ" (*H.E.* 1.1.7). By "economy" Eusebius means God's ordered dealings with creation, which culminate and have their focus in the incarnation of Christ. He discusses the incarnation briefly in the preface, and more extensively in the later sections of book 1, when he begins the actual history of the church with the human life of Christ (*H.E.* 1.2.17–27; 1.5–13). By "theology" Eusebius means the confession of the divinity of Christ (*H.E.* 1.2).[26] Christian theology, which is "the beginning of the economy of Christ," is, Eusebius says, "more divine than most people imagine"; it will require particular instruction and the inspiration of the Holy Spirit (*H.E.* 1.1.8). Theology and the economy are not, for Eusebius, two different modes or sets of Christian doctrine, as they are often imagined in modern scholarship.[27] Theology is the result, or the interpretation, of the economy, and it is the beginning of the economy in the sense that the being and will of God and Christ are the beginning and foundation of the economy; hence, the incarnate Christ is the basis of true theology (*Proof* 3.6). Eusebius presumably sees his discussion of Christ's divinity and preexistence in *Ecclesiastical History* 1.2–4 as "theology," followed by a full treatment of the incarnation, or the "economy," in section 5, both of which are "too lofty and great for humans to conceive" (*H.E.* 2.pref.1).[28]

Eusebius summarizes his theological confession of Christ many times in the *Ecclesiastical History* (on which more below), and again in the *Proof of the Gospel*. The very nature of Christian faith is to believe "that our Lord and Savior Jesus is truly the Christ of God," that the human Jesus is the preexistent Christ (*Proof* 1.1.8). Eusebius clarifies and expands this movement from the economy to theology in the *Proof of the Gospel*. In his interpretation of the Old Testament, he plans to speak first of prophecies concerning "events that came to light" much later, namely, Christ's incarnation or economy; after which he will prove that the prophets also saw things that were not present as though they were present, meaning the precosmic life of God and Christ, which is the subject of theology (*Proof* 1.pref.2). Several times in the course of the work, Eusebius moves from one to the other: he begins the main argument in book 3, for example, with prophecies of the incarnation of Christ, after which he turns to the "more mystical theology" concerning him; likewise the economy treated in book 4.10–17 is followed by theology in book 5.[29]

On the basis of this method of confessing theology from the divine economy, Eusebius's main argument in the preface to the *Ecclesiastical History* is that Christ is divine and "older" than all creation, and that the Christian life is also ancient. Eusebius addresses this argument to skeptical pagans, who believe that Christianity is newfangled, and he develops it at greater length in the long apologetic works. The surest way to demonstrate the antiquity of the faith, then, is to show the divinity of Christ, the only-begotten Son and the Word of God (*H.E.* 1.2.1). The preface thus argues that Christ is incredibly old, despite the recentness of his human appearance (his *politeia* in the flesh), and Eusebius later goes on to argue that Christ's teaching is likewise ancient (*H.E.* 1.4). The Christian manner of life and conduct (βίος) also are not recent but are as old as the true religion of humanity from the beginning (*H.E.* 1.4.4). Eusebius wants to demonstrate both the uniqueness of the Christian revelation and its continuity with the Hebrew (and, by derivation, Greek) heritage. He envisions the foundation of the history of the church—and of the cosmos as a whole—to be the divinity of Christ and the corresponding way of life that Christians live. On this basis he narrates the divine power of Christ that has been lived out by the church's leaders, often against heresy, both through the church's successes and through the witness of its martyrs, ending with its triumphal restoration by Constantine and Licinius.

Eusebius begins the preface with an important Christological summary, which is similar in many ways to Origen's doctrine. Christ's manner of existence is twofold,[30] much like a human body that has both a head and feet. On the one hand, Christ is known to be God by those who believe, and yet for our salvation he put on "human existence capable of suffering as we do" (*H.E.* 1.2.1).[31] In order to be complete, the history of the church—which is really the history of Christ—must contain both the embodied, corporate life of the church, which is like Christ's feet, as well as an account of Christ's divine identity, or Christ's head.[32] Christ's divinity, moreover, is his most important aspect and, in Eusebius's view, the determining factor in the story that follows (*H.E.* 1.2.1). In this opening sentence of the preface, Eusebius has succinctly stated that Christ exists in two different ways, that the guiding and determining factor of Christ's existence is his divinity, and that he has become human to save us through his suffering. This narrative account of the identity of the one Christ, focused on his divinity, is what Eusebius believes will best convey to pagan readers the rationale of Christianity and the church in Roman society—that it is both ancient and of divine origin, just as Christ's divinity is the dominant theme of the older books 2–7.

The primary theological and historiological factor in Eusebius's early works is therefore Christ's divinity. In the remainder of the preface, Eusebius defines Christ's divinity in very strong terms, beginning with a series of biblical titles and descriptions taken mainly from Origen. The "being and nature" of Christ, his birth (γένος) and his supreme worth, exceed the capacity of human speech and knowledge, so that the Son is known to the Father alone, who begat him (Matt 11:27; Isa 53:8). Christ the Son is precosmic Light, noetic Wisdom existing before the ages, and "the divine Word that was living and existing in the beginning with the Father." He is "the first and only offspring of God, prior to every creature and thing made, whether visible or invisible," the captain of the heavenly host, the "angel of mighty counsel," the one who does the Father's will, the second cause of the universe after the Father, and "the true and only-begotten Son of God, the Lord, God, and King of all creatures." Having received "supreme authority, dominion, divinity, power, and honor from the Father," Christ the Son is indeed God, as the "mystical theology of the Scriptures" of John 1:1 states (*H.E.* 1.2.2–3). In the remainder of the preface and his apologetic works, Eusebius provides several related terms to express Christ's divinity. Christ is "a human being who is also God" (*H.E.* 1.2.23).[33] "Christ" is also a divine title in the Old Testament, even if the Hebrews did not recognize Christ's divinity (*H.E.* 1.3.2; *Proof* 4.1). Christ is "the Word of

God and himself God," who speaks with the voice of God (*Proof* 3.7). The apostolic preaching is that *God* came on an embassy in a human body; Christ is the Word of God by nature and works wonders as God, and he is the one principle (ἀρχή) of the universe (*Proof* 3.7; 4.1).

An additional indication of Christ's divinity is that he is worshipped along with God the Father. Eusebius writes that, following Abraham, the righteous ancients knew the Son and imagined him by the pure eyes of the mind, and they paid him the reverence (τὸ σέβας) that befits a child of God, and that when the Son appeared to Abraham by the oak of Mamre, Abraham fell down and worshipped (προσκυνεῖ) him as God (Gen 18:1–2; *H.E.* 1.2.6–7). Again, only Christ, among all those "christs" who were high priests, kings, and prophets, receives the honor of worship (σεβάσμιος) (*H.E.* 1.3.10, 19). Eusebius has thus expressed the divinity of Christ in extremely strong terms, whose fuller meaning we examine below.[34]

Because of the misrepresentation of Eusebius's doctrine during the Arian controversy, it is important to be clear about two additional points concerning Christ's divine status relative to other beings caused by God the Father. First, Eusebius stresses throughout his works that, as the Son and Word of God, Christ is absolutely unique, just as the Father is unique. As his title "only-begotten" indicates, he is the only offspring and the true child of God, the only one "through whom all things were made," and the only Savior, which no other being is. Three brief textual references will settle the point: God surrenders to Christ "and to no other than his divine and first-born Word" the making of inferior beings; only Christ receives the honor of worship due to the Father; only Christ is called "God" together with the Father (see John 1:1), and he alone is the Son of God by nature (*H.E.* 1.2.4; 1.3.10; *Proof* 5.4). The second point concerns the precosmic existence of the divine Son. We will take up the question of the Son's eternity in greater detail in the context of Eusebius's later works, but for the time being we simply observe that, contrary to the caricature imposed on a wide variety of other positions by the pro-Alexander alliance during the Arian crisis, Eusebius does not conceive of Christ's generation from the Father in any temporal sense. He has a different sort of priority or anteriority in mind, which we further analyze in its proper place.

In addition to simply proclaiming the divinity of Christ in the preface of the *Ecclesiastical History*, in terms similar to those found in books 2–7, Eusebius explains more fully what that divinity entails. Christ is divine not as an independent deity (as one god among others), but as the direct result of a specific relationship with God the Father. Eusebius explains that Christ is the "true and only-begotten Son of God, the Lord and God and King of all creatures, who has received from the Father the supreme authority and dominion, together with divinity [θεότης] and power and honor" (H.E. 1.2.3). The next ten sections of the work then present biblical descriptions of Christ's relationship to the Father. John 1:1 mystically "theologizes" Christ in saying that the Word was in the beginning with God the Father (ὁ θεός), was himself God (θεός), and was the instrument of creation. According to Moses, God has given over to Christ the divine Word, and to him alone, the creation of all things through a sort of interpersonal conversation (Gen 1:26; Ps 33:9; 148:5). In response to the instruction and command of the Father, the divine Word serves the Father's sovereign will as one who "exists secondly" (δευτευρεύοντα) in relation to the Father and to whom the Father entrusted the creation and governance of the cosmos (H.E. 1.2.4–5). In these sections, Eusebius emphasizes both Christ's derivation from and dependence on the Father—a relationship that he has no trouble demonstrating from the biblical text—and also Christ's divinity and "likeness" to the Father—that is, the Father's priority as the "God over all things," including the only-begotten Son and Word, who stems from him, as well as the Son's full sharing in the Father's divinity.

On the one hand, Christ is the divine "Lord, God and King of all creatures," sharing in the divinity of the Father as none of the creatures does;[35] he receives the worship due only to the unique child of God; and Moses calls him "God" (Gen 22:28–30; H.E. 1.2.3, 6, 9). Eusebius even identifies God's self-revelation to Moses in Exodus 3 as the revelation of the *Son*, not the Father, so that it is Christ who says, "I am the God of your father, the God of Abraham, the God of Isaac, and the God of Jacob" (H.E. 1.2.13; Exod 3:6).[36] Yet, on the other hand, Eusebius is equally insistent that Christ is not God the Father. With a host of New Testament passages informing his reading, Eusebius continues to explicate the Old Testament in order to show the antiquity of Christianity. The God who appears to God's people is not the Father but the Son, who uniquely brings the knowledge of God the Father and who even shows piety, obedience, and subservience to the Father. Hence, the God who appeared to the Old Testament saints was also the Son of God. Here Eusebius voices the normative view of second- and third-century theologians that God the Father cannot have appeared in human form and certainly cannot have become incarnate as Jesus or suffered creaturely existence in any way (the traditional opposition to patripassianism). It is contrary to *logos*—both biblical "teaching" and sound "reasoning"—that "the ingenerate and changeless being of God Almighty" and the "first cause of the universe" should take on human form, or even pretend to appear as a creaturely figure. Rather, this is the special character and office of the Son: "the God and Lord who judges all the earth" and is seen in the shape of a human being (Gen 18:1–2) can only be the preexistent, divine Word (*H.E.* 1.2.8).

One implication of this scheme—and closely related to the divinity of Christ in ways that will hold important repercussions in the centuries ahead—is a point that Eusebius turns to late in the preface, namely, that the divine Son exists as a being or hypostasis who is distinct from the Father. In order for Christ to be divine at all and to be a being who reveals himself in creaturely ways, he must, in Eusebius's view, be distinct from the Father. If Christ is exactly the same thing as God the Father, then he cannot be said to be a divine figure appearing to us, and there is no divine revelation such as Christians confess to have received through Jesus Christ. Eusebius notes the basic witness of Scripture, which lies behind all such reasoning. Most of his exegesis in the preface to the *Ecclesiastical History* shows what the second- and third-century antimonarchians knew well: that the biblical text depicts an interrelationship between two incommensurable figures, whose distinct identities it would be impossible to deny without an extreme degree of allegorization of the text that substitutes another theological scheme for what the Bible plainly relates. So Christ ministered to God the Father in the creation of all things as a precosmic being (*ousia*) who lives and subsists (*H.E.* 1.2.14; 1.3.18–19). For evidence, Eusebius refers to Proverbs 8:22–31, a traditional Christological source for Origen that was already becoming controversial in the Arian controversy and which Eusebius himself addresses at much greater length against Marcellus.

It is also noteworthy that Eusebius mentions the Son's distinct subsistence only briefly, near the end of the preface, as if merely to state what is implied throughout. At this point in his career, Eusebius is not advancing a deliberate antimodalist polemic, such as he will later against Marcellus. In the *Ecclesiastical History*, he simply echoes this point of traditional antimonarchian doctrine from his earlier sources, such as we saw in Origen's correction of Beryllus in the older book 6. By comparison, he does not emphasize it nearly as strongly as he does Christ's divinity or the nature of the Father-Son relationship. The main point remains clear as Eusebius introduces the "mystical theology" of Christ at the beginning of the *Proof of the*

Gospel book 4. Even the Jews have a doctrine of Christ, as seen in the Old Testament; but what they fail to recognize is his divinity and the cause of his becoming human (*Proof* 4.1). The *Theophany* likewise continues to emphasize Christ's divinity. As its title indicates, the whole work is a proof of "the divine manifestation of the common Savior of all, Jesus Christ," that both his words and deeds are divine (*Theoph.* 5.1, 35, 51). For the early Eusebius, it is the divinity of Christ that makes all the difference.

Eusebius famously conceives of Christ's unique revelatory function as being the mediator and image of God toward creation, sometimes in ways that have suggested a philosophical sort of ontological mediation. There are several such statements in the early works. The Word of God "alone, according to his rank [κατὰ τάξιν], knows how to serve God, and stands midway between the ungenerated God and the things that are generated after him" (*Proof* 4.10, 167.34–35). Eusebius refines the point even further in his third apologetic work, the *Theophany*, and the corresponding oration at the Church of the Holy Sepulcher in 335: God the Father is above and beyond all existence and cannot be approached by material and recently created beings who are therefore inferior in nature to God. In response, Eusebius says, the good God puts forth the Word as a kind of medium of divine power, who is able to "associate perfectly and closely with the Father and partake of his ineffable qualities," and can also descend and conform to the imperfect, and with perishable, physical matter, making contact with the universe (*L.C.* 11.12). Again, the Word functions like an unbroken bond between the chasm separating God and creation (*L.C.* 12.7–8; *Prep.* 7.15; *Proof* 4.2, 5; *Theoph.* 11.5, 24).

Since the nineteenth century, several scholars have argued that Eusebius's emphasis on the Father's transcendence and the Son's function as image and mediator of God represents a philosophical hierarchy of being that Eusebius has merely dressed up in Christian guise.[37] In this view, the Son fills the place of the mediatory second God, who stands in between the supreme God and creation, and is able to bridge the gap between the two on account of his being a lesser being than the first God but greater than the cosmos. Yet there are two problems with this interpretation. First, it takes his apologetic texts excessively literally, ignoring their rhetorical interest in expressing Christian ideas in terms that would be familiar to a pagan audience. If we refrain from projecting philosophical sources too heavily on Eusebius's apologetic texts, then we will be in a better position to notice, second, that Eusebius does not in fact describe the Son in terms of ontological or divine mediation in any of his works. He does not espouse a philosophical scheme of ontological mediation. The Son's ability to manifest himself to creatures is not a matter of his being "less divine" than the Father, like a kind of buffer or way station along the scale of being. What Eusebius does say is that, for some unknown reason of the Word's identity, he is uniquely able to reveal the Father and to appear in creaturely ways *without being any less divine than the Father*. The point applies as well to Eusebius's various expressions of the Son as existing "secondary" to God the Father, which he probably derives from Justin Martyr and Origen rather than any philosophical source (*H.E.* 1.2.3, 9, 11; *Proof* 1.5.10). For Eusebius, the difference between the "primary" and "secondary" status of the Father and the Son, like that between ὁ θεός and θεός in John 1:1, is not one in degrees of divinity but is what we might call a *structural* difference within the Trinity. Eusebius makes this point especially clearly in an important passage in the *Proof of the Gospel*: God the Father is "first" in that he alone is self-subsistent divinity by nature; only the Father is God from no other source than himself. The Son, on the other hand, is "second" to the Father because he receives divinity from the Father, as the image of God, not because he is less than the Father. This structure of derivation ensures that there is only one God: the Father, who shares his divinity with the divine Son and Spirit. Consequently, Christians confess that there is only one divinity in both Father and Son according to its paradigmatic nature or condition in the Father (*Proof* 5.4.14).[38] The Son shares fully in the Father's divinity, possessing the same divinity and no other, so that there is only one God in both. Rather than diminishing the divinity or being of the Son, as is often assumed without warrant in Eusebius's text, the Son's derivation from the Father and his character as the image of God is precisely what causes him to be divine in the first place, sharing fully in the divinity of the Father, who is "the only true God."

In each of these early works we see that Christ's divinity arises from the particular relationship in which he stands to God the Father. The Father generates the Son as his unique, divine offspring, unlike all of creation, and delegates, as it were, the creation, rule, salvation, and final judgment of the universe to him. He is the source of the Son's distinct existence and his divinity, so that it is through the Son alone that the Father is known, under both the Old and New Covenants. Christ is therefore divine *as* the Son of God, neither as an independent second God (which is polytheistic) nor as a mere extension or aspect of the Father (which is modalist). The Son is both divine and also distinct and ordered under the Father because of his begetting from the Father.

Finally, we may note that Eusebius's basic theological system, as laid out in his early works, is structurally Trinitarian. He establishes the pattern right away as he begins his exegetical treatment in the *Ecclesiastical History*: the divine Spirit announces that the generation of the divine Son from the Father is ineffable (Isa 53:8; *H.E.* 1.2.2). One of Eusebius's most interesting Trinitarian statements—and a point on which he will be followed by Gregory of Nyssa—concerns Christ's anointing. By his participation in the unbegotten divinity of the Father, Christ receives a divine anointing with divine chrism through the divine Spirit (a Trinitarian process) (*H.E.* 1.13.13, 15). This anointing, as depicted in Psalm 64:7–8, indicates the unity of the anointer (the Father), the anointed (the Son), and the anointing oil (the Spirit) (*Proof* 4.15). The Son is therefore "Christ," the Anointed One, precosmically, apart from the incarnation. Eusebius's Trinitarian scheme is clear as well from his frequent reference in the apologetic works to Jesus's instruction to baptise in the name of the Father, Son, and Holy Spirit in Matthew 28:19. Eusebius elaborates on this Trinitarian structure in his later works, but for now we can see the main building blocks in place.

Scholar that he was, Eusebius strove to represent the traditional theology of the second and third centuries, as read chiefly through Origen. It is highly significant, not only for our interpretation of Eusebius's work but also for our understanding of the development of patristic Christology, that the antimodalist strain of Eusebius's doctrine precedes the Arian controversy (it is not an Arianizing *reaction* to Alexander and company) and even any acquaintance with the later-third-century modalism of Sabellius, of whom Eusebius seems to be ignorant except for brief mentions in the letters of Dionysius of Alexandria.[39] That Eusebius's doctrine is traditional in this sense can be seen in the Caesarean creed that he introduced into the proceedings of the Council of Nicaea. Eusebius presents the creed as representing the faith in which he was formed as a catechumen and a young presbyter, having received it from prior bishops of the Caesarean church, and which he himself now teaches, and there is no reason to doubt the truth of this statement. The creed has several commonalities with Eusebius's doctrine as outlined above: the divinity of the Son based on his derivation from the Father ("God of God, Light of Light"); the Christological titles Word, only-begotten (μονογενής), and firstborn of all creation; and the Son's generation "before all ages" and his instrumentality in creation; as well as emphasis on the Son's true subsistence distinct from the Father, the singularity of Father and Son, their true fatherhood, sonship, and "spiritness" with reference to Matthew 28:19, and a caution against the partition of the divine nature.

The second way of Christ's being, Eusebius says, is that he became human for our salvation (*H.E.* 1.2.1). Although Eusebius echoes the second-century opposition to docetism, he generally does not argue for Christ's humanity per se, beyond a few passing remarks. In the preface to the *Ecclesiastical History*, he writes that the body which Christ assumed in the incarnation "in no way differed in its existence [οὐσία] from our nature [φύσις]" (*H.E.* 1.2.23). On a related point, though, he is keen to defend the goodness of material creation and human bodily life in general—a point to which he later returns in his defense of Christ's eternal kingdom against Marcellus, and which we will consider further in connection with martyrdom. Yet Eusebius gives a great deal of attention to Christ's humanity with reference to his saving work (*H.E.* 1.5–12). Over the course of his career Eusebius presents a multifaceted doctrine of salvation that will come to have far-reaching effects, influencing both the work of Athanasius and that of the Cappadocians. At the outset, Eusebius regards the present human condition as being so unavoidably corrupt and subject to death that only God can save us by his own initiative (*Theoph.* 2.1, 3, 52, 64, 83). In the final works of the early period, the *Theophany* and the oration for the dedication of the Church of the Holy Sepulcher, Eusebius summarizes the thoughts that he has long held. There are, he says, several causes or reasons why Christ became incarnate, lived, died, and rose from the grave, each of which constitutes our salvation (*Theoph.* 3.39). These reasons cluster into two main sets: why Christ became human and why he died and rose again.

The first cause of the incarnation was so that the invisible and incorporeal Word of God could manifest itself to creatures who could no longer perceive it. As Eusebius understands the human condition without Christ, our perception is fixated on sensory things and we are trapped in idolatry, "immersed in the depths of evils and in the corporeal substances" of nature (*Theoph.* 3.39). Rather than contemplate the Creator-Word, as God intended, we have instead sought God in creatures; delighting in the things of sense and seeking God in idols, we have failed to recognize the Word and Savior of all (*Theoph.* 3.39; 2.21). Out of compassion toward our idolatry, the invisible Word of God took on a corporeal instrument in order to recapture our earthward attention and converse with us again (*L.C.* 14.1).

Hence, Christ assumed our nature and came among us, "showing God through human existence [ἀνθρώπου ἐπιδεικνύμενος], which is a great wonder for all people" (*Proof* 4.10, 168.15–19). He was "seen by the very eyes of flesh" and manifested himself in ways beyond human power to perceive. He lived a life in common with us, in no way forsaking the existence that he had before, and yet preserving his divinity (τὸν θεόν) in his human existence (τῷ ἀνθρώπῳ). At the first moment of his descent among us, Christ mingles with God the divine glory of our birth (*Proof* 4.10, 165a–c). The Word took on a body, a "perceptible dwelling for the intellectual power" of God, which is a physical instrument, a holy temple and a pure image (*Theoph.* 3.39; *L.C.* 14.1). Without such an instrument, Eusebius asks, "How could the eyes of the body look upon the incorporeal nature of God?" (*Theoph.* 3.9). Christ's body thus serves as a kind of mediator and interpreter of incorporeal, divine knowledge and a means of rescuing our misdirected perception. Through the incarnation, the Word "made his Divinity sensible" and became known among mortals as an equal (*Theoph.* 3.39).[40] So the Word entered into communion with mortals through the instrument of a mortal body, in order to save humanity through the resemblance (*L.C.* 13.16).

In addition to this first cause of the incarnation, Eusebius lists three causes of the crucifixion and resurrection. Although he speaks frequently of Christ's revelatory function, Eusebius regards the passion and resurrection to be Christ's greatest work and "the very crown of all," and an integral part of the divine knowledge that Christ reveals (*L.C.* 15.1). When Eusebius first refers to Christ's "two manners of existence" at the beginning of the preface to the *Ecclesiastical History*, he writes that the divine Word has taken on human nature that is capable of suffering like us, intimating that his death on the cross would be Christ's ultimate saving act. Later in the preface Eusebius elaborates that Christ "did and suffered" such things as the prophets foretold, from his miraculous deeds and teaching of true piety to his death, resurrection, and ascension (*H.E.* 1.2.23).

The causes of the crucifixion are again multiple, including the fulfillment of Old Testament prophecy and Christ's own promises to his disciples; Christ's death also prevents his earthly sojourn from seeming to have been an illusion, were he simply to vanish without a trace. But the chief reasons for the crucifixion are two. The "first and greatest reason" for Christ's passion and "the great cause of his death" was so that the Word could defeat death and mortality on the cross and transform fallen human nature into immortal life. By dying on the cross, Christ frees the human race from its decaying nature and transforms our mortal condition into immortality by the divine power of the Word (*L.C.* 15.1–3; *Theoph.* 3.60). In the last conflict with death, Christ delivers his own body from corruption through its participation in the Word. Through his death, Christ also finishes the work that he had begun against evil powers. During his earthly ministry Jesus subjugated the demons to his divine authority; now, in his final act on the cross, he defeats death itself. Along with emphasizing the defeat of mortality in Christ's person, Eusebius is equally insistent that the crucifixion was necessarily a public event proclaimed abroad by the disciples. If Christ had died in secret, Eusebius says, there would have been no benefit to his followers (*L.C.* 15.5). This is one of the most interesting aspects of Eusebius's soteriology, because it shows the crucial importance of the proclamation of the cross and resurrection. There is no sense in Eusebius's work that Christ's death had an automatically redeeming effect on anyone—except for the transformation of his own mortal humanity into immortality. Only because Christ died a public death is he able to persuade his followers that they need not fear death but can trust and look forward in hope to the heavenly life that awaits them too after death. For this reason, the death of Christ on the cross is "the first and most mandatory doctrine of all" (*L.C.* 15.7). The crucifixion thus provides the reality of heavenly life in Christ himself, who is "the prototype of immortality," as well as the message of his victory over death, which are together the source of Christian virtue and hope in the face of death (*L.C.* 15.9; *Theoph.* 3.41–57, 62).

The reason for Christ's resurrection was then to vindicate the divine power of the Word that dwelt in Jesus. Whereas many other people who heroically faced death have come to be regarded as gods, Christ rose from the dead in order to demonstrate that he truly was God in human form—to show that the divine power dwelt in the body of Jesus and that it is superior to death in every form. It is the demonstration of Christ's real, divine power that persuades people to confess that he alone is "the God of truth" who now wears the crown of victory on his head (*L.C.* 15.10; *Theoph.* 3.58). Christ's risen body is thus "a trophy of victory over death and the demonic host" and a safeguard against former human sacrifices (*L.C.* 15.13).

The second main cause of the crucifixion is Christ's redemptive sacrifice for the sins of the world. Eusebius takes up this theme in book 1 of the *Proof of the Gospel*. In order to explain how Christians understand the nature of religious sacrifice, he contrasts the true and perfect sacrifice of

Christ with the animal sacrifices of the Old Testament, which were but a temporary measure provided by the Holy Spirit as a symbol and a type of Christ's true sacrifice. Drawing primarily on Isaiah 53 and its echo in John 1:29, Eusebius understands Christ as a sacrificial lamb who bears the sins of the whole world, a ransom and a propitiation for Jews and Greeks alike, who has also taken away the curse laid on those who were under the Jewish law (Gal 3:13; 2 Cor 5:21). In the *Proof of the Gospel* Eusebius explains that the Word took on human nature "able to suffer like us" specifically in order to be a sacrifice for sin through Christ's suffering and "the crowning trophy of the Cross" (*Proof* 3.5). After the crucifixion, God then gave to Christians the Eucharist in which to celebrate and remember Christ's self-offering (*Proof* 1.10; 3.2). In the *Theophany* and the Holy Sepulcher sermon, Eusebius reiterates his atonement theory. Christ was the sacrifice consigned to die for the souls of the human race, the sheep slain for the whole flock, and "the great offering superior to all other sacrifices." Yet Eusebius's notion of sacrifice also contains the idea of the Word's saving power; for Christ's sacrificial death in turn destroys the power of demons and dissolves "the whole vain, earthly system of error" by its mighty power. At the same time, in discussing Christ's sacrifice, Eusebius is careful to distinguish between the human sacrifice of Christ's body and the Word and power of God, who is the great high priest who performs the sacrifice, even apart from the incarnation, much as Origen had done. The difference is signified by the two names—"Jesus," which refers to the sacrifice of salvation, and "Christ," which refers to the preexistent high priest. Christ's sacrifice, finally, is something that is taught in "mystical terms"; it cannot be fully explained (*Theoph.* 3.59). Like Athanasius, Eusebius regards Christ's atoning sacrifice as an absolutely necessary and holy act, foretold by the prophets, and yet at the same time an act that belongs to the larger and deeper mystery of Christ's defeat of death. Christ died for the sins of the world, but his ultimate victory, in Eusebius's mind, was to defeat death and the devil.

For all these reasons God instituted the "primary mystery" of Christ's body (the incarnation) and "the signal mark of the victory of the Cross" (the crucifixion), and also the "remembrance," which Christ called "the commemoration of the life that is eternal and immortal" (the Eucharist) (*Theoph.* 3.61). Eusebius concludes his account of Old Testament prophecies in the preface to the *Ecclesiastical History* by considering Christ's final kingdom from the prophet Daniel (*H.E.* 1.2.24–25). Eusebius makes no argument here for the endurance of Christ's kingdom, as he will later against Marcellus; he refers to Daniel's text merely to show again both the divinity and the unity of Christ: that Daniel's words clearly refer to the Savior "who was 'in the beginning with God,' God the Word, and who is called Son of Man because of his incarnation at the last" (*H.E.* 1.2.26–27). In this text Eusebius briefly indicates the sort of apocalyptic views concerning Christ's second coming that he held throughout the early period and that are plenty evident in his other works on the prophets (*Ec.Proph.; Proof*). It is likely that similar material appeared in the last ten books of the *Proof of the Gospel*, which are no longer extant.[41]

LATE CHRISTOLOGY (337–339): *AGAINST MARCELLUS* AND *ECCLESIASTICAL THEOLOGY*

Eusebius's debate with Marcellus of Ancyra at the end of his life brought out his fullest doctrinal exposition. Written between 337 and Eusebius's death in 339, *Against Marcellus* and the *Ecclesiastical Theology* respond to the reversal of Constantine's ecclesiastical policy, when the exiled bishops were recalled after his death. These late works expand and in some ways shift the emphasis of Eusebius's early position; in particular, he gives a fuller account of his Trinitarian doctrine. Here Eusebius no longer seeks to explain or defend the faith to outsiders or assailants; this time he writes about the faith of the church as an insider speaking to another insider— though someone who, on account of his errors, Eusebius regarded as dangerous nevertheless. If Eusebius's apologetic works, spurred on by the attack of Porphyry, involved him in trying to show how the gospel relates to traditional Greek modes of thought, his polemical works against Marcellus take him in the opposite direction, eschewing extraneous influences and even seeking to protect the faith from them when he spies them in Marcellus's doctrine. *Against Marcellus* seeks to show the absurdity of Marcellus's position mainly by letting him condemn himself in his own words. The work may in fact be the case against Marcellus that Eusebius prepared for the synod of Constantinople in 336 at the time of Constantine's Tricennalia, when Marcellus was deposed; or it may be that Eusebius wrote it after the council to justify its actions.[42] Later, realizing that the first work did not do the job (*E.Th.*, ep. Flac.), Eusebius went on to write a fuller refutation in the *Ecclesiastical Theology*, which is also, as the title indicates, a summary statement of the faith of the church as he understands it.

The Interpretation of Scripture

Eusebius was first and foremost a biblical scholar, like his master, Origen. That he derives his theology and his view of human history chiefly from the Bible is clear from both the *Ecclesiastical History* and the apologetic works, and it is even more apparent in the late works against Marcellus. As already noted, Eusebius began his career as a dedicated biblical scholar in the tradition of Origen and Pamphilus, and he remained such until the end of his life. While he happily practiced a spiritual and theological interpretation of Scripture, he placed an especially high regard on the literal or historical sense of the text, even when referring certain Old Testament texts to Christ. Both aspects of Eusebius's exegesis have their roots in Origen's work.[43]

In his works against Marcellus, Eusebius shows the same exegetical principles as in his early work, giving a more sustained treatment of many passages than he had previously. It is on these grounds that Eusebius could oppose Marcellus most clearly and convincingly, for, as possibly the greatest biblical scholar of his generation, he was well placed to show the weakness of Marcellus's position at its most sensitive point: his claims about the Bible. If Marcellus's doctrinal position could seem appealing at first glance—that God is one; that the Word of God is fully divine, eternally dwelling in the Father; that one day God will be "all in all"—the underlying logic of these claims could best be exposed by confronting just how Marcellus understands the Scriptures. Patristic debates are usually known in terms of the doctrinal arguments and formulas at stake, yet Eusebius perceived that the dispute between himself and Marcellus was chiefly over the interpretation of Scripture. In *Against Marcellus*, Eusebius focuses on several egregious exegetical mistakes in order to undermine Marcellus's credibility as a theologian. In his view, the source of Marcellus's erroneous doctrine is his faulty interpretation of the Bible (*C.Marcel.* 1.2).

Eusebius points out first of all that the "wondrous historian" Marcellus mistakes basic facts of the biblical narrative, such as confusing the priest Joshua son of Josedek in Zechariah 3:1 with Joshua son of Nun, or failing to notice that Elisha was not the first to rise from the dead, since Elijah had already raised the widow's son earlier in the story (1 Kgs 17:22). Marcellus also confuses Solomonic proverbs with prophecies (*C.Marcel.* 1.2). Glaring as these mistakes may be, even more serious is the fact that Marcellus uses pagan Greek proverbs to understand the proverbs of the Bible, "trying to interpret the divinely inspired Scriptures through Hellenic models," the evidence for which takes up an entire section of the work

(*C.Marcel.* 1.2–3). Instead of pagan Greek sources, Eusebius recommends the "spiritual" interpretation of Scripture, as taught by Origen, according to which difficulties in the text are meant to exercise the interpreter's understanding, not send him looking for pagan Greek historical information; after which Eusebius defends Origen directly in the following section (*C.Marcel.* 1.4). Most egregious of all, however, Marcellus strays from the plain and obvious sense of the text and is ignorant of the story that has been narrated (*C.Marcel.* 1.2; 10.13).[44] Marcellus's lack of exegetical discipline involves referring certain biblical sayings, such as Colossians 1:15 and Proverbs 8:22, to the incarnation or the flesh of Christ in ways that both strain the literal meaning of the text and miss their true "theological" sense—about which Eusebius will have much more to say in the *Ecclesiastical Theology* (*C.Marcel.* 2.3). This litany of exegetical blunders is meant to show that Marcellus's interpretation was ridiculously bad.[45]

In *Against Marcellus*, which is heavy with direct quotations from Marcellus's work, Eusebius had hoped to expose the errors of Marcellus's theology through the sheer weight of its absurdity. But it was not enough, and so Eusebius explained himself in much more detail in the *Ecclesiastical Theology*. He again argues that Marcellus's doctrine is unsupportable by the Scriptures and charges Marcellus with regularly interpreting them falsely (*E.Th.* 1.pref; 1.17, 19–20). For his part, Eusebius means to base himself on a careful interpretation of Scripture: God's words in Scripture are sufficient, he says, for telling us what we need to know about the generation of the Son (*E.Th.* 1.12). It is the Scriptures that teach us that Christ is primarily the Son of God, and not the Word, in the reductive sense that Marcellus understands it, and through the Scriptures the only-begotten Son reveals the Father and himself (*E.Th.* 1.15; 1.20.v). In this way, Eusebius maintains an Origenist belief that the Scriptures plainly teach all saving doctrine, even as God has placed obscurities in the text to exercise the understanding—while he is clearly less interested in the sort of speculations beyond the text that so entertained Origen. Eusebius regards the Scriptures as the foundation of all Christian doctrine, containing the revelation of the mystery of Christ to the church. Consequently, most of the *Ecclesiastical Theology* is devoted to exegetical argumentation.[46]

Eusebius's exegetical approach is fairly clear and distinctive. Unlike the *Proof of the Gospel*, which concentrates on the Old Testament, and closer instead to the *Ecclesiastical History*, Eusebius begins his doctrinal exposition by appealing first to the New Testament. After giving a systematic summary of his own doctrine, Eusebius makes his first exegetical argument by means of a quick pass through the New and Old Testaments in order to show that Christ is called many things other than "Word" apart from the incarnation (*E.Th.* 1.20). It is not a difficult case to make. He begins with John's gospel and proceeds to Paul and Hebrews before turning to the Old Testament prophets, psalms, and proverbs, finding a host of titles that include God, light, life, only-begotten, rock, high priest, image of God, justice, Wisdom, tree of life, and Lord. All these things, Eusebius concludes, are said in Scripture about "the divinity of the Son of God"— they refer to the divine Son in his transcendent existence alongside God the Father—not to his incarnate state, or his flesh, as Marcellus thinks (*E.Th.* 1.20.xiii; 2.10–11).

Among the New Testament passages that Eusebius uses for constructive doctrinal purposes, the most telling single text is 1 Corinthians 8:6: "For us there is one God, the Father, from whom are all things . . . and one Lord Jesus Christ, through whom are all things."[47] Eusebius adopts this statement of Paul as a summary of the faith in the main doctrinal discussion in book 1 (where it is also the first text of any length that he discusses), and it is the first text he cites when he turns to Marcellus's doctrinal errors in book 2 (*E.Th.* 1.6; 2.2). Several elements of this verse provide important doctrinal information. First, Paul identifies the "one God" as the Father of Jesus Christ. Second, he explicitly refers to Christ as the means of creation— Christ being (especially in Paul) the Son of God, not the Word internal to the Father's being, as Marcellus would have it—showing that the Son preexisted the cosmos. Third, both the Father and Christ are signified as each being "one" entity, which further clarifies their distinct existence, again as opposed to Marcellus's denial of the same. And finally, Paul regards the confession of the one God, the Father, and the preexistent Christ as the saving faith of Christians ("for us"; *E.Th.* 120.viii). For Eusebius, much as it had been for Origen before him, Paul's statement clearly indicates that the one God is specifically the Father, in a primary or initial sense; that Christ preexisted creation as God's only-begotten Son and his incarnation as a human being; and (in some contrast to Origen) that the same Christ is now a human being, as a single subject of existence.[48]

Of particular importance in the later works are Jesus's sayings in John's gospel, especially in chapters 5 and 6. Two verses stand out as strong indications of Christ's distinctness from and dependence on God the Father as the preexistent Son: John 6:38 ("I have come down from heaven not to do my own will but the will of him who sent me") and 5:30 ("I can do nothing of myself; . . . I seek not my own will but the will of him who sent me"). Eusebius observes that Jesus is speaking of himself as having existed before his incarnation, as being dependent on the Father, who sent him, and as now being the incarnate Christ—a single subject of existence. He notes, more-over, that the Father and the Son in these passages are clearly distinct char-acters, or πρόσωπα. In keeping with the continuity between the preincarnate and the incarnate Christ expressed in the text, Eusebius takes Jesus to be referring not to his fleshly or human will, as Marcellus holds, but to his will as the divine Son of God, in relation to that of God the Father. In Eusebius's view, Jesus cannot be referring to himself merely as a human being, without implying that his flesh has literally descended from heaven, which is preposterous. These and other passages in John show, again, the irreducible presence of two divine figures in relation to one another, both before and during the incarnation, much as Eusebius had also discussed in the first book of the *Ecclesiastical History* (1.2.4–5). John's gospel shows, finally, that the Father is superior to the Son in some sense (John 14:28; 20:7), and yet, paradoxically, that the Son is also God and worthy of honor and worship along with the Father. Such examples could easily be multiplied.[49]

The debate with Marcellus comes to a head over the interpretation of the Old Testament, for Marcellus had appealed to classical monotheistic statements in the Old Testament in order to attack the pluralistic doctrine of Asterius and others and to defend his own monistic theology. For Eusebius the mystery of Christ, the only-begotten Son of God, had been definitively revealed to the church only in the New Testament; before this, only a select few of the Old Testament prophets knew the Son as such, and even then they did not proclaim him clearly, as he would be later in the incarnation. In light of the New Testament revelation, however, Christians are in a position to discern the Son throughout the Old Testament—along the lines of Paul's argument in 2 Corinthians 3, which was the dearest hermeneutical text to Origen: for those who are in Christ, the veil over Moses's face has been lifted, and the glory of God is now visible.

Eusebius's survey of biblical texts aimed to expose Marcellus's exces-sively narrow reference of many passages solely to the economy of the incarnation. While this involves the New Testament as well, it was over the Old Testament that the interpretive battle was fought most acutely.

The central text at hand—an important piece of Christological exegesis since before Origen, a point of heated contention between Marcellus and Asterius, and a passage destined to be a flashpoint of controversy for decades to come—was Proverbs 8.[50] Marcellus had attacked Asterius's exegesis of this text. In response, Eusebius makes Proverbs 8 the focus of his dismantling of Marcellus's exegesis in book 3 of the *Ecclesiastical Theology* and the cardinal example of Marcellus's hermeneutical foibles. Marcellus seizes on the statement of Wisdom that "the Lord created me at the beginning of his ways for his works" (Prov 8:22) and refers it to the incarnation in order to distance the subordinationist connotations of the passage from the eternal Word of God. In reply, Eusebius observes that throughout the chapter Wisdom plainly speaks of her heavenly existence with and in relation to God, not of the incarnation of Christ, as do several of the prophets.

Eusebius notes, first, that Wisdom speaks in this chapter as a distinct character or persona (πρόσωπον) who subsists and lives in herself. Second, the passage, as it continues after verse 22, plainly speaks of the establishment of Wisdom before the creation of the heavens and the earth, and that Wisdom was with God "like a master worker" when he created the earth, the sky, and the seas, "rejoicing always before God" and being "daily his delight." The passage uniformly refers to a past, or precosmic, state of affairs, not to a future Messianic event, as Marcellus claims. It thus conveys "mystical knowledge" about the Son's divine life before the creation. Moreover, Eusebius argues that the goal of the Old Testament is not yet to teach the new mystery of Christ's incarnation, but to teach monotheism against the polytheism of the nations (*E.Th.* 2.20). To think otherwise strains the obvious sense of the text, forcing a meaning on it that doesn't fit. Equally significant for our understanding of Eusebius's doctrine, he does not conclude that the Son, as Wisdom, was therefore created in anything like the Arian sense. Eusebius takes pains to reckon with the verb "created," turning to the Hexapla to work out the problem. He sees that the Hebrew text does not say "he created me" but "he possessed me," which is also reflected in the Greek translations of Aquila, Symmachus, and Theodotion; Eusebius then takes this statement to refer to the Father's appointment of the Son as the head, foundation, salvation, and providence of the creation, as the greatest and most honored possession of the Father (*E.Th.* 3.1–2).

In order to make his interpretation work, Marcellus allegorizes many of the other details in the passage, such as the terms "foundation" (which he refers to Christ's fleshly economy), "the earth" (human flesh), "the abysses" (the hearts of the saints), the "fountains of waters" (the apostles), and so on (*Frag.* 17–23). In Eusebius's view, this maneuvering is unnecessary and absurd, twisting the sense of the text by heavy-handed allegory and moving needlessly beyond its literal meaning (*E.Th.* 3.3). He has found Marcellus's weakest point. For by insisting that God is, strictly speaking, "one" apart from the incarnation and Pentecost, Marcellus is forced to interpret Old Testament passages that speak of two differentiated figures in relation to one another as referring to God and the incarnate Lord, often at great strain to the plain sense of the text. Eusebius defends the narrative sense of the text and exposes Marcellus for excessive allegorizing—a point that is especially ironic, given Marcellus's accusations against Eusebius and his colleagues for undue allegiance to Origen, the fabled allegorizer. Eusebius's treatment of Proverbs 8 is so central to his argument that it occupies approximately one-sixth of the entire work (*E.Th.* 3.1–3),[51] and his arguments against Marcellus's overly allegorical, economic exegesis continue through *Ecclesiastical Theology* 3.7–8.

The most famous corollary of Marcellus's theology and exegesis is his view that in the final consummation Christ will hand over his kingdom to the Father; he will cease to exist as a human being; the Word will return to being within God the Father; and God will be "all in all" (1 Cor 15:48). Eusebius takes on Marcellus's treatment of this verse, bringing even more doctrinal ammunition to bear. How can it be, he asks, that the saints will dwell with God forever, but Christ is not allowed to keep his own humanity? Eusebius points to many other texts in support of the endurance of Christ's eternal kingdom. In this case as well, he finds Marcellus ignorant of the Scriptures (*C.Marcel.* 2.1, 3–4). More examples could again be added.

By adhering more closely to the literal sense of the text and opposing Marcellus's excessive allegorization, Eusebius shows his greater acceptance of the thick narrativity of Scripture and its full range of meanings. In this respect Eusebius's exegesis is more Christologically inclusive than Marcellus's, and it reflects a greater sense of the continuity between the Old and New Testaments.

The Theology of the Son

The guiding principle of Eusebius's biblical exegesis, from the early *Prophetic Extracts* and the *Ecclesiastical History* to the late *Ecclesiastical*

Theology, is the revelation of the only-begotten Son of God. Commenting on the Old Testament as a whole, he writes that "the grace of the proclamation of the theology concerning [the Son] was preserved for his coming, which his Church, as if receiving some mystery that was long ago kept hidden in silence, now sows throughout the world . . ., a mystery that was hidden for ages," in a pastiche of Pauline phrases (*E.Th.* 1.20.xxix).[52] The central message of the New Testament, and consequently that of the Old Testament as well, is the revelation of the mystery of the Son of God; through the grace of Christ, the church has now received the theology of the Son, or the true confession of his divinity and preexistent life with God the Father.

This means that the Scriptures yield theological meaning about the Son apart from the incarnation: they give the knowledge of the Son in his preexistent, divine life, not, as Marcellus maintains, only economic meanings that refer all such statements about Christ or the Son to the incarnation. As Eusebius puts it, Marcellus "refers to the flesh the apostolic statements through which [the apostle] gives the divine teaching regarding the Son of God," such as Colossians 1:15–17. Through his excessively economic interpretation, Marcellus refuses to theologize the Son (*C.Marcel.* 2.3), and his Sabellianism makes him "a stranger to both the knowledge and grace of Christ" (*C.Marcel.* 1.1). By contrast, Eusebius argues that the Christian mystery is not the eternal Word internal to the being of God, which even Jews and Greeks believe God possesses; nor is it the incarnation per se, as if the flesh of Christ had any permanent value on its own. Rather, the mystery of God that has been revealed in the New Testament and through the human Jesus is the divine Son (and distinctly existing Word), who alone reveals God the Father. In this regard, the prophets, proverbs, and psalms of the Old Testament provide their own preliminary "theologies" of the Son, visible in light of the New Testament theology of the Savior, which has now been revealed for all to see.

Eusebius's biblical exegesis thus yields the Trinitarian "mystery of the Son," who is distinct, divine, and dependent on the Father. As we have seen since the *Ecclesiastical History*, Eusebius's theology and his understanding of history are centered on the person of Christ, who is the only-begotten Son and the divine Word of God—even as the Son serves chiefly to reveal the knowledge of God the Father. As he analyzes Marcellus's exegesis, he concludes that the result of Marcellus's faulty interpretation is effectively to deny or blaspheme the Son. This is Eusebius's chief criticism of Marcellus in the two works against him (*C.Marcel.* 1.1; 2.1, 4; *E.Th.* pref; 1.1; 2.2, 16). By this he means that Marcellus has denied that the Son preexists the incarnation at all and has any continuity with the life of God apart from his human form (instead of being only the Word), and has therefore denied both the divinity of Jesus and the humanity of the Son who became incarnate in Jesus (*C.Marcel.* 2.1). As evidence, Eusebius points to Jesus saying in John's gospel that eternal life consists of faith in the Son of God, who alone knows the Father (John 3:16, 36; *E.Th.* 1.12; Matt 11:27). As in the case of the martyrs, true "theology" is to confess the divinity of the Son, and it is here that Eusebius believes Marcellus has strayed from the gospel.

Christ and the Trinity

Eusebius argues for the theology of the Son and the faith in the Holy Trinity against Marcellus's monism and his denial of the Son. In the opening sections of *Against Marcellus*, Eusebius defines the gospel of Christ (Gal 1:6–9). The "one gospel" is that which Jesus gave his disciples in the Great Commission: to "make disciples of all nations, baptizing them in the name of the Father and of the Son and of the Holy Spirit" (Matt 28:19)— that is, it is the faith in the Trinity. Through the "mystical regeneration" (of baptism), Christ has given the church "the grace of the knowledge of the Holy Trinity"—a grace that neither Moses nor any other prophet, let alone any pagan philosopher or oracle, has revealed. As John's gospel states, in the first verse cited in Origen's *First Principles* (John 1:17–18; *Princ.* pref), only Jesus, the Son of God, has proclaimed "the paternal grace," that is, the grace of the knowledge of the Trinity. Whereas Moses and the prophets served chiefly to move the Jewish people from polytheism to belief in one God, Christ has proclaimed the saving grace, which is the "angelic and transcendent" knowledge (of the Trinity) and the "mystery hidden" from the ancients, "the blessed and mystical Trinity of Father and Son and Holy Spirit," which the church receives as its saving hope—and which it now preserves against the likes of Marcellus (*C.Marcel.* 1.1).

Yet apart from this brief opening discussion of the Trinity, *Against Marcellus* chiefly aims to expose Marcellus's work on his own terms, not to present a direct counterargument (*E.Th.*, ep. Flac.). It is in the *Ecclesiastical Theology* that Eusebius presents his Trinitarian doctrine with unprecedented fullness and clarity. Now, in order to refute Marcellus more fully, who defended the one God in one book against Asterius, he presents the "true theology" of the church by "honoring the all-holy and thrice-blessed

Trinity" in as many books (*E. Th.*, ep. Flac.). Whereas Marcellus insists on the oneness of God, citing familiar Old Testament texts in his defense, Eusebius replies that the one God (the Father) has been "in Christ reconciling the world to himself" (2 Cor 5:19) all along, communicating with his people constantly through the Son. After referring to John 17:3 as further evidence of the Trinity, Eusebius summarizes the gospel again for Marcellus—who, he intimates, ought to know it by now, as a long-standing bishop of the church. The mystery of the Son of God that was "hidden for ages and generations" (Col 1:26) from the ancients, but which has now been vouchsafed to the church by divine grace, includes "the teaching concerning the Holy Trinity of Father and Son and Holy Spirit" (*E. Th.* 2.22). The mystery of the divine Son, who is begotten from God the Father, is simultaneously the mystery of the Trinity as a whole.

Eusebius gives an important doctrinal summary at the opening of his argument in the *Ecclesiastical Theology*. Whereas the Jews (and Marcellus) received the confession of one God, as opposed to Greek polytheism, the saving grace that the Christian church has received is to confess "that the same God is father of an only-begotten Son," and in turn to confess that Christ is the divine Son. The confession of Jesus's sonship is not, Eusebius argues, a statement about Jesus's earthly or fleshly identity: it is not according to the birth of the flesh that he assumed, which is the "form of a slave" and the "Son of Man," but "according to his birth from God the Father himself before all ages and unknowable to all" (*E. Th.* 1.2). For by this divine begetting, the divinity of the Father constituted (hypostasized) him as Son and also God—even "God from God," as Eusebius's Caesarean creed, and later the Nicene Creed, states. To know that Christ's divinity derives solely from God the Father is the true "theology" (*E. Th.* 1.3).

At the outset of both later works, Eusebius presents the essence of the Christian faith as having to do chiefly with Christ's transcendent relationship with God the Father, as he had earlier in the *Ecclesiastical History* and the *Preparation for the Gospel* and *Proof of the Gospel*; and in the face of Marcellus's denial of the subsistence of the Son, this relationship takes priority over the simpler proclamation of the Son's divinity, which was so central before. The Son's relationship with the Father is both the result and the organizing principle of the church's interpretation of Scripture, according to Eusebius. Whereas Marcellus locates Christ's sonship in his incarnate, human status, Eusebius holds that the focus of the church's faith is instead on the divinity of the incarnate Christ and his precosmic begetting from God the Father, which are known only through the incarnation and the revelation of the mystery of the Son to the church.

In a second summary passage, Eusebius writes that Christians believe three basic things (ὑποκείμενα)—a list that is apparently meant to describe the ascending order of faith: (1) the one from the seed of David and the Holy Virgin (the human Jesus), (2) the preexisting and essentially subsisting Son of God who has come to dwell in Jesus, and (3) God, who is Father of the Son and who sent him. This list of terms recapitulates the basic faith expressed in 1 Corinthians 8:6. For Eusebius, theology thus proceeds by starting with (1) the man Jesus; followed by (2) the confession that he is the Son (or Christ) of God, as stated in Peter's confession (Mark 8 and par.); through whom believers are enabled (3) to know God the Father, whom the Son alone reveals as such (*E.Th.* 1.6). As for Origen, this is the very nature of faith: to confess that the human Jesus of Nazareth is the only-begotten, divine Son of God, creator and redeemer of the world. Only such a confession, Eusebius continues, avoids the major Christological errors of docetism (Christ is divine but not really human), psilanthropism (Christ is human but not divine), and modalism (Christ does not exist as a distinct being at all)— particularly a modalism that arises from a fear of polytheism, as in the case of Marcellus (*E.Th.* 1.3, 7, 14). Eusebius thus continues to oppose the same heresies mentioned in the *Ecclesiastical History*. The Christian gospel proclaims that there is one God the Father over all, that Jesus Christ is the only-begotten Son and God from God, and that the Son of God also became Son of Man (that which he was not) because of the Father's love of humankind (*H.E.* 1.3). The "mystery of regeneration" is belief in one God (against Greeks) who is Father (against Jews) and who rules over all (against Gnostics), the only-begotten Son of God, Jesus Christ, who coexists with the Father and is not the same as the Father—God from God, Light from Light, Life from Life (*H.E.* 1.8; *Ep.Caes.*; *E.Th.* 2.6).

Against Marcellus's denial of the Son and the Trinity, Eusebius has presented the Son's generation from the Father and the Father's role as source and cause of the Trinity—what will later be called the monarchy of the Father. The Father's generation of the Son and sharing of his divinity with the Son causes the Son to exist in himself and also to be divine like the Father (*E.Th.* 1.11). Yet, for Eusebius, it is always the Father's divinity that the Son shares: Christ's glory, by which he is known as the only-begotten Son of God, "exists in him from no other source than God the Father" (*E.Th.* 1.20.iv; 2.17). Paradoxically, the Son receives all things from the

Father and is not without source in the Father, and yet as a result the Son also has life in himself, not from without, "springing forth in himself from the life that is in the Father" (*E.Th.* 1.20.v–vi; 2.1). Hence, the Son can be ὁ ὤν even as the Father is (Exod 6:2–3; *E.Th.* 2.20–21). The result of the Father's generation of the Son is that the Son is also God, and that at the same time he prays to, obeys, and gives thanks to the Father, and the Father glorifies him in return (*E.Th.* 1.10; 2.7, 11).

In his late works, Eusebius locates the generation of the Son in the transcendent realm of God and the divine substance, by comparison with which creatures are lower and unable to comprehend what is highest—a fact that is most evident when we consider that we cannot even understand our own affairs (*E.Th.* 1.12). The Son therefore belongs with the Father as transcendent deity. Even so, the unity of God still lies in the Father: he is the one true and self-subsistent God in the proper sense (see John 17:3), the cause of his own being and that of the Son, even though he gives the Son also to be God, as Eusebius reads in John: "For as the Father has life in himself, so has he granted the Son also to have life in himself" (John 5:26; *E.Th.* 1.11).

As in the early works, it remains the Son's nature always to mediate the divine will and being toward creation, and, vice versa, to mediate the knowledge of God held by creatures. However, contrary to the subordinationist interpretation of his work, Eusebius specifies that, as image, the Son is equal, not inferior, to God. The Son is "true God" and the one "in the form of God" (Phil 2:6), while the Father is "the only true God" (John 17:3) and the archetype of the image (*H.E.* 2.23). Much like Athanasius in *On the Incarnation*, Eusebius maintains that God wills to convey the saving knowledge of himself through the same mediator through whom he created the world in the first place (*E.Th.* 2.21). As image, the Son is the necessary mediator of divine knowledge, for structurally Trinitarian reasons, and this occurs because the mediator too is divine, sharing the Father's divinity as only an only-begotten Son can. The idea of Christ as image of God also conveys the monarchy of the Father and avoids the thought that there are two gods (*E.Th.* 1.20.xiv). Rather than suggesting polytheistic subordinationism, as is often thought, Eusebius's image doctrine actually serves to prevent it, by keeping the divinity of the distinct Son absolutely dependent on that of the Father.

Eusebius has often been accused of neglecting the Holy Spirit, but such an impression could be sustained only from the narrowest reading of the apologetic works alone, which do focus on Christ and the doctrine of

God. In fact, the Spirit plays an important role in Eusebius's theological and historical works, from the *Ecclesiastical History* forward, making his work solidly Trinitarian from the start. As soon as he issues his summary statement about Christ at the beginning of the preface to the *Ecclesiastical History*, Eusebius cites the words of "the divine Spirit" in Isaiah as evidence of the Son's ineffable generation, and he repeats the phrase several times in the preface (*H.E.* 1.2.2, 4, 24).[53] With this title, which runs across his corpus, Eusebius names the Spirit in the strongest terms that one could expect at this time, calling it divine (θεῖον) but otherwise not wanting to move beyond the language of Scripture to call it "God" (θεός) outright.[54] Eusebius's position is further evidence of his Origenism, in which he was followed by Basil of Caesarea and matched by Athanasius, beyond which significant development would have to wait until the work of Gregory Nazianzen in the 370s.[55] The Spirit's inspiration of the Bible runs like a refrain through Eusebius's works, and he speaks regularly of the Spirit's coming to believers who are worthy.

It is true that Eusebius does not discuss the Spirit's divinity or subsistence to the extent that he does the Son's. This is due to the fact that the Spirit is less a point of contention for much of the fourth century, as is often noted, and also to the greater attention to the Son in the New Testament. Nevertheless, Eusebius accords the Spirit a key role in his work, as he learned to do from Origen, more so in fact than it plays in Athanasius's work before the 350s.[56] In the third book of the *Ecclesiastical Theology*, Eusebius clarifies the Holy Spirit's place in the Trinity, saying that it too preexisted creation, although it is not the same thing as the Son, on account of having been produced by the Son as well (*E.Th.* 3.2–6). Excelling all other rational substances in honor, glory, and privileges, the Spirit is thus included in "the Holy and thrice-blessed Trinity," coming after the Son in order; the Father, Son, and Holy Spirit are all "spirit"; and God reigns over all together with the Son and the Spirit (John 4:24; *E.Th.* 3.5–6). In sum, Eusebius traces a sequence of divine action that runs from the Father through the Son and to the Holy Spirit, similar to that found later in the Cappadocians (*E.Th.* 3.5). The Christian gospel is therefore a revelation of the divine nature of Christ, the Son of God, and his relationship with God the Father, and at the same time a revelation that the one God, whom Jews have long known as such, is in fact the Father of Jesus Christ. Together with the Holy Spirit, by whom all of this is known (as Eusebius regularly states since his early work), it is thus the faith in the Trinity.

While he was in the capital for the synod that deposed Marcellus, possibly on the evidence of Eusebius's own *Against Marcellus*, and for Constantine's Tricennalia, Eusebius delivered a panegyric to Emperor Constantine. In the midst of the speech he speculates on the numerological implications of the Tricennalia, based on the numbers one and three, and makes a statement of the Trinity that summarizes much of his final thinking on the subject. The number three, Eusebius says, is "an image of the mystical, all-holy, and royal Trinity, which, because it depends on the nature that is without source and unbegotten, possesses the seeds, the principles, and the causes of the essence of all begotten things" (*L.C.* 6.13). The entire Trinity derives from God the Father (the unbegotten nature), and because of this divine derivation it can be the basis of all other existences.

Near the end of the *Ecclesiastical Theology* Eusebius summarizes the Trinity in a way that shows the believer's involvement in the divine mystery. Because of who Christ is—the image of God, the one "in the form of God," bearing the stamp of the Father's hypostasis (Col 1:15; Phil 2:6; Heb 1:3)—whoever is purified by the Holy Spirit will be enabled to see the power of the only-begotten Son, in whom "the fullness of the Father's divinity dwells" (Col 2:9) and who is like the Father in all things; and, on seeing the Son, will also see the Father (John 14:9) in a way beyond all reason (*logos*) and image. That person will see the Father himself through the Son, being sanctified by the Holy Spirit (*E.Th.* 3.21).

Excursus: On Time and Eternity

One of the major interpretive problems in Eusebius's theology—and indeed a flashpoint of controversy between the pro-Arian and anti-Arian alliances—has to do with the language of temporality and eternity used for the Son. Scholars have debated whether Eusebius held the view that Alexander and Athanasius attributed to Arius, that "there was a time when the Son was not," by contrast with the network around Alexander, who agreed that the Son must be "eternal" just as the Father. Since his earliest works, Eusebius had spoken of the Son as "preexisting" the cosmos but not being strictly "eternal." In keeping with his apologetic argument toward the pagans that Christianity is the most ancient religion, as well as biblical statements that the Son is the instrument of creation, Eusebius teaches that the Son existed before the cosmos and was begotten from the Father "before the ages" (*C.Marcel.* 2.2; *E.Th.* 1.2, 8). Yet, on the other hand, he also teaches that the Father "preexists" the Son, an idea that has caused some readers to equate Eusebius's position with that of Arius. In the *Proof of the Gospel*, for example, Eusebius contrasts the Son's relationship to the Father with that of a ray emitting from a light. Whereas a light and a ray are inseparable from one another, the Son subsists distinctly (ἰδίως) alongside the Father; he does not exist merely as an activity of the Father but has his own proper existence (καθ' ἑαυτὸν οὐσιώμενος). Moreover, the ray coexists with the light as something that completes it (for they necessarily go together); whereas the Father preexists the Son and has presubsisted the Son's genesis, since only the Father is unbegotten (*Proof* 4.3; *C.Marcel.* 1.1; *E.Th.* 1.4).

What seems to have confused interpreters is that Eusebius uses prefixes and prepositions that often carry a temporal meaning (such as "pre-" and "before," or "co-" and "with") in a nontemporal sense. Eusebius is clear that the Son exists before and beyond all creation and time ("before the ages"); he does not believe that "there was a time when the Son was not." Moreover, he prefers to use biblical rather than philosophical terms for describing the Son's transcendence of creation and time, such as those found in Proverbs 8, where Wisdom says that she was with God "before the ages" (Prov 8:23), or in John's gospel, that "the Son abides unto the ages [εἰς τὸν αἰῶνα]" (John 8:35).[57] Eusebius uses terms that may appear to be temporal in order to express the basic structure of the Father-Son relationship, which, as we have just seen, he believes is central to the faith: namely, the Father's self-existent divinity (the fact that he has no source) and the Son's derivation from the Father. The narrative sequence of the Father's begetting of the Son in such passages reflects not a temporal priority but an order of divine generation, which is often conveyed in the Scriptures as a sequence of divine will. This emphasis is clear in another passage from the *Proof of the Gospel*: the Son does not cosubsist with the Father, Eusebius writes, "without source [ἀνάρχως], because the one is unbegotten and the other begotten, and the one is Father and the other Son, and everyone would agree that the Father pre-exists and pre-subsists the Son" (*Proof* 5.1, 215c). The idea of the Father's "pre-"existing the Son is for Eusebius an expression of the relationship of origin and derivation, not of a temporal interval.[58] An additional part of the relationship of dependence between the Father and the Son that Eusebius wants to preserve is the freedom and actuality of the Father's will in generating the Son. Here again, the language of preceding represents the Father's autonomy in generating the Son, rather than temporal precedence. Through such expressions Eusebius preserves a robust sense of source, sequence, and dependence within the Trinity.[59]

We may also observe that, in keeping with his close proximity to the literal sense of Scripture, Eusebius's sequential language maintains the epistemic priority of the biblical narrative in a way that is more immediately effective than abstract expressions of the Son's eternity are likely to be (*Proof* 4.1). For in Eusebius's scheme, one is constantly forced to remember the causal ordering of the divine generation, even as one also recognizes that the generation altogether transcends the realm of creation. Put somewhat differently, Eusebius's language preserves the economic basis of theological knowing with respect to the inner structure of the Trinity, resisting the leap to an artificial, abstract vantage point suggested by the conceptuality of pure eternity, as if the theologian did not himself or herself always exist in time. In this way Eusebius prevents us from forgetting how we come to know the Son's transcendence, which is an epistemic rootedness that is important and far-reaching. Likewise, the stronger language of eternity that Eusebius does apply to the Father again reflects the epistemic structure of theology, since the Father, through the Son, is both the ultimate object of theological knowing and worship and the source of all things, including the Son. Epistemically speaking, the Father *is* eternal; he is not involved in the process of knowing in the same mediatory way that the Son is.

An interesting question then remains as to how Eusebius understands the ongoing nature or the finality of the divine generation—whether he can speak of a continuous, "eternal" generation in the sense that the Cappadocians will later, or even in the sense of Origen, which is different yet again. Eusebius obviously does not seek to do so through the language of eternity, but the transcendent language that he does use would not rule out such a concept, since the alternative (that the Son's generation is not eternal) inevitably throws one back into the temporal framework that Eusebius firmly denies. On the whole, Eusebius follows Origen by insisting on the mysteriousness of the Son's generation, and it is this line that Arius transgressed in trying to pin down its temporality, in a manner that is very far from the approach of Eusebius.

The question of time, sequence, and eternity becomes particularly acute in Eusebius's debate with Marcellus. Interestingly, it is Marcellus who presents a temporal scheme that contrasts most starkly with Eusebius's view. Marcellus imagines that, although the Word exists eternally in God, the Son comes to exist at a certain time for the purpose of the incarnation, and will later become one with God again after the fleshly economy is over

(*C.Marcel.* 1.1). At one point the debate turns over the teaching of Origen, whom Marcellus criticizes for not learning about the eternity of the Word from the prophets and apostles, and for contradicting himself by saying elsewhere that the Father is always Father. Eusebius argues in return that the Son is in fact not begotten in time but before all ages (*C.Marcel.* 1.4). Here, at least, Eusebius does claim to know Origen's teaching on the Son's eternal generation and to replicate it more faithfully than Marcellus does, which is not surprising, given Marcellus's sharp criticisms of Origen in general. Eusebius recognizes that Marcellus's view of the Son's temporality suffers from what we might call a problem of mythologizing. Eusebius asks, if the Word was no longer "in God" during the incarnation (having extended itself to become the Son), then when did it coexist with the flesh (*C.Marcel.* 2.4)? Eusebius recognizes that Marcellus is imagining a sort of temporal change in God (*E.Th.* 2.9). Moreover, by denying that the Son is generated from the Father at all, apart from being born of a human mother, Marcellus is even further from affirming the eternal generation of the Son (or even the Word, which is not "begotten") than Eusebius is. Rather, Eusebius submits, the Son "always co-exists and is present with the Father, deep within as if in the most profound and inaccessible recesses of the Father's kingdom," and the Spirit too "always stood by the throne of God" (*E.Th.* 3.4). Perhaps Eusebius's strongest statement of all comes in his panegyric to Constantine: "The only-begotten Word of God endures with his Father as co-ruler from ages that have no beginning to ages that have no end" (*L.C.* 2.1). Not only is Eusebius clear that the Son's generation transcends all time, but his handling of these matters shows several theological strengths that have been almost universally overlooked by those who take their lead from the polemics of Athanasius.

The Unity of Christ

One of the most interesting shifts that occurs in Eusebius's late works concerns his sense of the unity of Christ. Although his earlier Christology is already predominantly unitive, Eusebius goes to greater lengths in his later works against Marcellus to make the unity of Christ unmistakably clear. Beginning with the *Ecclesiastical History*, Eusebius normally speaks of Christ's economic activity as a single subject of existence. In the interest of confessing the divinity of the incarnate Lord, Eusebius naturally stresses the continuity between Jesus Christ and the preexistent Son of God. When Christ became incarnate, he was "the same teacher" that Israel and the righteous of old had known all along (in a veiled way) (*H.E.* 1.2.23). Likewise, the incorporeal Word himself overcame mortality, by means of human armory and a mortal body—that is, as a single subject (*Theoph.* 3.61). In such arguments, Eusebius establishes not only an identity between the Creator-Word and the redeemer-Word, much as Athanasius will do later in *Against the Pagans* and *On the Incarnation*; but he is equally concerned to show the continuity between Christ the redeemer and the God of Israel, which is largely absent from Athanasius's early work. Christ's obedience to the Father shows the consistency between his human life and his divine relationship with the Father's will, reflecting his self-emptying love in accordance with the will of the Father (*Proof* 10.8). The identity of Jesus's human existence with the life of the divine Word in turn causes Jesus's earthly submission to be reflective of his divine identity as the Word of God and his submission to the will of the Father. Eusebius's early vision of the unity of Christ represents perhaps his most significant correction of Origen's theological program, and it appears that he was helped in this regard by avoiding Origen's doctrine of Jesus's human soul, as many other theologians of the time did as well.

Yet, in keeping with Origen's Christology, Eusebius occasionally qualifies his unitive statements in order to make clear that the Word did not suffer, change, or diminish through the incarnation. Such dualizing qualifications occur with special frequency in the *Theophany* and the Holy Sepulcher sermon. Eusebius insists that Christ's incorporeal power suffered nothing in his own essence nor received anything from the mortal body; light did not become the clay that it shone on, nor was the sun polluted by commixture with the body (*Theoph.* 3.39–40). Again, the Word is not subject to the passions of the body like a human soul when it "spiritually touched a human body" (*L.C.* 14.4, 7–9, 11). In the *Theophany* Eusebius even states that, in the crucifixion, the Word left the body of Christ on the cross and then returned later to raise him from the dead—a scenario that depends on a less than unified bond between the two, not to mention the soteriological questions implied in the Word's deserting Christ at the most crucial moment (*Theoph.* 3.61). We may understand such statements in the context of Eusebius's concern to explain Christianity to a pagan audience, who would have deep-seated aversion to suggestions of divine suffering, much as Origen had done.

In the late works, however, Eusebius's Christology becomes more consistently unitive. He writes in the *Ecclesiastical Theology* that Christ was the only-begotten Son of God, existing in something like a divine statue, which is the instrument of his body (*E.Th.* 1.13). Even more unitive is Eusebius's treatment of Jesus's statements about himself in John 3. "The one who comes down from heaven," Eusebius argues, cannot be the flesh of Jesus; it must be "he himself, namely the light and Word and God and only-begotten and Son, himself being all these things" (*E.Th.* 1.20). The reason for Eusebius's particular expression, again, seems to be contextual, namely, in reaction to the strongly dualistic Christology of Marcellus. Eusebius opposes the sharp distinction Marcellus makes between Christ's flesh and his spirit (*E.Th.* 3.10–11). To make matters worse, Marcellus even allows that the incarnate Son *disagrees* sometimes with God (*C.Marcel.* 2.2). Here again, Marcellus's resistance to theological interpretations of certain biblical texts—refusing even to ascribe the titles "Jesus" and "Christ" to the Word at all—also pushes in a dualistic direction (*C.Marcel.* 2.2–3). And finally, there is the matter of Christ's ceasing to exist as a human being, when the Word returns to the Father, which is an eminently dualist picture (*C.Marcel.* 2.4). There is an interesting parallel between Marcellus's Christological dualism and that of his anti-Arian associate Eustathius of Antioch.[60] When faced with a Christology like that of Marcellus, Eusebius has second thoughts about putting things quite so dividedly. Nevertheless, his transmission of basic Origenist categories and his strong appeal to the unity of Christ—correcting Origen and countering Marcellus—make Eusebius a major Christological teacher in the early fourth century.

At the same time, Eusebius does account for the presence and functioning of Jesus's human soul. While he often speaks of the Word as the sole agent of Jesus's words and deeds, as Athanasius tends to do, Eusebius envisions Christ as having a human soul that can undergo suffering, and already in the *Ecclesiastical History* he speaks of Christ possessing a complete human mind (*H.E.* 1.2.1). Later, in the *Proof of the Gospel*, he writes that Christ "descended to our world and received in turn our rational nature on account of his own likeness to it" (*Proof* 4.10; 16.8–10); and in the Holy Sepulcher sermon, "The divine image . . . partook of life and intellectual existence" (*L.C.* 14.2–3). On the question of whether or not Jesus possessed a human mind or soul, Eusebius is no Apollinarian, in the sense that Athanasius was, even though it is equally true that he does not reflect in any depth on how the agency of the divine Word works together with human free choice. Such problems will occupy theologians of later centuries at some length.

CHRIST AND CULTURE

Eusebius has long been recognized as a key figure in the developing relationship between Christianity and the surrounding culture. He has been called "the first political theologian of the Christian Church,"[61] and his political theology was enormously influential during the Eastern and Western Middle Ages. Less widely recognized, however, is the connection between these aspects of his work and his understanding of Christ. We have already seen that Eusebius's Christology directly engages with aspects of the wider Roman culture; it should come as no surprise that it figures centrally in how he deals with the challenges and triumphs of the church in society.

Martyrdom

Eusebius's understanding of Christ is far from an abstract concern. It is intimately tied up with the surrounding Greco-Roman society in ways that call on Christians to witness to Christ with their bodies as much as with their minds. In the initial argument of the *Ecclesiastical History*, Eusebius means to show not only that Christ is the divine Word who appeared to the saints of old, but also that the Christian "way of life" (βίος) is itself both ancient and holy. Together with the knowledge of the Father, Christ gives Christians a "heavenly way of life" through the doctrines of truth (*H.E.* 1.3.12). Eusebius's definition of a "Christian" is one who excels in righteousness, godly conduct, and virtue and who worships the one God of all, just as each of the Old Testament saints did (*H.E.* 1.4.6–7). As the *Ecclesiastical History* unfolds, Eusebius focuses more and more on the lived witness that Christians bear to Christ. The lived quality of his Christology hinges on his central use of the idea of divine power. Christ is "the power of God and the Wisdom of God," Paul writes (1 Cor 1:24). To confess that Christ is divine and the Word of the Father is to confess that he is God's power who came among us and who is now present with the church through its members. For Eusebius, to confess Christ is to proclaim his divinity both with words of faith and with the actions of one's life, just as Christ himself taught the victory of life and immortality by dying and rising. Eusebius calls it the most miraculous thing of all that believers honor Christ not only with their voices and words, but with all the affection of their souls and the witness (μαρτυρία) of their very lives (*H.E.* 1.3.20). This lived witness to Christ advances the argument of the book just as much as the doctrinal statements of Christ's divinity.

Among several main themes, the *Ecclesiastical History* narrates the persecution of Christians from the first generation of Christ's followers through the Great Persecution of Eusebius's own lifetime. While he celebrates the successes and the growth of the church, Eusebius is also careful to highlight the repeated confrontations and sufferings that Christians faced over time. Several times he speaks of Christ's kingdom being in tension with the powers of the Roman world. Vespasian did not rule the entire world, as an oracle declared, but Christ did (*H.E.* 3.8.10–22). When Domitian was persecuting some Jewish Christians, the persecutors inquired about Christ and his kingdom, to which the Christians replied that it was not of this world or anywhere on earth and would be established only at the end of the world (*H.E.* 3.20.4). The same sentiment is repeated in different ways several times throughout the work.[62] The conflict between Christ and the world then comes to a head most decisively during the Great Persecution, in which Christian martyrs wage a battle for true worship and honor against the forces of evil (*H.E.* 8–9).

The twin themes of Christ's power and suffering appear at the beginning of the main narrative, in book 2, and run throughout the story of the church. In his account of the apostles following the ascension of Christ, Eusebius focuses immediately on Stephen, the leader of the first seven "deacons" and the first martyr of the church, as well as on the martyr James, the brother of the Lord. He connects Stephen's martyrdom directly with Christ's death: he was "the first after the Lord . . . to be put to death, stoned by the Lord's murderers," and "the first to win the crown called by the same name as he, which is reserved for the victorious martyrs of Christ" (*H.E.* 2.1.1). Eusebius then relates how Thaddeus healed King Abgar by the word of Christ and performed "wonderful miracles," leading the inhabitants of Edessa to "reverence the power of Christ" (*H.E.* 2.1.6–7).[63] From this display of Christ's power, Eusebius turns again to persecution, as suffered by the Jerusalem church and inflicted by Paul (*H.E.* 2.1.8–10). Several other figures stand out in the original books 2–7. When the Jews demanded that James the Lord's brother deny Christ, he confessed instead that Jesus was the Son of God, for which he was killed by being thrown from the pinnacle and clubbed to death (*H.E.* 2.23.1–3). And Eusebius's mentor, Pamphilus, earned "the crown of martyrdom" as a great confessor of the faith (*H.E.* 7.32.25). At the conclusion of the original edition in book 7, Eusebius summarizes the argument as having shown "the successions from our Savior's birth to the destruction of our places of worship" (*H.E.* 7.32.32)—successions, by this point, including bishops, Christian doctrine, and the witness of the martyrs intermingled together.[64]

With the Great Persecution the story becomes more complicated. Eusebius ascribes some of the blame to the church itself, and God plays the role of righteous judge. Eusebius writes that the persecution arose as a result of the church's success, which we know occurred at record levels during the early years of the reign of Diocletian. When the faith became more widely received and rulers began to allow places of worship to be built, Christians became slothful and their leaders quarrelsome. As a result, God "exalted the hand of his enemies" against the church in what became the Great Persecution under Diocletian (Ps 89:42; *H.E.* 8.1). As with the Babylonians who invaded Israel in the Old Testament, the persecutors are enemies of God whom God nevertheless uses to discipline his people (*H.E.* 8.12). After he "scourged the people" with severe trials, God finally showed himself gracious again (*H.E.* 9.8). Yet in another sense, the church has simply been "ravaged by a destroying demon," and the protector Word "restored her again" (*H.E.* 10.4). When Constantine finally defeated Maximin, Christians danced and sang and honored God and the pious emperor, who had "wiped the world clean from hatred of God" (*H.E.* 10.9). Throughout the persecution, Christ's kingdom is very clearly "not of this world," even as the church must shoulder some of the responsibility for its trials.[65]

In the *Ecclesiastical History* books 8–9, Eusebius narrates at length the horrors of the persecution, many of which he witnessed himself. It was true devotion and love of God that provided the "philosophic determination" of the martyrs (*H.E.* 8.9.8). Many church leaders endured heroically, and thousands of martyrs showed enthusiasm for the worship of the true God. Many prosperous Christians, Eusebius notes, preferred to confess Christ rather than to maintain the "outward glory and prosperity" that they enjoyed, putting everything second to "true religion and faith in our Savior and Lord Jesus Christ" (*H.E.* 8.3). Here Eusebius takes care to show that, for all its newfound prosperity, the church maintained the true faith through the persecutions. Despite all the suffering, Eusebius saw "the ever-present divine power of him to whom they testified, our Savior Jesus Christ himself, visibly manifesting itself to the martyrs" (*H.E.* 8.7). The martyrs "bore Christ" (*H.E.* 8.10) and preferred to confess Christ rather than to heed the imperial command to commit idolatry, battling all over the world for the true worship of God (*H.E.* 8.11–13; 9.1). Through their brave sufferings, the martyrs "furnished in themselves unmistakable proof our Savior's truly divine and ineffable power" (*H.E.* 8.12.11).

The witness of the martyrs in the *Ecclesiastical History* is for Eusebius the ultimate confession of Christ's divinity and saving work. By means of their actions, the martyrs practiced the same reverence of God through the divine Word that Abraham himself had practiced (*H.E.* 1.4.14). Likewise, the battle against false doctrine is also a struggle to witness to Christ. During a certain time of prosperity, Eusebius writes, the devil, who had formerly persecuted the church from without, was now fomenting spiritual corruption within through impostors such as Menander, Saturninus, and Basilides, whom Irenaeus rightly opposed as heretics. But against these errors the truth established itself, and the catholic church grew in size and power, and "slander against the faith" died down over time (*H.E.* 4.7.1–14; 7.31.1). Right doctrine, the Christian way of life, and the most extreme confession of martyrdom are thus interrelated witnesses to the divinity and power of Christ (*H.E.* 7.32).

Church Buildings

The fact that Eusebius's career overlapped with Constantine's sweeping building program had almost as great an effect on the latter part of his life as the Great Persecution did on the first part. Just as the witness of the martyrs is a tangible proof of Christ's divinity and power, so too the force of Christ's incarnation, passion, and resurrection is further demonstrated by the new changes taking place (*L.C.* 16). Our most important source here is Eusebius's oration for the dedication of the Church of the Holy Sepulcher. Only recently, Eusebius recalls, imperial persecutors had destroyed church buildings in an effort to eliminate Christian congregations (*L.C.* 17.2). Then, after the persecutors perished and edicts of toleration were issued, God immediately erected "victory trophies everywhere on earth, adorning the entire inhabited world once again with holy temples and the solemn dedication of oratories," which came to be called, appropriately, "the Lord's houses" (κυριακῶν) (*L.C.* 17.3–4). Just as Christ's bodily resurrection is the trophy of his victory over death, so now the new churches are further trophies of the same, adorning city and town with civic ornamentation of Christ. At the same time, Christ was also persuading monks, nuns, and priests to dedicate themselves to his service through lives of virtue (*L.C.* 17.5–6).

Just as Christ vanquished the demons through his incarnation and, finally, defeated death on the cross, so too the new church buildings—in many cases, literally—won the victory over former pagan temples and sacrifice. Many of Constantine's new churches were built on the sites of old temples, some of which were torn down just for the purpose, and many were funded by confiscated temple treasures, a policy for which Constantine was apparently being criticized by certain pagan citizens. Within the churches were set up further trophies of Christ's death—some sort of crosses or crucifixes to decorate the new church buildings (*L.C.* 11.2).[66] This architectural victory over paganism parallels the victory that Christ achieved over idolatry, demons, human sacrifice, and war (*L.C.* 13), so that the new buildings are "the living acts of the living God" (*L.C.* 17.1). Eusebius regards the public deeds of the Christian church, now reestablished in Roman society at a level that was previously unthinkable, as an epitome of "the divine powers of our Savior," and proof that the true Son of God has been "seen on earth" in his churches (*L.C.* 17.15).

All of this is yet another demonstration of Christ's sovereign power made manifest in the world. At the beginning of his oration at the Holy Sepulcher, Eusebius states that the true reasons, or principles (λόγοι), of the new church buildings that Constantine has sponsored are "the reasons of the power of our Savior God" (*L.C.* 11.7). The purpose of the new churches is, again, the power of Christ, which can be understood only through "the power of the divine Spirit" (*L.C.* 11.3). The divine power that comes from God the Father through the Son and the Holy Spirit (a Trinitarian enterprise) is the source and explanation of the new churches being built. In this light, the benevolent Word of God has placed new schools of divine knowledge everywhere, to bring the knowledge of God to those who are ignorant of him (*L.C.* 11.5). Hence, there follows, in between these opening statements and Eusebius's later remarks on the buildings, a full Christological exposition, which we have already discussed (*L.C.* 11.7–12.16).

Glorious new churches such as the Holy Sepulcher are thus further "witnesses" to Christ's divinity and power, in continuity with the martyrs. When the cave of the resurrection was rediscovered and unearthed, the "martyrion" of the resurrection was revealed, through its own resurrection (*V.Const.* 3.28), and the shrine built by Constantine over it was a "manifest testimony [*martyrion*] of the Savior's resurrection" (*V.Const.* 3.40). There is an especially interesting connection here with Eusebius's positive regard for the human body and marital relations. Several times in the *Ecclesiastical History* he registers his opposition to those who denigrate the body or marital relations. He opposes the so-called Nicolatians, who taught that Christians must treat the flesh with such contempt that marriage is regarded as an evil to be disposed of, in order to renounce such desires, and he concurs with Clement of Alexandria (his source of information about the

Nicolatians), in support of the good of marriage (*H.E.* 3.29–30). In *Ecclesiastical History* book 4, Eusebius again opposes those who seek to impose a rule of celibacy on the Christian community (*H.E.* 4.23, 28). Similarly, in his treatment of church architecture, Eusebius is imagining something like the full "embodiment" of Christ in human society—an act that, in his time, would necessarily require the approval of the Roman government, which does not usurp the theological authority of the bishops. One could oppose to this notion a more rigorous and even ascetical separation of the church from the support systems of wider society; we will find just such a scheme in Athanasius, who depicts a more extreme asceticism in the monk Antony, by contrast with Eusebius's moderate, scholarly spirituality.

The new building of churches around the eastern Mediterranean, and especially in the Holy Land, witnesses that Jesus's divine power is greater than all the pagan gods and heroes. Christ's power has spread by virtue of his saving teaching, the philosophic life that Christians now lead, the geographical spread of Christianity, and finally the defeat of the pagan gods and the political system that they support, which once had attacked the church but has since been vanquished—thanks in large part to the ministrations of Emperor Constantine (*V.Const.* 17.3–4).

Imperial Favor

The last decade of Eusebius's career convinced him, beyond any shadow of a doubt, that Christ's power could ideally be manifest through official support and the legalization of Christianity, just as it had been by the martyrs. This common witness in what could hardly be more different circumstances was not, for Eusebius, the contradiction that it is for many modern people. Scholars of Eusebius tend to favor one side or another of a dilemma between Eusebius the innocent churchman who wrote the *Ecclesiastical History* and Eusebius the political sycophant, who emerged after the Council of Nicaea and went on to write the obsequious *Life of Constantine*. If we read Eusebius's political works in the context of his wider corpus, however, they make more sense as expressions of his Christology, and they appear less brazenly manipulative and power hungry.[67]

When he wrote the first edition of the *Ecclesiastical History*, Eusebius focused on the power of Christ manifested through martyrdom, at the same time that he had a vision of the public success of Christianity. These two visions are not as conflicting as they may seem, for one of the main effects of persecution or oppression can be to make the victims appreciate times of peace and favor all the more. This is just what happened to Eusebius, who had seen horror after horror inflicted on the followers of Christ. During times of cultural oppression, Eusebius believes that Christians will witness to Christ through righteous suffering in solidarity with Christ's own death; whereas during times of social stability and cultural support, Christians witness by prospering and entering more fully into the fabric of public life, which is a miracle no less divine than the miracles Christ performed when on earth.

Eusebius's main account of Constantine's place in history is in his oration at the Church of the Holy Sepulcher, which repeats long sections of the *Theophany*. When Constantine defeated the emperors who were persecuting the church and built new churches in place of pagan temples, he appeared to Eusebius as the veritable culmination of human history. Eusebius had been seeing the fulfillment of Old Testament prophecy in contemporary events all his scholarly life. His view of human history—which we have here identified as being rooted in the divinity and power of Christ—adjusted easily to the good fortune of having a Christian on the imperial throne. Both his *Commentary on the Psalms* and *Commentary on Isaiah*, written after Constantine's accession as sole emperor, focus on Old Testament predictions of the church's success: the buildings at the tomb of the Savior, the cessation of pagan sacrifices, the downfall of the persecutors, the end of the worship of demons, the appointment of Christians as provincial governors and generals—and a Christian occupying the imperial throne and supporting the church.[68] In the oration at the Holy Sepulcher, Eusebius gives a broad statement of God's power being exercised through Constantine's activities to suppress pagan worship and to support the true faith, such as we saw with the construction of new church buildings. Among Constantine's pro-Christian measures was to give church councils legal status, forbidding provincial governors to contravene their decrees (*V.Const.* 4.27), and he intervened in theological controversies, sometimes with good effect.

Constantine's patronage of the church is, in one sense, not at all unusual, since emperors had systematically promoted religious practices for a long time, including the support of religious buildings, and this had even increased under Diocletian in the previous century. For Constantine it was not a question of whether the emperor would support religion, as some modern Westerners imagine; the decision was whether to support the old gods of Greece and Rome or the God of Israel and Father of Jesus Christ. Although Eusebius was not as close to the emperor, in the political sense, as he claims, he does appear to have been fairly close to him in terms of theological influence—as can be seen from Constantine's remaining theological documents excerpted in the *Life of Constantine*.

According to his own theological rationale, Eusebius's glowing acceptance of Constantine's sponsorship is not disconnected from the martyr spirituality of his earlier period. Besides having defeated Maximin and Licinius, who were persecuting the church, Constantine shared a great appreciation for the faith of the martyrs. This attitude can be seen in his letter to the bishops of Palestine in 324 (*V.Const.* 2.24–42), which extols the power of God and the success of Christianity against the backdrop of its former persecution and the attacks of Porphyry—much as Eusebius himself thought. In addition, Constantine dedicated his new capital to "the God of the martyrs" (*V.Const.* 48.1), and he himself prayed at the shrine of the martyr Lucian in Helenopolis as his death approached (*V.Const.* 4.61).

For Eusebius, a profound continuity exists between the church's identity before and after the rise of Constantine, for the same power of God is manifest in each time and setting, even if in different ways. Accordingly, Eusebius ends his narrative of the persecutions with a prayer of gratitude for God's deliverance and the hope that troubles will stay away (*H.E.* 10.1). He now celebrates what many righteous people and martyrs of God "longed to see on earth and did not see" (though they attained better things in heaven)—the amazing and bountiful grace of God. Already in his early apologies, Eusebius spoke strongly for the universality of Christianity's mission and achievement thus far, spreading throughout the Roman world and beyond. Christianity transcended the limitations of all other known religions, offering a New Covenant between God and all nations, and as such it was destined to exert divine power in the world, whether through the martyrs' deaths or the establishment of Christianity in the Roman empire (*H.E.* 1.1.6–7; *Proof* 2.3).

Eusebius's political theology inevitably strikes the modern ear as distastefully flattering, morally questionable, and socially dangerous. But it was not at all so in its own time. Eusebius merely took up the old practice of theologizing kingship and gave it a Christian meaning; nor was he the only one to eulogize Constantine, as he was joined by pagans and other Christians alike.[69] Judging from his biblical interpretation, Eusebius most likely regarded all rulers as instituted, or at least permitted, by God, as Paul taught in Romans 13. Both Diocletian's persecution and Constantine's favor are divinely willed or sanctioned. Given the former, it should be no surprise to see the latter. Moreover, Constantine may even use force to enact justice, as Paul also argues, and, in an unexpected blessing, to defend the church from its enemies. On both counts Eusebius reflects a traditional view of active divine providence operating through what moderns think of as secular power.

Eusebius's public theology and his imperial oratory were of a piece with what he had done all along: to speak authoritatively to the surrounding culture on behalf of the divine power of Christ, defending Christianity against virulent persecutors from Porphyry to Diocletian and arguing for the social viability and supremacy of Christianity over the pagan past. With the reign of a powerful Christian emperor, the possibilities for achieving these goals were unprecedented and irresistibly exciting. Thanks in part to his own influence, Eusebius would certainly not be the last to find it so.

3. Nicaea (325) and
Athanasius of Alexandria

The church of Alexandria again played a leading role in the major theological and ecclesiastical developments of the fourth century, while the city remained the chief commercial center of the eastern Mediterranean. The new imperial capital of Constantinople, founded in the 320s, would eventually rival both Rome and Alexandria for prominence, but not until the latter part of the fourth century. Meanwhile, the metropolitan see of Alexandria continued to produce formidable bishop-theologians who greatly affected the course of patristic theology: Athanasius, who was bishop of the city for nearly half of the century (328–373), and, in the following century, Cyril, whose Christology we will discuss in chapter 6. Contrary to the conventional accounts, the theological climate of the Alexandrian church remained heavily determined by the legacy of Origen, even though Athanasius caused significant shifts in the Origenist tradition there.

Despite the fact that he incurred the condemnation of his bishop and decamped to Caesarea in the 230s, Origen retained a surprising authority in the Alexandrian church during succeeding generations. Bishop Demetrius defined his episcopal ministry to some extent in opposition to Origen, and his successor, Heraclas, apparently upheld Origen's condemnation; yet the following bishop, Dionysius, was a staunch Origenist and a defender of his legacy. Like Origen, Dionysius opposed modalism and was accused of positing more than one first principle. By the middle of the third century, if not before, Origen had reestablished himself as the chief theological authority in the city of his first renown, only now his influence resided both in the episcopate and in the continuing catechetical school, which was tightly controlled by the bishop. Between Demetrius and the turn of the fourth century, every Alexandrian bishop began as head of the school: Heraclas (231–247), Dionysius (247–264), Maximus (264–282), and Theonas (282–300). In addition, two heads of the school near the turn of the century appear to have been moderate Origenists as well. Theognostus, who served as head shortly before Peter became bishop in 300, wrote a lost work titled *Hypotyposeis*, which sought to prove the possibility of the incarnation. Pierius (d. 303?), who was a presbyter of bishop Theonas and teacher of Pamphilus of Caesarea, may also have written on the incarnation in a work on Mary the "Theotokos," or God-bearer, and in particular on Christ's virgin birth, a theme important to Origen. Jerome held Pierius in high esteem and dubbed him "Origen Junior" (Jerome, *Vir.Ill.* 76), and Athanasius later considered him an excellent teacher (*Decr.* 25). Although he was once regarded as an anti-Origenist, Bishop Peter (bishop, 300–311) likewise carried forward Origen's theological legacy. The remaining fragments of Peter's works show that he wrote on the divinity of Christ, the soul, and the resurrection—the very topics that Pamphilus's extracts from Origen focus on—and he opposed the preexistence of souls (as Dionysius also had), making him in all likelihood a moderate Origenist as well.[1] We know little about Peter's successor, Achillas, who served as bishop for only six months in 312.

By the early fourth century, episcopal orthodoxy in both Alexandria and Caesarea was thus defined by a moderate Origenism that carried forward Origen's emphasis on the divinity and distinctness of Christ against radical subordinationism, monarchian modalism, and Gnosticism, and a defense (or correction) of Origen against accusations of holding heretical views on the soul and the resurrection. While it is less clear how third- and early-fourth-century Origenists conceived of the incarnation, fragmentary evidence indicates that they most likely continued in the master's train of thought. The liturgical evidence of fourth-century Alexandria also confirms the continuance of Origenist theology in the region.

ARIUS, ALEXANDER, AND THE
COUNCIL OF NICAEA (325)

In the late 310s or 320s, a theological dispute arose within the Alexandrian church that soon grew to enormous proportions. The so-called Arian crisis activated preexisting tensions, the nature of which we do not fully understand, and quickly escalated into an international conflict that culminated in the Council of Nicaea of 325. The Arian problem eventually came to define future Alexandrian theology, chiefly through the apologetic efforts of Bishop Athanasius, and indeed "Arianism" remains the archetypal heresy of the church in the minds of many modern Christians to this day. Exactly how the controversy erupted is difficult to discern; despite a great of amount of scholarly attention on the matter in recent years, many questions remain.[2]

When the Arian crisis began, Bishop Alexander was already in a precarious situation, and relations between the Alexandrian church and certain other sees were tense. Alexander began his episcopate in a state of conflict and deep in the throes of controversy. His diocese was doubly schismatic, divided from the continuing Meletians and a group associated with Colluthus the presbyter. Meanwhile, Eusebius of Beirut (later of Nicomedia) showed signs of aggression against Alexander, possibly over Alexander's appointment as bishop. Writings of the later historians show traces of a possible rivalry between Arius and Alexander at the time of Alexander's election as bishop in 312, and it is possible that Eusebius of Beirut may have supported Arius as a candidate for bishop.[3] For multiple reasons, it seems, Alexander had cause to struggle to maintain his authority as bishop. It is impossible to confirm the situation, but such a picture best fits the fragmentary evidence that we have.

By the spring of 322 at the latest, we find Alexander in open conflict with Arius. Real theological differences existed between the two men, but it was not a cavernous divide; nor were their differences of a degree of seriousness that warranted international ecclesiastical or political intervention, had it not been for the larger networks and alliances that came into conflict as a result of this minor episode. Alexander's response to Arius has often been portrayed as a much needed regulation of the disastrously infectious teachings of a wayward presbyter, but on closer examination it is difficult to imagine that Alexander's episcopate, let alone the faith of the church as a whole, was so deeply threatened by Arius's theology alone, had the dispute not been taken as a proxy for larger local and international conflicts already at work.

Once the conflict had escalated somewhat, Alexander invited a group of Egyptian and Libyan bishops together in synod in order to condemn Arius. Around the same time Eusebius of Nicomedia inaugurated a letter campaign involving other Eastern bishops in support of Arius and against Alexander. As we shall see, the deeper theological fault lines of the church at this time, for which many a bishop and confessor had been willing to suffer for more than a century, lay elsewhere. The course of the ensuing controversy, and especially the career of Athanasius, in large part brought about the confusion, rather than the clarification, of received orthodox tradition, in which Origen had played a major role. It fell to the next generation of theologians to make some sense of the mess, which required drawing directly on the theological stream that Athanasius for many years condemned as Arian. The little evidence that we possess of Alexander's theology shows him already in the midst of debate with Arius.

Originally from Libya, Arius became a presbyter and the regular weekly pastor of a congregation in the Baucalis region of Alexandria, beginning either in the early years of Alexander's episcopate or just before, during that of Achillas (Eusebius, *H.E.* 1.15). At this time Alexandrian presbyters functioned as supervisory pastors of their congregations with a relative degree of independence, and the bishop served as a sort of first among equals. In this context, Arius appears to have been a popular pastor and preacher (Epiphanius, *Panar.* 69.3.1).[4] Of his original teaching and written works, we now possess only four examples. At least three of the four texts are products of the controversy after it was already under way, and each has been preserved only in the works of Arius's opponents. The dating of Arius's works and the overall course of the debates before Nicaea are notoriously difficult to reconstruct, and a scholarly consensus has yet to emerge.[5] Arius's four surviving works, in approximate chronological order, are:

1. The *Confession of Faith of Arius and His Associates to Alexander of Alexandria*, written probably from Palestine around 321 (Urk. 6)[6]
2. The *Letter of Arius to Eusebius of Nicomedia*, written in 321 or 322 (Urk. 1)
3. Two fragments of Arius's doctrinal poem the *Thalia*, which may also have been composed in Palestine in order to secure support from allies and potential supporters, probably around 323[7]
4. Arius and Euzoius's *Letter to Constantine*, written after the Council of Nicaea of 325 (Urk. 30)

It is challenging to give a comprehensive and reliable account of Arius's theological views. Nevertheless, in what remains we can discern a distinct pattern of thought that gives a fairly reliable sketch of at least some portion of his ideas. Thanks to the attacks on his theology by Alexander and Athanasius, Arius is best known for his views of the Son. As portrayed by the Alexandrian bishops, Arius is the archetypal heretic who denies the

Son's divinity, chiefly by denying the eternity of his existence with or in God the Father, asserting the Son's creation ex nihilo, and so claiming that the Son is a creature on the same level as all other creatures. This account of Arius's doctrine is by and large a caricature designed to forward the interests of his opponents. Among modern interpreters, Arius has also been linked with Origen and is sometimes seen as the real continuator of Origen's thought in early-fourth-century Alexandria. The determining factor in Arius's theology, however, is not the identity of the Son at all, but the nature of God the Father; nor, as we shall see, does he represent Origen's thought with even a modest degree of faithfulness.

Arius's main focus on God the Father is clear in each of the extant documents, including his public letters, in which we might expect him to accommodate himself to his opponents' concerns about the Son if his aim were to reach some compromise with their views. Arius begins his statement of faith to Bishop Alexander emphatically: "We recognize one God—alone unbegotten, alone eternal, alone without source [*anarchos*], alone true, alone possessing immortality, alone wise, alone good, alone sovereign—who is judge, controller, and administrator of all things, immutable and unchanging, righteous and good, God of the Law and the prophets and the New Covenant" (Urk. 6.2). Most of the lengthy first paragraph of his confession, in fact, concerns the unique transcendence of God (the Father). Arius then states his views about the Son in the same paragraph, as a kind of appendix, collapsing the first two articles of a typical confessional statement into one and implicitly suggesting that the Son is merely an extension of the Father's activity.[8]

Despite these structural indicators of a different theological project in his public letters, Arius presents himself as a traditional Alexandrian theologian, and even as a faithful disciple of Bishop Alexander (Urk. 6.3). Much of what he says about both the Father and the Son accords perfectly well with a moderate Origenist theology, and it is possible that his opening statement about God echoes certain elements of a traditional Alexandrian creed. As he goes on to explain in the *Confession of Faith to Alexander*, God the Father is unique within the Trinity as the source of the Son and is himself without source; God is ontologically, though not temporally, "prior to" (*pro*) the Son,[9] much as Origen held. Also in keeping with Origen's thought, Arius is concerned to avoid any suggestion that there are two sources or first principles in the Trinity. It is for this reason that he argues against Alexander's claim that the Son does not exist "eternally," "coeternally," or "co-unbegottenly" with the Father. As the last term suggests, Arius takes Alexander to be asserting not temporal coexistence, or the absence of temporal sequence, but the absence of *any* sense of sequentiality, including causality (Urk. 6.4; 1.2).[10] Arius does not, therefore, assert the temporal priority of God over the Son, as he is routinely accused of doing. Alexander's and Athanasius's further comparison of Arius's work with that of Eusebius of Caesarea and others on these grounds— arguing that they all held a similar view of the Son's divinity and position within the Trinity in virtue of their denial of his eternal generation—has created one of the most misleading impressions in all of Christian theological history. Where Alexander and Athanasius tried to suggest that much more was at stake in Arius's doctrine, amounting to the definition of the Son as a mutable creature, and inasmuch as modern scholars follow their lead—for example, by viewing Arius as crucially rejecting a middle Platonic ontology of mediation by making the Son a creature—they are all wrong.[11] To deny the Father's causality of the Son, in Arius's view, risks making the Son a second divine principle; such was the view of Origen as well. For Arius, God ontologically preexists the Son and is himself without source (προυπάρχει ἀνάρχως). Similarly, Arius echoes the traditional anti-Gnostic and anti-Marcionite confession of one God of both the Old and New Testaments, and he opposes the suggestion that there can be any material division of God's substance. He therefore rejects the idea that the Son comes "from" or "out of" (ἐκ) the Father, because of its suggestion of division, emanation, change, or materiality in the Father (Urk. 6.5). He also maintains that the Father, Son, and Holy Spirit are three hypostases (Urk. 6.4) and similarly opposes Sabellian modalism (Urk. 6.12). In his most public face, Arius clearly maintains the priority of God (the Father) within the Trinity, and he knows that, up to a certain point, Alexander must surely agree, just as Origen would have.

Much of what Arius says about the Son also sounds traditional in some respects. The Son is neither unbegotten nor formed out of any currently existing substratum (ὑποκείμενον), but he is made to subsist (or hypostasized) by the will and counsel of God "before all times and ages, [that is,] timelessly" (Urk. 6.4).[12] The Son received his life and existence from God, who is the source of all things, and like God the Son is immutable and unchanging (Urk. 6.2–4). He is the only-begotten and unchangeable God (Urk. 1.3–4) and the one through whom God made all things. Moreover, the Son's generation (whether it is called begetting or creation) is unlike that of all other beings: he is "a perfect creature [κτίσμα], yet not as one among the creatures," and "an offspring [γέννημα], yet not as one of the offspring" (Urk. 6). Arius also opposes the idea that the Son somehow preexists but is only later made into a Son, which represents either an opposition to a contemporary like Marcellus[13] or possibly an echo of Origen against a similar Word-only Christology. Again, Origen could easily have said the same. Overall, Arius's main emphasis in the public letters is on the distinction between the sourceless God and the begotten Son. In each of these respects, as far as they go, Arius not unreasonably claims to be a traditional Alexandrian theologian.[14]

But there is another side to the story. Aside from the caricatures of his enemies, the greatest difficulty in assessing Arius's actual theological position lies in the fact that he has adjusted the received Alexandrian tradition in a rather stark direction. Already in his public letters we see indications of this shift. Arius maintains the unique definition of God (the Father) to an extent that not even a moderate Origenist would recognize. For God's unique qualities include not only his self-subsistence (and/or self-existence) and his causality of the Son, but also the quality of uniqueness or singularity: God is supremely unique (μονώτατος), yet the Son does not share this quality. On this point Origen, Eusebius, and Alexander would all disagree.[15] In addition, the public letters contain what became perhaps Arius's most damning claim of all: that God brought the Son into existence "from nothing" (ἐξ οὐκ ὄντων). In Arius's mind, the phrase may simply reiterate that the Son derives only from the will of God and not from God's substance or from any previously existing substratum (Urk. 1.5), both of which, as we have seen, reflect traditional Alexandrian catechesis.[16] However, in his choice of terms, if nothing else, Arius clearly distinguishes himself from Origen's theology or that of Origen's Alexandrian followers (as far as we know).[17] For Origen plainly denies that the Son is created from nothing, a view that he *contrasts* with generation by the divine will; so the phrase cannot explain generation by will in any Origenist sense.

Yet it is in Arius's theological poem, the *Thalia*, that we see the extremity of his doctrine most clearly. Here we see that Arius regards God as being so far superior to the Son that he is inaccessible to him, which is a claim that not even a moderate Origenist would recognize. It is difficult to interpret the remains of Arius's *Thalia* because of their fragmentary nature, the fact that they appear in Athanasius's works, and the possibility that they were altered in order to make Arius appear even more heterodox than he was. Yet while any interpretation can be at most provisional, the *Thalia* does not contradict the position Arius evinces in his public letters even when we allow for such alterations. In addition to the more traditional differentiation of the Father from the Son based on the Father's unique role as sourceless cause (*Thal.Frag.* 5–6), the *Thalia* shows aspects of the Father-Son relationship that Arius conceals in the two open letters, by which God is much more radically separated from the Son. It is even possible that Athanasius selected these particular verses of the *Thalia* in order to show the side of the Father-Son relationship that Arius deliberately played down in his public letters. In much starker terms, Arius states in the *Thalia* that God is "essentially foreign to the Son" and that the Son is "unlike" the Father, does not participate in him, and has nothing that is proper (*idios*) to God (*Thal.Frag.* 12, 2/3, 7). Consequently, even their glories are unique and unmixable (*Thal.Frag.* 11), and they are not consubstantial (*Thal.Frag.* 7). The Father and Son are therefore not only unequal but truly incomparable to one another (*Thal.Frag.* 4). The Father exists independently of the Son: he is God apart from the Son's existence (*Thal.Frag.* 14–15), though, as already noted, this independence need not be taken in a temporal sense. On these points Arius is nowhere near Origen's thought. Most telling of all, however, is Arius's repeated claim, which would be hard to fabricate persuasively from whole cloth, that the Father is unknown, ineffable, and invisible to the Son (*Thal.Frag.* 9, 22). Despite the fact that Arius speaks once of the Son's ability to see God by the power of God's own vision (*Thal.Frag.* 10), there is very little sense here in which the preincarnate Son could be construed as the image of God, as Origen stressed.

At its most basic level, Arius's Christology is determined by an apophatic doctrine of God the Father, who appears throughout as a remote and solitary deity. The radical transcendence of God over the Son is so central that the Son cannot be said even to know God in his own being or activity. Arius's apophaticism is not obviously Platonic or Gnostic, although it is ultimately closer to Plato and Valentinus (despite verbal echoes of Scripture) than it is to the positive mysticism of light and the image Christology of Origen. In this respect, Arius's Christology is nearer to the doctrine of Philo and Clement than it is to Origen's, although he characterizes the Son's ignorance even more strongly than Clement did.[18] Given the determining role of his apophaticism, Arius could hardly be more unlike Origen in the ways that matter most; his fabled indebtedness to Origen and the received Alexandrian tradition of Origenist theology runs only skin deep. Despite appearances, Arius's theology is not an Origenist program to any significant degree, as many have claimed, beginning in the fourth century with the likes of Epiphanius. In fact, it was the theology of Origen himself that Alexander decisively leveled *against* Arius in the crisis of the 320s. Nevertheless, Arius's theology remains a puzzle. Why he chose to pursue this particular theological agenda no one has yet explained. At the very least we can say that, within the prevailing stream of Alexandrian Origenism, Arius's theology was retrograde.

Alexander's episcopate, as we have already noted, began in the midst of a double controversy and schism. In addition to these difficulties, by the early 320s Alexander was deeply embroiled in a dispute with his presbyter Arius. Our knowledge of Alexander's theology comes almost entirely from documents that stem from this tense debate. We possess only two works that purport to be by Alexander. Both were written near the spring of 323, after Alexander had secured Arius's condemnation by a synod of Egyptian and Libyan bishops (a condemnation, however, that was not unanimous), Eusebius of Nicomedia had launched a letter campaign on Arius's behalf, and Arius had submitted his *Confession of Faith* to Alexander. On account of their pronounced differences in style and content, only one of the two documents has a strong claim to having been written by Alexander himself, the so-called *He philarchos* (named after the opening words), which is a letter addressed to Bishop Alexander of Byzantium. The second document, a circular letter titled *Henos somatos*, was almost certainly written by Alexander's deacon and protégé Athanasius;[19] we will consider it below in our treatment of Athanasius. It is difficult to determine when each letter was distributed, or whether they were distributed together.[20] Alexander may have authorized Athanasius to write a doctrinal and ecclesiastical attack on Arius and his allies, and Alexander himself may have written *He philarchos* as a summary statement of his position, to be sent as a cover letter for Athanasius's text.

Alexander's *He philarchos* is especially important for our understanding of his theological position at this stage in the debate, because in it he gives a formal statement of faith (*Phil.* 46–54), and he appears to have asked other bishops to sign this statement, perhaps in a condensed form, at a later point (in the *Tome*). The most conspicuous characteristic of Alexander's statement of faith, by contrast with the one that Arius presented to Alexander, is its traditional form. It contains three clear articles (basic thematic units), in keeping with the form of the rules of faith found in the mainstream catholic tradition of the previous two centuries, including the rule that Origen gives in *First Principles*. Following the traditional form, Alexander professes his faith in God the Father, the Lord Jesus Christ, and the Holy Spirit in three distinct articles, adding further qualifications to each.

The statement as a whole is deeply Origenist and may be regarded, alongside Pamphilus's work, as another key witness to the state of moderate Origenist tradition in the early fourth century. Whereas Pamphilus has oriented his presentation to certain attacks on Origen, Alexander has pitched his version against Arius; yet, as we have noted, the two sets of opponents are in some ways remarkably similar, as are the Origenist positions that Pamphilus and Alexander each bring to bear on those opponents. Alexander confesses faith in one God the Father, who is unbegotten and without cause, unchanging, constant, and Lord of both covenants; one Lord Jesus Christ, the only-begotten Son of God, who is also unchangeable, equal to the Father except in the fact of his having been begotten, eternally generated without corporeality or division, not generated out of nothing, and the exact image of the Father; and one Holy Spirit of both the Old and New Testaments; together with belief in one catholic and apostolic church, the resurrection of the dead, and the incarnation of the Son, who remained divine when he became human. Moreover, Alexander prefixes each article with the numeral "one," to emphasize the singularity of each of the three against monarchian modalists and Gnostics (as even Arius had done). On each of these points, without exception, Alexander presents himself as a thoroughgoing Origenist.

There are additional Origenist elements as well. Alexander cites key Origenist proof texts from Scripture, and like Origen and Eusebius, he interprets Proverbs 8:22 as referring not to the incarnation, but to the preexistence of Wisdom (*Phil.* 7). Christ is the Son of God "by nature," and he is the natural Son of God "according to the nature of the *Father's* divinity" who shares or participates in the Father's divine nature, as opposed to all other children of God, who are so by adoption and who increase in virtue by the free gift of God. Moreover, the Father and Son are equal in divinity and unequal only in their causal relation. In sharp contrast with Arius's radical apophaticism, for Alexander the Father and Son are inseparable; the Son's generation is an ineffable mystery, transcending the comprehension of the evangelists and even the angels; and Son is like the Father in all things, as the image and mediator of the Father, the imprinted character of the prototype, and the light shining from the brightness of the Father (*Phil.*

7, 9–10). Alexander thus shares Origen's central belief that the Son, by virtue of the character of his preexistent divine nature, serves mainly to reveal the knowledge of the Father, again unlike Arius's apophaticism. Alexander's Origenism is so comfortably mainstream, furthermore, that he is happy to call the Father and Son two distinct hypostases, even though Arius did the same, and he can speak as well of their being "two natures" (*Phil.* 4, 9); he also echoes the conventional defense against holding two unbegotten first principles (*agenneta*) against Gnostics and modalists (*Phil.* 11), as Arius did as well. Particularly interesting, in light of later developments, is the fact that Alexander never speaks of the Son's being (*ousia*). In sum, Alexander brings to bear against Arius the traditional Alexandrian orthodoxy of Origen, and on the whole he has very little trouble doing so.

Alexander does make three and a half amendments to the traditional Origenist program. The first half an amendment is really just an amplification. Alexander borrows a phrase from Paul to emphasize the unique nature of Christ's sonship: he is the "proper Son" (*idios huios*, Rom 8:32) of the Father (*Phil.* 8), meaning the only son who is truly the Father's own in a way that reflects the Father's divine nature, much as only a human child is the proper child of a human parent, as no other species can be. This emphasis leads Alexander also to highlight the term "Father" a bit more than Origen does on balance, although this is a matter of only slight difference and not one of theological substance, particularly given the paucity of Alexander's literary remains.

In addition to this basic Origenist framework, then, Alexander makes three crucial adjustments, which pull him away from the Origenist mainstream represented by Pamphilus, Eusebius, and for the most part Alexander himself. Each of these points is a central feature of Athanasius's later work against the "Arians," and it is possible that on all three points the young Athanasius has already influenced his bishop. The glimpses that we have of their relationship at this stage makes such an influence possible; however, unless more works by Alexander are discovered, we will probably never know the truth of the matter.

First, Alexander abandons Origen's idea that the Son is generated by the will of the Father. He apparently makes this shift simply to counter Arius's use of the idea, since it was not strictly necessary in order to maintain the full divinity of the Son, his eternal generation from the Father, their shared divine nature, and the other traditional points that Arius denies, as the case of Pamphilus illustrates.[21] On this point both Arius and Alexander have departed from Origen: Arius by denying the Son's common divine nature with and participation in the Father, and Alexander by denying the Father's generation of the Son by the divine will; for Origen had held both. Alexander has also relaxed the traditional Alexandrian resistance to the depiction of the Son as coming "out of" (*ek*) the Father, brushing aside its corporeal, animal, and other divisive connotations.

Second, Alexander makes a decisive change in the language of eternity in reference to the Son's divine generation and existence. He argues that in order to confess the Son's equality with the Father and his identity as the Father's exact image, it is necessary to hold that the Son "always exists from the Father." At first glance, this appears to be the very idea of eternal generation that we found in Origen, Pamphilus, and Eusebius, but the term Alexander uses here is different. Rather than confess the Son's "eternal" generation, using the typical biblical and philosophical term *aidios*, as the others did, Alexander uses the Greek term that can also denote pure nonsequentiality, *aei*, or "always." And it is over this term in particular that he and Arius disagree. Here we see Alexander being pushed to the limits of his Origenist good sense (most likely by the forceful pleading of Athanasius), for he indicates that he is aware of the misleading nature of the term and that he prefers the traditional language of eternity. He further explains that human language can express eternity only through a lengthening of time (as *aidios* and *aionios* do), but it cannot directly express "the Divinity or the antiquity [*archaiotes*], as it were, of the only-begotten," noting that the Scriptures (and possibly other theologians) use this traditional language, not that of pure nonsequentiality (*aei*), to speak of the Son's relation with the Father. Consequently, he admits that "always" (*aei*) can suggest that the Son is unbegotten and that there are two principles of divinity (*Phil.* 48–52).

Third, Alexander maps the ontology of being versus nonbeing onto this newly formed distinction between time and absolute eternity/nonsequentiality. He argues that if the Son were created from nothing, as Arius claims, he must have been created in time, which Arius did not believe. Yet, while Alexander links nonexistence with the temporal sphere, he makes the point only briefly in *He philarchos*, and he does not exploit the opposite side of the pair. He does not discuss the Son's being (*ousia*); he does not argue that the Son is of the same being as the Father, or even like the Father in being; and he is otherwise unconcerned to mount a full ontology of the Trinity or of divine substance in general. His motives appear to be more polemical than systematically or constructively theological (*Phil.* 6). All three points, however, will figure centrally in the later debates waged by Athanasius.

At the same time that he argues positively for orthodox doctrine in these terms, Alexander also makes his case by depicting Arius's position in a rather distorting way. His portrayal of Arius, much like Athanasius's later, amounts to a caricature of Arius's actual views, and it is this caricature that has informed the Western imagination ever since. Alexander's caricature of Arius's theology is not merely of interest in Arius's own case, however, for the position described here became in many respects the arch-heretical position against which true orthodox theology was defined, in the minds of many, for centuries to come. Alexander accuses Arius of considering the Son to be a creature no different from any other human being who is mutable and capable of vice, except that God foresaw the Son's virtue in advance (*Phil.* 2–3). Similarly, he accuses Arius of holding that the Son was created in time: in the famous phrase, "there was a time when he was not" (*Phil.* 2). And he alleges that Arius bases these views on those passages of Scripture that speak of Jesus's human vulnerabilities and sufferings (*Phil.* 1, 9). Finally, Alexander likens Arius to Jews, Greeks, and the modalist Paul of Samosata, all of whom deny Christ (*Phil.* 2, 9). Each of these accusations is untrue and appears to be the result of polemically motivated smear tactics.[22]

At its heart, Alexander's response to Arius was the redeployment of mainstream Origenism against a very different sort of theologian—though altered in significant ways. Yet even with these alterations, Alexander remained quite close to Eusebius of Caesarea on most points, including the divinity of the Son. Nevertheless, the adjustments (whether they were originally Alexander's or Athanasius's) managed to create a wide chasm between the Alexandrian bishops and those like Eusebius who based themselves on the received catholic tradition as expressed by Origen, with great consequences for the future of patristic Christology. In this regard, Alexander was a moderate Origenist very much like Eusebius who allowed himself to be pushed to the extreme.

Under normal circumstances, Alexander's dispute with Arius would have remained a local matter between a bishop and one of his presbyters, but these were hardly normal circumstances. In ways that we can now discern only very dimly, the debate seems to have gathered to itself rivalries that transcended the politics of the Alexandrian church and even the theological matters at hand, forcing the lines of hitherto well-established

Origenist tradition to be redrawn in surprising and startlingly abrupt new ways. Moreover, the advent of a new Christian emperor brought with it new possibilities and expectations for international church relations and raised the stakes immensely as to who would represent and guide the new theological consensus.

In the span of a few years, the controversy escalated into an international conflict involving the bishops of practically every see of any size in the eastern Mediterranean—Byzantium, Nicomedia, Antioch, Beirut, Tyre, Caesarea, and Alexandria, among others—until it eventually resulted in the famous Council of Nicaea of 325. Like most church meetings before the fifth century, the Council of Nicaea is shrouded in a fog of historical uncertainty. We have precious little information about the events leading up to the council, the council itself, and how most bishops received its results immediately afterward. Our main contemporary source is Eusebius of Caesarea, whose *Life of Constantine* narrates some of the preceding events and reproduces some of the correspondence that followed the council. We also possess the letter that Eusebius wrote to his church in Caesarea shortly after the council, which gives a few hints of the doctrinal debates and provides the only copy of the council's famous creed from a contemporary witness. Together with Eusebius we have the remembrances of Athanasius, which he recorded at a much later date and which are more strongly polemical. Athanasius probably attended the council as Alexander's deacon; he may or may not have attended its formal sessions. Finally, there are the often conflicting reports of the fifth- and sixth-century ecclesiastical historians.

Emperor Constantine either initially summoned the council or arranged for a council previously planned for Ancyra to move to Nicaea, where he could keep a closer watch on its proceedings. When he took up the Eastern throne as sole ruler of the Roman empire and the first (or second) Christian emperor, Constantine found to his dismay that the church in the East was in the heat of bitter controversy, which it had been unable to resolve through conciliar proceedings since the previous emperor, Licinius, had banned such gatherings of church leaders. Although Christianity did not yet command anything near a numerical majority in the Roman empire, it was sizeable and influential enough to make sharp discord in major urban centers a threat to the orderly running of society. Constantine therefore expected that the council would resolve the matters that threatened the unity of the church and the peace and harmony of his new empire.[23] Accordingly, the council's main business appears to have been threefold: to set a common date for Easter throughout the empire, to heal the Meletian schism in Alexandria, and to resolve the doctrinal dispute over Arius. Problems in Alexandria thus commanded most of the council's attention.

Eusebius appropriately describes the gathering as the first "ecumenical council," since it was the first time that bishops of most provinces of the church had gathered in synod. The bishops who attended represented an area that runs from western North Africa to Syria, Palestine, and Egypt, while the bishop of Rome was represented by two emissaries. Yet, despite the modern connotations of the phrase, the council's purposes were imminently occasional and practical, and no one harbored the idea that the meeting would produce a binding universal doctrinal standard. As far as we can tell, most of the bishops who attended the meeting expected the problems it addressed to be resolved as soon as the council's business was concluded. The authoritative status of the Nicene Creed was not in the mind of the original participants but took decades and even centuries to construct. Up to now, no doctrinal controversy had so consumed the church at an international level, and those that did arise, bishops tended to handle at the local level or in regional synods,[24] such as the Egyptian-Libyan synod that Alexander convened to oppose Arius or the synods that Origen once attended as a theological consultant. However, given the steady growth of Christianity, it seems inevitable that a meeting of this scale would have occurred at some point, even apart from the sponsorship of a Christian emperor.

Most of the churches around the Mediterranean celebrated Easter on a date set by the Roman calendar: the Sunday that followed the new moon immediately after the spring equinox; however, many churches in Asia Minor celebrated Easter on the Sunday that most closely coincided with the Jewish Passover, around 14 Nisan (also known as the "Quartodeciman" calculation). For obvious reasons, Constantine desired a united celebration throughout his empire. He imposed the Roman date on the Western church through the Council of Arles in 314, and shortly after the agreement reached at Nicaea he made it legally binding throughout the empire (Eusebius, *V.Const.* 3.5, 17–19). The council similarly resolved the Meletian schism in the manner we would expect, favoring Alexander as the rightful bishop, while allowing prior ordinations by Meletius to be recognized as long as the clergy remained under Alexander's authority.[25] Aside from these matters, the greater weight of the council fell to adjudicating the doctrinal dispute associated with Arius.

The results of the council's doctrinal work are expressed in its creed and accompanying anathemas. The Creed of Nicaea later came to be of defining importance; at the time, however, it simply represented the doctrinal definition on which most of the bishops present could agree and which sufficed to oppose Arius in strong enough terms. These functions required that the creed be (1) traditional, (2) uncontroversial enough to compel broad assent, yet also (3) directed against Arius and those associated with him (such as Eusebius of Nicomedia) in certain obvious ways. The Nicene Creed is particularly noteworthy for its scriptural idiom, its simplicity, and its resemblance to a rule of faith or baptismal creed, with certain technical emendations. Interestingly, the creed is noticeably unlike the three most recently published statements of faith by Arius, Alexander, and the Council of Antioch in 324, although it contains a threefold structure like Alexander's. The initial source of the creed is difficult to determine and has been debated by scholars. The most likely candidate is the local creed of Caesarea, which Eusebius of Caesarea presented to the council at some point during its proceedings. In his letter to his church, Eusebius reports that he presented the creed of his own community and that it was accepted with the addition of *homoousios* as required by Constantine (*Ep.Caes.*). This seems the most plausible train of events, especially if we assume that Eusebius is interpreting the required emendations for his own apologetic purposes.[26] Eusebius describes the Caesarean creed as the simple and scriptural faith that he learned from previous bishops, confessed at his baptism, and has since taught others as a presbyter and bishop (*V.Const.* 2.69.1–2). It bears clear marks of an Origenist statement of faith. A threefold confession like Alexander's, it proclaims faith in "one" God the Father, "one" Lord Jesus Christ, and "one" Holy Spirit; the Son is described as God, light, and life who derives from the same things in the Father; and the creed calls the preincarnate Son "the first-born of all creation" (Col 1:15), a remnant of Origen's theology that will very soon become a flashpoint of controversy in the hands of Marcellus and Athanasius. (Interestingly, Christ is defined first as the Word of God.) Eusebius's further comment highlights the distinct existence or subsistence of the three persons: "each of these is and exists, the Father truly Father, the Son truly Son, and the Holy Spirit truly Holy Spirit," although it does not contain Origen's terminology of three hypostases (*Ep. Caes.*). In addition to wanting to influence the council's deliberations, Eusebius had the pressing motive of needing to clear himself of charges of heresy that had been levied the previous year at a council in Antioch.

Assuming that Eusebius's creed was the initial document used, the council adjusted the creed in several ways in order to achieve its ends. The final creed of Nicaea reads as follows:

> We believe in one God the Father Almighty,
>   maker of all things visible and invisible;
> And in one Lord Jesus Christ, the Son of God,
>   begotten from the Father as only-begotten, that is, from the being [*ousia*] of the Father,
>   God from God, Light from Light, true God from true God,
>   begotten, not made, of one being [*homoousios*] with the Father,
>   through whom all things came to exist, things in heaven and things on earth;
>   who for us humans and for our salvation came down and was incarnate and became human, suffered and rose again on the third day, ascended into the heavens, and is coming to judge the living and the dead;
> And in the Holy Spirit.[27]

Appended to the creed is a list of views about the Son that the council anathematizes: that "there was a time when he was not" or "he was not before being begotten," that he came into being "from nothing," that he is "from another *hypostasis* or *ousia*" besides the Father, and that he is alterable or changeable.

The creed presents the traditional threefold confession, and most of its phrases are also biblical and traditional; it resembles the creed of Eusebius to a fairly large extent, and to a lesser degree Alexander's as well. The particular adjustments and explanations that the council added are fairly conspicuous and give a clear indication of the force that it intended the creed to carry in the immediate polemical situation. They represent the theological program of the anti-Arian alliance. The creed was strictly a polemical document; it was not intended for use as a baptismal confession and was never used as such; nor did it enter into the church's liturgy.

Most obviously, the creed and its anathemas aimed to repudiate the doctrine of Arius, according to a caricature similar to the one we identified in Alexander's work: the Son was not generated in time, nor was he "made," and he cannot change—all three statements that Arius likely did not make.[28] Arius did argue that the Son was created out of nothing, but he probably did not intend the implications that the council saw in the statement, and in any case none of Arius's former associates sought to repeat or defend the claim. Rather, the council repudiated the version of Arius's theology that Alexander and Athanasius had constructed, and it was also their theological position that is most discernable in the specific phrases added to the creed.

Three key phrases stand out for comment. The first, and the least obvious from the perspective of later ages, is the statement that the Son is "true God from true God." At first glance, this would seem to be an innocuous repetition of the affirmation of the Son's full divinity that had already been made in the phrases "God of God and Light of Light," both found in the creed of Eusebius (with the addition of "Life of Life"). However, Origen had argued that "true God" properly refers to God the Father alone, much like the Greek term ὁ Θεός in John 1:1, for the simple reason that Jesus plainly calls the Father "the only true God" in John 17:3.[29] The phrase therefore appeared to be a logical term for expressing the Father's unique identity as unbegotten divinity. Despite the fact that the phrase refers to Jesus himself in 1 John 5:20, its application to the Son by Nicaea marks a departure from the received Origenist tradition.

The second and third additions are more significant and arresting. The further definition of the Son's generation as being "from/out of the being of the Father" (*ek tes ousias tou patros*) is not only the first nonscriptural phrase to appear in the creed, but it is a shocking addition given the theological disposition of most of the bishops in attendance (as far as we can tell). As we have seen in the previous two chapters, catholic tradition leading up to the 320s sought to resist any suggestion that the Son was an emanation from or division of the Father's essence, in opposition to monarchian modalists and to Gnostics. In order to assert his incorporeal and nondivisive generation, most writers denied that the Son was generated out of the Father's being. So Eusebius's creed reads that he is "from the Father" alone; nor does Alexander use *ousia* language in reference to the Son in *He philarchos*. Additionally, the phrase could be seen to run counter to Hebrews 1:3, which speaks of the Son as coming from the hypostasis of the Father, but not his *ousia*. "From the being of the Father" would certainly have appeared shocking to both Arius and Eusebius of Nicomedia, and it clearly did not excite Eusebius of Caesarea either; we do not know how it appeared to most of the other bishops at the council. The most plausible explanation for its inclusion is to point to the influence of the young Athanasius on his bishop, Alexander. Of all those in attendance, Athanasius was the only one that we know of whose doctrinal system could make sense of such an expression.

The term does appear in *Henos somatos*, which was circulated in Alexander's name but which, as most scholars now agree, was authored by Athanasius. Moreover, years later Athanasius showed a clear memory of the phrase's addition into the creed at the council, and he went on to defend it as such; whereas the other attendees discreetly let it drop in the years following the council. Marcellus, Ossius, and Protogenes, for example, were quite prepared to move beyond Nicaea at the Council of Serdica in 343.[30]

Even more famous, because of its inclusion in the later ecumenical creed of Constantinople of 381, is the addition that the Son is "consubstantial/of one being with the Father" (*homoousios to patri*). Earlier catholic tradition, particularly that identified with Origen's teaching, had associated the term *homoousios* with Gnostic emanationism, a sense that it carries in the work of Pamphilus and Eusebius of Caesarea as well. (The modalist or Sabellian associations of the term come later through the work of Basil of Ancyra and Basil of Caesarea.) Again, Arius and Eusebius of Nicomedia would clearly not accept the term; hence its usefulness to the council. From what we can piece together of the council's proceedings, it appears that Alexander or one of his associates must have initially proposed the term, on the prompting of Athanasius,[31] and then Emperor Constantine himself either sponsored or forced the term's final inclusion in the Nicene Creed—although he could hardly have been aware of the full implications of doing so, and it did not very well represent the generally Eusebian theological position he expressed in his later speeches and letters. In his letter to his church in Caesarea, Eusebius gives a crafty explanation of how he was able to subscribe to the creed with this phrase, reading it within the sense of his own theological tradition. Eustathius of Antioch later defends the term against Eusebius of Caesarea, even though it was not a natural expression of his own theological system either. Here again, only the theology of Athanasius truly makes sense of the term, and only the backing of Constantine could have achieved such unanimity on such a traditionally contested and highly charged phrase. Given the radical nature of these additions, it is interesting that the creed does not proclaim the equality of nature among the three persons, nor the eternity of the Son's generation in positive and clear terms, as even Origen had. In sum, we could describe the Nicene Creed as a heavily Athanasian and Antiochene confessional statement that was built on an originally Origenist-Eusebian model.

Needless to say, all three special additions to the creed would have suggested (or at least have risked) a Gnostic or modalistic theology to any traditional Eastern theologian,[32] which explains why Nicaea was strongly resisted in certain quarters for several years to come. At a council in Antioch in 341, the gathered bishops reintroduced some of the traditional markers of anti-Gnostic and antimonarchian theology that Nicaea had dropped, even as it reaffirmed the Council of Nicaea and the denunciation of Arius; and it was this tradition that eventually fed into the stream of Cappadocian theology later in the fourth century. But for those in 325 who sought the censure of Arius—and, perhaps more important, the favor of Constantine—the Creed of Nicaea was an acceptable palliative, if not an ideal statement of faith. The council concluded by excommunicating Arius and two associates and deposing Eusebius of Nicomedia, although Arius was later (temporarily) restored and Eusebius was restored and in 338 transferred to the see of Constantinople. Yet most of the alliance of bishops that Alexander had opposed were left firmly in place, and in this regard the council can be seen as a disappointment as much as a success from his point of view.

Despite the long-standing impression that the council at Nicaea was a great watershed in the development of Christian doctrine, the bishops assembled there did not return to their sees with the sense that a great work of positive doctrinal definition had just been accomplished; in fact, the council was largely ignored for many years. It was more than twenty years later, almost solely through the determination of Athanasius, that Nicaea came to be seen as a great conciliar standard. For the remainder of Constantine's reign, until 338, those who had resisted Alexander's prosecution of Arius were in the ascendancy. The two most prominent casualties of these years were Eustathius of Antioch and Marcellus of Ancyra, both of whom were deposed. Yet the church of Alexandria was hardly willing to accept the status quo, and Athanasius continued the prosecution that he had helped to begin, from the time of his accession to the episcopate in 328 until his death in 372.

ATHANASIUS I (PRE-339): *AGAINST THE PAGANS— ON THE INCARNATION*

Nearly two-thirds of the way through his long career as bishop of Alexandria, Athanasius issued what appears to be an eminently sensible recommendation: "Why don't we include all the fathers in the pious faith— those who deposed the Samosatene as well as those who proscribed the Arian heresy—instead of creating a divide between them and refusing to think rightly of them?" (*Syn.* 47). He could hardly have asked a more ironic question. Before the late 350s, when, under enormous pressure, he began to look for greater compromise, Athanasius could not have answered his own question, and even afterward he could do so only half-heartedly. Indeed, the case is much worse than this, for over the previous thirty years it had been Athanasius himself, more than any other church leader, who was responsible for the very polarization of theological parties that he laments in the twilight of his career, through a long and aggressive campaign to demonize all who did not strictly agree with his own position. Near the end of his career, Athanasius appears finally to have seen the futility of his warmongering and to have begun to seek some measure of peace with his former enemies; but before 359 or so, "those who opposed the Samosatene," that is, antimodalists of the Origenist-Eusebian tradition, were, in his own words, the spawn of the devil, anti-Christs, and worse than Jews. No other Christian bishop in the fourth century employed such extreme, ad hominem rhetoric with such fervor and consistency.[33]

Like Alexander, Athanasius began his ministry, even before becoming bishop, in a state of conflict. After his consecration, he was soon accused of tyranny by the Meletians. Yet before long he adopted the strategy of blaming most of his troubles on an Arian conspiracy directed by Eusebius of Nicomedia with the support of Eusebius of Caesarea; conversely, Eusebius of Caesarea can be seen pointing anonymously to Athanasius as the source of his own troubles late in his career (*V.Const.* 4.41–48). The growing monastic movement in rural Egypt likewise presented a destabilizing element for Athanasius, and he spent much energy extending his episcopal control to include the monastic communities. Athanasius is one of the most controversial figures in early Christian historiography and an icon of the Christian imagination. It would be hard to imagine a bishop or theologian more convinced of his rightness for such a long period of time, and who persevered in his own cause at such great labor and hardship. Athanasius was not well educated, nor was he very gifted theologically. But he had studied the Scriptures with zeal and possessed an unstoppable determination to impose his interpretation of them on others; he also had the temperament of a fighter, and he did not hesitate to bring into service an acid tongue and vitriolic rhetoric.[34] We will gain the clearest view of his Christology by examining his work in three distinct phases.

The first is defined by Athanasius's dual work *Against the Pagans–On the Incarnation*. In this well-known treatise, written sometime between his episcopal ordination and his first exile (328–335), Athanasius gives his first, and in some ways his most complete, extended theological exposition.[35] Contrary to a fairly common view, the work is not catechetical in nature, despite its apparent simplicity of style and self-presentation; it does not give a summary of the key points of the faith as Origen's *First Principles* had or as Gregory of Nyssa would provide later in his *Catechetical Oration*.[36] These basic principles, Athanasius says at the beginning and end of the work, can best be acquired from the teachings of Christ in Scripture, just as Origen had said at the beginning of *First Principles*; and he refers the reader to the "many treatises of our blessed teachers composed for this purpose," which is surely a reference to the work of Origen, among others such as Dionysius (*C.Gent.* 1). Athanasius thus declares his intent to be a traditional Alexandrian theologian. He is less concerned to make a conceptually airtight argument than he is to produce an occasional, albeit fairly synoptic, work. The dual work is in essence a traditional Christian apology.[37] The closest comparison for the genre of Athanasius's work is earlier Christian apologetic literature, and especially Eusebius's *Theophany*. Eusebius's third and final apology, together with his *Preparation for the Gospel*, is also the main direct influence on Athanasius's two treatises. The second major influence is Origen, and as we shall see, the arguments of *Against Celsus* lie behind several of Athanasius's key points. Although *On the Incarnation* contains several paragraphs directed against the Jews, this section is pro forma, which is why Athanasius makes less use of Eusebius's *Proof of the Gospel*, which defends the truthfulness of Christianity mainly against the Jews by appealing to Old Testament texts. Athanasius's argument is ostensively aimed at pagan objectors to Christianity. Yet despite this implied rhetorical audience, Athanasius is not really seeking to convert pagan readers, as Origen was; he clearly intends the work to be read by Christians. *Against the Pagans—On the Incarnation* therefore seems to function something like a doctoral dissertation, by which Athanasius means to establish himself as an apologetic and didactic, if not yet an experienced pastoral, theologian—and in so doing to make his mark on contemporary orthodoxy, given the recent debates.[38] Despite its early position in his career, the dual work remains Athanasius's most systematic work.

Athanasius takes the main subject and the twofold argument of his work directly from Eusebius's *Theophany*.[39] As we observed in the previous chapter, Eusebius's work is a proof or explanation of why Christ became human, lived, died, and rose again for humanity's salvation, aimed particularly at idolatrous pagan culture. Eusebius gives the following two explanations. Christ became human in order to manifest the invisible and incorporeal

Word of God to creatures who are fixated on sensory things and trapped in idolatry, by taking on a human body as a temple, instrument, mediator, and interpreter of God. Second, Christ died and rose from the dead (the chief reason for the incarnation) (1) in order to defeat death and mortality on the cross and to transform fallen human nature into immortal life by the divine power of the Word, and to complete the defeat of the devil and evil powers, as a public event that Christ's disciples proclaim. The resurrection then vindicates the power of God and proves that God indeed dwelt in the body of Jesus and that Jesus is superior to death. Christ also died and rose (2) as a redemptive sacrifice for the sins of the world. He took a human nature in order to be able to suffer for sin, and the Eucharist is thus a remembrance of Christ's self-offering. Athanasius's two proofs of the incarnation are the very same as those of Eusebius, and like Eusebius's work, Athanasius's contains a thoroughgoing Logos Christology.

We could best describe Athanasius's double work as an *apologia crucis*, or a defense of the cross,[40] against pagan objections. The chief objection to which Athanasius responds is that Christianity is worthless and irrational (*alogos*) and that the cross of Christ in particular is a disaster that deserves nothing but mockery and scorn. We have no knowledge of contemporary Alexandrian pagans who attacked Christianity in this way, although it is not impossible; in any event, Athanasius's primary opponents are cultured critics of Christianity such as Celsus and Porphyry, to whom Origen and Eusebius had responded. In reply to this objection, Athanasius's main argument is that faith in Christ, and especially his crucifixion, which is "the chief point of our faith" (*Inc.* 19), is both rational (*logikos*) and the salvation of all creation (*C.Gent.* 1; *Inc.* 41 and passim); the cross of Christ should therefore increase, rather than decrease, true faith and piety.[41]

The Proof of Divinity and the Logos of God

What is so distinctive about this work, indelibly marking Athanasius's Christology for the rest of his career, is the way in which he shows Christianity to be rational and good. The centerpoint of his argument is that "the one who ascended the cross is the Word of God and the Savior of the universe" (*C.Gent.* 1), as opposed to Christ's being understood in merely human terms. Very much like Origen, Athanasius wants to point his readers away from the humiliations—and even the humanity—of Christ, which are regarded as a kind of problem, and to draw their attention instead to Christ's divinity. To mock the cross on the grounds of Jesus's suffering and humiliations is thus a fault of aesthetic perception (ἀναισθησία) (*C.Gent.* 1.20), because one sees Christ in human terms rather than perceiving both his divinity on the cross and his power at work in the world today. Against pagan mockery, Athanasius contends, Christ provides an even greater witness of his divinity, by showing that what people think impossible is possible, what seems unsuitable is suitable, and what may appear merely human is really divine. And so Christ persuades "those who mock or do not believe to recognize his divinity and power" (*Inc.* 1). The substance of the Christian faith, and the burden of Athanasius's apology, is thus to "apply one's mind" to his divinity, which will show the properness and dignity of Christianity, much as Origen had sought to answer Celsus's objections.

One of the most consistent and far-reaching aspects of Athanasius's Christology is his emphasis on Christ's identity as the eternal Word of God. Unlike Origen and even Athanasius's predecessor, Alexander, Athanasius by and large treats the idea of God's Word and Wisdom as the most fundamental and proper designation of Christ's divine nature, rather than the title "Son" and the idea of sonship. In this regard, Athanasius mirrors Eusebius of Caesarea's apologetic works but not his *Ecclesiastical History* or his late works, which show a clearer Son Christology. For Athanasius, Christ is divine not so much as the only-begotten Son, but as the Word of God. In order to argue for the divinity of Christ, he mounts a thoroughgoing Logos Christology that dominates *Against the Pagans–On the Incarnation* and spans the entirety of his career. The idea of Christ as the divine Son of God, which anchored Origen's and Alexander's Christologies and was recently confessed at Nicaea—and which dominates the Christology of the New Testament—appears only infrequently and with surprisingly little effect in Athanasius's dual work.[42] In this respect Athanasius takes the reverse approach of Origen: he understands divine sonship through the major category of the Word rather than the other way around (for example, *Inc.* 19, 48). Thus he distances himself not only from the great Alexandrian master and his immediate predecessor, but also from Eusebius's early and late Christological works. Indeed, *Against the Pagans–On the Incarnation* is one of the high-water marks of Logos theology in all of Christian tradition.

Athanasius constructs an entire Christology and anthropology around the Logos idea. The Word is truly from or of the Father (*C.Gent.* 41, 44). It is the demiurge of creation and is present in all things as the principle of existence and the means of God's providence (*C.Gent.* 29, 42, 46). God created human beings through the Word and in the image of the Word

(*Logos*), as rational (*logikos*) creatures, and they in turn know God through rational contemplation of the same Word, beyond all sensible things and apart from any intercourse with the body (*C.Gent.* 2).[43] When human beings sinned and turned away from God toward death and corruption, the Word came to restore the fallen image of itself in humankind (*Inc.* 13–16). Even before Christ's coming, the Word gave knowledge of itself in many ways; it can be seen throughout the Old Testament, and its divinity is visible everywhere (*Inc.* 11; *C.Gent.* 45). The proper titles of Christ are therefore the Word and Wisdom of God, although in virtue of his condescension in the incarnation, he is also known as Door, Shepherd, Way, and so on (*C.Gent.* 47).

Three other things stand out about Athanasius's understanding of the Word in *Against the Pagans–On the Incarnation*. The first is that the Word is explicitly and quite centrally mediatorial, as the image of God, the instrument of creation (God the Father creates through the Word), and the necessary means or channel of the knowledge of the Father. In this regard Athanasius adopts the traditional Alexandrian theology that we have seen from Origen right through to Alexander. He does not thematically explain the idea of the Word as image and means of divine knowledge, as Origen did, but it is operative throughout the work and central to its argument (*C.Gent.* 46; *Inc.* 1, 3, 11, 41, 57). Moreover, Athanasius uses the Word's identity as image of God to explain his full divinity: he is the "exact image" of God (*Inc.* 41, 46), as Origen had argued in slightly different terms and Alexander had stated explicitly—and as Athanasius himself had proposed in *Henos somatos*. Second, Athanasius is absolutely clear about the structure of priority between the Father and the Word: the Father is the source of all things and all divine action, and the Word serves to carry out the Father's actions, both in creation and in redemption. Third, Athanasius gives only slight indications of the Word's distinct subsistence in the dual work. On the whole, the sense of the mind-reason metaphor mitigates against such an emphasis (by contrast with the Father-Son metaphor), as in Athanasius's emphasis that the Word is uniquely "in" the Father (*Inc.* 17). There are some indications that he envisions the Word as distinctly existing in the Origenist sense; for example, the Word acts as the interpreter and messenger of the Father—yet even here the comparison is to the function of reason communicating what is in a person's mind (*Inc.* 45). On each of these points the course of Athanasius's thought will be highly significant for the eventual construction of orthodox Christology.

In its immediate implied context, however, Athanasius's Logos doctrine serves to explain why Christianity is not "irrational" (*alogos*), for it is about Reason (*Logos*) through and through. Christianity is therefore not only rational, it is the *only* true expression of reason in human history. Yet it is also a Christological conception that has made a deep impression on Athanasius's mind, and it remained with him for the next forty-five years.

Salvation through the Incarnation

Within this Logos framework, Athanasius describes Christ's saving work in a powerful and memorable way in *On the Incarnation*. These rich sections of the work show how Athanasius understands the nature of the cosmos, human sin and brokenness, and Christ's identity and saving work, in what has since become a classic text, even though it exercised little influence in the fourth century. As already noted, Athanasius follows Eusebius's twofold understanding of salvation, presenting two rationales, or "two ways of philanthropy," for understanding Christ's saving work. Christ saves human beings by defeating death on the cross and renewing us, and by revealing the knowledge of God (*Inc.* 16).

The first rationale of the incarnation, which Athanasius calls "the primary cause of the Savior's becoming human" (*Inc.* 10), focuses on Christ's death on the cross. Accordingly, Athanasius explains the human predicament in terms of our need for the Word of God to conquer death and mortality. Originally, God made all things out of nothing through the Word. However, despite the fact that human beings were created by the Word, the rationale (*logos*) of our existence is oriented toward death and nothingness, and we are by nature mortal, since we were created out of nothing. In order to compensate for this weakness, God gave us the extra grace of creating us after his image, the Word, by endowing us with reason and making us rational (*logikos*) beings by the presence and philanthropy of the Word and our participation in it (*Inc.* 4–5, 11). We were therefore enabled to know God, to remain in paradise, and to look forward to heavenly immortality through our original rationality (*logos*). God then secured the grace of the Word by imposing on us a law and a particular location; if we turned away from God by disobeying his law, we would suffer the corruption and death that is natural to our created condition and die outside of paradise (*Inc.* 3). Through the gift of rationality, which is a participation in the divine Word, God intended and empowered us to live "as God," which is to live a virtuous life. However, we forsook the grace of being in the image of God, and so we "turned to what was natural for us," which is "corruption toward non-being," and consequently received the condemnation of death (*Inc.* 4, 7).

Our current condition of physical and moral decay is therefore the result of our forsaking the Word that was given to us. Over time our corruption became stronger, even against the threat of punishment provided in God's law, and we became "insatiable in sinning" (*Inc.* 5). Death prevailed, according to the provision of the law, and God's work of rational humanity was perishing. The situation thus posed a dilemma. On the one hand, it was obviously improper for creatures who had originally partaken of the Word to die and return to nonexistence; such a result would only show God's weakness and undermine his goodness. Yet on the other hand, it would not be reasonable (*eulogon*) for God not to fulfill the punishment of death that the law required (*Inc.* 6–7). Were God to demand only our repentance from sin, his honor and truthfulness would be violated; and even if God could justifiably forgive our sins, this would fail to solve the real problem, which is our decaying mortal condition. At the deepest level, we have by our own choice deprived ourselves of the grace of existing in the image of God, which is the Word; therefore, only the Word, who created us from nothing in the first place, can re-create us and bring us from corruption to incorruption (*Inc.* 7). For this reason, the incorruptible Word of God condescended to appear among us in a human body. In order to defeat the reign of death in our very nature, the Word "took to himself a body" like our own and made it to be a temple and an instrument of his saving work. Because the Word took on a human body, when Christ was crucified, all of humanity died in him, and God's law was fulfilled and finally abolished (see Rom 6:8), and his resurrection conferred the grace and promise of the resurrection on us all. Although the Word itself cannot die, being God, it took on a human body that could die, in order to fulfill the law and pay the debt we incurred by our sin (*Inc.* 20); and because the Word dwelled in the human body that was crucified, Christ's death is also the death of us all, as when a great king enters a city and honors the city by dwelling in one of its houses (*Inc.* 8–9). This act of salvation thus shows God's goodness, just as a good king would come to rescue a city that had been besieged by bandits, even if it was due to the neglect of its inhabitants, for his own honor and goodness matter more than the wrong of their negligence.

The second rationale of the incarnation concerns our inability to know God directly through the Word, as God originally intended. Here again, the purpose of the incarnation relates to our original created condition. Because we were created out of nothing and are fundamentally corporeal (no different from irrational animals), we are naturally unable to know God, who is self-existent (unbegotten) and incorporeal. In order that we would be able to know him, God gave us a share of the Word and created us according to his image and likeness. In this way, we received the grace to understand (*noein*) the image of God and consequently were able to gather a notion (*ennoia*) of God the Father, and by recognizing our maker were able to lead lives of blessedness. However, when we turned away from God, we lost the concept of the true God and fashioned for ourselves other gods instead, beings who are made of corporeal matter and who themselves do not exist and thus represent the realm of nonexistence (*Inc.* 11).

Whereas we were formerly able to know God directly through our rational participation in the Word, in our irrational, fallen condition we are able to know God only indirectly, through God's works in creation and through the law and the prophets (*Inc.* 12). Again, like a good king, God could not allow his creation to be subject to others (false gods), so he sent messages, his friends (the law and prophets), and when necessary eventually himself (*Inc.* 13). Here again, in order to restore the created image that has been marred, the original image is required, just as the original model is required to restore an image painted on wood that has been marred (*Inc.* 14).

Described in terms of knowledge, the nature of our sin and wickedness is that our eyes now gaze only downward, making idols of created things, and we are blind to God, our creator. The Word of God—the original image and the means of our knowledge of the Father—therefore took to himself a human body, made of earthly material, so that we could again know him through the works of the body (*Inc.* 14), like a good teacher who condescends to communicate by simpler means what his students are incapable of learning otherwise. Because we can see only in human terms, the Word appealed to our sense perception (*aisthesis*) by being born, living, dying, and rising from the dead as a human being (*Inc.* 15). Having caught our attention as a recognizable human being, the Word could then show us that he is not only human, but also the Word and Wisdom of the true God, since his works are divine works (*Inc.* 16). Yet, after laying out the two rationales of the incarnation, Athanasius notes that it is especially Christ's death that shows that he is the divine Son of God, and he makes clear that the second rationale depends on the first, Christ's defeat of death (*Inc.* 13, 19). In sum, God has achieved human salvation in two ways: by conquering death through Christ's death on the cross and restoring us to a life of incorruption by his resurrection, and by correcting our negligent earthly gaze through his teaching and works of power (*Inc.* 10).

The Word versus Its Flesh

At first glance, Athanasius appears to have made a strong move in the direction of asserting the unity of Christ, more so than Origen did. Most of his basic, nontechnical confessional statements are unitive: the Word became human in order to die for our sins, and he appeared in a human body to lead us to the knowledge of God. This unitive tendency is evident from the work's opening confessional statement, "the one who ascended the cross is the Word of God and the Savior of the universe" (*C.Gent.* 1), and it is evident in later passages as well, such as, "The Word of God, who is incorporeal by nature, was revealed in a body for us and suffered for our sake" (*Inc.* 38).[44]

Athanasius repeatedly speaks of "the Word, our Lord Jesus Christ" as a single figure,[45] and the Word is the chief acting subject in Christ throughout his earthly career: condescending to become manifest, submitting to our corruption, and ultimately conquering death by offering his own body on the cross (*Inc.* 8–10). Like Origen, Athanasius shows a clear impulse toward the unity of the incarnation to some extent, since it is the indwelling of the Word that makes Christ's death the death of all people, and the Word manages to reveal itself in an unprecedented way through the body it has taken on.

Yet for the most part Athanasius's argument presses in the other direction, toward a highly dualist conception of Christ, again like Origen. In his treatment of the two ways of salvation, he takes pains to distinguish between the human body of Christ and the Word who dwelled in it. Like Origen, he stresses the incorporeality of the Word and its inability to undergo human experiences and suffering. Because the Word itself cannot die, it took on a human body that could, and because the Word transcends bodily circumscription, it did not suffer at all when it was born or died (*Inc.* 17). Toward the end of the discussion of salvation, Athanasius makes the distinction even more explicit: when we say that the Word ate or drank or died, it was the body that did these things, not the Word; the Word was "with" the body that acted so but was not itself a human being. Such things, therefore, are *said* of the Word because the body belonged to the Word and it was a real human body (*Inc.* 18). The Word did not surrender himself to death, but only his temple and human instrument (*Inc.* 20). Hence, Athanasius upholds the strict distinction of the *communicatio idiomatum* as Origen defined it, and the cross-references indicated in unitive statements to not extend beyond the level of verbal association.[46]

Most importantly, Athanasius is keen to avoid the suggestion that the Word suffered in the crucifixion. Rather than show any signs of passivity or vulnerability, the Word instead purified and illuminated our dying human nature through Christ's death on the cross, remaining purely active (*Inc.* 17).[47] The Word does not die, but delivers his body to death on our behalf (*Inc.* 37). Athanasius's stress on the Word's pure activity is reinforced by his anthropology as well, since apart from the grace of the Word, human beings are by nature mortal, reflecting their origin from nothingness; and, epistemically speaking, the knowledge of God is unbodily (noetic) anyway. Athanasius preserves the distinction between the two also in terms of the Word's divine nature: he makes clear at the beginning of *On the Incarnation* that the incarnation is not a consequence of the Word's divine nature, but results from the mercy and goodness of the Father alone (*Inc.* 1).

Athanasius's dualistic Christology is central to the overall argument of *Against the Pagans–On the Incarnation*. Against imagined pagan detractors, Athanasius aims to show that the crucified Jesus is in fact the divine Creator-Word, *as opposed to* a pathetic and dying man.[48] Christ's sufferings are an obstacle to, rather than a vehicle for, perceiving his true, divine identity. Accordingly, Athanasius carefully maintains the distinction between the Word and his mortal human body, and he preserves the Word from any improper involvement in Christ's human suffering. From this perspective it is also significant that Christ's body "participated" in the Word,[49] which is the same sort of relationship that all human beings were originally created to have,[50] so that the indwelling of the Word in Christ is not structurally any different from its indwelling in Adam. Athanasius summarizes the argument in the conclusion of the work. The proof of the Christian faith is to see that the crucified Christ is not a suffering human being, but the divine Word of God. For Athanasius this means recognizing that Christ's works are "not human but of God," that the Word himself was not harmed in any way, because he is impassible and incorruptible, but instead cared for us by his impassibility. And it is in this sense that Athanasius imagines that the Word became human so that we might become divine, as he famously says near the end of the work, dying to defeat death and giving us an idea of the invisible Father. Athanasius's apology for the cross is therefore not so much a defense of the crucifixion as it is an explanation of the divine manifestation of the Word and a vindication of divine power *despite* Christ's death, rather than through it. So he can describe Christ's dying body, at the beginning of the double work, as a cloud that *hides* the sun (*C.Gent.* 1), rather than as an image that reveals it.

In the end, Athanasius's Christology is remarkably like that of Origen. He regards Jesus's human limitations and suffering as the defining problem of the incarnation, much as Origen had; he carefully defines the Word's impassibility; and against the *communicatio idiomatum* he repudiates the suggestion that the Word actually experienced human suffering. Yet the work shows the difference that Athanasius has no use for Jesus's human soul. In his mind, Christ is a combination of the Word with a human body, in which the Word operates as the sole intellectual principle of Christ's human existence. The consequences of this difference will become apparent below.

A Dualist Cosmology and Anthropology

In his understanding of Christ and his saving work, Athanasius adopts a view of the cosmos and the human person that is similarly dualist-tending. In his effort to express orthodox tradition, Athanasius takes his cue from Origen and the Eusebius of the apologies, each of whom, as we have seen, adheres to a strong distinction between the intelligible and sensible realms and the corporeal limits of human knowledge of the incorporeal God. However, Athanasius presses these distinctions much further than even Origen did, aligning the extremities of divine and human existence with dichotomies between incorporeal, intelligible, and rational (*logikos*) realities and corporeal, sensible, and irrational realities, and even between male and female (*C.Gent.* 10).[51] In our fallen condition, the physical world and the human senses are in themselves a distraction from the knowledge of God, so that God can reveal himself only through divine works or actions (*Inc.* 14, 18–19, 32). In this way God captures and reorients our perception away from sensory things and toward the incorporeal Word and

Father (*Inc.* 15, 43). Above all, Athanasius casts the universe into a radical division between being and nonbeing or nothingness; only God exists in himself and gives existence to creatures, while nonbeing means death and decay, in the case of humans who are created from nothing, and even outright evil, in the case of demons and idols (*C.Gent.* 9). Similarly, in our bodily existence human beings are oriented toward death from the beginning, as our natural and potential condition even apart from the fall, and our corruption resides in the human body (*Inc.* 44). Consequently, it is only through our rationality, which is the image of the Word, that we can avoid the corruption of nonexistence.

On an important related matter, Athanasius radically divides God's being or nature from his works in creation. Although God is known by his works,[52] as an artist can be known from the things he or she makes, Athanasius is insistent that we cannot see or know God in his nature, even through the works. To be sure, there is an inconsistency between Athanasius's argument that the Word reveals itself through its bodily acts and his denial of any knowledge of God's essence. There is a real tension between the unitive aspects of Athanasius's Christology and the metaphysical dualism that he constructs to sustain what is ultimately a dualist program.

As modern scholars have observed, Athanasius's version of Christian Platonism is not the result of a sophisticated, deep reading of classical sources. He is on the whole unfamiliar with classical Greek culture.[53] He seems to have cobbled together bits and pieces from what he found derivatively in earlier Christian sources such as Origen and Eusebius and from current philosophical textbooks, and his knowledge of ancient or Second Sophistic rhetoric is even less. The bluntness of his cosmological scheme, whereby everything imaginable is divided so starkly in this way, reflects the superficiality of his philosophical borrowings. We will comment below on the Christological liabilities of Athanasius's cosmological dualism.

Triumphalism and Super-Humanity

We see the effects of Athanasius's dualist position most graphically in the way he regards Christ's human nature and redeemed humanity in general. In various ways, Athanasius elevates Christ's humanity to a superhuman level. Even before the resurrection, Christ has attained a superhuman status. His humanity (human body) is *already* incorruptible, from the time of his conception on; he does not become humanly incorruptible only after the resurrection (*Inc.* 44). Even though he has taken on a body like ours, Christ is not naturally mortal as we are (*Inc.* 20), and his human body is immune from suffering, unless the Word chooses for him to undergo suffering and death, by surrendering his own body to death (*Inc.* 8, 21, 31). Not only does the Word remain uninvolved in the body's natural attributes and passions, but it divinizes them (*Inc.* 43), as Athanasius stresses in many passages throughout his career. Accordingly, he resists the plain sense of Hebrews 2:10, which states that Christ was "made perfect through suffering." Rather than take the verse to be referring to Christ's humanity, as most interpreters do, Athanasius wants to avoid the suggestion that Christ improved in any way as a human being, and so he applies it to the Creator-Word instead (*Inc.* 10).

Here, Christ is apparently meant to mirror the original condition of humanity. Because of their participation in the Word, the original humans would have remained invulnerable to natural corruption, had they only adhered to the grace of the Word (*Inc.* 5). Christ, then, is likewise humanly incorruptible, because of the indwelling of the Word in his human body. In the background of this scheme we may spy Paul's idea of Christ as the Second Adam (1 Cor 15:47) and possibly Irenaeus's use of the same idea. That idea in itself, in some version or other, is practically ubiquitous among patristic theologians; however, what is so significant about Athanasius's version is that he understands Christ to have become incorruptible at his birth, rather than at his resurrection, as Eusebius and most other theologians of the period held. Athanasius thus presents us with a fairly unique example of what many modern readers have assumed most of the Greek fathers held, namely, divinization and salvation (of a sort) at the point of incarnation rather than in the passion and resurrection. Likewise, Athanasius presents Christ's saving effects as being universal for humanity as a whole. Christ's human immunity from suffering and death, then, supplies a further proof that the cross is divine and not shameful. In the face of imagined objections, Athanasius imagines Jesus as a kind of superhero who isn't really vulnerable to the kind of death that the gospels report. In this regard he distinguishes the incarnation and the passion as two key points of Christ's transformation. At the point of incarnation, Christ has already defeated death in his own person, since death has no power over him as a human body, yet he conquers death and corruption for us all by voluntarily undergoing an actual death.

Just as Athanasius views Jesus's humanity as incorruptible and invulnerable even before his passion, so too he describes the Christian church in the early fourth century as if it had already achieved a state of total cultural victory. *Against the Pagans—On the Incarnation* is famous for its buoyant optimism and hyperbolic triumphalism. Athanasius asserts that the whole world is filled with the knowledge of Christ, who now shines as brightly as the sun. Christ's cross has been set up; the demons flee from its presence; and the opponents of Christianity, now shamed, are constantly converting to the truth. Here again, the church triumphant serves as proof against imagined pagan objections: at the denouement of the work, Christian faith and the sign of the cross crush death in numerous, public ways (*Inc.* 29–30, 55). Athanasius may be borrowing Origen's argument in *First Principles* book 4, which points to contemporary examples of conversion and martyrdom as proofs of the divinity of the Christian Scriptures. Yet he elevates the point to an almost hysterical key, making the work both psychologically and culturally pugnacious. A work such as this seems possible only in a political environment like that under the new emperor, Constantine, and from a theologian as young and idealistic as Athanasius. Here we are witnessing Athanasius's euphoria comparable to the enthusiasm that Eusebius showed in some of his late works on Constantine.

Conclusions

We see in Athanasius's first theological work an interesting and powerful vision of salvation in Christ, which is centered on and determined by the concept of the Logos of God. Athanasius's Logos Christology is basically dualist, as we have seen, with the result that he stresses the absolute impassibility of the Word. He is so focused on the Word's impassibility and divinizing power over the body that he tends to skip over the exigencies of Christ's human suffering—and by extension that of Christians as well—repelling them like armor rather than taking them into his own divine existence in order to heal them. Athanasius's Christ superhumanly "pushes through" death, as it were, shirking it off as a large animal might a fly. The key point here is that Christ is already immortal *as a human being* in Athanasius's scheme, and so his passion functions as if he were just humoring us to undergo a death that in reality has no power over him apart from his willing choice. In addition, we can see that Athanasius's Trinitarian doctrine is vulnerable to modalism and that it notably omits the language of hypostasis still current in other Origenist traditions. In his dualism and his protection of divine impassibility, Athanasius remains closely aligned with Origen, although he has jettisoned Origen's antimodalist and anti-Gnostic

Trinitarian plurality, which concentrates on Christ's identity as Son rather than Word. Athanasius has shifted Origen's ontology and cosmology from a largely epistemic qualification to one of moral ontological difference, and from a primarily volitional ontology to an essentialist one.[54]

The ultimate goal of the work is to show the rationality and seemliness of Christ's crucifixion, and by extension the present life of the church, as Athanasius understands them. His main argument, at multiple levels, is to point the reader away from Christ's humanity and suffering and toward the divinity and power of the Word in order "to see Christ's divinity." He aims to keep Christ's humanity, and that of his followers, respectably free from suffering, ignorance, and shame. Christ's lowliness and suffering are ultimately an embarrassment to the faith, and so for Athanasius the incarnation is both an ontological and a moral-cultural problem, even more than it was for Origen.

One of the unsolved mysteries of Athanasian studies is why he began as this sort of theologian. One explanation is clearly the Alexandrian tradition, from which he took the bare bones of his Christological scheme. Yet equally formative was Athanasius's stance in the Christological debate with Arius. By contrast with Alexander's *He philarchos*, Athanasius shows himself to be already more extreme and impetuous in his earliest engagement, in the *Henos somatos*. At some point—how early and by what possible sources, we do not know—Athanasius moved in his own particular, and somewhat unique, direction (as we saw in the language of Nicaea), which downplayed what is arguably the most central aspect of Origen's work, his antimodalism and image doctrine, while amplifying its least durable aspect, divine impassibility and the ontological problem of the incarnation. By contrast with Athanasius's excesses, Alexander and Eusebius remained closer to the heart of the master.

ATHANASIUS II (339–362): THE *ORATIONS AGAINST THE ARIANS* AND OTHER WORKS

The second major phase in Athanasius's theological career began around 340, during his second exile. While staying in Rome, he found important allies in the city's bishop, Julius, and in the exiled Bishop Marcellus of Ancyra. Marcellus provided not only the general support of an ally in the current conflict, but also the concrete aid of his work *Against Asterius*, which became Athanasius's main source for his own three *Orations against the Arians*. Athanasius may have first met Marcellus at Nicaea as a member of the pro-Alexander alliance, in which Marcellus was clearly involved by that time.[55] Interestingly, the fact that Marcellus did not discuss Arius's theology (as far as we know) could be seen as further evidence that the real theological conflict was about different matters than what Alexander and Athanasius made them out to be in the 320s.

Marcellus's main work is his now lost treatise *Against Asterius*. This treatise marks the second of three key stages of theological polemics against Arius and the "Arians," the first being Eustathius's lost *Against Arius*, from the 320s, and the third Athanasius's *Orations against the Arians* from around 340. We possess about one-sixth of the original from the quotations given in Eusebius's *Against Marcellus* and *Ecclesiastical Theology*. It has recently become clear to scholars that Marcellus's *Against Asterius* was the main source of Athanasius's anti-Arian argumentation and much of his exegesis in *Against the Arians*; Marcellus's work not only helped to give a new polemical form to Athanasius's initial Christology, which we saw in *Against the Pagans—On the Incarnation*, but it also provided several key ideas that helped to shift Athanasius's thinking in distinct ways.

It is not necessary to provide a comprehensive summary of Marcellus's life and work; our purpose here is merely to highlight aspects of his Christology so that we can trace their influence on Athanasius. Marcellus was a member of the ecclesiastical alliance that Alexander brought together in defense of his claims against Arius. The association of Marcellus and Alexander on the same side of the debate is surprising, for in most respects the two bishops were very different theologians. Above all, Marcellus virulently opposed Origen's teaching and his legacy as the Eusebians had claimed it by the 320s; whereas, as we have seen, Alexander was an Origenist through and through. In his opposition to Asterius, Paulinus of Tyre, and Eusebius of Caesarea, Marcellus identifies Origen as a key source of the errors in his opponents' positions (*Frag.* 19). In particular, he accuses Origen of teaching the Father's temporal preexistence of the Son, and thus of elevating his own opinions above the teaching of Scripture, which Marcellus believes teaches the Word's eternity (*Frag.* 20). The charge is false, of course; yet instead of vindicating Origen against Paulinus, Marcellus produces evidence that Origen did teach the eternity of the Father-Son relation, only to accuse him of contradicting himself (*Frag.* 21). In sum, Marcellus charges Origen with adhering to the doctrine of the philosophers, rather than to the Christian Scriptures (*Frag.* 22). The accusation that Origen erred because of his tutelage under Plato appears to be traditional by this point, and we have already examined the way in which Platonist cosmology made itself felt in Origen's Christology. However, in Marcellus's case the charge is doubly ironic, because he shows himself to be familiar with Plato as well, and it turns out to be Marcellus, rather than his Origenist opponents, who bases himself on pagan literary norms and a predetermined theological scheme, against the plain sense of Scripture.

The chief principle in Marcellus's Christology, as evident in his argument against Asterius, is the eternity of the Word of God and the priority of the idea of the Word above all other titles and descriptions of who Christ is, including "Jesus," "Christ," and "Son of God." In this respect he is similar to Athanasius (but not Alexander), although possibly for different reasons. Marcellus's work is not a mutation of Origenist tradition, but represents instead a very different approach, possibly influenced by Irenaeus. In one fell swoop, Marcellus mounts a comprehensive defense against every Christological point that his opponents make on the basis of terms such as Son, only-begotten, and image of God, by insisting that Christ can truly be understood only as the Word of God. In terms that echo Origen, Asterius had emphasized the uniqueness of the three persons of the Trinity in their interrelationships with one another: "the Father is truly Father and the Son is truly Son, and likewise regarding the Holy Spirit" (*Frag.* 60). Marcellus declares in reply, "No other name befits the eternity of the Word than this very one that . . . John spoke in the beginning of his gospel." Logos, or Word, is therefore the primary and original name of Christ; all others are "new and more recent" and the result of the Word's economy in the flesh (*Frag.* 3). For "before he came down and was born through the Virgin, he was only Word" (*Frag.* 5).

There are several relevant corollaries of Marcellus's Logos doctrine. The first is that his view of the Trinity is highly monistic. One of his chief concerns against Asterius and company is to defend the unity of God against any sense of plurality among the Father, Son, and Holy Spirit. For Marcellus, God is absolutely one and cannot be differentiated in his eternal existence in any way. The "Monad," as Marcellus regularly calls God, is one, as Jesus states in the First Commandment, quoting Deuteronomy: "The Lord our God, the Lord is one" (*Frag.* 91; Mark 12:29; Deut 6:4). One of the chief points that Scripture shows is "the Monad of the divinity" (*Frag.* 97) and the fact that there is only one figure or character (*prosopon*) speaking throughout (*Frag.* 92). In his eternal existence, God is therefore indivisible and not to be differentiated in any way, even on the basis of the terms Father, Son, and Holy Spirit (*Frag.* 85). The Word, then, is "one and the same" with God and does not possess its own distinct existence (*Frag.* 73). It is "within" God, as opposed to "outside" him (*Frag.* 76, 90). Because the Word is, as the metaphor suggests, internal to God, whose Word it is, and because it is counterintuitive to imagine God ever existing without reason, Marcellus concludes that Christ is both one with God the Father and unequivocally eternal.

From its eternal and absolute unity, the Monad broadens into a Triad in the divine economy, for the acts of creation, redemption, and final consummation (*Frag.* 48). For Marcellus, the Trinitarian plurality is only an economic plurality; it has no reality in God's eternal life apart from the economy. And so consequently the title "Son" is only an economic title, and the Trinitarian confession in Matthew 28:19 referring to baptism "in the name of the Father, Son, and Holy Spirit" is the confession only of the economy, not of God's permanent identity as Trinity. There is no sense of an eternal generation of the Son from the Father, or of Christ's being the eternal image of God; these notions are strictly limited to the economy. The "new mystery" of the Christian faith, then, is not the eternal Trinity, as Eusebius argued (following Origen), but the economy and the incarnation (*Frag.* 31, 38). Despite his claims to oppose Sabellius (*Frag.* 69), many of Marcellus's contemporaries and later readers recognized that in fact he represented the sort of modalism that had been condemned in Sabellius and opposed even earlier by Origen.

An important aspect of Marcellus's Logos doctrine is his understanding of the relationship between the Word and the man Jesus. At the same time that he envisions the Word within the pure singularity of the divinity, Marcellus regards the human Jesus as existing independently of the Word. First of all, Jesus possesses a full human nature, including a human mind and will; he is not merely the Word acting through a human body, as in Athanasius. Moreover, Marcellus imagines Jesus's existence as being so distinct from the Word that Jesus's will can even disagree with the Word's divine will, so that there is a division between the Father and the Son (which are, again, economic titles). When Jesus prays to the Father in the Garden of Gethsemane, asking that the cup of his impending suffering might pass (Matt 26:39), this shows a real disagreement between himself as a human being and God's divine will, a disagreement that is reinforced by Jesus's final statement of acquiescence, "Yet not as I will, but as you will"

(*Frag.* 74–75). The Christology of Marcellus is therefore even more strongly dualist than that of Origen, who at least argued that the independently existing man Jesus did the will of the Father in all things.

Marcellus's Trinitarian monism and Christological dualism are supported by a particular hermeneutical procedure. In a sweeping way, Marcellus interprets a vast number of biblical statements about Christ as referring to the economy as opposed to the eternal life of the Trinity. This includes all references to Christ as Son, image, only-begotten, firstborn of all creation and references to Christ in the Old Testament (*Frag.* 13, 26, and 52). Under this rubric, Marcellus counters the Eusebian interpretation of Proverbs 8:22, which derived from Origen and with which Alexander agreed. Marcellus argues that Wisdom's statement that God "created me as the beginning of his ways" does not refer to the eternal existence of the Word, but to the economy of Jesus's human life. Here, Wisdom is proleptically referring to her future incarnation, her "creation," as a human being. Marcellus spends page after page making his case that Proverbs 8 as a whole refers to the incarnation. In order to do so, he gives an allegorical interpretation of many details, such as the terms "work," "foundation," "waters," "earth," and so on, arguing that each one refers to something in the human economy of Christ or the church (*Frag.* 23)—all the while claiming that this is the obvious, literal meaning of the text. It does not take a very sophisticated reader to see that Marcellus is stretching the point. There is little if any indication in Proverbs 8 to suggest that these features refer to Jesus and his disciples; the plain sense of the narrative refers more naturally to the preincarnate life of Wisdom, a meaning that Marcellus acknowledges in other passages (*Frag.* 88, 110). When we take into account the fact that Marcellus prefaces his exegesis of this chapter with an extended discussion of the enigmatic sense of proverbs in general, based on examples from pagan literature, then his claims to be articulating the obvious sense of Scripture, together with his accusation that Origen misread the Bible because of his use of pagan philosophy, appear more than a little far-fetched. Yet on the exegesis of this very passage Marcellus would prove extremely influential on the future work of Athanasius and others.

The most famous aspect of Marcellus's Logos doctrine is his view that Christ will eventually cease to exist as a human being. The kingdom of Christ began in time, and it will also come to an end in time, after the last judgment (*Frag.* 100–1, 104), for in the ages to come the flesh that the Word assumed in the incarnation will have served its purpose and no longer be of any benefit. This is how Marcellus interprets Paul's statement that Christ will eventually subject all things, including himself, to God the Father, and "God will be all in all" (1 Cor 15:28), as well as Jesus's own statement that "the flesh is of no avail," but only the spirit gives life (John 6:61–63; *Frag.* 105). This view also corresponds with Marcellus's sense of Christ's saving work: that just as a human being (Adam) was originally deceived by the devil, lost his earthly kingship, and incurred the punishment of God, so Christ as a human being defeats the devil through the power of the Word, recovers the lost kingship (*Frag.* 99, 101, 106), and undoes the punishment that stands against errant humanity, as only the divine Word can do (*Frag.* 124).

In time Marcellus was best remembered for denying that the human Christ continues to exist at the right hand of God, a limitation that eventually led his opponents to specify in the creed of Constantinople of 381 that Christ's "kingdom will have no end." But Marcellus's understanding of the temporal limits of the incarnation versus the eternity of the Word also holds further implications in his Christology as a whole. Above all, it shows the extent to which he maintains a barrier between the divine economy and the eternal life of the Trinity. When the fleshly kingdom of Christ ceases to exist, Marcellus says, the Word will no longer be "separated from the Father by [his] activity because of the flesh" (*Frag.* 104). The Word's incarnation in Jesus Christ, in other words, represents a kind of division or separation from its eternal life in the Father, from which Christ's human disagreement with the will of God is yet a further step of removal. Marcellus not only maintains a consistently dualistic Christology and monistic Trinitarian doctrine, which proved to be structurally indistinguishable from monarchian modalism, but he verges on mythologizing the incarnation as an earthly episode in the life of the Word, in a way that is deeply antithetical to the Origenist tradition. Through his interaction with Athanasius in Rome, however, several of Marcellus's ideas came to influence the later course of fourth-century theology well beyond his own sphere.

In the late 330s Athanasius made the second major shift of his career, the first being his entry into the Arian conflict with Alexander. Marcellus's *Against Asterius* provided the crucial impetus for a new plan of attack, by which Athanasius could advance his theological and ecclesiastical interests. He set himself squarely against a group that he identified as "Arians," whose core teachings he now found in the works of Asterius, together with the original caricature of Arius's doctrine. In this general approach, and in much of his specific argumentation, Athanasius directly followed Marcellus, even as he modified Marcellus's thought in some ways and integrated it into his own systematic concerns. An additional new source of Athanasius's work at this point appears to be Eusebius of Caesarea's *Ecclesiastical Theology*. Athanasius echoes and occasionally corrects several of Eusebius's concerns, and it is likely that he modeled his own work in three books on the same structure he found in Eusebius.

In his *Orations against the Arians* Athanasius attempts to reconstruct and reassert his theological authority as the exiled bishop of Alexandria, in the face of continuing conflict and direct assaults on his office. To this end, he presents himself as a catholic theologian who stands in opposition to the traditional heresies defined by the received Alexandrian tradition, and who therefore can best bring that tradition to bear in the current situation. He does this by referring to his own "succession of teachers" in Alexandria (*C.Ar.* 1.3) and by declaring early on his opposition to the traditionally defined heretics, from Marcion to the Gnostics and including the Novatians in Rome (where he is currently being sheltered) and the more recent Meletians in Alexandria, both of whom were opposed by prior bishops of Alexandria (the Novatians by Dionysius, the Meletians by Alexander) and were identified as heretics in the canons of Nicaea.[56] To this list he then adds Arius. Yet in his use of the antiheretical tradition, Athanasius heightens the stakes: the heretics that concern him are in fact no longer Christians at all, but are merely known by the names of their founders: the Marcionites, Valentinians, Meletians, and so on. So too, those who supported Arius in opposition to Alexander have "left the Savior's name" altogether and are no longer Christians; instead, they are now merely "Arians" (*C.Ar.* 1.3, 10). Among all the heretics, Athanasius says, the Arians stand out, because they have denied the divinity and the oneness of the Word (*C.Ar.* 2.41).[57] In order to paint Arius as truly heretical, Athanasius must also declare that Arius's own denunciation of earlier heresies was merely a pretense used to insinuate his false teaching into the stream of catholic tradition (*C.Ar.* 1.8). In this way Athanasius claims for himself the authority of the catholic tradition, despite his exile, and he casts his opponents out of that tradition by labeling them Arians.

The rhetorical strategy of *Against the Arians* has influenced later readings of fourth-century theology even more than its substantive argumentation. Building on the *Henos somatos*, Athanasius takes on the Arians with an acerbity that is pungent even by ancient standards. Not only does he accuse them of denying the Son and thus violating the basic faith of the church

(*C.Ar.* 1.4; 2.34), but he blasts them with anger and bitterness that have unfortunately colored his theological legacy for centuries. Athanasius finds the Arians so offensive that he repeatedly calls them madmen, the offspring of Satan, stupid as women, worse than Jews, and deserving of the hatred of any sensible person.[58] The work is peppered throughout with inflammatory and vitriolic language of a degree that one rarely finds in other polemical writings of the period, on any side of the debates. The extremity and violence of Athanasius's rhetoric is another sign of his lack of classical education, which would have taught him a more controlled, engaging, and playful use of invective speech. In terms of substance, most of the work is devoted to countering Arian biblical interpretation, going over the same theological ground dozens of times. Athanasius aims to persuade his readers by a combination of sheer volume and the emotional force of his case, both of which make the work extremely tedious to read. Unfortunately, Athanasius's influence has colored much other patristic literature, especially examples of theological polemic, in the minds of modern interpreters, making it seem more repulsive than it in fact is. *Against the Arians* is an embattled work in more ways than one.

Nonetheless, the *Orations against the Arians* are justly regarded as a major dogmatic work. Here Athanasius reiterates the basic Christological scheme of *Against the Pagans–On the Incarnation* and makes several key shifts in response to the new polemical situation and the influence he derived from Marcellus and Eusebius. The doctrine he presents remains largely unchanged over the next three decades of Athanasius's career. His basic position in the orations remains Logos Christology, although he modifies it in some important ways.

The Image of God

One key difference from his earlier work is that Athanasius further develops the image doctrine that he largely assumed in *Against the Pagans–On the Incarnation*, which focuses on the human image in need of redemption rather than on the divine image. The work of Eusebius may have persuaded Athanasius that he needed to engage directly the Origenist image doctrine that played an important role in his opponents' Christology. Whether he also made a further study of Origen at this time is unclear. Either way, given the centrality of the idea in the work of Origen, Alexander, and Eusebius, it would certainly bolster Athanasius's case as a catholic theologian to explain in what sense Christ is the image of God, both in order to counter his opponents' views and to give credence to his own.

Athanasius affirms that Christ is indeed the image of God apart from the incarnation, as Origen and Eusebius taught and against the denials of Marcellus. He makes the point using a variety of terms: in his eternal existence as the Word of God, Christ is "the image and form of the Divinity"; the character, the "form and appearance," and even "the exact image" of God the Father.[59] In so doing, he stipulates that the Word uniquely communicates and reveals the divinity of the Father to creatures. He likewise affirms that the divinity that the Word conveys as image is the divinity of the Father in a primary sense. The Word is the image, Word, Wisdom, and offspring *of* the Father, the brightness of the Father's divine light, and so on.[60] Thus Athanasius consistently preserves the notion that the Father is the source and principle of the Word, so central to Origenist tradition (*C.Ar.* 1.9, 14–15, 19–20 and passim), and it is for this reason that the Son does the works of the Father (*C.Ar.* 1.61; 2.29; 3.6, 12). What's more, he makes the interesting supposition that the Word is the image of God to God the Father himself: that the Father sees himself in his image and takes delight in what he sees (see Prov 8:30; *C.Ar.* 1.20; 2.82).

Yet, although Athanasius's language reaffirms this basic principle of Origenist theology, his real concern is not with the Word's communicative nature or role within the Trinity, as Eusebius was, but only with how that role bears on the question of the Word's divinity. His many references to the Word's identity as image serve to argue that *if* it is the image of God, then it must be fully divine, against what he takes to be Arian denials of the Word's divinity on the basis of its mediatorial status. In one passage, for example, he argues that just as the image of the emperor shows the form and appearance of the emperor, and anyone who worships the emperor's image in fact worships the emperor himself, so too the image of God shows the form of God and leads only to the worship of God (*C.Ar.* 3.5). Once the Word's divinity has been established, it is as if its identity as image is forgotten.

In fact, the most striking thing about Athanasius's image doctrine, when we read the *Orations against the Arians* against their traditional background, concerns his treatment of the language of mediation. Even though he affirms that the Father is the source of the Word and that the Word is the eternal image and brightness of the Father through whom the Father is known, Athanasius simultaneously denies that the Word is in any sense a "mediator" of the Divinity to creatures, except in its incarnate form

(*C.Ar.* 1.59; 2.31), as Marcellus held. Athanasius argues at length against the Arians and Eusebians that God does not require a mediator for his work of creation and redemption. His favorite tactic is a reductio ad absurdum: if God requires a mediator, then wouldn't the mediator require yet another mediator, and so on ad infinitum (*C.Ar.* 2.26)? To suggest that God needs a mediator, moreover, implies that God is weak and incapable of action; on the contrary, God's will is sufficient in itself to achieve its desired effects, period (*C.Ar.* 2.29). Notably, Athanasius makes this argument most clearly in a passage in which he also recognizes that all things come to be through the Son or Word of God, that the Word remains the radiance of God's light and the expression of his substance, and that the works of the Son reveal the divinity of the Father (*C.Ar.* 2.25–26, 30, 32–33, 80). At the same time that Athanasius accepts that the Word is image, structurally speaking, he paradoxically *denies* that it serves as a mediator of divinity in any sense. Instead, the Word's identity as image merely proves that it is fully divine. Here lies a point of deep tension in Athanasius's doctrine, which will send repercussions through several centuries of theological reflection and conciliar decrees. The force of his argumentation for the Word's divinity leads Athanasius to ignore the other side of catholic theology. Athanasius has either missed or consciously avoided the idea of the Son's mediating, full divinity, which Origen identified and Alexander plainly accepted, and his primary reason for doing so seems to be a defensive and desperate reaction against what he experiences as a growing Eusebian conspiracy. In his attempt to argue for the Word's divinity without any sense of mediation, Athanasius's position is ultimately inconsistent. He does not care to acknowledge that the same question could be put to his own Trinitarian scheme: why does God need an image or Word at all in order to convey his divinity to creatures? And why does the existence of the Word not also show God the Father to be weak? These are inconsistencies that Athanasius studiously avoids.

Athanasius defines how the Word is fully divine and the "exact image" of the Father by adding several key qualifiers. Both Alexander and Eusebius had already affirmed that the Son is "like" the Father, as had the Eusebian tradition after Nicaea. In *Henos somatos* Athanasius introduced the qualification (negatively, by way of listing what Arians and Eusebians deny) that the Word is "like [the Father] according to *being*" (*homoios kat' ousian*; Urk. 4b.2), whereas Alexander had avoided speaking of the Father-Son relationship in terms of being. In the tradition of Origen, the more common way of saying that the Father and Son are each fully divine, and that the Son fully possesses the Father's divinity (the one and only Divinity), is to use the language of divinity or to say that they share a common divine nature. This terminology has the advantage not only of biblical precedent (Rom 1:20; Col 2:9), but also of avoiding the implicit denial of the Father's and the Son's distinct modes of existence, which are seen as fundamental to any assertion of the Son's divinity—he can't be divine if he doesn't exist at all but is merely an extension or attribute of the Father. In the 320s, at least in Alexandria and Caesarea, the term *ousia* retains this sense of the particular manner of existing, or a thing's own proper existence, much as it had for Origen. This is the only sense in which Alexander, for example, uses the language of being in his confession of faith (here in its verbal form): the Son is "begotten from *the one who is* Father" (*ek tou ontos Patros*) (*Phil.* 12). Alexander calls the Son "God" (*theos*), the exact image of the Father, like the Father in every way except in being unbegotten, and the Son by nature; but to call the Son like the Father in *ousia* would have meant that he was no longer Son but Father. As already noted, this was probably the view held by many other bishops at Nicaea.

The traditional sense of *ousia* remains in Athanasius's *Against the Arians* as well (*C.Ar.* 1.29, 58; 3.6). Yet, for polemical reasons, if nothing else, he decides to press the matter further and insists that in order for the Word to be the exact and true image of the Father, it must be like the Father in his being, as well as in every other way. This is a complicated shift to interpret for several reasons. On the one hand, Athanasius's Logos Christology left him vulnerable to modalizing tendencies since *Henos somatos* and *Against the Pagans–On the Incarnation*. By 340, his continuing struggle against the Arians made him even less inclined to affirm the distinct subsistences of the Father, Son, and Holy Spirit in the traditional terms of hypostasis, which the Eusebians were championing, let alone to countenance any sense in which they are three "existences" (*ousiai*) in the Origenist or Eusebian sense. Third, Athanasius's collaboration with Marcellus of Ancyra encouraged him to strengthen his position in this direction, the effects of which we will discuss below. *Against the Arians* contains only a few explicit antimodalist statements; otherwise, Athanasius is shockingly silent on this key point of traditional catholic theology.

It is evident, on one level, that Athanasius wants to preserve the traditional confession that the Son is fully divine because he shares and possesses the Father's divinity (*C.Ar.* 1.45; 2.18, 73; 3.5). This idea represents the basic structure of the Trinity as determined by the Father's role as source of the

Word and the Spirit (*C.Ar.* 2.21; 3.1, 3, 6). And he continues to echo the Origenist phrases that the Son is God "by nature" (*C.Ar.* 1.9, 15; 2.9, 14). Yet, on another level, Athanasius has crafted a new metaphysical system, building on his work in *Against the Pagans–On the Incarnation.*[61] Using several technical terms, he sharply distinguishes God from all else in a sort of mutually exclusive way. In order for the Son to be the "proper" (*idios*) and true Son of God the Father, he must be seen as coming from the Father rather than from nothing.[62] Similarly, Athanasius uses spatial language to describe the Son as "within" the Father, whereas everything else is "outside" him— terms that could easily play into a modalist view. But above all, Athanasius concentrates in a new way on the language of being (*ousia*). As the proper Son of the Father, Christ must, Athanasius argues, be seen as existing from the Father's being or essence, and so "like in essence" (ὅμοιος κατ' οὐσίαν) to the Father (C.Ar. 1.20–21; 3.26) and "proper to the essence" (ἴδιος τῆς οὐσίας) of the Father (*C.Ar.* 1.26; 3.67) by contrast with originate things (τὰ γενητα), which are not like the Father's essence; for what is from nothing cannot have any likeness with what brought it out of nothing (*C.Ar.* 1.21). Athanasius explains further that the Word represents the perfection and fullness of the Father's essence, in the sense that a light always has its radiance and a subsistence (*hypostasis*) always has its expression or character or image (see Heb 1:3), or the Father has his truth (John 14:6): none of these things can exist without the second term (*C.Ar.* 1.20).

The Son's title of image, then, is not merely a name, but a real "indication of a similar essence" (ὁμοίας οὐσίας γνώρισμα), which is also the sense of the phrase "like in all things"—a phrase that the Arians cleverly deny, by saying that the Son must also be a father of other sons; whereas in the Divinity the Father is truly father and the Son truly son.[63] These expressions of the Father's and the Son's essence serve to indicate that the Son is from the Father, like a human child from its parent, rather than from without (*C.Ar.* 1.27). The Nicene term *homoousios* appears only once in *Against the Arians*, and Athanasius takes it to mean the same thing: the proper offspring of the Father's being (ἴδιον τῆς τοῦ πατρός οὐσίας γέννημα), a phrase similar to but not quite the same as Nicaea's "from the being of the Father" (*C.Ar.* 1.9).[64] Athanasius therefore leaves ambiguous whether the Father and Son have the *same* being, which would truly be modalist or Gnostic. His use of *ousia* in this way was quite novel, particularly against the backdrop of early-fourth-century Origenist tradition. Yet its novelty alone is not nearly as significant as the fact that Athanasius is beginning to argue that this is the *only* way to express Christ's true sonship and shared divine nature with the Father. This move would prove to be a major shift in Christian theology, for later generations would take from it a kind of foolproof metaphysic by which, they believe, they could penetrate the mystery of the faith, regardless of the artificially constructed nature of the terms.[65]

Athanasius makes an additional contrast that further marks his departure from Origen. He not only defines the Son's similarity with the Father's being and his generation from the Father by contrast with generation from nothing, but he also contrasts the Son's generation from the Father's being with generation by the *will* of the Father. This is another metaphysical construction that practically reverses the received tradition. Previously, the idea of the Son's eternal, divine generation by the will of the Father as opposed to his *ousia* served to assert that the Son comes from the Father alone (not ex nihilo), that the Father's being is in no way divided or materially conceived, that the Son fully shares the divine nature and the divinity of the Father, and that the Son can be considered as himself a being that can be compared to the Father—nearly everything that Athanasius argues for, in other words. Yet, in the new polemical situation, Athanasius has inexplicably reversed the conventional terms. In doing so, he also introduces the troublesome notions that God's will could somehow be distinct from his being (*C.Ar.* 1.29; 3.62); that generation by will is tantamount to generation from nothing, simply because God creates other things ex nihilo in effect by his will (*C.Ar.* 3.61);[66] and that the divine will is in effect precarious, such that if the Son were generated by God's will rather than his being, this would make the Son's existence fragile and uncertain. Athanasius makes a slight allowance for the traditional language, perhaps to leave room for Origen, but only as long as it does not stem from the heretical "Arians" (*C.Ar.* 3.58). Why he makes this enormous shift is not clear, except that his opponents maintain generation by will and not essence. And those who disagree with his position on this, again, show by their disagreement that they are the children of the devil (*C.Ar.* 3.59). Athanasius attempts to produce biblical evidence for the language of being in reference to the Son (*C.Ar.* 3.59), but to little effect.[67] Meanwhile, he introduces the notion that the Word *is* the will of the Father (*C.Ar.* 2.31; 3.66), which works directly against his argument for common divine attributes.

The Incarnation

The *Orations against the Arians* mark an important shift in Athanasius's understanding of the incarnation as well. The most significant component of this shift concerns his method of biblical interpretation, and it is here that the influence of Marcellus made itself felt most palpably.

In terms of its structure and purpose, Athanasius's understanding of the incarnation is basically the same as it was in *Against the Pagans–On the Incarnation*. *Against the Arians* assumes the doctrine of salvation that Athanasius laid out in the former work: in order to reveal himself to us and to defeat death and the devil on the cross, God sent his Word to become human in the fullness of time (*C.Ar.* 2.55). Here again Athanasius describes the incarnation in ways that at first sound unitive, and again this is largely because he imagines Christ as the Word of God operating through a human body in the place of a human intellect (*C.Ar.* 2.31; 3.61.44; 3.31 and passim). Out of goodness and pity for our condition, God "had his own Son put on himself a human body and become human and be called Jesus, so that in this body, offering himself for all, he might deliver all people from false worship and corruption and become himself Lord and King of all" (*C.Ar.* 2.14). In the second oration Athanasius echoes earlier language of joining to describe the Word's relationship with its body: in order to be saved, humanity needed to be "joined to God" (συναφθεὶς τῷ θεῷ) (*C.Ar.* 2.70), and in the third oration, which was probably written a few years later, he further specifies that in Christ the Word actually "sojourned in a human being," by contrast with the way it merely "came into" the Old Testament saints (*C.Ar.* 3.30). Having "made his own" the human flesh (*C.Ar.* 3.33), Jesus is himself "God in flesh" (*C.Ar.* 2.10, 12; 3.54).

Yet, as before, it is a dualist framework that ultimately governs Athanasius's Christology here. The *Orations against the Arians* are full of qualifications that protect the Word from undue involvement in human affairs. The distinctiveness of Athanasius's dualistic approach and the influence of Marcellus on his thought are clearest in his treatment of biblical references to Christ, which is, after all, the main burden of the work's argument against the Arians. Most of the orations consist in a painstaking disquisition on the correct interpretation of contested biblical texts (*C.Ar.* 1.37–3.67). Athanasius addresses himself to the caricatured method of Arian exegesis, which seeks to prove that Christ is not divine on the basis of the lowly passages of Scripture. The Arians' chief problem, in his view, is that they perceive Christ's human deeds and attributes

(τὰ ἀνθρώπινα) in Scripture—such as Jesus's statement "my soul is troubled" in the Garden of Gethsemane (Matt 26:39) or Luke's comment that
Jesus "increased in wisdom and stature and in favor with God and man"
(Luke 2:52)—and conclude from them that the Word of God must have
been a creature (*C.Ar.* 3.26–27, 54). In reply, Athanasius argues repeatedly
that Christ's human experiences, and especially his death on the cross, were
not the experiences of the Word, but of his human flesh alone. It was the
Word's humanity that was exalted after suffering death (Phil 2:9), since the
Word is always divine and needs no exaltation. Statements such as these,
Athanasius explains, are made "humanly" (ἀνθρωπίνως), with reference to
the flesh that the Word took on, while others are said "divinely" (θεϊκῶς),
such as "the Word was God" (John 1:1). Athanasius presses the distinction
so far as to say that the human statements do not really apply to the Word
but to *us*, and Philippians 2 does not indicate that the Word is exalted, but
that we are exalted (*C.Ar.* 1.41).

The key to producing a pious interpretation, Athanasius explains, is to
identify the correct figure, or person (*prosopon*), being referred to, as well as
the subject and time of what is being said. In the above example, the Arians
err by failing to attribute Christ's sufferings and exaltations to the *prosopon*
of his humanity, or his body, rather than to the *prosopon* of the divine
Word (*C.Ar.* 1.54–55). Divine and human statements, in other words, have
distinct referents, which Athanasius denotes in one passage as ἄλλο καὶ
ἄλλο (*C.Ar.* 2.62), and this hermeneutical distinction is essential for maintaining anti-Arian orthodoxy. In the third oration he explains that the Arians
fail to see the full scope of the faith, which serves as a rule (*kanon*) of interpretation for questionable biblical passages such as these, in order to arrive at
their correct meaning. Understood within their full scope, the Scriptures
contain a "double account" of the Savior: as the Word and Wisdom of God,
he is always divine, yet at a certain point in time he also became flesh for
our salvation (*C.Ar.* 3.28–29, 35). A given biblical statement, then, *either*
shows the divinity of the Word, *or* it says human things about Christ as
the Son of Man (*C.Ar.* 2.1). The Arians' trouble, according to Athanasius, is
that when they see human, creaturely statements spoken of the Word—
above all Christ's death on the cross (*C.Ar.* 1.45)—they take these statements
as an indication that the Word suffers some pathos or defect in its very
being (although no "Arian" actually seems to have held this). Athanasius
concedes that, on the one hand, human things are indeed spoken of the
Word, because the body "belonged to the Word and not to any other" (*C.Ar.*

1.45), and the Word was internal and not external to it, having become human. Yet on the other hand, the creaturely language that the Word endured does not properly belong to him, but to us: "it is not [the Word] who is created, but we in him" (*C.Ar.* 2.56). Ultimately, for Athanasius, the human references to Christ apply to us rather than to the Word in any proper sense.

Athanasius's debt to Marcellus in this exegetical argument against the Arians is significant. From Marcellus he learned to handle contested texts by distinguishing between human and divine referents. Of all the passages in question, Athanasius seizes on Proverbs 8 as a point of special concern, giving it his greatest attention, just as Marcellus had done.[68] Although Origen, Eusebius, and Alexander had each read Proverbs 8:22 as a plain reference to the divine generation and preincarnate existence of Wisdom, Athanasius follows Marcellus by insisting that it must apply instead to Christ's humanity (*C.Ar.* 2.44–45). Because proverbs are mysterious and difficult to interpret, one must be careful not to interpret them plainly in the obvious sense of the text (*C.Ar.* 2.44, 73, 77), just as Marcellus had warned; in particular, one must discern which person (*prosopon*) is being discussed in order to discover the pious mind of Scripture. In this case, Athanasius rules out that Wisdom's statement "the Lord created me" could refer either to the essence or to the generation of the Word; instead, it must refer to its humanity and economy, as Marcellus had also concluded (*C.Ar.* 2.45). In order to achieve this interpretation, Athanasius likewise stretches himself to apply to the incarnation (according to election) expressions of precosmic temporal priority found in Proverbs 8, such as "before the world," "before [God] made the earth," and "before the mountains were settled" (*C.Ar.* 2.75–76). Similarly, he refers to the incarnation the statement that Christ is "the firstborn of all creation" (Col 1:15), for the same reason that he wants to avoid any equivocal sense of the term "creation" (*C.Ar.* 2.62–64). Here again he follows Marcellus in a reading that runs against the plainer meaning of the text. Whereas Athanasius points the reader to Christ's incarnation, this section of Colossians in fact goes on to say that in Christ "all things in heaven and on earth were created" and that "he himself is before all things, and in him all things hold together" (Col 1:16–17)—a plain reference to Christ's divine or preincarnate existence, not the incarnation. Against the plain sense of the text, Athanasius claims that the Arians harbor "evil thoughts and words about the Savior" because they fail to distinguish properly between divine and human referents. And because they similarly misunderstand Proverbs 8 and Hebrews 3:2, they are like dogs who wallow in their own vomit, with no knowledge of Christianity, and they are no better than unbelieving Jews (*C.Ar.* 2.1).

In the *Orations against the Arians*, Athanasius thus strengthens his dualist Christology chiefly through his exegesis, and he sets an important precedent for future discussions of how to understand the biblical witness to Christ. Drawing reinforcement from Marcellus, he bases his biblical interpretation on a clear distinction between divine and human referents. As a result, he remains committed to a strictly verbal *communicatio idiomatum*. When the Bible says human things about the Savior, Athanasius specifies that, strictly speaking, they do not refer to the Word's divinity, but to his humanity (*C.Ar.* 3.32, 41). In so doing, he further enforces on the biblical text and the current debates a binary metaphysical scheme, echoing that of the dual apologetic work, all of which requires heavy allegorizing and clever conceptual maneuvering in order to make certain texts mean what they are supposed to. The forced quality of this approach shows some of the desperation of Athanasius's embattled situation in the early 340s, but it also reflects the polemical mind-set with which he began his career in the 320s.

The Limits of Suffering and the Loss of Humanity

The exegetical divide that Athanasius imposes on the biblical material has two major consequences for his Christology, both of which are further developments of ideas we saw in *Against the Pagans–On the Incarnation*. The first concerns the limitations of the Word, and the second concerns the humanity of Christ and Christians. The consequences of Athanasius's exegesis show themselves most clearly in his understanding of Christ's suffering and death. In order to preserve the Word's divinity from what he sees as the intrusion of lowly human affairs, on which the Arian heresy is supposedly based, Athanasius emphasizes that the Word did not die on the cross, but only its body or flesh did. Moreover, the real epiphany of the incarnation runs counter to Christ's suffering and death. Somewhat like Origen in *Against Celsus*, Athanasius is concerned to protect "the glory of Divinity" from the ignominy of death in his anti-Arian works, much as he did before in the dual apologetic work. Even though Christians may say that the Word suffered in the flesh, it is imperative to bear in mind that in fact the Word did not suffer in the incarnation, because it is by nature impassible.

The human passions did not touch the Word, but instead the Word destroyed the affections (*C.Ar.* 3.31–34). Hence, "it is not lawful to say that the Lord was in terror" (*C.Ar.* 3.56). As a rule, when Athanasius gives voice to the Word's suffering in the incarnation, he typically issues an immediate qualification to the effect that, of course, the Word didn't really suffer after all. Athanasius's repeated qualifications in this regard aim to preserve the Word from contamination by human suffering and to keep it safely removed from contact with the mess at hand.

Athanasius preserves the superior power and glory of the Word's divinity in a second way, which is to transform Christ's humanity beyond recognition. Not only does the Word suffer no human passion, but the humanity of both Christ and Christians must itself become impassible and immortal. In *Against the Arians* Athanasius assumes the doctrine of salvation that he articulated in *On the Incarnation* (*C.Ar.* 2.55 and passim), devoting his attention instead to developing the idea of divinization in Christ. In the first two orations, he argues that in the incarnation the Word deifies Christ's humanity, which is also our humanity. The Word took our sinful and mortal flesh (*C.Ar.* 2.14, 66) and promoted it, exalting and divinizing his humanity and ours (*C.Ar.* 1.38, 41–43). Because we suffer from the mutability brought in by the first Adam, we required the immutability that only the incarnate Word, the Second Adam, can provide (*C.Ar.* 1.51). Yet in the subsequent third oration, Athanasius amplifies the idea considerably, to a point that strains the definition and integrity of humanity per se. The result of the incarnation is that we are "no longer human," and "we participate in the life of the aeons no longer as human beings, but as proper to the Word." Not only are we delivered from sin and given the grace of eternal life and immortality, but "our flesh is no longer of the earth, but from now on has been made Word" (λογωθείσης) (*C.Ar.* 3.33).

Athanasius demonstrates what he means by this dehumanization, or trans-humanization, in his treatment of Jesus's own divinized state, even before his crucifixion. When Jesus asks for information in several gospel passages, such as how many loaves of bread the disciples have among them, or where Lazarus lay (see John 6:6; 11:14), Athanasius comments that he is not in fact ignorant, as he seems to be. Whereas ignorance is natural to the flesh, it is not to the Divinity, and for that reason "Jesus knew what was in everyone" (John 2:25). Jesus's prescience likewise applies to his claim that he does not know the day or the hour of his death (Mark 8:32). Although

Jesus protests that he is ignorant, Athanasius maintains that, in fact, he *does* know the time of his death (*C.Ar.* 3.42). The reason why Jesus said he did not know the hour of his death was "because of the flesh," because human existence is naturally ignorant of such things. Consequently, we "ascribe to his humanity" Jesus's ignorance, and everything else that he says humanly. Yet, Athanasius continues, Jesus's statement in John's gospel, "Father, the hour is come" (John 17:1), shows that he does in fact know the hour *as Word*. Here again Athanasius divides Christ into two distinct referents or subjects. Yet in terms of Jesus's operative psychology, the Word serves the function of Jesus's mental apparatus, as shown by the concluding explanation. Divinely, the Word knows all things, just as only the Son knows the Father (Matt 11:27), yet Jesus says "I don't know" in order to show that he had put on flesh that was ignorant (*C.Ar.* 3.44–45). Thus Jesus's divinity as the Word of God blots out any human ignorance that he might appear to suffer as a human being; he is not in fact ignorant, but only speaks as though he were.

Similarly, Athanasius rules out the possibility of real human development on Jesus's part. On Luke 2:52 ("Jesus advanced in wisdom and stature and in favor with God and man"), Athanasius comments that "Jesus Christ is not a human being like all other humans, but is God who bears flesh." To imagine that Jesus actually grew and developed like other people would be equivalent to the adoptionist doctrine of Paul of Samosata, which Athanasius believes the Arians hold, although they won't admit it. Because Jesus is the enfleshed Word, who once "existed equal to God" (Phil 2:6), he cannot possibly have advanced in wisdom and grace. At most, we can say that Jesus grew physically, in his flesh; whereas what may appear to be mental growth is merely the Word's gradual self-manifestation in the human body, which was God's temple. In this view, Jesus contains no developing human mind at all and so cannot be said to have these finite aspects of human mental life. Nor does he have any fear of death, as the gospels seem to indicate, and to think that he did is unseemly and impious. While we suffer and grow mentally and morally (presumably as a sign of weakness and passibility), Jesus's life represents "the shining forth of the Divinity" (*C.Ar.* 3.51–54). This purely divine condition, even in human form, is what Athanasius imagines to be the ideal into which we too are incorporated through Christ. On the model of Jesus himself, our divinization means ultimately the absence of any limits of finitude, as we are "made Word." Athanasius not only keeps the Word away from human suffering and limitation, but he aims to deliver us from anything recognizably human as well.[69]

Having invented the Arian heresy in the 340s, Athanasius discovered a second apologetic strategy during the 350s, which eventually became one of the definitive markers of Christian orthodoxy for the next fifteen hundred years—namely, the Nicene faith. At this time, roughly three decades after the Council of Nicaea, Athanasius came to identify the creed of 325 as the main standard of the faith and the necessary rallying point for the theological consensus that he was trying to build against Arianism (*Decr.; Syn.*). In the long run, Athanasius was astoundingly successful in this effort; later generations would follow his appeal to Nicaea, so that when the Council of Constantinople issued a new creed defining orthodoxy under Theodosius in 381, it would describe that creed as the Nicene faith; and to this day the "Nicene" Creed of 381 remains the only creedal document that is accepted as a norm of faith by Eastern and Western Christian churches. However, in his own time Athanasius's position remained heavily embattled, and the theological situation was much more complex than his black-and-white apologetics would lead us to believe. The faith of Constantinople in 381 was in fact based more directly on the theological tradition that stemmed from Eusebius of Caesarea, which Athanasius *opposed* through the 350s, and Athanasius's turn to Nicaea was a shift of public relations only; it did not represent any change in his own Christology. The Christology that Athanasius solidified in the *Orations against the Arians* persisted through the series of works he produced during the 340s and 350s.

In his work *On the Decrees of Nicaea* Athanasius links his doctrine with the Nicene phrases that the Son is begotten "from the being [*ousia*] of the Father" and is "of one being [*homoousios*] with the Father," and he begins to argue that Nicaea and its language are necessary and nonnegotiable markers of orthodoxy. At the same time, he continues to appeal to prior Alexandrian tradition in order to justify his authority. He refers to Theognostus, Dionysius of Alexandria, and Origen, together with the Roman bishop Dionysius, in support of his new use of the language of *ousia* from Nicaea, and he continues to argue for the eternal coexistence of the Word with the Father (*Decr.* 25–27). Under these new terms, the Word is either a creature, or it is *homoousios* with the Father (*Decr.* 23); to be merely "like in being" (*homoios kat' ousian*), as he had argued in *Against the Arians*, is no longer enough, even though his explanation of what the Nicene phrases mean is the same as he had argued in the earlier work. Athanasius continues to employ

an Origenist framework at one level, emphasizing the "oneness" of the
Father and of the Word and giving the standard list of primary titles of
Christ—Word, Wisdom, image, and power—that Origen originally identified (*Decr.* 17); and he continues to uphold the priority of God the Father
within the Trinity throughout the work. But the same metaphysic still undergirds the argument: the real problem with the Arian term "originate" is that
it means that the Word was created in time and ex nihilo (*Decr.* 28). In one
interesting passage Athanasius confirms that he is still fundamentally operating with a Logos Christology, by arguing that "Word" and "Wisdom" are
not merely names or titles of the Son (*Decr.* 16)—a view that departs from
both Origen and Eusebius, as we have noted, and probably Alexander as
well. In another passage he quotes an example of Dionysius of Rome's
interpretation of Proverbs 8:22 without seeming to notice that it contradicts
his own rule of economic interpretation. For Dionysius, as for Athanasius's
demonic Arians, the term "created" must not be taken in only one sense, and
so the verse refers not to the incarnation, but to the Son's divine generation
from the Father (*Decr.* 26)!

Athanasius's *Letters to Serapion*, from the late 350s, reiterate the dualist
hermeneutic of *Against the Arians*, giving the same interpretation of several
passages, including Proverbs 8 and Matthew 13:32 (*Ep.Serap.* 2.8–9). In
these letters Athanasius gives both genetic and generic explanations of the
meaning of *homoousios*: in one case he compares the relationship between a
human father and son (a common nature shared by derivation), and in
another the relationship among all human beings as members of the same
race (shared common nature from a common source and/or members of
the same class of beings) (*Ep.Serap.* 2.3, 5).[70]

One interesting development—interesting above all because it has so
little effect on his broader thought—occurs in the *Letters to Serapion* and *On
the Sayings of Dionysius*, a work in which Athanasius seeks to reclaim the
legacy of Dionysius of Alexandria from the Arians, who have argued that
his teaching supports their doctrine. In both works Athanasius shows a
greater attention to the differentiation among the Father, Son, and Holy
Spirit than he normally does. The *Letters to Serapion* develop the notion of
the different functions that the three persons each perform and the sequence
of divine action that runs from the Father through the Son to the Holy
Spirit (*Ep.Serap.* 1.9, 28, 31; 4.7). Just previously, he had emphasized the
plurality inherent in the Trinity: in God is a Triad, and it is a Triad in truth
and real existence (*hyparxis*), not just in name (*Decr.* 4.7; 1.28). Now he

argues that the Father, Son, and Spirit are each "one and only" so, and that the Father is always Father, the Son always Son, the Spirit always Spirit (*Ep.Serap.* 1.16; 4.5), in terms that are plainly Origenist and Eusebian and that represent a positive response to recent Eastern councils. Similar language is repeated in *On the Sayings of Dionysius*, in which Athanasius tacitly reproduces Origenist elements of Dionysius's doctrine, including the notion that God is always Father and Christ is always Word, Wisdom, Power, and Brightness, together with an emphasis on the relational quality of the three names, and Christological titles taken from Wisdom 7:25 (*Dion.* 9, 15, 17). Yet even here Athanasius continues to enforce his binary herme-neutic, quite apart from Dionysius's own intentions: we must discriminate, he says, between statements about Christ's divinity and his humanity (*Dion.* 9, 19, 26–27). Any creaturely language that Dionysius used for the Son must apply to his humanity, a move that Athanasius claims was meant to counter Sabellian notions that the Father became incarnate, which is extremely unlikely (*Dion.* 5). Even though Athanasius knows that he is dealing with a different polemical context (Dionysius's antimonarchianism), he neverthe-less continues to read every situation through the lenses of his anti-Arian polemic, and the main argument of the work is that Dionysius was an anti-Arian before his time![71] Athanasius's increased use of pluralist language for the Trinity, after the manner of Origen, Eusebius, and Dionysius, shows some further engagement with the positions of his opponents, although the extent to which he allowed their arguments to have any real effect was slight.

A third key turn in Athanasius's apologetic strategy involves a new openness toward a number of Eastern bishops whom he had formerly spurned. As the more radical Heterousians split off from the homoian tradi-tion of Eusebius, leaving a group of Homoiousians (who affirmed that the Son is like the Father in *ousia*) opposing them,[72] and Athanasius found himself in need of increasing support, he began to acknowledge that the Homoiousians could be his allies after all. In *On the Councils of Ariminum and Seleucia* Athanasius extends an olive branch to the likes of Basil of Ancyra. These bishops whom Athanasius formerly castigated as demonic Arians, he now regards as friends (*Syn.* 41). Yet in reality Athanasius's accommodation was more feigned than genuine, and what he gives with one hand he takes away with the other; for he insists that any agreement between the two tradi-tions must be on his terms alone. Likeness according to essence, which had been Athanasius's own doctrine in *Against the Arians*, is now orthodox only if it really means sameness of essence (*homoousios*), understood to mean from the Father's essence (*ek tes ousias tou Patros*)—the two Nicene technical phrases—and any who dissent from Nicaea are enemies of Christ (*Syn.* 40–41). Similarly, Athanasius attempts to co-opt all traditional Origenist language, which the Easterners had continued to use, into his Nicene framework: "truly Father" and "truly Son," as taught by the Eusebians, really mean what Nicaea meant (*Syn.* 39), and the entire tradition of third-century anti-Sabellian councils and doctrine, which Athanasius can no longer ignore, must also be understood in Nicene, homoousian terms (*Syn.* 43, 45). In order to persuade his detractors of the necessity of homoousian language, Athanasius attempts to make a reasoned argument for his case. He upholds the Father's role as source of the Trinity; he continues to speak of the Word as God's image apart from the incarnation; and he firmly denies that *homoousios* indicates that the Father, Son, and Holy Spirit either are members of a class or are some sort of third divine thing—all of which were central concerns of Origen and his later followers (*Syn.* 50–51). But on top of this, Athanasius wants to maintain that only the term *homoousios* expresses these ideas adequately: that essences cannot in fact be "like" each other and share the same nature but must be "the same" if they are not to relate merely by participation (*Syn.* 53–54), so that the homoousian doctrine is now the only conceivable way to express Christ's full divinity. Similarly, Athanasius defines orthodox tradition as that which agrees with Nicaea, against a series of "Arian" councils, including those in Jerusalem in 335, Antioch in 341 and 344, Sirmium in 351 and 357, Seleucia in 359, Niké/Constantinople in 359/360, and Antioch in 361 (*Syn.* 7, 21–32). What is particularly notable about this list is that it contains councils that adopted a range of doctrinal positions, including councils that Athanasius's newfound friends held dear and that even gave a positive response to Nicaea (Antioch in 341). At the same time, he persists in accusing Eusebius of Caesarea of duplicitousness in his signing of the Nicene Creed, calling him still "Acacius' master"; meanwhile, he conveniently omits Eusebius's opposition to Marcellus (*Syn.* 13; *Decr.* 3). Athanasius's Balkanizing perspective on the Eastern councils and theologians of the mid-fourth century had a profound effect on later perceptions of orthodoxy and heresy in this period. Despite his claims of traditional catholicity and his pretensions of reasoned debate, Athanasius plainly distorted the received tradition in a novel and absolutist way in order to bolster his own position. It was not the first time he had drawn a line in the sand, and it would not be the last.

ATHANASIUS III (362–373): THE LATE WORKS

In the third major phase of his career, from the Council of Alexandria in 362 to his death in 373, Athanasius's literary productivity gradually dropped off. Nevertheless, two sets of texts from this period are significant for the study of Athanasius's Christology. The first is the pair of synodal documents produced in connection with the council of 362, especially the *Tome to the Antiochenes*, which most scholars believe Athanasius authored. The second is a group of letters that he wrote to three different recipients around 371 or 372, which address a new set of Christological questions that arose for him at this late date.

The synod's *Catholic Epistle* is the least Athanasian of the two documents. It proclaims adherence to Nicaea, speaks of "one Divinity of the holy Trinity," and issues a denial that the Son and Spirit are creatures, which are typical of Athanasius's theology. Yet it also contains the novel phrase "the Trinity is consubstantial/*homoousios*" (*Ep.Cath.* 7), which Athanasius does not use elsewhere, and which is rather misleading if one takes it to deny the monarchy of God the Father.

The council's *Tome to the Antiochenes*, however, gives a much fuller picture of Athanasius's position at this time. The document attempts to reconcile the Antiochene schism between the party of Paulinus, with whom Athanasius shares communion, and that of Meletius, which represents the continuing Eusebian party associated with the very conciliar tradition that Athanasius castigated in *On the Councils of Ariminum and Seleucia*. Yet, as before, Athanasius's plan for reconciliation is exclusively defined by his own perspective and terminology. So the Homoiousians whom he hopes to include in the new Nicene initiative are former Arians (*Tom.* 1, 3), just as the Homoians and Heterousians are still Arians. The terms of reconciliation are to anathematize the Arian heresy, to confess the faith of Nicaea (denying the authority of the Council of Serdica), to anathematize those who say that the Holy Spirit is a creature and separate from the *ousia* of Christ (the divinity of the Spirit having recently come into question), and to anathematize the older heresies of Sabellius and Paul of Samosata, Valentinus, Basilides, and the Manichees (*Tom.* 3). The Eastern, Origenist language of three hypostases is now allowed, as long as one does not mean that the three are foreign in *ousia* to one another, divided from one another like three creatures, or three first principles (*archai*), which would indicate three gods. Here Athanasius makes a brief acknowledgment of the antimonarchian heritage that remained foundational for the Easterners: each of the three truly exists and subsists. Yet he is very quick to issue the qualification that the three must be understood in such a way that the Son is *homoousios* with the Father, and the triune relations are otherwise defined in terms of *ousia (Tom.* 5)—terms which are antithetical to the very tradition that Athanasius means to include. Likewise, the phrasing of one hypostasis is also acceptable, when this is understood to mean *ousia (Tom.* 6), which is the scheme that Athanasius himself prefers. Victoriously, the council agreed on these terms, anathematized Arius once again, thus defining itself against a presbyter who had now been dead for almost thirty years, and pledged itself in loyalty to Nicaea from now on (*Tom.* 6). The council's terms of reconciliation were not equally accommodating to all parties concerned.

Yet the council also saw some disagreement over the particular way in which the Word became incarnate ("the fleshly economy of the Savior"). Athanasius reports that the differing parties agreed that the Word did not "come to be" (ἐγένετο) in the sense that it dwelt in a holy human being (εἰς ἅγιον ἄνθρωπον), as it did in the prophets, but that "the Word himself was made flesh." Likewise, Athanasius continues, those who agreed to this idea also signaled their admission that Jesus did not lack an intelligent mind: he was not a soulless body lacking in sense (*Tom.* 7). The idea is that because the Word operated in Jesus's human body, it satisfied the need for a guiding intelligence; this does not appear to be an affirmation that Jesus possessed a *human* mind.[73] In this brief, veiled account, we are probably witnessing not a debate over whether or not the Word was fully present or united with Jesus's humanity, as it may appear after Christological discussions connected with later Antiochene doctrines, but rather a debate over whether the Word could have coexisted with a fully functioning human mind. This is probably the sense of dwelling "in a holy human being," that is, one who exists and possesses holiness at a human level, which would require the exercise of human choice. This may have been the first time that Athanasius squarely faced the question. In his response, he speaks, as before, of the Word doing some things humanly and others divinely, no human mind contributes to the picture.

Here again, Athanasius's rhetoric and self-presentation are overblown. He makes no mention of Meletius of Antioch, who led the larger community there, but only of Paulinus, Athanasius's ally; and there is no sign that the *Tome* effected any reconciliation in Antioch. The Alexandrian council may have been merely the reunion of certain exiled bishops. In his *Letter to the Emperor Jovian* written in 363 or 364, Athanasius reiterates the same position: Nicaea is the standard of the catholic faith; the Arian heresy still poses a threat; and the *homoousion* is the only sufficient formula to express true sonship.

There are new Christological developments in certain locations around 370, to which Athanasius responds in three letters. Some have identified the parties in question as either Antiochenes or Apollinarians, the latter being a group that was attracting significant international attention around this time (see chapter 4), but we cannot be certain who the opponents in view are, or even what exactly their doctrine was.[74] Here we find Athanasius as an embattled and rather bitter old man striving to defend the Christology that he had labored so hard to construct. In his letters to Bishop Epictetus of Corinth, Bishop Adelphius from lower Egypt, and a certain Maximus, Athanasius continues to wave the banner of Nicaea, which, he adds, successfully reiterated the earlier councils and fathers and now definitively expresses Christian orthodoxy. His rhetoric is as vitriolic as before, and he interprets the new Christological questions all as slights against Nicaea (*Ep.Epict.* 1; *Ep.Adelph.* 1; *Ep.Max.* 5). To the end, Athanasius maintains his Word-flesh Christology: he writes to Epictetus that, when God the Father says of Christ in the Jordan and on the Mount of Transfiguration "this is my beloved Son," God is showing that "the Son is the Word himself" (*Ep.Epict.* 12).

At this last stage of Athanasius's career, two Christological points stand out. The first is his insistence on the sharp distinction between the *ousia* of the Word and the human body of Jesus. Athanasius repeatedly denies that the incarnation took place as a result of the Word's being or nature. In the *Letter to Epictetus* he inveighs against the notion that the *ousia* of the Word hung on the cross; instead, it was the body. Similarly, he repudiates the idea that the incarnation was the result of the Word's divine nature: "he did not become human in consequence of his nature [*physeos akolouthia*]" (*Ep.Max.* 3). The erroneous views that Epictetus describes to Athanasius are confusing and even contradictory. At one moment it sounds as though Jesus's humanity was generated directly from the Word and possibly descended from heaven, while the next moment Jesus appears to be an independently existing human being with whom the Word associates itself (*Ep.Epict.* 2). In any event, Athanasius is keen to preserve the distinction between the Word and its flesh, and he reiterates his earlier views against the Word's suffering in the incarnation. In the *Letter to Epictetus* Athanasius speaks of the Word "suffering, yet not suffering" in the incarnation

(*Ep.Epict.* 6), yet his point is merely to account for the verbal *communicatio idiomatum* that we have already seen, nothing more.

The second notable point in the letters is how Athanasius opposes the suggestion that Christ was a complete human being. In the *Letter to Maximus* he reiterates his Word-flesh Christology against what appears to be a notion of Jesus's human death. The bottom line for Athanasius is that Christ crucified, whom Christians worship, is himself "the Lord of glory and the power of God and Wisdom of God" and "truly the Son of God." He explains further: "for the body that was seen was not that of some human being, but of God [ἀνθρώπου τινός . . . ἀλλὰ θεοῦ], in which he existed even when he was crucified." Again Athanasius writes that Christians are deified "not by partaking of the body of some human being, but by receiving the body of the Word himself"; and it is not the case that "some human being gave his life for us." The point seems to be that the only way for Christ's dying body truly to be the Word's is for the Word to be the animating and intellectual principle in it *and not* a human intellect. Athanasius assumes that if Jesus were a complete human being, he could not be the Word made flesh, and the faith and hope of Christians would be in a human being rather than in the Word of God (*Ep.Max.* 1–3). Even though Jesus "exhibited" behaviors that are proper to the human body, such as eating, drinking, and suffering, it was nevertheless the Word who sojourned among us. But if his divinity were denied and he were imagined to be "a human being existing alongside the divine Word,"[75] that would amount to the heresy of Paul of Samosata (who was accused of adoptionism) (*Ep.Max.* 4). It is in this way—as the Word plus human flesh alone—that Athanasius imagines the real difference between Jesus and the Old Testament saints, a view evident as well in the *Tome* of 362. In short, if Jesus were a complete human being, Christians could not claim to worship the crucified Lord (*Ep.Max.* 5).[76] As it is, they worship the Word together with his flesh.

Athanasius's late Christology does not advance the discussion, as is often supposed; if anything, it is recalcitrant and backward-looking. As the conversation moves on in various places, Athanasius fails to see either the possibilities inherent in others' views or the limitations of his own. Athanasius's Christology is not, in the end, more unitive than that of others, as it is sometimes imagined to be, for his anti-Arian polemic and his Logos Christology both require that the Word be kept separate from human experience and suffering, and that humanity as such be eliminated in order to make room for the Word's dominion. Athanasius imagines divine and human existence as mutually exclusive realms that cannot be brought together without compromising the one or destroying the other.

EXCURSUS: ATHANASIUS AND THE ALEXANDRIAN LITURGY

One of the most telling ways to evaluate Athanasius's Christology is to compare it with the eucharistic liturgies of the Alexandrian church and the surrounding area. Although our knowledge of Christian worship practices in the mid-fourth century is relatively sparse, we possess more evidence of northern Egyptian liturgies than we do of many other regions at this time.[77] On the whole, the liturgical material shows that the deepest theological stream at this time was some version of broad Origenism, and that Athanasius's Christology was relatively unusual and innovative.

The main eucharistic tradition of the Alexandrian church, the *Liturgy of St. Mark*, is extremely interesting in this regard. *St. Mark* is thought to represent indigenous Egyptian tradition distinct from the eucharistic liturgies that were developing in other locations, at least up to a certain point, when regional traditions began to influence each other. Three characteristics stand out in comparison with Athanasius's work. First, the prayer is replete with images and themes from Origen's Christology. It speaks of creation through the Wisdom, Light, and Son of God, all typical Origenian titles for Christ. Moreover, it expresses in very strong terms the distinctions among the Father, Son, and Spirit, which stood at the heart of Origen's anti-Gnostic and antimonarchian theology. The prayer gives thanks to God the Father *with* Jesus Christ and the Holy Spirit, and in the final version of the prayer Christ in his oblationary role is described as Wisdom, which was Origen's chief title for the Son. These passages also demonstrate the basic structure of Christian prayer that Origen had outlined in his work *On Prayer*, in which all prayer is ultimately addressed to God the Father through Christ and the Spirit. A further trace of Origenist antimonarchianism exists in the description of the Father, Son, and Holy Spirit as each "one," even in the final version.[78] In sum, the prayer appears to be deeply informed by the theology and spirituality of Origen.

Second, *St. Mark* contains no discernable Logos Christology. We find a similar phenomenon in the version of the second-century church order *Didache* that endured in Egypt. This document too uses parent-child language rather than the Logos idea to describe the Father-Son relation, as Origen had, and Christ as revealer is clearly subordinate in some sense. Nor do we find in *St. Mark* any language of deification, which became the focus of Athanasius's understanding of Christ's humanity and that of all Christians. The very heart of Athanasius's Christological program thus appears to have had no effect on the language of *St. Mark*.[79] Third, there is no reference to Nicaea as far as we can tell, up through the second layer of the prayer, the John Rylands Fragment and British Museum Tablet, which is normally dated around 400. The final version of the prayer does refer to Nicaea, which we would expect to find in the primary liturgy of any major see after the Theodosian settlement of 381 had legally established the Nicene faith. One trace of Athanasius's influence that we do see in the final version is his characteristic expression, borrowed from 1 Peter 4:1, that Christ died "in the flesh"; although the phrase is dropped in Coptic versions of the prayer, where Cyril's happy embrace of divine suffering overruled Athanasius's opposition to it. The primary liturgical tradition of Alexandria therefore shows amazingly little trace of Athanasius's Christology, and when it does at a late date, it is fairly unremarkable. Compared with the Christology represented in the Alexandrian liturgy, which remains predominantly Origenist, Athanasius's Christological program stands out as extremely innovative and rather unique.

The exception that proves the rule among the Egyptian liturgies is the eucharistic prayer attributed to Bishop Serapion of Thumis, one of Athanasius's associates. Like *St. Mark*, *Serapion* is also strongly Origenist. It addresses God as ungenerated Father and emphasizes God's incomprehensibility, ineffability, and invisibility; and it refers to Christ by the title "only-begotten Son." Moreover, its application of the phrase "the true God" to the Father but not to Christ ignores the new usage made at Nicaea and follows instead the pattern of Origen and Eusebius, and probably Alexander. Here too we have a strongly pluralist, antimodalist structure of Trinitarian prayer, where Christ and the Holy Spirit sing to God the Father "in us" who are praying. *Serapion* is famously distinctive, however, for the presence of an epiclesis to the Logos rather than to the Holy Spirit, as we find in most other epicleses. The prayer asks that God's Word would "come on this bread . . . that the bread may become body of the Word, [and] on this cup, that the cup may become blood of the Truth." The phrase "body of the Word" could certainly be an echo of Athanasius's Christology, and Athanasius's working relationship with Bishop Serapion could have made such a borrowing possible. Some scholars have speculated that the phrase could also be a genuine archaism from the region,[80] and Origen may still be in the background, since he did make use of Logos conceptions within a larger framework of Son Christology. However, beyond this phrase there is otherwise little sign of Athanasius's Christology, and the statement that Christ now "sits at the right hand of the uncreated"[81] is distinctly un-Athanasian; in his ears such a phrase surely would have sounded Arian. The dominant strain of the prayer is, again, an Origenist Christology.

ATHANASIUS *CONTRA MUNDUM*

Tension and conflict dominated Athanasius's career from the beginning to the end of his forty-five-year tenure as a theologian and bishop. This embattled state of affairs was not merely the result of his struggles with ecclesiastical enemies and his efforts to bring the church in Egypt under his episcopal control. It is also reflected in his Christology and quite obviously in his own character, and it makes for one of the most disturbing chapters in the history of the Christian church.

Athanasius sought to represent the traditional orthodoxy of the Alexandrian church through each of his controversies, adding Arius to the list of recognized heretics that he had inherited from his predecessor, Alexander. In some respects Athanasius did indeed carry forward the Origenist tradition, from Origen's image doctrine and his emphasis on the priority of God the Father within the Trinity to his sense of the threat that human suffering poses to divine impassibility. Yet in other ways Athanasius moved in a radically new Christological direction, which clouded the original stream in deeply complicating ways and exaggerated the exclusive power differential that Origen's system already contained. From the beginning of his conflict with Arius, which occupied his first work, *Henos somatos*, Athanasius committed himself to a metaphysical scheme in which God and humanity are so starkly opposed that any suggestion of the natural being and vitality of creaturely existence would compromise the all-consuming power of God. Structurally speaking, Athanasius ends up diverting the Origenist heritage in a modalist direction and augmenting the principle of Christological dualism and mutual exclusion that had long been masked by the unitive language in which it was sometimes couched. Over time, Athanasius solidified his mind-set in this regard, as he became carried away with inventing and maintaining the Arian heresy and the exclusive, universal orthodoxy of Nicaea. As a result, he fixated on a certain Christological and Trinitarian structure while ignoring the received anti-monarchian orthodoxy.

Athanasius sees Christ as the combination of a supremely triumphal and uniquely active divinity and a purely passive and naturally disintegrating humanity.[82] His is a Christology of grave contrasts in which the Word is all power, and human flesh can only await transformation into the Word itself.[83] It is also a scheme in which God lacks the desire and the ability to include human brokenness into the divine being without being threatened with decomposition himself, and humanity possesses no real and lasting nature of its own. In Athanasius's vision there is no room for a fully functioning human being, either in Jesus's case or, ultimately, in ours. Athanasius did not correct Origen's idea that divinity and humanity require a mediator to bridge the gap by making God immediately present to creation in Christ, as he is often thought to have done. For in Athanasius's scheme, God and creation are not less but *more* ontologically irreconcilable than they are for Origen, and in the end Athanasius's Christology is even less comprehensive than that of Origen or even Eusebius of Caesarea. This fact may be largely due to the relative narrowness of Athanasius's reading compared with that of Eusebius and the Cappadocians, who would provide the next generation of theological leadership. Similarly, Athanasius saw only black-and-white contrasts in the church at large, in a grand Arian conspiracy that was poisoning the true faith. There is an unmistakable correlation between the univocal and exclusive power of the Word in Christ's body and the all-or-nothing power of Athanasius's episcopate. Athanasius devoted much of his theological energy to enforcing this binary view of Christ and the church, and any who disagreed he accused of ingratitude toward God, Jewish unbelief, and being in league with the devil—all the while refusing to admit that there was more to the story, even when he came to regret the doctrinal polarization that was plaguing the church (*Syn.* 47).

Although it has long been regarded as the greatest dogmatic achievement of the fourth century, Athanasius's lifelong polemic against the Arians complicated the church's Christological tradition more than it clarified it.[84] A more balanced and traditional synthesis would have to wait until the next generation of leading theologians, who represented a very different mental and geographical region—the Origenist tradition that stemmed from Athanasius's enemy Eusebius of Caesarea. When Bishop Cyril of

Alexandria made use of Athanasius's *Against the Arians* book 3 and *Letter to Epictetus* at the Council of Ephesus in 431, he marked a new moment in the reception of Athanasius's theological legacy. By virtue of his quotations and his use of certain Athanasian concepts, Cyril helped foster the notion that Athanasius is the central authority in fourth-century orthodox tradition. Yet by this time Athanasius's doctrine was understood mainly in terms of the work of other theologians, even as his name remained attached to the finished product. This process of reception was immensely complex, and to understand it we must now turn to the work of the Cappadocian fathers, who provide a more lasting contribution to orthodox theology.

4. Gregory of Nazianzus, Gregory of Nyssa, and Constantinople (381)

The period from 360 to the early 380s was a crucial turning point in the development of patristic Christology. Here our attention shifts from Alexandria and Palestine to the regions between Constantinople and Antioch, where much of what later became orthodox Christian theology was defined with a degree of clarity and permanence that has seldom, if ever, been repeated. This achievement took place largely through the theological efforts of the Cappadocian fathers—Basil of Caesarea, Gregory of Nazianzus, and Gregory of Nyssa—together with the great Council of Constantinople of 381, which produced the so-called Nicene Creed that is known to many Christians today. The Nicene Creed of Constantinople provides the conciliar standard of orthodoxy for most later church councils; it is still recited in the liturgies of many Christian churches around the world; and it is the most widely recognized creed in modern ecumenical discussions. Despite the common designation of these theologians as the Cappadocian fathers, their work is distinctive in many respects. In this chapter we concentrate on the two who most directly influenced the development of patristic Christology, Gregory of Nazianzus and Gregory of Nyssa; however, since the latter Gregory continued his elder brother Basil's work in several respects, we will encounter some of Basil's thought as well.

Before we consider the theology of the Cappadocians, we must first come to terms with the two theological debates that provided the immediate contexts for the Christological works of both Gregories, much as we sought to understand Arius as the initial spur for Athanasius's work. The first debate concerns the "homoian" doctrine that Emperor Constantius established as the official orthodoxy of the empire in 360, and which remained in place in the Eastern empire until 379, thus spanning the formative period of the Cappadocians' theological careers. The second debate took place between two theologians in the vicinity of Antioch over the question of the unity and composition of Christ's person.

THE HOMOIAN DEBATE

The theological milieu from which the Cappadocians emerged was primarily shaped by the Origenist tradition of Eusebius of Caesarea, rather than that of Athanasius, as has often been assumed. Alongside the works of Origen and Eusebius, the most significant conciliar definitions for this tradition came from the Dedication Council of Antioch in 341. The Antiochene council expressed a positive regard for the meeting in Nicaea; it repudiated Arius; and it reasserted the traditional antimodalist doctrine that Eusebius had recently championed against Marcellus of Ancyra and that the Nicene language of consubstantiality threatened to violate.[1] The council's Dedication Creed affirmed the Origenist principles that the Father, Son, and Holy Spirit are three hypostases; Christ is the exact image of the Divinity, being, power, will, and glory of the Father; Christ is distinctive among the things created by God; and the Father does not precede the Son temporally.[2] The council's fourth doctrinal statement is even more accommodating to the wider debates: it employs no *ousia* language; it denounces Arius's doctrine of creation ex nihilo; and its antimodalism is somewhat toned down, although it still opposes Marcellus. These are the sort of principles that most deeply informed the Eusebian tradition that led eventually to the work of the Cappadocians.[3]

In the 350s, at the same time that Athanasius was discovering the usefulness of Nicaea as a conciliar standard and focusing on its language of being, the "Eastern" Eusebian tradition split in two directions. The first was an outgrowth of official "homoian" policy. During this time Emperor Constantius was attempting to build church unity around a new version of homoian doctrine, while prosecuting Athanasius wherever he could. Among the many councils of this period, two stand out as notable markers of homoian theology. The Council of Sirmium in 351 reiterated earlier condemnations of Athanasius, Marcellus, and Photinus, and it signaled unease with *ousia* language for describing the relation of the Son to God the Father.[4] Constantius tried to enforce the council's decrees, though he met with significant resistance in several quarters. In 357 another council in Sirmium then drew a thick line in the sand by explicitly refuting the Creed of Nicaea, which Eusebian tradition had long since accepted, and by prohibiting the use of *ousia* language altogether—thus leaving one able to say only that the Son was "like" (*homoios*) the Father, whence the term "homoian" for designating this view. Although the Eastern tradition had voiced unease with the Nicene *homoousion* because of its Gnostic and modalist connotations, the total prohibition of *ousia* language signaled an alarming degree of subordinationism for any moderate Origenist. The subordinationist doctrine of Sirmium was reiterated in the Dated Creed of 359, which limited itself to saying that the Son is "like the Father in all things," with no reference to being.[5] Constantius expected the Dated Creed to be ratified at a dual council in Ariminum-Seleucia, which he staged as a new general council intended to replace Nicaea. However, the bishops at both councils opposed Constantius's creed, Ariminum favoring Nicaea and Seleucia the Dedication Creed of 341, but in the end the bishops were forced to sign the Dated Creed nevertheless. At this point the unresolved debates moved to Constantinople, where a new council was held in 360.

Alongside these conciliar developments, some homoian theologians began to argue explicitly for an even greater subordination of the Son to the Father, by claiming that the Son is in fact "unlike" the Father in essence—a position that scholars have since termed "heterousian" (unlike in essence). The most prominent early heterousian theologian was Aetius, who had already earned a reputation as a strong subordinationist among Eusebians in the 320s. Eunomius, Aetius's former secretary and theological successor, went on to elaborate the heterousian doctrine, and it was he who became the main polemical target of all three Cappadocians, at the beginning of Basil's and Gregory of Nazianzus's public ministries in the early 360s and again when Gregory of Nyssa took up his brother's cause in the late 370s and 380s.

In reaction to the homoian, and especially the heterousian, movements, more moderate Eusebians such as Basil of Ancyra, Marcellus's replacement since 336, and George of Laodicea developed the Eusebian tradition in a very different direction by reaffirming the divinity of Christ. An important gathering of this group occurred at a council in Ancyra in 358. In addition to Basil, Eustathius of Sebaste (Basil of Caesarea's future mentor) was present, and George of Laodicea sent a message of alliance, expressing his concern about the heterousian persecution of others in

Antioch, which he termed "the shipwreck of Aetius" (Socrates, *H.E.* 4.13). Still clearly in the Eusebian mold, the council emphasized the distinctness of the Father, Son, and Holy Spirit and the Father's role as cause of the other two, and it endorsed the anti-Marcellan councils of Constantinople (336), Antioch (341), Serdica (343), and Sirmium (351). Yet, at the same time, it opposed the Heterousians by arguing for the priority of Father-Son language over that of creator and creature for understanding the relationship between Christ and God the Father. It argued, furthermore, that in order to confess the Son's divinity, one must hold that he is at least "like in being" (ὅμοιος κατ' οὐσίαν) (Epiphanius, *Panar.* 73.4.2) to the Father, a phrase that has earned this group the name Homoiousians. Yet the group did not go so far as to confess the Nicene *homoousion*, in order to avoid suggestions of modalism. Constantius accepted the council's doctrine for a time, until the Dated Creed and the Ariminum-Seleucia council of 359, at which point Basil of Ancyra signaled his resistance by adding the qualification "like in being" to his signature of the Dated Creed (*Panar.* 73.22.7). Basil and George then sent a letter reiterating their position (*Panar.* 73.16.3–4), which argues that heterousian doctrine is in fact the logical consequence of the homoian position. It also explains that the concept *ousia* is implied in Scripture; that "Father" is a more definitive term for God than the Heterousians' preferred term "unbegotten"; that this is what the language of three hypostases means to indicate ("the subsisting, existing properties of the persons"), rather than three gods or first principles; and that there is "one Divinity, which encompasses all things through the Son in the Holy Spirit" (*Panar.* 73.2.1–11.11)—all of which are standard elements of both Origen's and Eusebius's theology, as we have seen.

Thus by 360 a coherent effort had begun within the Origenist-Eusebian tradition to maintain the Son's divinity against radical denials of it, and it was this stream that led most directly to the theology of the Cappadocians over the next two decades. At this point, the Council of Constantinople in 360, under the presidency of the heterousian bishop Acacius of Caesarea, ratified the homoian doctrine produced the year before. It deposed several members of the homoiousian network, including Meletius of Antioch, Basil of Ancyra, Macedonius of Constantinople, Eustathius of Sebaste, and Cyril of Jerusalem, and appointed heterousian bishops in their stead, including Eudoxius of Constantinople and Eunomius of Cyzicus. The synod also issued a statement of faith, based on that of Niké/Ariminum, which remained the official standard of orthodoxy for the next two decades, until the Council of Constantinople of 381, excepting only the brief reigns of the pagan emperor Julian and the pro-Nicene Jovian from 361 to 364. The statement declares only that the Son is "like the Father according to the Scriptures" (not even "in all things") and prohibits the use of both *ousia* and hypostasis as Christological terms. Soon thereafter, Eunomius of Cyzicus published his *Apology*, which presented his theological position as he would have most likely articulated it at the council. Central to Eunomius's doctrine was the claim to know the essence of God exactly, and that God's essence is above all "unbegotten." Eunomius's *Apology* begins with the statement that God (the Father) is one, and that God is defined chiefly by the fact that he exists in and of himself, apart from any source either within or without. God is therefore "unbegotten being" (οὐσία ἀγέννητος) (*Apol.* 7). This designation of God's essence, moreover, is not merely a human concept that might denote God with more or less accuracy. For Eunomius, it is important to maintain the strict correspondence between such terms and the reality of God; otherwise, we cannot know God truthfully (*Apol.* 8). On the basis of these principles, then, Eunomius maintained that the Son cannot be like the Father in essence, since he is begotten and the Father is not.[6] Through the combined efforts of the imperial will and the theological labors of Heterousians such as Eunomius, Constantius's homoian program achieved a solid and lasting victory in 360. This doctrinal position was the target of Basil of Caesarea's and Gregory Nazianzen's polemical work for many years. Many other bishops throughout the church resisted the deep subordinationism that the official doctrine represented as well.

One of the most important results of these debates was not doctrinal per se, but rather procedural. It was the very idea of having a single creed or doctrinal statement produced by a council of bishops that would serve as a universal standard of orthodoxy.[7] Before this time, the generally held, catholic rule of faith served this purpose, and while bishops had long gathered in regional councils to settle matters of doctrinal dispute, there was no assumption that a contemporary council of bishops needed to, or even should, produce a new statement of faith apart from the rule of faith and the commonly held traditions of its interpretation. Athanasius, several Western bishops, and eventually the homoiousian network began at this time to identify Nicaea as the council that they considered a universal standard of the faith, and this expectation carried forward into the work of the great council of 381.

THE ANTIOCHENE CHRISTOLOGICAL DEBATE

The second major context for the development of Cappadocian theology is the Christological debate that occurred in the vicinity of Antioch between Apollinarius of Laodicea and Diodore of Tarsus.[8] Although Basil of Caesarea had some involvement in this exchange, it was the two Gregories who provided the most direct, visible responses. Together with the homoian regime of 360, the Antiochene Christological debate had a formative influence on the work of the latter two Cappadocians. Our knowledge of Apollinarius's and Diodore's work is limited because of the fragmentary nature of their literary remains and the scarcity of other historical information; nevertheless, we have enough information to reconstruct the debate with a fair degree of certainty.

Apollinarius was a leading member of the loose network of bishop-theologians who sought to promote the Trinitarian faith in the 360s and 370s. Basil of Caesarea once consulted him on how one should understand the strange Nicene term *homoousios* (*Ep.* 361, 363), and both he and Pope Damasus regard Apollinarius as "one of their own" when they later came to oppose his views (*Ep.* 92).[9] In the 340s Apollinarius was some sort of associate of Athanasius (Athanasius stayed at his home during his travels back to Alexandria), and around 360 he began to serve as the pro-Nicene bishop of Laodicea. Together with his father, Apollinarius is reported to have transposed much of the Bible into classical verse, in reaction to Emperor Julian's prohibition of Christians teaching classical literature.

Written probably between 358 and 362, Apollinarius's major extant work, the *Detailed Confession of the Faith*, begins with an antihomoian statement of faith and then proceeds to argue chiefly against the doctrine of Marcellus of Ancyra. Apollinarius reflects both the position of Athanasius—his Christology is in several respects a fuller expression of Athanasius's, including his infamous denial of Christ's human mind—and that of Eusebius, a combination that makes him a particularly important figure in the development of fourth-century pro-Nicene traditions.

Apollinarius's main theological position, which he defined before his knowledge of Diodore's work, centers around the confession that Jesus Christ is the divine Son of God, and that he is able to save human beings and is worthy of worship only because he is the eternal Son dwelling in human flesh (*Conf.Faith* 1, 6, 12). Apollinarius thus argues both that Christ is fully divine (similar to Athanasius and Eusebius) and that he is a distinct entity (*prosopon* or hypostasis) from God the Father (here following

Eusebius). Apollinarius also maintains a clear distinction between the human and divine properties in Christ, as Athanasius had, such that human properties cannot be literally predicated of the Divinity.

Yet, at the same time, Apollinarius conceives of the union between Christ's humanity and divinity more tightly than Athanasius dared to (*Conf.Faith* 3; *Union* 11), and herein lies the main structural principle of his Christology. Using a phrase that he may have found in Irenaeus, Apollinarius emphasizes that Christ is "one and the same" Son of God, both before and after the incarnation (*Conf.Faith* 36; *Frag.* 42); in other words, Jesus is the same divine Son who has always existed and through whom the world was created. Apollinarius also uses the language of mixture and unity in a new way in order to describe the relationship between the Word and its human flesh: in Christ, God and human existence are "mixed" with one another (*Frag.* 10, 93), and human flesh is united with the Word, so that they exist in "union" (ἕνωσις) with one another in the incarnation (*Union* 5, 11; *Ep.Dion.* 1.9). These terms may derive from a passage in Origen's *Against Celsus* (3.41) in addition to currents of Stoic and Neoplatonic philosophy, yet Apollinarius applies them to Christ with new emphasis among fourth-century writers.

Apollinarius's explanation of Christ's unity and identity as the Son of God is in one sense fairly simple. Like Athanasius, Apollinarius believes that the Word occupies the place of Jesus's human mind or soul (*Conf.Faith* 2; *Union* 12; *Frag.* 19).[10] Jesus Christ is the Word of God living out a human life in human clothing, as it were. In this respect Apollinarius clarifies and completes Athanasius's Christology—although he goes well beyond Athanasius's Trinitarian theology. This is the belief for which Apollinarius is infamous, and it is what later heresiologists and modern theologians mean when they refer to "Apollinarian" Christology: the view that Christ lacks a human mind. In addition, Apollinarius makes a technical qualification that will be important in later discussions. Because the Word serves the function of Jesus's mind, Apollinarius argues that Christ possesses only one, divine nature. The Word is the only acting subject in Jesus, and the flesh is a merely passive instrument (*Union* 7, 9; *Frag.* 38, 108–9, 117, 127). Yet this does not mean that Christ is made up only of divinity—the Word and human flesh remain distinct—but that the divine Word is Christ's primary identity even in his fleshly form. Consequently, all biblical references to Christ refer to the divine Son, and in the incarnation to the "whole Christ."[11] The unity of Christ can therefore be compared with a human soul and body, which are distinct yet combine to form one being.[12] However, despite later accusations to this effect, Apollinarius does not appear to have held that Christ's human flesh preexisted the incarnation.[13]

The Word-plus-flesh model serves several key purposes for Apollinarius. First of all, it easily explains the divine aspects of Jesus's life, such as his virgin birth, miracles, and resurrection, which can be understood as simply the direct, natural acts of the Word of God.[14] It also ensures that the Christian worship of Jesus is the worship of God and not of a creature, which would be idolatry, since Jesus simply *is* the Word of God with flesh and bones (*Conf.Faith* 31; *Frag.* 9, 85). Moreover, in order to save us, Christ must be God in his most fundamental identity, not God plus a distinct human being, which is a position that Apollinarius rightly regards as integral to the modalist doctrine of Marcellus and Photinus (*Conf.Faith* 28–30) and later Diodore. Apollinarius recognizes that this makes Jesus very different from us: he is not in fact a complete human being, possessing a human mind, soul, and body (*Frag.* 9, 42), but he merely came "in human likeness," as Paul writes (Phil 2:7). In one fragment Apollinarius uses the language of Nicaea to explain the situation: just as we are both consubstantial with irrational animals in the flesh and not consubstantial with them in our minds, so too Christ is consubstantial with us in our flesh and not consubstantial with us as the Word of God (*Frag.* 126).

In another sense, however, the structure of Christ's person fits perfectly well with both Apollinarius's general understanding of human existence and his theory of salvation. In his view, a human being is by definition an incarnate mind, or a union of mind and flesh (*Frag.* 69–72). In order for God truly to become human and dwell among us—rather than merely enlightening or inspiring an independently existing human being, which has occurred many other times—the Word itself must be the mind of a human being. In one place he writes, "If there were also a human intellect together with God, who is intellect, then the incarnation would not be accomplished" (*Frag.* 74). In the second place, Apollinarius argues that, even if it were possible for God to become incarnate together with a human mind, the presence of the divine Word would violate Jesus's self-determination and obliterate his human mind (*Frag.* 42, 87). It is therefore necessary for anthropological reasons that the Word assume only human flesh in the incarnation.

This model also justifies Apollinarius's understanding of human sin and salvation. In his view, it is the very nature of our fallen condition that our sinful flesh wields control over our minds, and the domination of passions of the flesh over the mind is the definition of sin. When we were powerless to control the appetites of the flesh, God sent his Son to provide a divine intellect, which alone is powerful enough to dominate the wayward flesh and thus to destroy sin in it, which Christ completed on the cross (*Frag.* 74, 76; *Conf.Faith* 2). Through faith and the imitation of Christ, Christians likewise conquer sin in the flesh by means of their minds (*Frag.* 74; *Conf.Faith* 2, 31). In order to accomplish salvation, Christ therefore is like us, and even "a human being" in the most important sense that he contains the same structural parts that we all share: intellect, soul, and flesh (*Frag.* 91). Yet Apollinarius issues the same qualification that Athanasius did: in order for the Word to conquer sin in the flesh, it is essential that it not be involved in the sufferings of the flesh (*Conf.Faith* 11, 30; *Union* 6, 8; *Frag.* 93, 117).

Apollinarius's Christology is thus a combination of Athanasian Christological structure and pro-Nicene commitment lodged within a broader, Eusebian Trinitarian theology, which opposes both the modalism and the Christological dualism of Marcellus. When Apollinarius came into contact with Diodore's Christology, possibly as late as the 370s, he found much the same problem that he had encountered in Marcellus.

We know even less of Diodore's early career than we do of Apollinarius's. He appears to have undertaken an ascetic lifestyle as a young man, in the company of his friend Flavian in Antioch. He may have studied in Athens, and he proved himself to be well trained in rhetoric.[15] Diodore first appears on the scene with any clarity as a presbyter of Bishop Meletius of Antioch in the 360s. He was clearly regarded as a leading member of Meletius's church, for he and Flavian assumed pastoral leadership of the community when Meletius was exiled during the years 365–366 and 371–378. At least once, in 372, Diodore too was expelled from Antioch, during which time he joined Meletius in Armenia, where he made a favorable impression on Basil of Caesarea.[16] While still a presbyter, Diodore worked as a Christian teacher of some sort, and it was in this capacity that he initiated a discernable tradition of Antiochene biblical exegesis and theology. Among his pupils were Theodore, future bishop of Mopsuestia, and John Chrysostom.

In 378 Diodore was made bishop of Tarsus, the hometown of St. Paul on the Cilician coast about 140 miles west of Antioch. In 379 he attended a council of bishops in Antioch which aimed to signal to the new emperor, Theodosius, that he should take his religious policy in a more fully

Trinitarian direction. The council received a collection of documents from Damasus of Rome and a series of Italian synods, which sought to establish doctrinal agreement and therefore communion between the two churches; Damasus had already exchanged letters with the rival pro-Nicene community of Paulinus in Antioch (*Ex.Syn.*). Among its other business, the council appointed Gregory of Nazianzus to travel to Constantinople in order to combat the problem of Apollinarian Christology, a commission that certainly bears the stamp of Diodore's theological agenda. Diodore played a major role in the events surrounding the great Council of Constantinople in 381, which was initially chaired by Bishop Meletius. When Meletius died, Diodore naturally would have been one of the chief spokesmen for the Meletian network. At this point he seems to have played a leading role in inciting discord over the appointment of Meletius's successor as bishop of Antioch. Although Meletius and Paulinus had agreed that whoever survived the other should become the sole bishop of the city (notwithstanding the rivals Eudoxius and now Vitalis, who had been ordained bishop by Apollinarius),[17] Diodore pressed for the candidacy of his friend Flavian. Gregory Nazianzen, now bishop of Constantinople and a crucial witness to these events, protested that the prior arrangement was not being honored. Yet Diodore prevailed nevertheless, and the council elected Flavian; Diodore later traveled to Antioch to help consecrate his friend bishop of the city. In response to Diodore's actions, among other things, Gregory resigned his presidency of the council, and a Roman synod in 382 excommunicated Diodore and recognized instead Paulinus as bishop (Theodoret, *H.E.* 5.23).[18] Yet the council of 381 condemned Apollinarius, Diodore's Christological rival. We can perceive Diodore's influence at the council and in the new religious establishment, finally, by his appointment as one of the arbiters of the orthodox faith in the new Theodosian legislation (*Cod.Th.* 16.1.3).

Despite the contemporary judgment of his orthodoxy by the council, we possess fewer writings by Diodore than we do by Apollinarius, thanks to the condemnation of Theodore of Mopsuestia and the disparagement of his teacher, Diodore, in the fifth century. Diodore's Christological works exist now only in fragments quoted in the works of later theologians and collections of sayings.[19] Most of the extant fragments show Diodore already in debate with Apollinarius, which most likely did not occur until the 370s, when Apollinarius became active in the Antiochene church and eventually attracted the opposition of the current leaders. Diodore's most pronounced disagreement with Apollinarius concerns the relationship of the Word of God with Jesus's human existence.

The central principle of Diodore's Christology is that the divine Word of God and the human Jesus are two distinct subjects or beings, and they must not be mingled or confused with one another. Jesus is clearly distinct from the Word; he is neither the Word present in human form, nor human existence literally or essentially united with the Word, as Apollinarius alleged. The human being Jesus of Nazareth is from the seed of Abraham and David (see Rom 1:3) and is human in his nature and being (*ousia*) (SD 3, 6, 11); whereas the divine Son is naturally begotten of God the Father and shares his being (SD 10–13). Jesus and the Son of God are therefore different in nature from one another, and each one is a perfect and complete entity: full God and a full human being (SD 5, 8). In reply to Apollinarius, then, Diodore strongly insists that the Word did not "unite" or "mingle" with human flesh, but rather "indwelt" the man Jesus as in a temple (BD 20; SD 4). Christ is the Son of God by grace, not by essence, nature, or union.[20]

Diodore's dual view of Christ is clearest in his interpretation of biblical passages that refer to him. His consistent pattern is to interpret such statements as referring either to the divine Son or to the human Jesus, but not to both. Paul's statement that "the Lord of glory was crucified" (1 Cor 2:8) and Jesus's cry of abandonment at Gethsemane (Matt 26:39) do not refer to the divine Word, but to the seed of David, while Jesus's statements that the Son of Man "descended from heaven" (John 3:13) and the one from Abraham is "before Abraham" (John 8:58) do not refer to the human Jesus but only to the eternal Son (BD 17–18, 24). At times Diodore goes to extreme lengths to explain that the biblical text does not mean what it appears to say. He argues, for example, that the risen Jesus did not really pass through the wall of the upper room when he appeared to the disciples, but snuck in through the door when they were not looking (BD 9–10)! Diodore applies this interpretive method with great consistency, and he is insistent that the divine and human subjects must not be confused with one another.[21]

It is not correct, therefore, to say, as Apollinarius does, that "one and the same" figure does both divine and human things (BD 2, 26; SD 10); Diodore wants to avoid any suggestion that only one being is the subject of Jesus's divine and human acts. For Diodore, Christ must be conceived as two subjects. In one fragment preserved only in Syriac, he writes that Christ is "one and another" (BD 2). The Greek original of this phrase may well be ἄλλος καὶ ἄλλος,[22] or possibly ἕτερος καὶ ἕτερος, which would make for a sharp contrast with the doctrine of Gregory Nazianzen and subsequent church councils, as we shall see. Diodore likewise rejects Apollinarius's comparison of Christ with the union of a human body and soul, partly on the grounds that a human soul does not rule without the body as the Word does, and partly because the comparison suggests that Christ is somehow composite, which Diodore also opposes (BD 2, 7, 26). Again, Diodore argues that Mary did not give birth to the Word (in any form), but to the temple of the Word, and that the Word did not have two births, but only one, from God the Father (BD 19). Mary is therefore not to be called "Theotokos," or Mother of God, except by a kind of distant, verbal extension (SD 2); rather, she should be called "Anthropotokos," since she was merely the mother of the human being Jesus (BD 1, 22).

In his debate with Apollinarius, Diodore denies that he views Christ as merely a prophet, since the Word filled Jesus with glory and wisdom permanently, rather than only temporarily, as in the prophets (SD 1–2). Likewise, he denies the accusation that he teaches two sons or a double worship (SD 6; BD 30). Nevertheless, it is difficult to reconcile these claims with his exegesis and other arguments. Some modern scholars have seen in Diodore and the subsequent Antiochene school of Christology an image of themselves, namely, someone interested in upholding the full humanity of Jesus against overly divinizing views or high Christologies. Yet this is not Diodore's agenda in his arguments against Apollinarius. More central is his concern to maintain the immutability and impassibility of the Word, which Apollinarius's language of union and mixture and his single-subject biblical interpretation seems to threaten (BD 19–20, 26; SD 2, 11). In sum, Diodore aims to preserve the distinction between two subjects in Christ, one divine and one human, in order to preserve the impassibility of the Word. Although he shows certain affinities with Origen and Athanasius in his concern for divine impassibility and his dualist exegesis, these may be due to similar philosophical interests rather than to direct borrowing.

GREGORY OF NAZIANZUS

The Christology that Gregory Nazianzen articulated in reaction to the homoian and the Antiochene debates remains one of the great theological achievements of early Christian tradition. In the period we are examining, Gregory is the first theologian to produce a lasting Christological synthesis after Origen. Among his many theological and humanistic projects, he is best known for his overall teaching on the Trinity. On account of his definitive articulation of Trinitarian orthodoxy, Gregory was accorded the title "the Theologian" by the Council of Chalcedon in 451, a title that he shares only with St. John the Divine and St. Simeon the New Theologian, who was being compared to Gregory. Gregory remains today one of the three "universal teachers" of Eastern Orthodoxy, along with Basil and John Chrysostom. In the fifth century Gregory became the main teacher of Cyril of Alexandria, providing the bulk of Cyril's Christological framework.[23]

Gregory's career was framed by both the homoian and the Antiochene Christological debates. He began his ordained ministry in 362 in order to assist his father, the local bishop, in a struggle over the homoian doctrine promulgated by the Council of Constantinople in 360. For the next ten years or so, Gregory sought to articulate the divinity of Christ and a full doctrine of the Trinity in clear and strong terms as the basis of the church's faith and life. In this endeavor he often worked closely with Basil, who produced the formal treatise *Against Eunomius* in the mid-360s. Following a period of retirement, Gregory later resumed his labors in Cappadocia and, after 379, in the capital, where he sought to consolidate various groups around the faith in the Trinity against the prevailing homoian orthodoxy. The Eunomians are the ostensive polemical opponents in Gregory's famous *Theological Orations*, which he delivered in the summer of 380.

Yet the major phase of Gregory's theological career, from 379 to 384, was in a more immediate sense determined by the Christological debate between Apollinarius and Diodore. The synod of 379 that gathered in Antioch under the presidency of the homoiousian bishop Meletius, which Diodore and Gregory of Nyssa attended, appointed Gregory Nazianzen to serve as bishop in Constantinople. The Antiochene synod commissioned Gregory with the specific responsibility of opposing the growing threat of Apollinarian Christology in the capital (*De vita sua* 607–31).[24] When Gregory reached the capital, however, he did not follow the orders he had been given. Rather than defending the Antiochene Christology of Diodore against Apollinarius, Gregory first noted the errors in both positions, hinting that the Antiochene view was on the whole the worse option of the two (*Or.* 22.4, 13); he then concentrated instead on the homoian situation, which he regarded as the more pressing concern.

At a deeper level, however, Gregory responded to all three opponents with essentially the same Christology. Although many students have been taught that Gregory's late Christological epistles, from 383 to 384

(*Ep.* 101–2, 202), are the key expression of his Christology, the main elements of his doctrine are in fact to be found throughout his mature works, from 379 onward. Four texts in particular provide key accounts of his Christology, three from the Constantinopolitan period, in addition to the late epistles:

1. *Orations* 29.18–30.21 (the third and fourth *Theological Orations*)
2. *Oration* 37.1–4
3. *Orations* 38–40, the Epiphany sermons of 381
4. *Letters* 101–2 *to Cledonius* and *Letter* 202 *to Nectarius*, the famous Christological epistles[25]

The Incarnation of the Son of God

The central principle and ultimate focus of Gregory's Christology is the union of God and human existence in the person of Jesus. The unity of Christ lies at the heart of Gregory's understanding of the Christian life as a whole, and it forms the basis of his polemical arguments against all three of his major Christological opponents: Eunomius, Diodore, and Apollinarius. As was the case for Eusebius, the confession, or "theologizing," of Christ's identity as the Son of God is the key to the knowledge of God and of all creaturely life, and in several respects Gregory's Christology is synonymous with his understanding of salvation and Christian spirituality.

A key statement from Gregory's third *Theological Oration* bears quoting at length, since it expresses several of the basic motifs of his Christology. Here Gregory is directly addressing the Eunomians, who denied that Christ is as divine as God the Father, yet he also has Diodore and Apollinarius in view:

> The one whom you now scorn was once above you. The one who is now human was at one time not composite [ἀσύνθετος]. What he was, he continued to be; what he was not, he assumed. In the beginning he existed without cause, for what is the cause of God? But later he was born for a cause—namely that you might be saved. . . . He took upon himself your thickness, associating with flesh through the intermediary of a [human] mind, and being made a human being who is God on earth [γενόμενος ἄνθρωπος ὁ κάτω θεός], since [human existence] was blended [συνανεκράθη] with God and he was born as a single entity [εἷς], because the one who is

more powerful prevailed [over his assumed humanity], so that we
might be made divine just as he was made human. (*Or.* 29.19)

As this passage shows, Gregory views Christ's identity in dynamic, narrative terms; his divinity is not a static thing, but the agent of the drama of
salvation who unites with himself the fullness of human existence.

For Gregory, human existence—and indeed the entire cosmos—is a
direct reflection of God's superabundant being, goodness, and light (*Or.*
38.7, 9; 40.5). Yet among all God's works, human beings are the fullest
expression of God's wisdom and generosity, even above the angels (*Or.*
38.11). The nature of human existence, moreover, is to grow constantly in a
transforming participation in the divine nature, a process that Gregory
boldly calls "divinization" (*theosis*), a term that he coined himself.[26] The
process of divinization is both the rationale of our creation and the final
destiny for which we were created. As Gregory puts it, a human being is "a
living being cared for [οἰκονομεῖν] in this world, and later transferred to
another; and, the final stage of the mystery, made divine [θεοῦν] by its
inclination towards God" (*Or.* 38.11). The very nature of human existence,
in other words, is a dynamic movement toward God rooted in our creation
and oriented toward a future consummation. The term "divinization"—to
become godlike or divine—itself indicates the close connection between
the definition of human life and God's divine life, and it takes place
through divine illumination, ascent, and ultimately union with the Trinity
(*Or.* 2.1–2). At the same time, divinization is a process of human participation in God, so that the difference between the creator and creation is maintained and never violated, as the term may otherwise suggest. Divinization
is thus our natural, created condition, which reflects the goodness and the
grace of God. Gregory's notion of divinization became the main foundation
for the later Byzantine understanding of salvation through Pseudo-
Dionysius and Maximus Confessor.

In the fall of Adam and Eve, however, human beings turned away from
God and interrupted the divinizing process that is our true nature and destiny.
As a result, we are no longer growing toward union with God and will face
the ultimate separation at Christ's final judgment (*Or.* 38.12; 39.13; 40.45).[27]
The purpose and rationale of the incarnation, then, is to save us from our
condition of death and alienation and to restore the process of divinization.
For Gregory, divinization includes a broad range of concepts for salvation,
and it serves as the organizing principle for all of them (*Or.* 38.2–4). Christ is

thus the means of our restoration to our created nature and our final destiny, and the goal of human life is to become divine as a result of Christ's having become human.[28] As Gregory exclaims in his funeral oration for his brother, Caesarius, "I must be buried with Christ, rise with Christ, be a joint heir with Christ—become a son of God and be called God himself" (Or. 7.23). Yet Christ effects our divinization not merely as a work that he accomplishes, but in and through himself. Christ's own identity is therefore the center point and the chief instrument of salvation and human fulfillment.

Just as our condition is not static but dynamic, so too for Gregory Christ's identity is not a static thing, but a dynamic process that is best understood in the same narrative framework of the divine economy. Gregory's chief argument against Eunomius is that in order to save us and reconnect us with the divine life, Christ had to be fully divine himself; and Christ's divinity is itself the act of the divine Son of God within the economy. As Gregory writes in the passage quoted above, however lowly and humble Christ may appear in his earthly, human condition, before his incarnation he was purely the divine Son of God, transcending creation ("above" us) and unmixed with creaturely existence ("not composite"). Now, however, he has assumed into himself our created, human existence, a form of existence radically different from his own ("what he was not"), and became a composite being (ὁ σύνθετος) (Or. 29.18). While remaining the divine Son, he became also a complete human being, with human flesh and mind, so that Jesus is himself God dwelling on earth as a human being (Or. 29.19).[29] Similarly, in the opening of his First Letter to Cledonius, Gregory confesses that Christ is "one and the same God and Son, at first not human but alone and pre-eternal, unmixed with a body and all that belongs to the body, but finally a human being as well, assumed for our salvation, the same one passible in flesh, impassible in divinity" (Ep. 101.13–14).

The aim and result of the incarnation, then, is the union that Christ achieves between himself, as the divine Son of God, and fallen human existence. The unifying action of the divine Son represents the structure, the mechanism, and the entire purpose of the incarnation. Against the dualist Christology of Diodore, Gregory emphasizes that when the divine Son takes on human existence, he remains a single subject or entity; he does not become two things or two sons. Rather, what were formerly two things, God and human existence, have become one thing in Christ (Or. 37.2).[30] Even as God and human existence remain distinct realities (ἄλλο καὶ ἄλλο), they became "one thing" (ἕν) when the divine Son became human, and the only-begotten Son continues to exist as a single subject of existence (ἄλλος), just as he always has been (*Ep.* 101.20–21).

Gregory defines the union of God and humanity in Christ in various ways, including the same term "union" (ἕνωσις) that Apollinarius and even Origen had used (*Ep.* 101.30). Just as frequently he speaks of the "mixture" (μίξις) and "blending" (κρᾶσις) of divinity and humanity in Christ,[31] terms that also appear in both Origen and Apollinarius. The language of mixture will eventually be prohibited by the Council of Chalcedon, on the prompting of Antiochene representatives, much as Diodore had opposed it in Apollinarius's work. Yet for Gregory such terms helpfully convey the dynamic unifying movement of the incarnation and the mysteriously intimate union of God with humanity in Christ. Similarly, Gregory indicates that in the incarnation the Son of God is now "composite." Each of these terms is significant in asserting that Christ is in fact a single entity, the divine Son of God made flesh, rather than two sons, as Diodore held. Moreover, only by being composite can the Son of God suffer the things of the flesh (*Vita* 638–41). Where Antiochene theologians like Diodore are concerned to protect the integrity and impassibility of the divine nature, Gregory confesses their marvelous and saving union in Christ, and he argues that any lesser notion is insufficient (*Or.* 6.38–41; 37.2).

One of Gregory's most telling expressions is the statement that Christ is "one and the same" Son of God both before and in the incarnation. He writes to Cledonius, "We teach one and the same God and Son," who was at first only the divine Son, but at a later time also became a human being, "so that by the same one, who is a complete human being and also God, all of humanity, which had fallen under sin, might be created anew" (*Ep.* 101.13–15). Here Gregory adopts a unitive phrase from his native Eusebian tradition, which appears also in Apollinarius, as we have seen, in a way that is unique among his Cappadocian contemporaries as well as Athanasius.[32] Likewise, he accepts Apollinarius's comparison of a human soul and body: like a human being, God and human existence are originally different natures that now exist in "one and the same" Son of God, and the two things are one entity (ἕν) on account of their mingling (*Ep.* 101.18–21). However, since Gregory believes that Christ possesses a human mind, he alters the comparison from a literal image (the Word is soul to Christ's human body) to a metaphorical comparison (the divine Son is united with Christ's full humanity in a way similar to the union of a human soul and body).

Finally, Gregory also tends to speak of Christ as possessing one divine nature, a choice that will have enormous repercussions in later centuries.[33] Gregory's preference for single-nature expressions reflects the crucial asymmetry that exists between God and humanity in Christ. Because the nature of the divine Son is radically transcendent of creation, the composition of divinity and humanity is not like a mixture of two similar types of things, like different ingredients in a food recipe, which the common term "natures" could suggest. Gregory's practice of speaking of Christ's one divine nature also emphasizes that Christ is fundamentally divine—he is "God made visible" to those who are able to perceive his true identity (*Or.* 30.20); and it reinforces the idea that Christ never exists as a human being independent of the life of the divine Son. While it is also possible to speak of Christ as possessing two natures, in Gregory's view it is less desirable. When Gregory does speak of Christ's two natures, it is almost always to express the two different things *from which* Christ is composed, after which he has become "one thing" (*Or.* 37.2). Otherwise, the distinction between two natures in the incarnate Christ is possible only through human abstraction, like differentiating a human soul from its body (*Or.* 30.8). The confession that Christ possesses a single, divine nature expresses his most fundamental identity, and in doing so it reiterates the basic rationale and saving purpose of the incarnation: the divine Son's union and mixture of fallen human existence within his eternal, divine life in order to heal and save it.

Christ's singular identity can be truly expressed only in deeply paradoxical assertions: the one who is uncontained now moves from place to place; the one who exists beyond time has come to exist within time; and the invisible one has now become visible (*Or.* 37.1–3). Nevertheless, Gregory's notion of the singular identity of Christ reflects the traditional rule of faith and most of the fourth-century creeds, including those of Nicaea in 325, Antioch in 341, and Constantinople in 381.[34]

Biblical Interpretation

In a famous sentence, Gregory describes Christ's unity in terms that have entered into the standard vocabulary of systematic theology: "Just as the natures are blended and flow into [περιχωρουσῶν] one another, so too do his [divine and human] titles, according to the principle of their natural union [συμφυΐα]" (*Ep.* 101.31). Although Pseudo-Cyril and John of Damascus will later apply the same term *perichoresis* to the relationships among the three persons of the Trinity,[35] Gregory instead emphasizes the difference between the intra-Trinitarian relations and the union of God and humanity in the incarnation (*Ep.* 101.20–21). With reference to Christ, Gregory uses terms of mixture and interpenetration (or commingling, *perichoresis*) to denote the mysteriously intimate relationship between the Son and his human existence, as well as to signal how biblical statements about Christ should be interpreted. The cross-referencing of divine and human statements about Christ in Scripture is not a merely verbal convention—and certainly not something that needs to be explained away—but rather a realistic indication of who Christ is. For Gregory, the *communicatio idiomatum* is true at the level of Christ's being. He explains further: the divine Son did not merely operate (*energein*) in Christ by grace, as in a prophet, but he "was and is joined together [with human existence] in his being [κατ' οὐσίαν συνάπτειν]" (*Ep.* 101.22).[36] In these terms "natural union" and "union in being," Gregory makes a powerful and crucial assertion of the reality of Christ's unity, on which his saving work entirely depends—or rather, which *is* his saving work. The Son of God has united to himself human existence, taking on our sin and death, in the deepest sense possible, in his divine nature.

Gregory's understanding of the unity of Christ thus reflects a particular method of biblical interpretation. Just before the passage quoted above from the third *Theological Oration*, Gregory explains how best to interpret the many different statements about Christ in Scripture: "Apply the loftier passages to his Divinity, to the nature that is superior to passivities and the body; and apply the lowlier passages to the composite [Lord], to the one who for your sake emptied himself and became flesh and, to say it just as well, was made human, and afterwards was also exalted" (*Or.* 29.18). The key to interpreting both humble and exalted references to Christ is to understand that both kinds refer to the same Son of God, only in different ways. Lofty, or divine, statements refer to the Son in his proper, divine nature (his divinity)—both apart from and in the incarnation, since the incarnate Christ remains divine—while lowly, or human, statements refer to the Son inasmuch as he is composite, or incarnate, that is, to Christ's "economy," as Gregory says a few lines below. Passages such as "In the beginning was the Word, and the Word was with God, and the Word was God" (John 1:1), or the titles "only-begotten Son" (John 1:18), "light" (John 8:12), "Wisdom," "power" (1 Cor 1:24), and "image of goodness" (Wis 7:26), convey Christ's identity as the divine Son of God and his eternal relationship with God the Father; whereas human expressions such as "slave" (Phil 2:7) and "he wept"

(John 11:35), and especially the story of his death on the cross, refer to the Son's human existence as Jesus of Nazareth.[37]

This rule of interpretation provides for the knowledge of Christ's divinity and humanity, as well as the union of the two natures in "one and the same" Son of God. Against the Eunomians, Gregory asserts that the lowly statements of Scripture do not contradict Christ's divinity, since they are spoken on account of his human existence in the incarnation. Against Diodore, the human statements do not refer to a separately existing human being, or even to Christ's humanity per se, but to the one divine Son in his human form, without threatening the divine nature. And against Apollinarius, these human statements indicate human mental activity as an expression of Christ's divinity, again without contradiction. Gregory's method of biblical interpretation preserves the unity of Christ at the same time that it distinguishes between the two different sorts of statements that apply to him.[38]

Gregory demonstrates his practice of unitive Christological exegesis in one of the most beautiful passages in early Christian literature. With rhythmic rhetoric and overtones of liturgical prayer, he recites a litany of seemingly contrary acts of the one Son of God:

> He was begotten, but he was also born of a woman. . . . He was wrapped in swaddling bands, but he took off the swaddling bands of the grave by rising again. . . . He is baptized as a human being, but he remitted sins as God. . . . He hungered, but he fed thousands. . . . He thirsted, but he cried out, 'If anyone is thirsty, let him come to me and drink.' . . . He prays, but he hears prayer. He weeps, but he makes weeping to cease. . . . As a sheep he is led to the slaughter, but he is the shepherd of Israel. . . . He lays down his life, but he has power to take it up again. . . . He dies, but he gives life, and by death destroys death. He is buried, but he rises again. (*Or.* 29.19–20).

In each case "one and the same" Son of God accomplishes both divine and human things, as a single subject of existence.

Gregory employs this method with great consistency throughout his works, usually in nontechnical ways. Often he speaks simply of "Christ" being and doing a host of human and divine things, both apart from and within the incarnation. For example, "Christ became like us. . . . He descended so that we might be exalted. . . . He ascended, so that he might draw us to himself" (*Or.* 1.5). Again, it is "Jesus" who created us and became human to save us; "Jesus" was "in the beginning with God and was God" (John 1:1); and "Christ" does miracles in both the Old and New Testaments (*Or.* 14.2; 37.2; 24.10).[39] The same Christ exists before the incarnation, becomes human to save us, and continues to call us as the risen Lord. Even more telling, however, are the reverse expressions, where Gregory speaks of the divine Son of God as the real, underlying subject of all of Jesus's human acts: "the One who is [ὁ ὤν, Exod 3:14] has come to be, the uncreated One is created, the uncontained One is contained" (*Or.* 38.13). The great mystery of the incarnation and the reason why the human Jesus can be described as the creator of the world is that he is in fact the Son of God. When making such deeply paradoxical statements, Gregory normally feels no need to differentiate constantly between Christ's divinity and his human form.

The Suffering of God

The most obviously paradoxical statements about Christ concern his suffering and death, and here we come to the heart of Gregory's Christology. For Gregory, the focus and climax of Christ's saving work is the cross. The whole purpose of the divine Son's incarnation was so that he could undergo a human death in order to save us. A key test case for how to understand Christ's suffering is Jesus's agony in the Garden of Gethsemane and his cry of abandonment from the cross: "My God, my God, look upon me, why have you forsaken me?" (Ps 21:1, LXX). Gregory strongly opposes the view that God truly abandoned Christ in his suffering and death—probably referring to Diodore: in such a case there would clearly be two different acting subjects. On the contrary, Gregory writes, Jesus's cry does not show God's abandonment of him—as if God were afraid of suffering—but rather his incorporation of Christ's human suffering into the divine life. This is the very heart of Christ's saving work, and his ultimate desolation shows just how fully the divine Son has assumed and represented our fallen condition, "making our thoughtlessness and waywardness his own" (*Or.* 30.5). The darkest hour of Jesus's suffering, in other words, does not indicate the absence of God, but God's inclusion of our abandonment within his saving embrace, and his healing presence in the midst of human desolation, despair, and ultimately death. Christ became human, Gregory maintains, to undergo our sin and death most of all—the suffering and alienation that the gospels display Jesus experiencing so vividly—so that the divine nature could destroy our sin and death as fire melts wax, through the union and intermingling of the incarnation (*Or.* 30.6).

At the same time, Gregory continues, these passages show that, in addition to having the divine will of the Son of God, Christ possesses a fully operating human will, and it is the process of human choice and self-determination as well that we see depicted in the gospel accounts of the passion (*Or.* 30.12). In this way, Gregory can confess that God has fully assumed fallen human existence, to the point that he even "submits" to human suffering and death (*Or.* 30.2). This assumption and submission presuppose that Christ possesses a complete human nature in every sense. In his *First Letter to Cledonius*, Gregory famously argues against Apollinarius that Christ possessed a human body, soul, and mind because we needed healing in all three, and that our mind needs healing above all, since it is the source of our sin, not our bodies (*Ep.* 101.50–55). In his understanding of salvation, Gregory differs considerably from Apollinarius (in his Athanasian dimension) and is instead closer to Origen. Borrowing a phrase from Origen, Gregory pronounces what has become a beloved saying among many Christian theologians to this day: "That which has not been assumed has not been healed, but that which is united to God is also being saved" (*Ep.* 101.32). Also following Origen, Gregory teaches that Christ's human mind acts as an intermediary between the divine Son and human flesh (*Or.* 29.19). Yet although it is justly famous, this passage is exceptional in Gregory's corpus, probably because he considers it obvious that Jesus is a complete human being, possessing normal mental capacities and limitations and operating with human self-determination, and he finds the denial of this basically absurd. His opinion on the matter is evident in the characteristically humorous dismissal, "Whoever hopes in a mindless person is mindless himself!" (*Ep.* 101.32).

With a full human nature in mind, then, Gregory announces in his first Christological statement in Constantinople that *God* was born for us, was nailed to the cross, was buried, and arose, the denial of which is Diodore's chief error (*Or.* 22.13).[40] Christ's human suffering shows the greatness of God's love for us, because in him God has died in order to forgive our sins (*Or.* 33.14). For Gregory, the central conviction of the Christian faith is that Christ is "God made passible for our sake against sin," and that we are "saved by the sufferings of the impassible one" (*Or.* 30.1, 5). To be sure, as God, the incarnate Son remains unconquerable; otherwise, he would be powerless to defeat death by dying (*Or.* 26.12; 45.13). Yet,

Gregory stresses again and again, paradoxical though it may seem, the effect of the Son's transcendent divine power is not to make him avoid creaturely suffering, but just the opposite: it leads him, out of love and goodness, to embrace our suffering and death to the very fullest. God therefore suffers for us an "impassible passion," as it were. Gregory describes the situation succinctly: "We needed an incarnate God, a God put to death, so that we might live, and we were put to death with him." Consequently, the great glory of the Christian faith is "to see *God* crucified" (*Or.* 45.28–29; 43.64). Only because Christ's death is the death of God can Christians be assured of their salvation; the death of a mere human being, however righteous, could not bring about such a result.

God Prevails

As Gregory indicates in several of the passages we have quoted, Christ is "one thing" because the divine Son (or the Divinity) "prevailed" over his assumed humanity. When he assumes human form, the Son of God blends it with his own divine nature and unites it to himself, taking on our finitude and mortality in such a way that he remains the divine Son and ultimately divinizes Christ's human existence through the resurrection (*Or.* 37.2). The unifying action of the incarnation is performed and made possible by the greater power of Christ's divinity compared with his humanity: "Both things are one entity by the mingling, since God has been 'in-humanized' and humanity 'divinized,' so to speak" (*Ep.* 101.21).

The nature of Christ's divinity has a further consequence for its relation to Christ's humanity. Because he is divine, Gregory argues, the Son is perfectly able to assume human existence without contradiction or threat to himself. It is this basic theological principle that Gregory brings to bear in his dispute with Apollinarius over the question of whether or not Jesus possessed a human mind. In Apollinarius's view, the Word cannot coexist with a human mind because they are mutually exclusive (*Ep.* 101.37). In response, Gregory challenges the assumption that the Word of God and a human mind are mutually exclusive in an ontological sense. For God, he argues, can coexist perfectly well with any creature, and one can even cite examples of two or more creatures that coexist with one another in the same space, such as a human soul and body. Christ's divinity and humanity can coexist with one another in their respective completeness or perfection with no trouble at all, since they are each of a different order of existence. Just as Moses can be a god to Pharaoh but the servant of God, so Christ's human mind can govern his body while also being subject to God, with no contradiction. On this point Gregory parts company with Origen and Athanasius as well, in that he does not regard the incarnation as an ontological problem. This will also be a major dividing line among later theologians.

Christ's basic identity, therefore, is his divinity. He is not a "lordly man," as the Apollinarians are reported to hold, but "our Lord and God." So too, he is not "a human being who is also God," but the "God-man" (*Ep.* 101.12; *Or.* 40.33), and Christians worship "a man-bearing God," not "God-bearing flesh" (*Ep.* 102.18–20). Gregory is insistent that the central, operative fact of Christ's identity is his divinity: "If I worshipped a creature, I would not be called a Christian. Why is Christianity precious? Is it not that Christ is God?" (*Or.* 37.17). The incarnation is above all the work of God, and Christ's identity as the "one and the same" Son of God who has assumed human existence is the central principle of Christian salvation and spirituality. Rooted in the unity and the divine identity of Christ, the salvation or divinization of all human beings is to ascend to God by means of the doctrine of Christ. Christology is therefore central to the Christian life as a whole. Through the knowledge of Christ as "God made visible," Christians are divinized and elevated through faith, being made God in response to the fact that Christ was made human (*Or.* 29.18–19).

THE COUNCIL OF CONSTANTINOPLE (381)

The so-called second ecumenical council produced what has remained the normative creedal definition of the faith ever since. It also bears a close relationship with the theology of Gregory Nazianzen, who served as its president for a time. When the Eastern emperor, Valens, was killed in the Battle of Adrianople in 378, the Western emperor, Gratian, invited the general Theodosius to take over leadership of the Roman army in the Balkans. Theodosius then became successor to Valens as Eastern emperor in 379. It is likely that the synod that met in Antioch in the same year—the same gathering that commissioned Gregory as bishop of Constantinople—had the intention of influencing the new emperor's religious policy. Theodosius finally entered his capital in November 380, and the following spring he called a council to meet in Constantinople in the summer of 381.[41] As with the Council of Nicaea, no official acts remain, nor do we possess more than a brief historical account written within sixty years of the meeting. Gregory Nazianzen's several references to the council and surrounding events are therefore our most important witness to what took place.

The meeting was initially composed of Eastern bishops drawn mainly from Asia Minor and the network of Meletius around Antioch. It was, in fact, largely the same group that attended the Antiochene synod of 379, and Meletius himself served as president. Its clear purpose was to solidify the ecclesiastical situation in the East at the beginning of Theodosius's reign. (Theodosius became sole emperor after the death of Western emperor Valentinian II in 392.) The council had three main items of business: to confirm Gregory as bishop of the imperial capital, to give a further definition of the faith (reaffirming Nicaea), and, as an extension of the second item, to reconcile with the fully Trinitarian movement certain bishops who opposed the full divinity of the Holy Spirit. Soon after Gregory's confirmation, however, Meletius died, leaving Gregory in charge of a meeting that soon threatened to come apart.

Early on the council was beset by strife among the Antiochene factions, which was sparked into flame by the question of Meletius's successor and fueled by the large number of bishops associated with the Antiochene church, from both Meletius's and Paulinius's networks. The Antiochene schism carried with it as well some old East-West tension, since Meletius (of the old Eusebian tradition) had the support of most of the bishops in Asia Minor, including Gregory in Constantinople, and Paulinus (of the old anti-Eusebian, Eustathian tradition) enjoyed the support of Alexandria—and both were now in communion with Damasus of Rome. Despite Gregory's efforts to broker a settlement between the rival groups, conflict broke out nevertheless, spurred on in large measure, it seems, by Diodore of Tarsus. When representatives from the church in Egypt arrived later at Theodosius's behest, in order to bring some order to the meeting, the further divisions that ensued proved insurmountable, and Gregory eventually retired in exasperation.

In its doctrinal work, the council produced a formal creed as well as a longer explanation (a *Tomos*) that we no longer possess (Theodoret, *H.E.* 5.9), together with four canons. The creed reads as follows:[42]

> We believe in one God the Father Almighty,
>   maker of heaven and earth, of all things visible and invisible;
> And in one Lord Jesus Christ, the only-begotten Son of God,
>   who was begotten from the Father before all the ages,

light from light, true God from true God,
begotten, not made, of one being with the Father,
through whom all things came to be,
who for us humans beings and for our salvation
    came down from the heavens
    and was incarnate from the Holy Spirit and the Virgin Mary
    and was made a human being;
he was crucified for us under Pontius Pilate,
    and suffered and was buried,
    and rose again on the third day according to the Scriptures,
    and ascended into the heavens,
    and is seated at the right hand of the Father,
    and is coming again with glory to judge the living and the dead,
    whose kingdom will have no end;
And in the Holy Spirit, the Lord and giver of life,
    who proceeds from the Father,
    who with the Father and the Son is worshiped and glorified,
    who spoke through the prophets;
    [and] in one holy catholic and apostolic church.
    We confess one baptism for the forgiveness of sins.
    We look forward to the resurrection of the dead
    and the life of the world to come.
Amen.

Several observations are pertinent to our study. First, the creed names the one God primarily as the Father—in whose being and life the Son and (possibly) the Holy Spirit may share, but not in a way that controverts the Father's priority in the divine unity. In this respect the Creed of Constantinople directly reflects the doctrine we find in Gregory, in which the Trinity as a whole is anchored in the existence and generating work of God the Father.

Second, the creed professes belief in Jesus Christ. Here two points stand out. First, the creed confesses Jesus to be "one," the term that Origen had often used to indicate the distinct subsistence of each of the three persons of the Trinity; only now it is applied to Jesus (as in the Creed of Nicaea as well), not initially to the divine Son, pure and simple. That Jesus is "Lord" is one of the very earliest Christian confessions (see 1 Cor 12:3), and the phrase does not specify anything technical about his identity here; similarly, calling him "Jesus Christ" is also so ubiquitous as to be noncommittal. The first key point about the confession of Christ, then, is that the Lord Jesus is one: there is only one Christ, considering and including everything else that is confessed in the remainder of this article of the creed. The second point that stands out is that the creed immediately identifies the one Lord Jesus Christ as the Son of God. The order of the names here is significant: Jesus is the basic object of belief ("we believe in one Lord Jesus Christ"), and this Jesus is confessed to be the Son of God, who is and did the following things described of him. The creed does not begin with belief in the divine Son of God, who then becomes human and is known as Jesus; it begins as the disciples did, with the earthly Jesus, and confesses him to be the divine Son. Here we have a process of "theologizing the divine economy" very similar to that which we saw in both Eusebius and Gregory.

The third significant aspect of the creed is that the second article—everything from "And in one Lord Jesus Christ" to "there will be no end"—is a single sentence made up of a string of verbs, all of which are spoken of the one Christ. The entire article, in other words, refers to the same subject, who is "Jesus Christ, the Son of God"; in grammatical terms, the Greek sentence, with its clean, simple syntax, makes a statement of identity through an appositive construction. Taking the second and third aspects together, then, everything that follows this opening phrase defines Jesus as the Son of God who preexisted from and with God the Father, sharing the same divine being, and who became human to save human beings, was crucified, rose, and will come again as judge. At no point is an additional subject introduced in order to differentiate between divine and human qualities or acts. It is the same "Jesus Christ, the Son of God," who is both eternally begotten of God the Father and who died on the cross for our redemption.

Fourth, the creed has more to say about the Holy Spirit than the Creed of Nicaea did. The meaning of the third article, however, was a point of sore contention at the council. Gregory Nazianzen urged the bishops to confess the Spirit's divinity in the fullest possible terms, by calling it "God" and/or "of one being with the Father," as the second article does of the Son. It appears that the council equivocated on this point under pressure to make room for the Pneumatomachians, for whom the confession of the Spirit's full divinity may have sounded modalist.[43] Nevertheless the creed had typically been read as a fully Trinitarian statement virtually since it was promulgated. A synod held the following year in Constantinople interpreted it in this way (Theodoret, *H.E.* 5.9), a fact that suggests the overall success of Gregory Nazianzen's mission in the capital.

Two additional elements of the creed, which are marked differences from Nicaea, deserve brief mention. First, the council added the phrase "whose kingdom shall have no end" (see Luke 1:33), which had by now become a stock refutation of Marcellus of Ancyra's idea (in light of 1 Cor 15:28) that the kingdom of the incarnate Christ would one day come to an end. In addition, the creed lacks the phrase that the Son was begotten "out of the being of the Father," which was the second of the two appearances of the term *ousia* in the original Nicene Creed. Athanasius had made extensive use of this phrase in his anti-Arian arguments, so its absence from the Creed of Constantinople is striking. These two details are further indications of the Eusebian theological tradition that had formed the majority group of bishops originally in attendance (before the arrival of the Egyptians), namely, the formerly "homoiousian" network associated with Meletius, which was so distinct from that of Athanasius. If the faith of Nicaea in 325 was (by later construction) largely that of Athanasius, the faith of Constantinople in 381 can be said primarily to represent Cappadocian and Antiochene theologians such as Meletius of Antioch, Basil of Caesarea, and Gregory of Nazianzus. Finally, the council reaffirmed the faith of Nicaea and denounced as heretics the Eunomians, Eudoxians, Pneumatomachians, Sabellians, Marcellans, Photinians, and Apollinarians (Canon 1).

In addition to its doctrinal work, the council brought about an ironic situation of church politics, which had a great effect on later developments and even runs against the grain of its doctrine. Following in the wake of Meletius's death, the disputes over the Antiochene succession, the Egyptians' attack on Gregory, and Gregory's retirement, the council resulted in a clear victory for the new Antiochene contingent associated with Diodore of Tarsus; meanwhile, Apollinarius stood officially condemned.

Soon after the meetings ended, Theodosius named the following bishops as official arbiters of the catholic faith: Nectarius of Constantinople, Timothy of Alexandria (the order making clear the new priority of Constantinople in the East), Pelagius of Laodicea and Diodore of Tarsus (from the diocese of Oriens), Amphilochius of Iconium and Optimus of Pisidian Antioch (in Asia), and Helladius of Caesarea, Gregory of Nyssa, Terennius of Scythis, and Marmarius of Marcianopolis (in Pontus).[44] Given that Nectarius was Diodore's appointee and that Gregory of Nyssa's

Christology, as we shall see, bore the Antiochene stamp more than any other, the council amounted to a major ratification of Antiochene ecclesiastical power. Since the council made Constantinople the chief see of the Eastern empire, this meant that the Antiochenes now controlled two of the three leading sees, and in doing so endorsed one side of the Christological dispute between Diodore and Apollinarius. The considered response that Gregory Nazianzen made to both Diodore and Apollinarius lay dormant in his literary remains, as a resource that would be called up several decades later, at the Council of Ephesus in 431, and reintroduced into later patristic tradition by the likes of Cyril of Alexandria. Once Gregory's Christology was recovered and championed by Cyril, the Antiochene dominance ratified in 381 proved unsustainable.

GREGORY OF NYSSA

The second Cappadocian theologian who came to have a strong influence on the course of Christological developments, in both the patristic and the modern periods, is Gregory of Nyssa. One of Basil's younger brothers, Gregory was a theologian of many interests, whose dogmatic, exegetical, and ascetical writings became especially well known in the twentieth century. There are notable differences among the works of the three Cappadocians, and these are especially pronounced when we compare the Christology of Gregory of Nyssa with that of Gregory Nazianzen.

Several things account for the distinctiveness of Gregory of Nyssa's thought. First of all, he did not receive nearly the same degree of formal education that Basil and Gregory Nazianzen did. While Basil advanced to the highest level of graduate studies in Athens, together with his close friend Gregory Nazianzen, Gregory of Nyssa by contrast received little formal schooling. His main tutors in Greek and Christian learning appear to have been Basil and their elder sister Macrina; Gregory learned much as well by his own study. His intellectual makeup was therefore different in several respects from that of the other two Cappadocians. One of the most pronounced is his attitude toward philosophy. Whereas Basil and Gregory Nazianzen regularly disparaged the philosophers, Gregory of Nyssa embraced the thought of Plato more wholeheartedly and to a greater extent than the other two.[45]

A second major difference stems from Gregory's closer association with the church in Antioch. As already noted, Gregory was present at the synod of 379, together with Diodore and Meletius, which commissioned Gregory Nazianzen (in his absence), and with Diodore he became one of the legal arbiters of the faith after 381. Gregory's position in the new, Antiochene-dominated religious establishment is further indicated by the fact that he was chosen to deliver the funeral sermons for Meletius, the former bishop of Antioch, as well as the wife and daughter of Theodosius. Gregory's alliance with the Antiochenes is evident above all in his Christology. A third distinguishing factor is Gregory's younger age, which enabled him to read and respond to many of the works of Basil and Gregory Nazianzen, as he saw fit.

Three texts in particular are most important for establishing Gregory of Nyssa's Christology. Sometime after Basil's death in 379, he composed his own *Against Eunomius*, which responds to Eunomius's *Apology for the Apology* and thus represents the fourth stage in the debate,[46] at the same time that it was also meant to complete, and occasionally correct, the work of Basil.[47] When Gregory took over his brother's debate with Eunomius, he often redirected the conversation in ways that would suit his own categories and thought patterns. As in Basil's and Gregory Nazianzen's anti-Eunomian works, Gregory of Nyssa's main concern in *Against Eunomius* is to defend the divinity of Christ; yet, as we shall see, book 3 of this work, which Gregory wrote probably between 381 and 383 (after the Council of Constantinople), also contains the basic elements of Gregory's Christology in a more comprehensive sense. The second key Christological text is Gregory's letter to Bishop Theophilus of Alexandria, which he wrote to enlist Theophilus's support for his struggle against Apollinarianism. In this letter Gregory offers a response to the Apollinarian charge that he teaches two sons; it dates from after 385, the year of Theophilus's consecration. Third, we have Gregory's *Refutation (Antirrheticus) of Apollinarius*, which is a phrase-by-phrase reply to Apollinarius's *Proof (Apodeixis) of the Divine Incarnation in Human Likeness*. In this final text, Gregory's main concern is to show that he does not teach that Christ is merely an inspired human being (an *anthropos entheos*) or that the crucified Savior had "nothing divine in his own nature," as he says he was accused of holding (*Antirrh.* 135, 169, 172). The *Antirrheticus* was most likely written after the *Letter to Theophilus*, in 385 at the earliest.[48]

Like Gregory Nazianzen, therefore, Gregory of Nyssa defined his Christology mainly in opposition to Eunomius and in response to the

Antiochene debate. The chief differences between them stem from their divergent stances toward the latter; for while Gregory Nazianzen defines himself chiefly against Diodore, as we have seen, Gregory of Nyssa identifies Apollinarius as his main opponent, as one would expect from a theologian of Antiochene sympathies. It is Gregory of Nyssa's particular stance toward this debate that has since given all three Cappadocians the reputation of being chiefly anti-Apollinarian theologians in modern historiography, a characterization that one still finds in fairly recent handbooks.[49] Gregory of Nyssa appears to have taken up several of Gregory Nazianzen's chosen terms and motifs, yet in the end he forges a rather different path. We will examine Gregory of Nyssa's Christology by following the chronological order of its development.

Against Eunomius

In book 3 of *Against Eunomius* Gregory of Nyssa presents his Christology over the course of a detailed exegetical and doctrinal argument that involves several points of contention between Eunomius and Basil. Because of its complicated nature as well as the fact that its dogmatic contours normally go unnoticed, we will examine Gregory's argument in some detail.

Near the beginning of the book, Gregory resumes his argument by focusing on the language of creation. His immediate aim is to counter Eunomius's claim that the Son is foreign in nature to God the Father because he is "something made" (τὸ πόημα) and "something created" (τὸ κτίσμα), whereas God the Father is the maker and creator (*C.Eun.* 3.1.8).[50] For the sake of argument, Gregory focuses mainly on the term "creature" (*C.Eun.* 3.1.12). Like many theologians at this time, whether in the Athanasian or the Eusebian tradition—though, interestingly, unlike Basil—Gregory strongly resists any suggestion that the Son of God was "created" apart from the incarnation, and, as usual, what is most at issue is the interpretation of Scripture, especially Proverbs 8 (*C.Eun.* 3.1.21–65). On the whole Gregory gives an economic interpretation of the text, much as we saw in Athanasius and Gregory Nazianzen; and since Gregory of Nyssa knew the work of Marcellus,[51] he may have chosen to follow him on this point just as Athanasius had done.

Gregory explains the meaning of Proverbs 8:22 in a way that at first sounds quite unitive. Wisdom's statement "he created me," Gregory explains, did not come from "the divine and unmixed one," that is, the Son of God apart from the incarnation, but from "the one who was mixed with our nature from the creation, according to the economy." In other words, the language of creation applies only to the incarnate Christ, whom Gregory here describes in fairly unitive terms. It is the economy that explains how the same voice (the figure of Wisdom) can say at first that she lays the foundation of the earth and prepares the heavens, and then also is "created" as the beginning of God's works. Gregory paraphrases the narrative thus: because human beings have rejected God's grace through disobedience, I, Wisdom, will remind you of what is done for your welfare, and "for this reason I was created, the one who for ever is" (C.Eun. 3.1.51). Here Gregory is directly mirroring the single-voiced narrative of the text of Proverbs, where Wisdom speaks both sorts of statements—seemingly divine ones about being the instrument of creation, and seemingly human ones about being created—as a single subject. If we were to take this passage on its own as a full statement of Gregory's Christology, it might appear that he shares the unitive, single-subject approach of Gregory Nazianzen. But Gregory of Nyssa's aim here is in fact to resolve a difficulty that the text presents, namely, that the same figure of Wisdom speaks, in a single voice, of having created the world and of having herself also been created, against Eunomius, who is able to cite this text in support of his claim that the Son is in fact "created" apart from the incarnation. Gregory is arguing, in other words, to solve a conundrum raised by the text as he sees it.

Gregory's further commentary and analysis in the following section give a clearer indication of his own view. Wisdom's statement that she has been created applies not to Wisdom in human form or to Wisdom economically, as the former passage might suggest, but to "the humanity" (τὸ ἀνθρώπινον) as distinct from the divinity of Christ. For Gregory of Nyssa, the two sorts of expression do *not* apply to "one and the same" figure, as they do for Gregory Nazianzen (C.Eun. 3.1.52–53). Gregory then turns to Christ's birth to clarify the situation further. Paul calls "the same one" (τὸν αὐτόν) both a "new man created according to God" (Eph 4:24) and "Christ"—a title that for Gregory of Nyssa normally indicates his divinity (C.Eun. 3.3.44)—"in relation to the divine nature, which has been enmixed [ἐγκραθεῖσαν] in the creation of this new man, *as if* the two expressions apply to one and the same figure" (C.Eun. 3.1.53).[52]

What Gregory is seeking to reckon with in Proverbs, in the letters of Paul, and elsewhere is the *communicatio idiomatum* that we have seen being treated since Origen. In various ways, the biblical texts clearly do refer both divine and human things to the same figure, and at times they even show

Wisdom or Christ saying both kinds of things in a single voice; this much cannot be denied. As Gregory explains in this passage of *Against Eunomius* book 3, the proper way to interpret such texts is to refer the "lowly" passages (to borrow Gregory Nazianzen's term) such as Proverbs 8:22 to the economy rather than to the divinity. Where the Bible predicates both kinds of statement to a single subject, Gregory resolves them into a form of double predication, which is the reverse of Gregory Nazianzen's method. In order to counter Eunomian exegesis, Gregory of Nyssa chiefly aims to differentiate the referents between Christ's divinity and his humanity. Only the method (*logos*) that "looks to the economy and protects what is fitting concerning the conception [ὑπόληψις] of the divine and the human" is truly pious, he says, and only by distinguishing the referents in this way can one "preserve thoughts befitting God" and "keep intact what is due to the understanding of the divine and the human" (*C.Eun.* 3.1.54).[53] It is a pattern that he will execute with a fair degree of consistency for the rest of his career.

A crucial further point of Gregory of Nyssa's Christology concerns how he imagines the unifying element of Christ. Here he foreshadows later developments during and after the Council of Chalcedon, which we will examine particularly in chapter 7 in connection with Leontius of Byzantium. Although he does not normally employ the term hypostasis or *prosopon* in such passages, Gregory tends to imagine the unifying element of Christ as something distinct from his divine nature per se—not exactly a third thing in the sense of a third nature, but almost as much.

Here Gregory is replying to a similar Eunomian exegetical argument, that Christ, the Son of God, was not ashamed of his human birth and "often called himself 'Son of Man.'" In order to understand such expressions, Gregory points us to Paul's statement in 1 Timothy, that Christ is "the Mediator of God and human beings" (1 Tim 2:5). The name "Mediator," Gregory says, is "nothing like the title 'Son.'" The chief difference in Gregory's mind is that the term "Mediator" "fits each nature together equally, the divine and the human. For the same one [ὁ αὐτός] is Son of God and also became Son of Man by economy, so that by his communion with each thing he might join together through himself things that are separate in nature." This statement leaves open the important question of what Gregory imagines to be "the same one" that is both God and human. In contrast with Gregory Nazianzen and even Origen, for whom the Son's mediation very much begins in his status as *divine* image and mediator,

Gregory of Nyssa here conceives of Christ the mediator as a kind of third thing. On the one hand, he wants to say that the mediator "is" the Son of God properly speaking, who then becomes Son of Man, which is a lesser ontological status. In this view, it would be the divine Son himself who does the joining. But as Gregory spells out further, the one who acts as mediator is something distinct from each of the two natures, such that it can join them together in itself. Christ the mediator therefore has communion *with* each nature, which presumes that he is not himself either of those natures properly speaking (*C.Eun.* 3.1.91–92). Again, Christ participates in human nature (as the Son of Man) and also has communion with the divine essence (as the Son of God), and every characteristic of the superessential essence is "in him," just as the entire human compound is "in him"—as if he were something distinct from both natures or essences (*C.Eun.* 3.1.93). The phrase "one and the same" (or "the same") thus refers to this connecting element, the "single thing" (ἕν) that unites the divine and human natures. Gregory does not offer a technical term for this linking element of Christ, yet in his argumentation he has established a conceptual structure that later writers will fill in for him, by using the term "hypostasis," which Gregory employs elsewhere in reference to each member of the Trinity.

The most illuminating passage of the work, however, comes in Gregory's defense of Basil's exegesis of Acts 2:36, "God has made him Lord and Christ, this Jesus whom you crucified." Gregory's discussion of this verse takes up most of book 3, part 3. Following Basil's *Against Eunomius*, Gregory is again engaged in an effort to deflect Eunomian exegesis. Eunomius's approach to the verse is to ascribe the term "made" to the Son apart from the incarnation, that is, to the being of the Son, much as we saw above on the language of creation. When Basil denied that the term "made" could refer to the divine Son, Eunomius then accused Basil of being ashamed of the cross—specifically, ashamed of saying that the Son of God himself was crucified—and, consequently, of positing two Christs and two Lords. For Basil, Peter's statement in Acts refers to "him who emptied himself in the form of a slave, who was made to conform with the body of our lowliness, and was crucified in weakness" (*C.Eun.* 2.576D–77A), which appears to be a description of the divine Son ("who emptied himself"), as Gregory Nazianzen argues in *Oration* 29.18. Yet Basil argues further that Peter's statement is not given "in the manner of theology, but it presents the principles [*logoi*] of the economy," terms that, in Basil's usage, now suggest that Peter's statement does not refer to the divine Son after all. At this point Eunomius presses the matter of Christ's single subjectivity a step further. If what Basil says is the case, then how, he asks, can a slave empty himself to become the form of a slave, or a human creature become a human creature? Surely it must be the divine Son who empties himself to become the form of a slave. Moreover, Eunomius asks, how can we be saved by a mere creature? In short, Eunomius believes that by disallowing Peter's statement in Acts 2 from referring to the Son in himself, Basil has de facto introduced "two Christs and two Lords" (*C.Eun.* 3.3.22).

What is at stake at this point in the debate, therefore, is not merely the Son's divinity in relation to God the Father, but also the unity of Christ as both God and a human being. The desire to uphold the unity of Christ against perceived dualism has been a key position in the Eusebian tradition since Eusebius's arguments against Marcellus of Ancyra. Eunomius argues elsewhere in similar terms: "Although both Basil and those who disbelieve like him falsely proclaim two Lords and Christs, yet for us there is one Lord and Christ 'through whom all things were made' [1 Cor 8:6], who did not become Lord by advancement, but before all creation and before all ages existed as Lord Jesus, by whom are all things, which is what all the saints in harmony teach us and proclaim as the most excellent of doctrines" (*C.Eun.* 3.3.23). Here Eunomius cites the same verse that Eusebius used to demonstrate both the divinity and the unity of Jesus Christ against Marcellus (1 Cor 8:6), followed by equally typical proof texts from John 1, Philippians 2, and 1 Corinthians 2 ("they would not have crucified the Lord of glory") (*C.Eun.* 3.3.15–25).

Each of these accusations, then, reflects the basic Eunomian complaint that, by dividing the human Jesus from the preincarnate Lord, Basil and Gregory are "ashamed of the cross of Christ" (*C.Eun.* 3.3.26). Here again we are faced with a concern very similar to the one that exercised Athanasius and Origen: to explain and defend the crucifixion in a way that avoids theological problems and unnecessary scandal. In order to defend himself and Basil against the charge of avoiding the scandal of the cross, Gregory replies much as Athanasius had done, by pointing instead to Christ's divinity revealed there. Basil and Gregory do not disparage the cross because they honor "the God who is made manifest through the cross." In other words, the cross is not a scandal because it reveals God the Son (*C.Eun.* 3.3.30).

Eunomius bases himself to a significant extent on the traditional opposition to the possibility of God the Father's suffering in any way (*C.Eun.* 3.3.32)—a view that has significant resonance with Origen, for whom the Son is communicable as image in a way that the Father is not. For Eunomius, "the Father's nature abides purely in impassibility, and is unable to engage in any kind of sharing in the passion, while the Son, because he diverges in nature [from the Father] by his inferiority, is not unable to enter into the experience of flesh and death" (*C.Eun.* 3.3.38). If for Eunomius Christ's passion shows that he is not equal in divinity with God the Father, then for Gregory Christ's equality with God the Father demands that the sufferings of the cross not be predicated directly of the divine Son. We appear to be at a stalemate: either the divine Son suffers in a way that the Father cannot (thus preserving the unity of Christ at the cost of subordinationism), or the divine Son does not suffer, even humanly, because his divine nature is no less impassible than the Father's (thus preserving their equality at the expense of the unity of Christ).

Gregory seeks to resolve the debate over Acts 2:36 in favor of the Son's equality with the Father yet without opening himself to the charge of Christological dualism that Basil faced. He begins with the plain sense of Scripture: "The word of Scripture says that two things have been done to a single person [*prosopon*], the passion by the Jews, the honor by God— though not as if there was one who suffered and another who was honored by his exaltation." He recognizes the unitive sense of the Scriptures when they are taken at face value: they obviously ascribe both divine and human things to one and the same literary figure, "Jesus," who was crucified and yet was also honored by God. As Peter describes it in Acts, it is as though the same subject (ἄλλος)[54] experienced both things, which obviously supports Eunomius's position in some respect. Yet in order to resolve the problem, Gregory proceeds in the same manner of sharply distinguishing the actual referents against the grain of the biblical text. Surely the one who was exalted after being crucified (Acts 2:33) cannot be not "the lofty one" (ὁ ὕψιστος) or the Deity (τὸ θεῖον), but must be "the lowly one" (ὁ ταπεινός), namely, Christ's humanity (τὸ ἀνθρώπινον) (*C.Eun.* 3.3.43). In other words, Gregory is concerned to show that Christ's suffering, humiliation, and exaltation are *not* referred to the divine Son of God, but only to the human Jesus. In the end, Gregory offers an exegetical method of double predication, and this distinction between referents is itself the revelation of "the ineffable economy of the mystery" (*C.Eun.* 3.3.44). Just as for

Marcellus, the Christian mystery is the incarnation, the humanity Christ has taken on, rather than the divine life of the Son enacted in the incarnation, as it was for Eusebius.

The dualist sense of Gregory's Christology is clear in the succinct summary that he gives next. The Christian mystery, or the "ineffable economy," is to be understood as follows: "The Right Hand of God, who made all things that exist—which is 'the Lord through whom all things came to be' [see 1 Cor 8:6; John 1:3]—itself elevated to its own lofty height the human being who was united with it, by making him to be what it itself is by nature through the commingling [ἀνάκρασις]" (*C.Eun.* 3.3.44). The real mystery of the incarnation is that, through a kind of union and mixture, the divine Christ, who is the creator of the universe and equal with God the Father, transformed the human being Jesus and made him divine just as the Son was divine to begin with. Accordingly, Gregory concludes, Peter's words show that "the lowliness belongs to the one who was crucified through weakness," namely, the human being Jesus, not the divine Son of God. Yet because the human Jesus was "commingled with the infinity and boundlessness of the Good," he is transformed so as to transcend his own limits and to become "Lord rather than a slave, Christ the King rather than a subject, most high rather than lowly, God instead of a human being" (*C.Eun.* 3.3.45–46). In this way, God saved the human race "through the human being in which he had made his dwelling" (*C.Eun.* 3.3.51).

Gregory devotes himself primarily to establishing the clear distinction between Christ's divinity and humanity, as he continues to defend against the charge of teaching two Christs (*C.Eun.* 3.3.56–66). Where the Eunomians are in error is their failure to see that Christ's divinity and humanity remain unconfused (*C.Eun.* 3.3.63). "No one would say either that the flesh is pretemporal, or that the Word was born recently"; likewise, "the flesh does not design the existence of things, nor does the Divinity have the power to be passive." The *communicatio idiomatum* of Scripture, in other words, must be untangled and the divine and human referents kept straight, much as Diodore had argued. One must therefore keep these things distinct: the Word was "in the beginning with God" (John 1:1), while the human being (ὁ ἄνθρωπος) was "in the experience of death," and "the human is not from eternity, nor is the divine mortal" (*C.Eun.* 3.3.64). Basil's comments on Acts 2:36 that Peter is not doing theology but referring to the economy thus indicate the same distinction of referents, and "*this* Jesus" clearly points to the humanity (τὸ ἀνθρώπινον).[55] The emphasis that

Gregory gives this point in *Against Eunomius* book 3 indicates its central importance in his mind.

Having thus defined his exegetical practice in connection with the debate over Acts 2:36, Gregory applies the principle of exegetical distinction to a number of other examples. It was not Christ's human nature that brought Lazarus back to life, Gregory says, any more than the impassible power of God wept for the dead man (John 11:35–44): "the tear was proper to the human being, but the life to the true Life." In each example, Gregory asks, who is it who did such contrasting things, such as being weary from traveling versus sustaining the entire world, or being flogged during the passion versus being glorified in eternity? The answer, he says, is obvious. The lowly statements belong to the servant, and the honors belong to the master. The fact that the Scriptures do refer each sort of statement to the opposite referent is simply a reflection of their coming together in Christ and the fact that the servant is "in" the master and the master "in" the servant. As Gregory explains, both kinds of statement "become common to each referent, on account of their conjunction and attachment. So the Master takes to himself the bruises of the servant and the servant is glorified with the honor of the Master," as in passages such as 1 Corinthians 2:8 and Philippians 2:10 (*C.Eun.* 3.3.65–66). Yet, despite their conjoining, orthodox exegesis depends on clearly distinguishing the referents, which Gregory proceeds to discuss further in the following sections (*C.Eun.* 3.3.67–69). Gregory's handling of the *communicatio idiomatum* is thus closer to Origen and Athanasius than to Eusebius or Gregory Nazianzen, who were concerned to identify one, rather than two, ultimate referents and subjects of existence in Christ, allowing the literal sense of the biblical text to convey a true Christological meaning without needing constantly to be transposed into another key.

As indicated in the passages above, the language of mixture, union, and assumption in Gregory's work primarily indicates the transformation of Jesus's mortal human nature into immortal divine status at the resurrection, rather than any structural linking or joining of the two natures per se. This transformation provides a second main response to Eunomius's charge of teaching two sons. Gregory and Basil do not teach two sons because the flesh of Christ is transformed into divinity over the course of the incarnation: after his passion, the human Jesus was exalted and "made Lord and Christ by his union with the divine Lord and Christ" (*C.Eun.* 3.3.53–54).

Gregory describes this transformative, divinizing process using various metaphors. After the passion, the true life that lay in the flesh "flows back up" to itself, and the flesh containing it is borne up with it, like liquid that rises with bubbles, driven upward from corruption to incorruption. Christ's flesh "as it were conceals the tinder of life in its corporeal nature," and it is made to "flare up by the power of his own Divinity." In this way the form of a slave is made into the Lord, and the man born from Mary is "made Christ." In his mortal life, then, Jesus is truly human and receives the "lowly" references of Scripture, but in his resurrected state his humanity has become divine and the mortal nature is renewed to match the dominant element of his divinity. In a famous image, which we will discuss further, Gregory compares the transformation of Christ's humanity to a drop of vinegar that is mingled in an infinite sea and consequently is made into sea. Gregory teaches only one Christ and Lord, finally, because in the resurrection Jesus's humanity is transformed into divinity (*C.Eun.* 3.3.67–68). This is a theme that he will develop at much greater length in his later anti-Apollinarian works.

In the fourth part of *Against Eunomius* book 3, Gregory exposes an even deeper point of his rationale for keeping the human and divine referents in Christ distinct. Here he turns to a related Eunomian criticism: that by so strongly distinguishing the divine and human in Christ, Gregory and Basil hold that salvation was accomplished by an ordinary human being (*C.Eun.* 3.4.1). In these sections Gregory signals a typically Antiochene concern. What is ultimately at stake is not so much whether Christ is one thing, but whether God suffered in the incarnation. For Gregory, it is imperative that God not suffer at all. By suggesting that the crucified Christ can be the single subject and referent of both divine and human acts, Eunomius is violating the clean separation between the impassible God and passible creatures. By not referring Christ's sufferings to his human nature, the Eunomians "set the passible against the impassible" and "subject the Divinity itself to passion" (*C.Eun.* 3.4.3–4).

Here we gain an important further glimpse into how Gregory imagines the interpretive task, which reveals a deep similarity with Origen (whom Gregory certainly knew) and also Athanasius (whom he may or may not have known), as well as Antiochene theologians such as Diodore and, later, Theodore of Mopsuestia. Gregory argues that the way in which the Scriptures present Christ is problematic: "The conception [of Christ] is two-fold and ambiguous," specifically in terms of "whether the divine or the human was subject to passion."[56] What is most significant at this point is that Gregory understands the problem to be one of mutual exclusion: "the decision to reject one surely becomes an argument for the other" (*C.Eun.* 3.4.4), not unlike the ontological problem that Origen sees between Christ's humanity and divinity (*Princ.* 2.6). Either the Divinity suffered or the humanity suffered in Christ, and it cannot be that they both shared Christ's suffering. If the Eunomians criticize Basil and Gregory for ascribing Christ's suffering to his humanity alone, then by implication they are ascribing it to his divinity alone (although in fact they did not).

On the one hand Gregory claims that he does not regard the Savior as a mere human being, yet on the other he wants to protect "the pure and divine nature" from the taint of human passion and mortality (*C.Eun.* 3.4.6). In short, the view that Christ endured human passion and death in his divine nature threatens the doctrine of the Trinity: "if, on their showing, the divinity of the Son suffers, while that of the Father is protected in total impassibility, then the impassible nature is different in essence from the one that undertakes the passion" (*C.Eun.* 3.4.5). It is for this reason as well—in order to protect the shared divinity of the Trinity—that one must refer the lofty and the lowly sayings of Scripture to different referents, the one to the Word and the other to the flesh, and the distinctive qualities of each nature must remain (*C.Eun.* 3.4.7). Did the Divinity participate at all in Christ's passion, then? Gregory answers that it did, by serving as the active principle against the passivity of the flesh and its passion. But the passion of Christ does not, properly speaking, belong to it.

Gregory wants to make sure that no one misunderstands biblical statements to the contrary. When Paul writes that "God did not spare his only Son" (Rom 8:32), for example, we must realize the divine nature itself was not "in the economy of the passion," but only the human nature, which Gregory reads in Paul's statements elsewhere that God condemned sin "in the flesh" (Rom 8:3), and "since by a human being came death, by a human being also came the resurrection of the dead" (1 Cor 15:21). The division is very clear: "the human being tasted death, but the immortal nature did not admit the suffering of death" (*C.Eun.* 3.4.9–10), and must be applied to any such statements in Scripture. Whenever the Scriptures proclaim "the mingling of the human with the divine," they nevertheless observe the distinctive character of each, so that "human weakness is changed for the better through its communion with the unmixed [nature], while the divine power does not collapse through the conjunction [*sunapheia*] of its nature with the lowly" (*C.Eun.* 3.4.13).

As these remarks indicate, Gregory views Christ's suffering and death as a sort of potential threat to the divine nature, so that it must be literally "protected"—the term occurs frequently in *Against Eunomius*—from such defilement, much as Origen and Athanasius also held (most likely because of shared Platonic assumptions). Paul's statement that God "did not spare his own Son" (Rom 8:32) therefore not only distinguishes Jesus as God's true son, in contrast with all other sons and daughters, and shows his natural affinity with the Father, as Alexander had first argued, but it also indicates "that no one should impose the suffering of the cross on the undefiled nature." Paul's statement elsewhere that Jesus is the "Mediator of God and men" serves the same protective function: to show that Christ not only mediates God to human beings but also mediates human beings to God, protecting God from the defilement of our nature and mortal condition. By applying both terms, God and humanity, to the same mediator, Paul ensures that "the proper conception is thought concerning each one: impassibility for the divine and the economy of suffering for the human" (*C.Eun.* 3.4.14). In this way, "the experience of death is not referred to the one who had communion with the passible nature through the union of the human being with himself" (*C.Eun.* 3.4.16). Gregory's resistance to the idea of divine suffering in the economy is consistent, and it again marks him as a typically Antiochene theologian by contrast with the theopaschite assertions of Gregory Nazianzen.

Finally, Gregory summarizes his argument in *Against Eunomius* 3.1–4. He considers the incarnation to be primarily the manifestation of God, as seen above all in the resurrection of Christ, by which his humanity is transformed into divinity and he becomes "Christ and Lord" (*C.Eun.* 3.4.35). Peter's statement in Acts 2:36 therefore refers not to the pretemporal Word, but to Jesus's humanity, which existed only "after the economy" (*C.Eun.* 3.4.49). Already in his anti-Eunomian work Gregory evinces typical features of Antiochene Christology, features that he will develop further in his explicitly anti-Apollinarian works several years later.

Against Apollinarius

When Gregory turned to face Apollinarius directly in the years following the completion of *Against Eunomius*, he met with a very different sort of opponent. If Eunomius represented someone who emphasized the unity of Christ in such a way as to compromise Christ's divinity, then in Gregory's eyes Apollinarius represented essentially the reverse problem: he proclaimed the divinity of Christ so strongly and in such a way that it decapitated his humanity on the one hand while superstitiously elevating what remained of it on the other. In his anti-Apollinarian works, Gregory gives the clearest and fullest exposition of the basic Christological ideas that he first exhibited in his earlier work. Gregory's anti-Apollinarian argument is clearest in his *Letter to Theophilus*, since it is here that he makes his case in his own terms; whereas in the *Antirrheticus* he adheres to the sequence of Apollinarius's text. We will therefore follow the native argument of the earlier letter, supplementing it with the more expansive but less organic treatment found in the *Antirrheticus*.

Gregory's description of the Apollinarians' position and their charges against his own party at the beginning of the *Letter to Theophilus* is highly indicative.[57] According to his report, the Apollinarians argue that "the Word is fleshly, the Son of Man is the creator of the ages, and the divinity of the Son is mortal." They are, in other words, speaking of Christ in highly unitive terms, according to the *communicatio idiomatum* of Scripture, and violating the clean separation of divine and human referents that Gregory defined in *Against Eunomius*. At the same time, the Apollinarians have accused certain catholic theologians of teaching that there are two sons, "one who exists by nature and another who was added later." This is an obvious reference to the Christology of Diodore and, by extension, possibly Gregory himself, both of whom are now established catholic teachers under the Theodosian settlement, which, we must remember, had declared Apollinarius a heretic in 381. The Apollinarians have much ground to recover, and they seem to be going after authorities such as Gregory of Nyssa, much as they attempted to seize Gregory Nazianzen's church in Nazianzus in 383 or 384. Gregory protests ignorance of such charges, and in a plea for ecclesiastical support he urges Theophilus to cut short such accusations (*Theoph.* 120–21), Theophilus himself being the successor of another Theodosian moderator, Timothy of Alexandria. Gregory again faces the charge of dualist Christology, and again the unitive sense of the biblical text is being brought to bear against him.

Against the Apollinarians' Word-flesh Christology and their charge of two sons, Gregory argues first that the incarnation is a theophany, a theme that was fairly common in the Origenist tradition, as we have seen. The "economic epiphany of the only-begotten Son of God through flesh" does not indicate another Son, in the sense that multiple theophanies would mean multiple sons (*Theoph*. 121–22). For Gregory, "the vision of the superessential nature" always occurs according to the ability of each person to receive it—which is why the Son this time appeared in flesh to our fleshly species, emptying himself in such a way that he could be received. If all people could penetrate the darkness to perceive invisible things like Moses, learn ineffable and superrational things like Paul, or be elevated above the body like Elijah, then there would have been no need for God's epiphany in the flesh (*Theoph*. 123–24). But because our flesh is too weak to achieve such an ascent, the divine physician became weak by becoming flesh. If the incarnation is a theophany, then it cannot indicate two sons, since otherwise the multiple theophanies in Scripture would indicate multiple sons, which is absurd.[58]

Gregory's second reply to the charge of two sons is to point again to the transformation of Jesus's humanity into divinity.[59] The oneness (τὸ ἕν) of Christ consists in the fact that what is mortal and corruptible in him has been transformed into the impassible and divine. Because of this transformation, he cannot be "chopped up into a double difference" (*Theoph*. 125.10).[60] On the other hand, if "the divine that was born in the human" had allowed the mortal, corruptible nature of human existence to remain, *then* there would be grounds for alleging that Gregory "contemplates a duality in the Son of God," such that there are numerically two things that are distinct in themselves (*Theoph*. 125.5–6).[61] In light of his transformation into the divine life, Jesus shows forth a single divinity, which again reinforces the idea that there is only one epiphany, not multiple ones. It is this exaltation that Paul refers to in Philippians 2, where God raises Jesus and gives him "the Name that is above every name" (Phil 2:9), whereby the servant becomes a king and "God made him Lord and Christ" (Acts 2:36), as Gregory discussed at length in *Against Eunomius* book 3 (*Theoph*. 127). The oneness of Christ depends on the transformation of his humanity into divinity.

One of Gregory's most famous images for the incarnation serves to explain the transformation of Jesus's humanity. Christ's humanity is like a drop of vinegar that has been mixed in an infinite sea. When this happens, the vinegar is so diluted throughout the sea of divinity that it now really exists only "in the divinity" and no longer "in its own proper characteristics" (*Antirrh*. 126.21).[62] Because the sea is infinite, the finite drop of vinegar necessarily disappears as it is absorbed in the sea's infinitude. Gregory conceives of the image in two different senses. In his *Letter to Theophilus*, he emphasizes the fallen and decaying aspects of human existence, which are transformed into their divine counterparts like a drop of vinegar absorbed in the sea: corruption becomes incorruption, mortality becomes immortality, and so on. Accordingly, after the resurrection "whatever one sees of the Son is divinity, wisdom, power, holiness, impassibility" rather than ignorance, weakness, and sinfulness (passibility can be construed as a fallen quality or not). Yet Gregory also imagines Jesus's transformed human existence in a more basic sense as well. In *Against Eunomius* and the *Antirrheticus* especially, he speaks of the transformation of human creatureliness altogether, even apart from its broken or malformed condition. "*All* things that once appeared in [Christ's] flesh were transformed into the divine and pure nature," including weight, form, color, resistance, softness, circumscription in quantity, and every observable quality (*Antirrh.* 201).[63] While the Scriptures may refer divine and human things to Christ in a distinct way, after the resurrection his humanity is transformed to match the dominant element of divinity. Like a drop of vinegar lost in the sea, "the natural quality [ἡ κατὰ φύσιν ποιότης] of the liquid no longer remains within the infinity of the dominant element [τοῦ ἐπικρατοῦντος]" (*C.Eun.* 3.3.67–68). As the image illustrates, the all-powerful divinity has so fully incorporated broken and finite human nature within itself in Christ that one can no longer perceive Christ's humanness at all by its natural qualities. Because they are so mixed together, the drop of vinegar "becomes sea to the extent that it is transformed with the sea," and the risen Christ appears *only* as the Son of God, through the divine qualities of light, life, wisdom, holiness, power, and so on. Christ's natural flesh has been completely changed into divinity, as the apostle says: "mortality was swallowed up by life" (2 Cor 5:4; *Antirrh.* 201).[64] In sum, there cannot be two sons because, in the end, there is only divinity in Christ anyway: the oneness (τὸ ἕν) of Christ cannot be "distinguished into a double signification, since no difference divides the number" (*Theoph.* 127).

Gregory downplays Christ's risen humanity in an additional way, by contrasting his earthly condition with what comes before and after it. "Christ," the anointed one—who is for Gregory the divine Son, not the incarnate Lord, as for most other theologians—exists always, as the Father eternally anoints the Son with the Spirit, both before and after the economy. "But he is not a human being either beforehand *or afterward*, but only during the time of the economy. Neither does the human being exist before the Virgin nor does the flesh still exist in its own properties after the ascent into heaven," as Paul says: "If we have known Christ once in the flesh, we know him no longer" (2 Cor 5:16).[65] Christ's human nature has been changed for the better, being altered from corruption to incorruption, from the temporal to the eternal, from the corporeal to the incorporeal and unfigured (*Antirrh.* 222–23). Christ is transformed beyond the visible and earthly forms of human life. He will come again not bodily but "in the Father's glory" (Matt 16:27), which is "purified of all form that can be contemplated visually," for "the divine lies beyond every bodily conception" (*Antirrh.* 230). While his treatment of Christ's resurrected body clearly echoes that of Origen, in a deeper respect Gregory is closer to the doctrine of Marcellus and Athanasius, for whom Christ's flesh is not so much spiritualized into a heavenly body as it transcends bodily limitations altogether by becoming God.[66]

A third reply that Gregory offers is that Christ is one because of the union of God and humanity in him. Gregory uses several terms that we have already seen in the work of Gregory Nazianzen. He speaks fairly regularly of the "mixture" (μίξις) or "conjunction" (κρᾶσις) of the divine and human natures in Christ, and, with less frequency, he calls this transformative process a "union" (ἕνωσις), even "the exact union" (*Theoph.* 127.15–16). It is possible that Gregory adopted these terms from Origen or from Apollinarius himself, as Gregory Nazianzen seems to have done, or he could have taken them directly from Gregory Nazianzen. In one passage Gregory of Nyssa registers his agreement with Apollinarius's statement that "we are not saved by God unless he intermixed [ἐπιμιχθέντος] with us," and he agrees that mixture essentially means union (*Antirrh.* 217).

Gregory disagrees with Apollinarius in several respects about the nature of the incarnation. What, then, does he mean by the union of Christ? It does not mean that in Jesus the Word of God directly lived a human life without the presence or mediation of a human mind. In one respect, the union of Christ is essentially the "assumption" of human nature by the divinity (*Antirrh.* 184, 193). Gregory spells out what he means in contrast to Apollinarius's view. Unity and assumption both have many meanings, he says, but the proper meaning of both terms should be clear. They both refer to a kind of relation: "For the unity occurs in relation to [πρός] something, and the assumption is of something completely. Each [term] signifies a relation with another thing [σχέσις πρὸς ἕτερον]; the one who assumes is united with what is assumed and the one who is united is united through assumption" (*Antirrh.* 184).[67] Here the language of assumption connotes the narrative sense that we saw in Gregory Nazianzen, and it makes clear (by implication at least) that the divine Son works as an acting agent in the process ("the one who assumes"). Also in terms similar to Apollinarius and Gregory Nazianzen, Gregory of Nyssa often describes the incarnation as a "mixture" of the divine and human. Through the Virgin, the Son of God is "mixed with" the human (*Antirrh.* 217), and by mixing with the divine nature the human flesh "became one" (ἕν ἐγένετο) with it (*Antirrh.* 207, 152). Yet, despite the possible suggestion of a thorough combination or blending, Gregory seems to envision this mixing more lightly than Gregory Nazianzen does; so he equates it with the idea of the Word's "communion with" (κοινωνία πρός) the humility of our nature (*Antirrh.* 151).

In the second place, Gregory argues against Apollinarius that the union of Christ includes a full human existence. "The assumption is of something completely"; the Son has united himself to Jesus's human soul and body and remains joined to both even at Jesus's death (*Antirrh.* 184, 153). The divine nature "dwelt closely in the nature [ἐμφύειν] of both the soul and the body, and became one thing with each of them through the commingling, . . . and separates from neither of them but remains with them in perpetuity" (*Antirrh.* 224).[68] Gregory also indicates that it was soteriologically necessary that Jesus have a freely choosing human mind, in order to heal our propensity for change toward the worse (*Antirrh.* 133). Since the whole flock departed from God in sin, the whole flock is restored by Christ, not merely its hide without its entrails, as Apollinarius imagines (*Antirrh.* 152). When Gregory speaks of the union of Christ as a "natural" union, this is chiefly what he means. The human Jesus is "naturally related" (προσφυῆναι) with the divine power, that is, as a complete human being, not one merely half-human, as Apollinarius alleges (*Antirrh.* 172).[69] Yet, at the same time that he opposes Apollinarius's reduced version of Christ's humanity, Gregory concedes another point—that Christ is not in fact exactly like us in every way. Playing off the title of Apollinarius's work, *Proof of the Divine Incarnation in Human Likeness,* which echoes Philippians 2:6, Gregory admits that Christ is "found to be *like* a human being—a human being, to be sure, even if he is not human in every way [δι' ὅλου]." A major difference between Jesus and all other human beings is that Jesus was born of a virgin, and consequently he is not a slave to the laws of human nature in all respects (*Antirrh.* 160).

In one sense Gregory shows quite a strong doctrine of the union, in that Jesus's life and death are seen as the acts of God himself. A striking example comes in the *Antirrheticus*, using language that we have already seen in Athanasius. Gregory writes that the Lord appropriates (οἰκειοῦται) the lowly things of human cowardice and suffering, "showing that what belongs to us truly pertained to him [ἦν περὶ αὐτόν] and confirming the nature from the community of the passions" (*Antirrh.* 182). Here it appears that in Christ, the Son makes our humanity and even our sufferings truly his own. The idea is reinforced through Paul's narration of Christ's self-humbling: "The highest humbled himself through his unity with the humility of our nature." When he is unified with the form of a slave that he assumed and becomes one thing with it, "he makes the passions of the slave his own" (*Antirrh.* 160). Gregory then offers a comparison that is highly unitive indeed. He likens the Son's union with the form of a servant to the natural cohesion of human limbs, in which pain in the tip of the finger is felt throughout the body. On the face of it, the divine Son is here depicted as being the ultimate center of subjectivity at the heart of Jesus's human life, just as the human mind or soul experiences whatever happens to the body. Such an idea is further suggested by Gregory's use of the language of being "in" God, which is never far removed from anyone reading John's gospel. The Word was blended with a human being and "received all our nature in himself" (*Antirrh.* 151, 221). Yet, even as he makes such unitive assertions, Gregory immediately qualifies himself in the other direction, much as Athanasius was wont to do in the third of his *Orations against the Arians* and later writings. Even as the union of Christ is like our mind and body, on the other hand it was *not* the case, Gregory explains, that the Divinity was bruised; rather, the one injured was "the human being who was naturally related with the Divinity through the union," because only human nature is capable of suffering so (*Antirrh.* 161).

The situation is not as paradoxical as it may seem. In Gregory's scheme there is good reason to qualify what he means by union. He gives us a clearer view of the matter in his discussion of Christ's role as mediator between God and human beings, by way of a reflection on the image of Christ the Good Shepherd. When the Lord found what was lost, he took it upon himself ("on the divinity of the Lord") and "became one with it." As a result, Christ the Shepherd "speaks to the sheep even in the voice of the flock," since human weakness could not have contained (ἐχώρησιν) the approach of the divine voice (*Antirrh.* 152). On the one hand, Gregory wants to say that it is God who speaks to his sheep in Christ, yet on the other, he is concerned to keep the two safely distinct; so, in the end, it is only a *human* voice that speaks to human beings. Gregory explains further: in Christ "the human being mediated to other humans through his own voice what was said," because human nature is not able to mix with "the unmingled co-essentiality of God" (*Antirrh.* 203).[70] At first glance this appears to be a statement of Jesus's actual mediation of the divine-human difference that is otherwise unbridgeable; but in fact Gregory is saying that *Christ's* humanity as well cannot sustain the divine presence any more than ours can. Christ is the mediator between God and human beings because the two cannot meet rather than because they *do* meet in him. Even as God is thought to speak in Christ, there is a more important sense in which the two must remain different and distinct. Gregory explains the contrast in ontological terms. He notes that Paul describes the divine Son as *being* in the form of God (ὑπάρχων, Phil 2:6), not *having* the form of God. By contrast, Paul writes that Christ *assumed* (λαβών, Phil 2:7) the form of a slave, which is something else by nature (*Antirrh.* 159). In Gregory's Neoplatonic ontology, the difference between being and possessing indicates the infinite difference between God and creatures. Similarly, Gregory is concerned to deny that the Son made a corporeal impression, since he himself is incorporeal. Instead, he "puts around himself" the nature of the body (*Antirrh.* 159–60).

In *Against Eunomius* Gregory defends the Son's full divinity by preserving a clear and strong distinction between divine and human referents, against the more unitive aspects of Eunomian exegesis. Here too, against the Apollinarians, he faces what he takes to be an improperly unitive approach that, again, results in Christological error. Although he adopts fairly strong terms for the relationship between divinity and humanity in Christ, such as union, mixture, and assumption, there are clear limits to what these terms can mean. As soon as he voices his agreement with the statement that "human nature was saved by being united to the Word by mystery," for example, Gregory quickly qualifies himself from the other direction. Union does not mean that the Son of God is fleshly in himself in terms of his own properties.[71] Regardless of the fact that this is not what Apollinarius meant (that the Word actually changed into humanity and ceased being God), what is significant for our understanding of Gregory is that this is what he *takes* to be the risk at hand. He is wary of allowing any suggestion that the Word of God might receive human description in any literal sense.

The limits of the union of Christ are especially clear in Gregory's treatment of Christ's passion. Not surprisingly, he is most resistant to Apollinarius's single-subject exegesis as it applies to Christ's suffering and death. In short, he recoils at the suggestion that in Jesus the Divinity actually undergoes human experiences. To say that the Son of God was born and wrapped in swaddling clothes; that he felt pain, hungered, thirsted, and did not know the day or hour of his death; or that he was beaten, bound, and nailed to the cross—to think that such things are "proper by nature to the pretemporal Divinity" (*Antirrh.* 167)[72] is in Gregory's mind outrageous. It is inconceivable that Christ could have undergone such things in his divinity.

Gregory recognizes that the pressing question is, who really suffered these things? Who is the subject of Jesus's human experiences? On this point he vehemently presses Apollinarius: "*Who* is it that is ignorant?—let him say! Who feels pain? Who suffers tribulation in hardship? Who shouts that he is forsaken by God . . .?" (*Antirrh.* 168). For Gregory, the answer cannot be the divine Son of God; it must be the human Jesus instead. The real risk of such an idea is evident in Gregory's next comment, which brings us to a fixed point of Gregory's doctrine of Christ's divinity and of the Trinity together. According to his understanding of the Trinity, it is impossible that the Father and Son could be divided against each other in any way. When Jesus cries, "My God, my God, why have you forsaken me?" (Matt 27:46), it can only be the human being calling out to God; it cannot be the divine Son taking into himself and his divine relation with God the Father the alienation and despair that the human Jesus experiences. Gregory thus reads Christ's agony in Gethsemane very differently from Gregory Nazianzen. Not only does the identity of the divine nature shared by the Father and Son prohibit such a division, but so too does the inconceivability that God the Father might suffer. In Gregory's scheme it cannot be that the divine Son could suffer without the Father himself also suffering—although he does not explain the corollary either, how the Son could be incarnate at all without the Father and the Holy Spirit also becoming flesh. The most that Gregory will say here is that the impassible God persists "in communion with human passions," but he does not undergo them himself (*Antirrh.* 167–68). Gregory plainly does not want to say that God speaks through Christ's human voice in his suffering. For Gregory, God is the sort of pure activity that cannot undergo or contain human passivity, much as we found in Athanasius. When applied to the person of Christ, this dichotomy results in a clear differentiation of divine and human, active and passible elements: "That which is passible in the [human] nature admits of death; that which does not admit passion actualizes [ἐνήργησεν] impassibility in the passible" (*Antirrh.* 138).

Gregory's comments that follow are especially illuminating with regard to how he understands Christ's saving work. In the next few lines—a section in which one can see Gregory making on-the-spot arguments as the debater that Basil trained him to be—Gregory claims that the death of God would not be effective for human beings anyway. What humans require for salvation is the death of a human; God would die only for other gods. Gregory's next question is extremely significant. He asks, "Is the one praying a human being *or* God?"—the assumption being that it cannot be both. Similarly, on Jesus's agony in the garden, Gregory insists that Jesus's fear belongs only to human weakness and is unworthy of the Divinity. The Word who "appropriated our passions says what is suited to the weakness of our nature as if from a human being," but Jesus's plea to be spared the passion is ultimately the product of a human will, not the divine will (see Matt 26:39). Despite his differentiation between Christ's divine and human natures, when Gregory considers Jesus's plea to the Father, he assumes that Christ's fear in the face of death is unacceptable and, more importantly, that such questioning would mean that the same subject is both willing and not willing the same thing, without allowing that Jesus's human questioning might even be in accord with the divine will.[73] What the Divinity provides in this scenario is the active force for Jesus to endure the passion; but the passion itself has no place in the divine nature (*Antirrh.* 78–82).

Against Apollinarius's charge that the death of a human being alone cannot suffice to save fallen human beings—"the death of a human being does not destroy death" (*Frag.* 94)—Gregory simply dismisses the question as absurd: "He says this to establish what?" For Gregory, it is inconceivable that the Son's divinity could suffer human passion and be crucified, as if this would make him cease to exist as God during his three days of burial—and this despite his acknowledgment that Apollinarius had opposed Arius very strongly in defense of the one Divinity of the Trinity. In Gregory's eyes, the human death of God would threaten God's existence altogether: "if [the Divinity] was mortified in this human being, there would be none left at all." So he repeatedly opposes the realistic sense of theopaschite language that Gregory Nazianzen held to be so central to the faith: "We confess that the Divinity exists *in* the one who suffers, but certainly not that the impassible nature became passible" (*Antirrh.* 223). For Gregory of Nyssa there is no "impassible passion," and in this regard his response to Apollinarius fits quite well with broader Antiochene concerns.[74]

The limits of the *communicatio idiomatum* in Gregory of Nyssa's Christology are especially clear. Although Gregory senses the traditional force of theopaschite statements, he is careful not to commit himself to their realistic sense (*Cat.Or.* 11), and he is generally concerned to qualify such statements so as to avoid the suggestion that God might have really undergone any human passion (*Cat.Or.* 13, 16, 32). Apollinarius therefore should not have said that the man Jesus is God, that God was born of a woman and crucified by Jews, or that the divine is subject to human passions (*Antirrh.* 155, 168, 170, 182). At most, such expressions in Scripture show the union of the two natures in Christ. The way in which Scripture calls the human by divine names and the divine by human names, Gregory says, shows "the true and indivisible unity," which consists chiefly in the transformation of Jesus's humanity into divinity after the resurrection (*Theoph.* 128). This clean division extends even to the point of the names of Christ. In a famous phrase, Gregory writes that the human being who corresponds with Christ (ὁ κατὰ Χριστὸν ἄνθρωπος), that is, the human nature, was called "Jesus," whereas the divine nature remains incomprehensible by name. Yet since "the two have become one thing through the blending," God too is named based on the human nature, and the human Jesus becomes superior to a name, as is proper to the Divinity. This also explains the singular worship given to Jesus: creation applies the worship of divinity to him who is united with the Divinity (*Antirrh.* 161). But it does not extend to a realistic application of the *communicatio idiomatum*, even one that preserves the integrity of the two natures.

Given Gregory's typically Antiochene concern to protect the divine nature from human suffering and his consistent double predication of biblical texts, it is not at all surprising that Apollinarius accused him of holding that God did not really become human and that God had no real contact with human passions in Christ, much like Marcellus and Photinus.[75] Nor is it surprising that Gregory in return argues that Apollinarius has violated the divine impassibility by claiming that God has died (*Antirrh.* 136, 138). He might have just as easily laid the same charges at the feet of Gregory Nazianzen.

Part III
The Construction of Orthodoxy

5. Augustine and the West

The formal tradition of Latin Christology got a late start in comparison with the Greeks. While there were important advances by Tertullian and Novatian in the third century, it was mainly due to the efforts of theologians such as Hilary of Poitiers, Ambrose of Milan, Jerome, and above all Augustine of Hippo that Latin theology came into its own in the late fourth and early fifth centuries. The tradition of pro-Nicene Latin theology gained new momentum in reaction to the Council of Sirmium in 357 and the homoian Western synods of Constantius in the late 350s and when several theologians who had traveled East later returned to the West, in particular Hilary of Poitiers, Eusebius of Vercelli, and Lucifer of Cagliari. In this chapter we consider the full flowering of Latin Christology in the work of Hilary, Ambrose, and especially Augustine, with special attention to how these figures relate to the lines of Christological thought already traced in the major fourth-century Greek theologians.

HILARY OF POITIERS

In the mid-fourth century, Bishop Hilary of Poitiers (c. 315–367/68) brought about an important transmission of Greek Christology to the Western church. Elected bishop in 350 and a firm opponent of homoian "Arianism," Hilary developed his mature Christological position during his exile in the East from 356 to 361. At that time he was influenced above all by Basil of Ancyra and other Homoiousians—theologians of the Origenist-Eusebian tradition who strongly opposed the reigning homoian orthodoxy of Emperor Constantius, which asserted that Christ was "like" (*homoios*) God the Father but no more (neither like in substance nor sharing the same nature), as well as the Christology of the emerging Heterousian group (Aetius, Eunomius, et al.), who were even more extremely subordinationist than the Homoians. When the Council of Sirmium in 357 formally promulgated the homoian agenda, the situation became a matter of acute concern to Basil of Ancyra and his homoiousian associates. Under the influence of the Homoiousians, Hilary came to oppose both homoian and Photinian (Marcellan) theologies and brought these concerns back to the West in 361. In his opposition to both homoian subordinationism and Marcellan modalism, Hilary carries forward the revitalized Eusebian tradition of Basil and his Greek associates—a tradition initially based, as we have seen, in the theology of Origen, who had championed both the full divinity and the distinct subsistence of Christ, all rooted in his divine generation from God the Father, which defined itself against the modalism of Marcellus of Ancyra in the 330s, and which, on the advent of the new homoian program of the late 350s, reasserted the Son's divinity and shared (similar) nature with God the Father against what it felt to be an unacceptable subordinationism.

Hilary's *The Trinity*, the final version of which dates from after 358, was a major theological work for its time. It can be compared with Basil's *Against Eunomius* (mid-360s) in terms of scope and method of execution. As for the Greek Homoiousians, Hilary's Christology finds its center in the Son's relationship of divine generation from God the Father, together with the Origenist conviction that the Son's generation is closely tied to his role as the unique revealer of the Father. Hilary follows the Greek Homoiousians in making a fundamental distinction between the Father-Son relationship and that between the creator and creatures. Although God has created many heavenly beings, there is only one only-begotten Son, Hilary writes. Moreover, his true and unique sonship derives exclusively from his origin in God the Father. The distinct identity of the Father as father and the Son as son, which was deeply rooted in the Origenist-Eusebian tradition, becomes in the hands of Hilary, as it did for Basil of Ancyra and Basil of Caesarea, a weapon equally useful against the Homoians and any others who denied the Son's divinity: "You hear of the Son; believe that he is the Son. You hear of the Father; remember that he is a Father" (*Trin.* 3.22; 7.11, 37). Here the names "Father" and "Son" are given precedence over others such as "creator" and "creature," much as Basil of Caesarea and Gregory

Nazianzen later came to argue against the heterousian Eunomius. "Remember that it was revealed to you," Hilary concludes, "not that the Father is God, but that God is the Father," a statement that could just as soon have come from the lips of Origen, Eusebius, the Homoiousians, or the Cappadocians (*Trin.* 3.22). When speaking of the unity of the Father and Son, as in Jesus's statement "I and the Father are one" (John 10:30), Hilary argues that they are one not as a single thing, in a Marcellan modalist sense, but "they are one as are one who begets and one who is begotten." They are one, in other words, in and by virtue of the Father's generation of the Son. An even better statement of their equality and oneness, in Hilary's mind, is Jesus's statement a few verses later, "The Father is in me and I in the Father" (John 10:38).

As the image of the Father's substance, the Son is distinct from the Father but not dissimilar from him in nature, Hilary concludes. For the Father and the Son to be "in" each other as Jesus says means that there is "a perfect fullness of divinity" in each one. The Son's identity as image of the Father as well as their shared divinity arises exclusively from the Father's generation of the Son: "The Son received everything from the Father, and he is the form of God and the image of his substance." Only that which is from God can be like God, Hilary adds, and in this way the names Father and Son convey their similar divine nature (*Trin.* 3.23; 2.3, 5, 8; 6.23). Hilary's doctrine of the Son's divinity is thus a clear example of the monarchy of God the Father, very much as we saw in Gregory of Nazianzus, as in Basil of Caesarea and the earlier Homoiousians. And as for the Cappadocians, the monarchy of the Father gives rise to both the unity of the Father and Son (against the Homoians) and the distinctions between them (against the Photinians). They are one God because there is one principle, God the Father (*Trin.* 5.10; 7.32), and the Word's relationship to the Father ensures that they are not the same thing, as the Photinians held (*Trin.* 2.15; 7.11). Drawing on the earlier Latin writers Tertullian and Novatian, Hilary argues that the Father and Son are "one thing" (*unum*—that is, God or divinity), as the gospel saying has it (John 10:30), but not "one figure" (*unus*, *Trin.* 7.5, 31), a statement that is very similar to the language that Gregory Nazianzen gives in Greek: the Father, Son, and Spirit are each one figure (ἄλλος) while all three are one thing (ἄλλο). Like his Greek counterparts, Hilary likewise exhibits a prevalence of Origenist theology in general: Christ is the incorporeal and invisible Word, Wisdom, and Power of God, the living (subsisting) image of God whose divine identity is constitutive of his revelatory work toward creation (*Trin.* 7.11, 37; 8.48–49; 9.12). Not surprisingly, then, the Son as image retains a unique sense of what we called communicative divinity, as in Origen's work. Theophanies in the Scriptures are most immediately revelations of the Word, and the Word is God as he reveals himself (*Trin.* 4.23–25, 35–40; 5.11, 39).

Yet, although Hilary's theology in these ways bears a striking resemblance to that of Basil of Ancyra, Basil of Caesarea, and Gregory Nazianzen, his understanding of the incarnation of Christ distinguishes him from them, making him closer instead to the anti-Eunomian arguments of Gregory of Nyssa in some interesting ways, while in other ways being unlike any of the above.[1] Famously, Hilary argues that Christ's humanity was "like," but not in fact identical with, ours in substance. The most pronounced issue, which has earned Hilary criticism from various quarters for centuries, concerns the reality of Christ's humanity, and particularly his suffering.

The structural basis of Hilary's Christology is a particular understanding of Paul's language of the "form of God" and the "form of a servant" in Philippians 2. In the incarnation, the Son of God emptied himself of the form of God, as Paul says, and assumed the form of a servant and a "living human being" (*hominem viventem*), and so the Son of God was born as the Son of Man (*Trin.* 8–10). Yet, while Jesus possesses a full humanity, he did not assume what Hilary calls the "weak soul" that other human beings have. Just as Jesus was conceived in a unique way (by the Holy Spirit), so too he suffers in a unique way, which accords with his distinct human nature (*Trin.* 10.14–15).

Hilary believes that the nature of Jesus's human soul must be very closely tied with his conception by the Holy Spirit; otherwise, the Son of Man would be too distinct from the Son of God. In this regard, Hilary's ascription to Jesus of a very different sort of human soul, one that is impregnable, as it were, serves to preserve the unity of Christ. Christ was born "in the likeness of sinful flesh" (Rom 8:3), and in this way he possessed a flesh that is suitable to the Word. It is this unique quality that makes Christ's human flesh "the Word's flesh" (*Trin.* 10.26). As in the thought of Apollinarius, this unique quality of Christ's humanity is reinforced by the obvious differences that one can see between Jesus as he is depicted in the gospels and other human beings, such as his ability to perform miracles, to walk on water, or to pass through closed doors. A further aspect of Jesus's unique humanity is that he truly receives human blows and wounds, but he does not feel the pain of human suffering (*Trin.* 10.23). Even though he is a human being, Jesus's humanity is not corrupt like other people's, and consequently his soul is not weak like ours.

Much of Hilary's concern here is the homoian claim at Sirmium that the Son "took of Mary a man, through whom he suffered" (*Syn.* 11), and the general homoian argument that Jesus's suffering shows his subordination to the Father. Accordingly, in *The Trinity* book 10 Hilary considers a series of biblical texts in which Jesus is described as suffering. There is a trace of theopaschite language in book 9: "God willed to suffer"; "God suffers for the sake of our innocence, and finally dies for the sake of our revenge"; and "God dies through the flesh" (*Trin.* 9.7). Yet Hilary reasons away such notions in book 10. For example, in considering Jesus's sadness in the Garden of Gethsemane and his prayer "Let this cup pass from me," he argues that Jesus was sad only to the extent that he could show solidarity with others, and particularly with his disciples, who would suffer too after his passion: he is sad for others, but not really for himself (*Trin.* 10.36–39). Hilary clearly believes that Jesus did not possess a corruptible human substance. Significantly, he accepts the homoian premise that were Jesus actually to suffer, then this would indeed prove that he is less than God. In other words, Hilary agrees with his opponents that God and human suffering are incompatible.

Up to this point, Hilary's treatment of Jesus's suffering mirrors that of his earlier *Commentary on Matthew*, which preceded the Council of Sirmium and his contact with the Homoiousians. Yet, in the passages that follow, Hilary takes a new approach, in which he gives a fuller account of the unity of Christ (*Trin.* 10.44–50).[2] He turns first to a consideration of the nature of Christ's body and to a point of theological method. Hilary opposes the homoian claim that the Word became flesh with no human soul, with the result that the Word underwent some change and diminution (as Hilary characterizes it), as well as the Photinian idea that Jesus was merely inspired like a prophet and is not really the Word made flesh (*Trin.* 10.51). Hilary means to maintain the unity of Christ: one should not "separate Christ Jesus, so that Jesus himself is not Christ"—a notion similar to Gregory of Nyssa's idea of the eternal Christ—but one also should not "absorb God the Word into the soul and body" of Jesus. Instead, "In him is the whole God the Word, and in him is the whole man Christ, while one holds fast to this one thing in the mystery of our confession: not to believe that Christ is anything else than Jesus and not to proclaim that Jesus is anything else than Christ" (*Trin.* 10.52).

Soteriologically, Hilary understands Christ's divinity as serving chiefly to make his humanity sinless, and this sinlessness is what achieves the saving effect. Yet the most striking aspect of Hilary's understanding of Christ's humanity is that it shows how extreme is his resistance to Christ's suffering, in ways that go beyond even Athanasius and Gregory of Nyssa, who also believe that God must avoid or somehow do away with suffering rather than take it into himself and heal it. Hilary retained his deep antimodalist sensibilities, even when he pressed beyond the Homoiousians by adopting the idea of Nicene consubstantiality in order to oppose the Homoians,[3] on which point he anticipated Gregory Nazianzen as well as the later Latin pro-Nicenes. Yet in the end Hilary's resistance to Christ's suffering froze his Christology in a particular dualist position that other Latin theologians would soon reject.

AMBROSE OF MILAN

Ambrose of Milan is notable among the Latin fathers of the church for a variety of reasons. Not only was he the influential bishop of the Western imperial capital who possessed enough personal gravitas to excommunicate Emperor Theodosius I when he learned that the emperor had ordered a retributive massacre of seven thousand citizens of Thessaloniki. Ambrose also made pivotal contributions to pastoral theology, Christian ethics, and the development of church hymnody, and he was the chief instrumental cause of the conversion of St. Augustine back to catholic Christianity. He played a major role as well in transmitting Origenist theology to the West. Ambrose studied Origen extensively and drew heavily on him for his typological and spiritual interpretation of Scripture. Ambrose's most important contribution to patristic Christology was twofold. On the one hand, he championed the Nicene faith against homoian "Arian" opponents, using arguments similar to those we have seen in Gregory of Nyssa and Hilary of Poitiers. Yet, on the other hand, he modified this heritage and made additions of his own that moved in a more unitive direction.[4] He devotes the first and longest section of *On the Sacrament of the Incarnation of the Lord*, a work put into its final form probably in 382, to a consideration of the unity and duality of Christ, chiefly in opposition to Apollinarius (*Inc.* 1–78). In composing these sections Ambrose made particular use of Athanasius's *Letter to Epictetus*; in the later, anti-Arian portion of the work he drew mainly on Basil's *Against Eunomius*.[5]

Ambrose attempts to maintain a fairly strong sense of Christ's unity
even as he is arguing for two complete natures against Apollinarius. He
gives the following summary of the church's faith, in which he famously
compares Christ to a two-natured giant, a metaphor that draws on Philo's
commentary on Genesis 6:4, in which giants have a compound nature
(*Giants* 15.65; 13.60). In his statement of faith, Ambrose first identifies
Christ as the Son of God, who is both eternally generated from God the
Father and also born of the Virgin Mary, just as the Nicene Creed of 381
does. He then comments that Christ is like a giant (see Ps 18:6), "because
he, one, is of double form and of twin nature, a sharer in Divinity and
in the body" (*Inc.* 5.34).[6] At this point it appears as though the main subject
in view—the "he" of the sentence—is the Son of God: "In going through
the duties of our life, although he was always God eternal, he assumed
the sacrament of the incarnation," an interesting and characteristically
Ambrosian phrase. The one who assumed the incarnation (or assumed
human existence) would naturally be the divine Son. Yet Ambrose
continues: "He is not divided, but is one, because both are one figure (*unus*),
and the one figure is in both—that is, with regard to both divinity and the
body".[7] Suddenly, it is not clear who the subject, the "one figure," is: is he a
third thing who is "in" divinity and "in" humanity? Ambrose's rhetoric
pushes the limits of the ideas being discussed. But he means to conclude on
a unitive point: it is not the case that one figure (*alter*) is from the Father and
the other (*alter*) from the Virgin, but *the same* is of the Father in the one
respect and from the Virgin in the other (*Inc.* 5.35).[8] Ambrose's language
here is quite close to that of Gregory Nazianzen.

On several other points Ambrose argues from a unitive position. His
most significant argument repeats one of Gregory Nazianzen's central
claims, and differs from the view of Origen: that Christ's divine identity
need not conflict with his human existence. His eternal generation from God
the Father does not rule out his being born of Mary as a human being,[9] nor
does his flesh necessarily conflict with his divinity, just as the divine will was
not opposed to Christ's passion, or vice versa. Ambrose summarizes in a
parallel statement that closely resembles the pattern of Gregory Nazianzen's
litany of Christ's divine and human acts: "For the same one suffered and did
not suffer, died and did not die, was buried and was not buried, rose again
and did not rise again" (*Inc.* 5.36).[10] Even when Ambrose adds qualifications
of the different natures involved, the Son of God remains the subject of all
of Christ's acts "in the body." Whatever died rose again, but what did not

die, that did not rise again, Ambrose explains. "Therefore *he* rose again according to the flesh, which having died rose again." But "he did not die according to the Word, which had not been destroyed on earth, but remained always with God." That is, the Word did not die as Word; it did not die a divine death, as it were, but merely a human one (*Inc.* 5.36). "Thus he died according to the assumption of our nature, and did not die according to the substance of eternal life. He suffered according to the assumption of the body, . . . and he did not suffer according to the impassible divinity of the Word, which is entirely without pain" (*Inc.* 5.37).

Commenting on Jesus's cry of dereliction in the Garden of Gethsemane, Ambrose fills out the picture dramatically. When Jesus cries to the Father "Why have you forsaken me?," this does not mean that the Father has abandoned the Son in a divine sense, but that "the same one"— the divine Son, not a different subject—had been forsaken "according to the flesh, in the incarnation" (*Inc.* 5.37–38). It is as if Christ were saying, in Ambrose's words, "Since I have assumed the sins of others, I have assumed also the words of others' sins. So I say that *I*, who am always with God, have been forsaken by God the Father" (*Inc.* 5.37–38).[11] In these words, the "I" is clearly the divine Son and Word of God: the one who is always with God takes on the abandonment, and so the statement of abandonment, that belongs properly to human beings, and so to Christ's flesh. Because of his assumption of human flesh in the incarnation, the same divine Son is both God and a dying human being. "He was immortal in death, yet impassible in passion," and the one who "trembled on the cross" is the same one "before whom the entire world trembled" (*Inc.* 5.39). Christ's work in the passion is thus "a kind of new operation" (*novo opere quodam*) that the Son effects. Though he was dead, he opens the tombs of the dead, and while his body lay in the tomb, "he himself" was free among the dead. This shows that although the flesh was not itself the Word of God, it was "the Word's flesh" (*Inc.* 5.40). Again like Gregory Nazianzen, Ambrose's rhetorical and liturgical sensibilities are evident in the rhythmic, antiphonal way he puts these phrases, and here we have a similar statement of the Son's impassible passion. The exegetical manifestation of Ambrose's Christology, such as we see in these comments on the passion, will be an important precedent for Augustine's even more expansive practice of the same. We should notice as well that, unlike Hilary, Ambrose fully embraces the Son's suffering in his humanity; he does not seek to protect the human Jesus from the pain and injury of the passion as Hilary did.

Together with this unitive approach, there are also dualistic strains, which come as no surprise, given Ambrose's reading of Athanasius and his use of Basil of Caesarea, who contains both. So we find, soon after the passage just discussed, several qualifications of the divine impassibility much like those Athanasius routinely issues after hearing his own nearly unitive statements. At his most extreme, Ambrose asks, "Why do you attribute [adtribuis] the calumnies of the body to divinity and connect the weakness of human pain even with divine nature?" Here he believes the Apollinarians have gone too far in claiming that it was the Word of God, in place of a human soul, that experienced the pain and agony of the crucifixion, because he believes this implies that when Jesus died the Word ceased to exist as well (although Apollinarius did not himself believe this). The Wisdom of God is not confined to the space of hell but resides always "in the bosom of the Father" (*Inc.* 5.41–42). These remarks are not a full qualification of the Son's human suffering, such as we saw in Gregory of Nyssa; Ambrose's unitive scheme prevails, though a certain uneasiness with a fully unitive Christology is evident nevertheless.

In reaction to the Apollinarians, Ambrose does, however, oppose the language of mixture. "Therefore do not mingle the darkness of our nature with the splendor of [Christ's] glory," lest we lose sight of what in Christ is passible and what is not (*Inc.* 5.44; *Virg.* 3.1.2). Such expressions of "mixing" the human with the divine, which we saw both Gregories accepting but which will in just a few decades be formally proscribed by the Council of Chalcedon under pressure of the Antiochene contingent, follow in the footsteps of Diodore's original resistance to the idea in Apollinarius. Yet even so, Ambrose does not adopt an Antiochene position, and he is happy, in this anti-Apollinarian work, to declare that "the Word of God suffered by the flesh." Since Ambrose is here referring to 1 Peter 4:1 ("Christ has suffered in the flesh"), he would be justified in restricting himself to saying that Christ, but not the Word, suffered so, but he does not; he makes a full, unitive confession, even while adding that the Word does not thereby undergo any change in the process (*Inc.* 5.44–45). Ambrose also opposes Apollinarius's denial of Christ's human mind by making a similar soteriological argument found in Gregory Nazianzen. Since the human soul is more responsible for sin than the body, it is all the more imperative that Christ possess a human mind (*Inc.* 7.68). So the Apollinarians not only divide Christ; they divide Christians as well and "separate the nature of man from man" (*Inc.* 2.11). Against this view, Ambrose maintains that

Christ assumed a human mind in the incarnation specifically in order to amend it (*Inc.* 7.67). In Ambrose's own environment, the Italian synods of the 370s under Damasus's leadership had already mooted the idea in opposition to Apollinarius (Damasus, *Il. sane* 73), and this may be a common source for both Ambrose and Gregory.

Again like Gregory, Ambrose understands the salvation that Christ wrought as involving his divine nature in a more integral way than we saw in Hilary. Ambrose writes that the Son of God "assumed what was mine so that he may impart what is his": he took on our humanity so that he could convey to us his divinity (*Inc.* 4.23). The function of Christ's divinity is not merely to render Christ's humanity sinless, so that it may effect salvation through the sacrifice of the cross. In moving rhetoric, Ambrose describes the complicated double work of divinity and humanity for salvation: "He received from us what he offered as his own for us, that he might redeem us from our own, and that he might confer upon us what was not our own from his divine liberality. According to our nature, then, he offered himself, that he might do a work beyond our nature. From what is ours he took the sacrifice, from his the reward" (*Inc.* 6.54). Here it is the same one Son of God who effects the entire mystery of salvation, both in his divinity and in his humanity (*Inc.* 7.75). Very shortly we will see Augustine replicate this same deeply inclusive understanding of Christ's ministry on our behalf. Likewise, Ambrose understands Christ's work of mediation not merely as reconciling humans to God, but as positively conveying his divine nature to us. For this reason, Christ must be equal in divinity to God the Father. "Can he grant anything that he does not have?" (*Inc.* 8.82, 85). In terms of the knowledge of God, Christ's incarnation serves as well to reveal God himself. The Word "took on what was outside the nature of divinity so that he might be seen according to the nature of the body" (*Inc.* 8.82, 85). The incarnation thus "inaugurates [human] nature" through baptism, so that Christians can "bear God" in their own bodies (*Exp.Lk.* 5.24).

Even if one grants such qualifications and a few inconsistencies concerning divine impassibility,[12] the Word typically remains the subject of Jesus's human actions in Ambrose's work. Ambrose asserts Christ's unity in a homily on Psalm 61. Both Christ's divinity and his humanity remain "one and the same";[13] there is not one figure (*alter*) from the Father and another (*alter*) of Mary. The duality of Christ, he explains, is manifest in the distinction of his works, but not in a difference of person (*varietate personae*) (*In Ps* 61.5). The dualist elements of Ambrose's work can safely be ascribed to his reading of Origen and Athanasius, and certain texts by Basil of Caesarea, yet his unitive instincts, which were possibly nourished by Gregory Nazianzen, win out in the end. In sum, Ambrose advances a strong, if not entirely consistent, unitive Christology in his own right,[14] and he provides a key turning point in Latin Christological tradition from certain forms of antihomoian argumentation, such as we saw in Hilary, toward the magisterial work of Augustine.

AUGUSTINE'S EARLY CHRISTOLOGY: *EXPOSITION OF PSALM 56*

Very few individuals approach the magnitude of St. Augustine of Hippo (354–430) in their theological and ecclesiastical influence: there is hardly an area of the Christian life on which he failed to leave his distinctive mark. It is therefore all the more remarkable that, until fairly recently, modern interpreters have tended to overlook, downplay, or simply misunderstand Augustine's Christology.[15] This bizarre state of affairs arose partly because Augustine's understanding of Christ is so deeply interwoven with his many other concerns that one has to read quite extensively in Augustine's works to discern its overall shape. Except for a few, lesser-known short treatises, Augustine did not produce any concentrated account of Christ alone, and certainly nothing on the scale of his famous *The Trinity*—although, as we shall see, that work is very much about Christology, if read attentively. As we have just observed, Ambrose had a significant effect on Augustine's Christology, though it may not be so obvious if one examines only their overt literary connections. For long before he took the trouble to read those works of Ambrose that he could get a hold of, Augustine had sat at the feet of Ambrose the preacher at a crucial time in his faith development, as he famously recounts in the *Confessions*. Ambrose's sermons taught Augustine a great deal about how to approach the Scriptures, and the Scriptures, as Augustine would argue in *Christian Doctrine* and his *Expositions of the Psalms*, are preeminently focused on Jesus Christ.

In order to elucidate Augustine's Christology, we will concentrate here on five key texts: his early *Exposition of Psalm 56* and his four major works, *Christian Doctrine*, *Confessions*, *The Trinity*, and *The City of God*. An important advance in the study of Augustine's Christology occurred when scholars identified the point at which he began to adopt the idea that there is one *persona* and two natures in Christ, which was quickly becoming a conventional formulation in the wider church.[16] This is a notable shift in terminology, to be sure, but in another respect it is less significant than it may seem, for if we examine its meaning rather than merely the terms used to express it, Augustine's Christology is remarkably consistent across his career. Virtually from the beginning of his priestly ministry in 391, Augustine advanced a strongly unitive Christology, and the unity of Christ serves as the linchpin for several major themes of his theology as a whole.

For an initial résumé of Augustine's Christology we could do no worse than to look at his early homily on Psalm 56. The *Exposition of Psalm 56* probably dates from 393 or 394, near the beginning of his ordained ministry and well before he altered his language to express the unity and composition of Christ. This early piece is an illuminating example of how Augustine operated with a fundamentally unitive Christology early on and the full range of hermeneutical and ecclesiastical issues that it involved. It is also a classic example of how groundbreaking theological reflection takes places in the liturgy and can even be inspired by something as serendipitous as the choice of Scripture readings given in the lectionary.

Augustine begins his homily on the psalm by referring to the gospel reading from the day's service (from John 15), which tells how much Christ loves his disciples and how they in turn are to love one another. For Augustine, this is an all-encompassing proposal, since love is both the ultimate meaning of all the Scriptures and the chief and final aim of the Christian life, both now and in the age to come (*Doctr.* 1–3). He therefore means to read the psalm in view of the church's life in the fullest sense. As we shall see, Augustine's understanding of Christ is intimately bound up with his understanding of the way in which and the ends for which believers are to read the Scriptures. Yet, at the same time, the very thought of Christ's love is wrapped up in a consideration of who he is. Before Augustine can even make the connection from Christ's love of his disciples to their love of each other, he interjects a brief statement of Christ's identity: "He is God with the Father; he is a human being with us" (*En.Ps.* 56.1).[17] Because of who Christ is, the one who is both divine and human, connected with God the Father and with us human beings, for *that* reason, Augustine says, Christ's perfect love of us enables us to love one another.

Augustine's approach to the question of love runs deeper than may at first appear. It is not a merely behavioral or ethical appeal: he aims to convey in a clear and compelling way how it is that human beings can imitate the love of *God*, and to move his hearers toward that kind of life. The crucial link between the divine love and the love that we show toward each other, as witnessed in the psalm and in every other respect, is Christ himself; and the key factor that makes Christ this link or mediator is his own divine-human identity. The point runs both ways. Even though Christ is radically different from us, in that he is our creator, nevertheless he is also like us, because he became human for our sake. In Augustine's view, Christ is truly imitable not merely because he is human; that is a necessary but hardly adequate condition for making someone worth imitating. What really makes Christ an effective model, Augustine says, is that he is *divinely* human: "he was human in such a way that he was also God" (*En.Ps.* 56.1).[18] Augustine comments later in the homily that the human Jesus is himself the Son of God in human existence (*En.Ps.* 56.8).[19] As for Ambrose, the main subject in view is the Son of God. Thinking again of the psalm, Augustine writes that, being divine, Christ is far above the psalmist David, but he (meaning the divine Son) deigned to become human from the line of David (*En.Ps.* 56.3). Thus, it is Christ's divine-human existence, or the unity of Christ, that undergirds the entire sermon, and indeed the whole of Augustine's theology and spirituality from the beginning of his career.

This particular psalm is a poignant text with which to consider the nature of Christ, for it is a prayer to God for deliverance from one's enemies. Jesus himself had of course prayed to God using the words of Psalm 21, crying out, "My God, my God, why have you forsaken me?" In that psalm as well, the psalmist speaks of his enemies who are persecuting him (vv. 6–8, 12–13, 16–18). By referring Psalm 56 also to Christ in his passion, Augustine raises acute questions surrounding the nature of Jesus's sufferings and particularly the unity and complexity of the incarnate Lord in the midst of them, much as they have been raised in similar ways for other theologians we have been considering. Augustine focuses in particular on the psalmist's opening cry for help, which he hears also as the voice of Jesus in the passion: "Have mercy on me, O God, have mercy, for my soul trusts in you" (Ps 56:2). His commentary on Christ's prayer to God gives us a full view of his Christology and its wider significance. "The one who together with the Father has mercy on you—he is crying out *in* you, 'Have mercy on me!' For that which in him cries out, 'Have mercy!' belongs to you: he took this from you; he clothed himself in flesh to set you free![20] This very same flesh is crying, 'Have mercy on me, O God, have mercy'—the human being itself [*homo ipse*], body and soul. For the Word assumed complete human existence [*totum hominem*], and the Word became a complete human being [*totus homo*]" (*En.Ps.* 56.5). In this brief passage, Augustine gives a simple but clear description of Christ's identity and saving work. Because he is God together with the Father, Jesus has mercy on us, and at the same time he also cries out for mercy *from* God on our behalf. The very same figure, in other words, both has mercy and begs for mercy. We might say that the two actions have different voices, so to speak, even though they come from the same speaker. Christ has mercy on us because he is God, and he begs for mercy from God because he has truly assumed a complete human existence from our own kind. On account of this assumption, Christ, the divine Son, speaks also with a human voice on our behalf. Christ's two modes of existing are so closely involved, in fact, that the divine Son has mercy on us precisely by crying out for us.

Augustine's further comments indicate that it is a full human being who cries to God for mercy, not merely the Word mimicking a human voice, as in an Apollinarian scheme. Both the Word and its human existence were "one human being," and at the same time they were also "one God" (*En.Ps.* 56.5).[21] In Christ, God and human existence come together in a single entity, and that single entity is himself completely God and completely human: he is the one God, as Son of the Father, and yet also an existing human being. Augustine is obviously aware of the potential difficulties involved, but as a pastor and a theologian he is equally clear that what is being claimed is of central importance for understanding the gospel and for the faith of his congregation. If any are confused about how all of this applies to Christ and to their own lives, or perhaps are anxious about their chances of obtaining mercy from God, Augustine encourages them: "Let us not be afraid of the voices that plead for mercy and grant it, for the same one pleas because he grants it,[22] and he became human because he is merciful—not that he was born out of any necessity of his condition, but he liberated us from our condition of necessity" (*En.Ps.* 56.5). There is no need for fear or confusion, Augustine says, precisely because Christ is both the petitioner and the guarantor of divine mercy. Even as a human being hanging on the cross, Christ was at the same time "God above the heavens" (*En.Ps.* 56.13).[23] Note that Augustine does not say, as Athanasius or Hilary might, that the Word was safely governing in the heavens while the human being Jesus died on the cross. He argues that *God* was both a human being on the cross while also reigning from the heavens.[24] It was God who died on the cross as a human being, and the crucified Christ was himself God, as well as a human being.

Not only is Christ able to grant the mercy that he himself pleads for, but, Augustine says, he takes on our suffering and need for God because he means to grant it. God became human in Christ out of mercy in the first place. Moreover, because he is both God and a human being, Christ prays to God in order to teach us how to pray, particularly in our times of most acute need and distress. "Just as he suffered to teach us how to suffer, and rose from the dead to teach us to hope for resurrection," so too Christ begged for mercy from God to show us how to do the same (*En.Ps.* 56.13). Christ is our exemplar because he takes upon himself, as God, our human condition and models in himself how we too are to relate to God. The unity of God and humanity in Christ, in other words, is the very ground of both faith and hope—and, as we shall see, of love as well. But all of this is possible only because, in Christ's passion, "*God says to God, 'Have mercy on me!'*"[25] (*En. Ps.* 56.13, emphasis added).

In the same homily, and in several of his other works on the Psalms, Augustine gives a famous definition of how Christ relates to the multiple voices in Scripture. This vision of the incarnate Christ represents Augustine's own characteristic approach to the hermeneutical questions that have occupied theologians since Origen. Just as he begins to discuss the witness to Christ's passion in the psalm, Augustine explains the full sense of Christ that is implied in such an approach: "The whole Christ (*totus Christus*) is both the Head and the Body." As Paul intimates (Col 1:18, 24), Christ includes both himself properly speaking—"our Savior himself, who suffered under Pontius Pilate and who now, after having risen from the dead, is seated at the right hand of the Father"—as well as his body, which is the church as it extends throughout the world and includes the faithful who have gone before and those yet to come. Even though he can no longer be seen, Christ the head rules his body from heaven, and his body is united with him in love. Because Christ himself includes the experience of his church, the multiple voices expressed in Scripture are therefore all the voices of the same Christ. One can see this most vividly in the Psalms, where prayers, praises, and lamentations are offered to God, interspersed with God's voice to his people, which is why Augustine explains the idea most clearly in his *Expositions of the Psalms*. In this way Christ includes even the historical voices of the original authors. The prophet David also spoke Psalm 56, Augustine explains, but only because Christ was speaking it in him. Even when David speaks of his own accord, he speaks the words of Christ because Christ has given him to speak them (*En.Ps.* 56.13). This way of reading Scripture is the direct result of the incarnation; that is to say, it is founded on Christ himself.

It is centrally important, Augustine tells his congregation, to understand who Christ is—that he is God who has been made human and who even includes his church—so that one can hear the many contrasting and even disturbing voices of Scripture as all belonging to him. As one reads the Psalms and other Scripture, one must first perceive Christ as the incarnate Lord or "hear the voices of the Head," so that one can then "hear the voices of the body as well." Christology, in other words, is the key to biblical interpretation, much as it was for Gregory Nazianzen and (in a different way) for Origen. The intended result of this way of reading Scripture is very specific and is itself unitive. Believers are to perceive the *totus Christus* as they read or hear the Scriptures for the sole reason that God "does not want us to speak separately from him any more than he wants to be separated [from us]" (*En.Ps.* 56.13).[26] If Christ is "with us, even to the end of the ages," as he said he would be (Matt 28:20), Augustine reasons, then "he speaks in us, he speaks about us, he speaks through us, because we too speak in him; and we speak the truth only because we speak in him" (*En.Ps.* 56.13).[27] Through the Scriptures and the prayers of the church, the speech of believers and the speech of Christ are wrapped up together in Christ's truth, and all because of who Christ is for us.

Given Augustine's unitive approach, it is significant that, in the same sermon, he is perfectly comfortable speaking of Christ's divine and human voices as coming from two *personae*, or two "persons," simply transliterated. For example, in his comment on Psalm 56:4, "he sent from heaven and saved me," Augustine writes that Christ speaks in the persona of a human being praying (*En.Ps.* 56.8). The term *persona* not only suggests a speaking and acting subject, but it can translate the Greek *hypostasis*, which, as we have seen, has often been used to designate the distinct subsistence of the divine Son. Fairly soon, at the Council of Chalcedon, both terms will be used to name what is one in Christ. In light of this wider context, it would appear, then, that Augustine is showing dualist tendencies in conflict with the position we have just discussed. But this is not at all Augustine's meaning; he uses the term to mean something like a literary persona or voice. Augustine's use of the language of multiple *personae* is so interesting because it shows how unreliable technical terms can be for assessing the real nature of a theologian's Christology. He will eventually conform his usage to the emerging norms of the wider church, but in the meantime, it is obvious that his Christology is as unitive as one could imagine.

Finally, we see in this piece a further suggestion that echoes and presages other "orthodox" positions. Augustine uses the imagery of the psaltery and lyre in order to comment further on Christ's divine and human deeds. Even though one can easily find two different sorts of action in Christ, such as miracles versus sufferings, it is the same Lord who performs them both: "The Lord works two kinds of deeds through his flesh" (*En.Ps.* 16).[28] While the miracles obviously reflect the work of God and the sufferings are human experiences, Christ did the miracles *through* his body, and both divine and human actions can be recognized in the one flesh of Christ. Augustine's teaching here resembles the earlier thought of Gregory Nazianzen on Christ's two wills, and Maximus Confessor will later expand on the same.

Thanks in part to the influence of Ambrose, Augustine has allowed himself to remain closer to the biblical idiom; he is more open to its full signification via the *communicatio idiomatum*, along the lines of Gregory Nazianzen, than the sort of approach that we have found in Diodore, Gregory of Nyssa, and Hilary.[29] For Augustine, the unity of "the whole Christ" is the central principle of the entire spiritual, ecclesial, and exegetical project. From the beginning of his ordained ministry, he shows a thoroughgoing unitive Christology, in which the divine Wisdom of God, Jesus's human existence, the life of the church, and the full range of voices in Scripture all belong to one and the same figure—the incarnate Son of God. In his own terms, Augustine has thus given full voice to the kind of single-subject exegesis that we have seen in Gregory of Nazianzus and that will be replicated very soon by Cyril of Alexandria.

AUGUSTINE'S MATURE CHRISTOLOGY: *THE TRINITY* AND *CHRISTIAN DOCTRINE*

The fuller meaning of Augustine's Christology is climactically expressed in his magisterial work *The Trinity*, which is one of his richest and most complex productions. It belongs with the *Confessions*, *Christian Doctrine*, and *The City of God* as one of his major theological opera, and it is easily one of the most significant theological treatises in Christian tradition. Augustine wrote the work gradually over a period of two decades (399–419), parts of it obviously at speed and much of it lacking the sort of revision that he would have liked. Nevertheless, it is carefully organized on the large scale, if not in every detail. As its title indicates, the entire work concerns the Trinity, yet it is also focused on Christ in a distinct way. Book 1 sets out the basic themes of the inquiry, including some key principles of Augustine's Christology and hermeneutics. As a foundation for the rest of the work, books 2–4 then treat the revelations of God, or theophanies, framed in a discussion of the meaning of "sending" or mission, first in the Old Testament and then culminating in God's sending of his Son to be incarnate and crucified and to rise again for our salvation. Because of the structure of Augustine's argument, we will consider his treatment of Christ in books 1, 4, and 13 more or less in order.

Augustine begins the work with several remarks on his approach and method, which characterize the way he understands Christ. His opening point is that his consideration of the Trinity throughout the entire work will be based on faith rather than on reason. Here he is particularly critical of human attempts to ascend to the knowledge of God (the divine substance) by means of our ideas and concepts of the universe. Such attempts are futile, Augustine believes, since the unchanging divine substance cannot be known in terms of concepts that are changing and finite (whether they are ideas of bodily or spiritual things). Many theological errors have arisen for just this reason—that people have applied to God ideas that derive from mortal and limited creatures (*Trin.* 1.1).

Instead of this route, which he often identifies with the philosophers, Augustine will instead base himself on the more reliable language of the divine Scriptures. Against the falsehoods obtained by reason alone, the Scriptures convey true knowledge of God by using the very creaturely concepts that reason has so wrongly employed. In this way the Scriptures communicate divine things by adapting them to our limited, creaturely understanding, and in so doing they purify our minds and spirits of false-hood (*Trin.* 1.2). In order to bring us to the knowledge of the transcendent God, Scripture leads us along more familiar and palpable roads—in partic-ular, the road of faith. For Augustine, as we have seen, the presentation of divine things by Scripture is also the presentation of Christ himself. The full truth of divine things is contained within the familiar, creaturely words, yet in another sense it is also hidden in them. Thus Augustine takes Paul's state-ment that "all the treasures of wisdom and knowledge are hidden in Christ" (Col 2:3). That is, to those whose minds are still being purified (of wrongful attachment to earthly things), God reveals himself through Christ in a hidden way that is accommodated to our condition: not in his full divine strength, as the divine Son equal to the Father, but "in the human weakness through which he was crucified" (1 Cor 2:2; 3:1–2; *Trin.* 1.3).

At this point Augustine mentions some who are discontented with the path through Christ and the Scriptures that he has just described, people who regard such things as senseless and beneath them. He defines the purpose of the work to "give the reasons" for the Trinity that they seek, which he briefly defines here in terms of the Nicene Creed: "that the Trinity is the one, only, and true God, and that it is right to say, believe, and understand that the Father, Son, and Holy Spirit are 'of the same substance' or 'essence'" (*Trin.* 1.4). The knowledge of the Trinity is available only through "the righteousness of faith" (Rom 4:13), which is to say through God's revelation and saving work in Christ. Augustine therefore means to identify himself with the Nicene faith of the catholic church, and here again, the legacy of Ambrose and others is foundational.

The object of the book's overall quest is "the unity of the three, the Father, Son, and Holy Spirit" (*Trin.* 1.5). Contrary to how he is often characterized as a theologian, Augustine is not beginning with the divine unity, at least not on the face of it; he is beginning with the three and aiming to discover or show the unity among them. Again, he offers a summary of the received faith in the Trinity, which is based on the Scriptures and taught by previous catholic commentators. First, the Father, Son, and Holy Spirit make up a divine unity in the inseparable equality "of one substance" and are therefore one God, even though, second, they each have different relations to one another (for example, the Son is begotten from the Father) and they are therefore not the same thing. Third, each of the three persons has a different set of actions or roles in the divine economy: only the Son was born of Mary, crucified, and rose again, and so on. And fourth, the three nevertheless always work together in their various economic acts (*Trin.* 1.7, 14).

After laying out the general theme in the opening sections, Augustine spends the remaining, longer portion of book 1 on basic questions concerning the identity of Christ as he is described in Scripture. The main question in view is the same one that has occupied theologians since Origen, namely, how we are to understand the various statements about Christ in Scripture. Augustine summarizes the problem in this way: in some passages the Son is described as less than the Father (for example, John 14:28)—and even less than himself (Phil 2:7)—while in others he is equal to the Father. In other words, we again have the lowly and the lofty statements of Scripture. In response, Augustine gives his own rule of Christological exegesis by looking to Paul's narrative about Christ in Philippians 2: that Christ, who was "in the form of God" and equal to God, emptied himself and "took the form of a servant" and was born in human likeness and form, and later died on the cross and was exalted by God and given "the name above every name" (Phil 2:6–11). Augustine's use of this passage is especially important for our understanding of Latin Christological tradition, on account of the different way that it will be used by Leo of Rome and through him the Definition of Chalcedon.

The key to interpreting the testimonies about Christ is to distinguish between those passages that "sound [*sonet*] according to the form of God in which [the Son] exists and is equal to God the Father," and those that sound "according to the form of a servant that he assumed and which is less than the Father." Augustine's rule of biblical interpretation, which he employs against (real or imagined) "Arian" denials of the Son's divinity and hence the unity and coequality of the Trinity, is identical in principle with the one that Gregory Nazianzen gave in his arguments against the Eunomians' denials of the same. On the one hand, one must distinguish between statements of the Son's proper divinity and statements of his assumed humanity, lest one take the lowly passages of Scripture as evidence that Christ is not fully divine. This distinction aims more directly at Arian exegesis. Yet, on the other hand, underlying the distinction is the unity of Christ and the continuity of the Son's existence through both "forms." While this distinction between forms is fundamental to a right understanding of Christ, the Scriptures are equally clear, through the *communicatio idiomatum*, that both types of texts apply to the same subject. Paul's statement that the rulers of this age have "crucified the Lord of glory" (1 Cor 2:8), for example—which speaks of God being put to death—makes it clear that the Son of Man, according to the form of a servant, is "himself the same" (*idem ipse*) Son of God according to the form of God (*Trin.* 1.28).[30] Augustine holds the two points together without flinching: "To be sure, he was crucified because he was in the form of a servant, but the Lord of glory was crucified. For such was the assumption that made God a human being and a human being God" (*Trin.* 1.28). Hence, the *communicatio idiomatum* in Scripture is, in Augustine's view, perfectly correct and certainly should not be explained away, as we have seen Origen, Diodore, and to some extent Athanasius do. This rule of biblical interpretation thus enables one to understand how a whole variety of biblical passages are "Scriptures about the Son of God" (*Trin.* 1.22);[31] that is, they all apply to the divine Son.

Structurally speaking, Augustine's Christology reflects his exegetical procedure directly. The incarnate Christ is both God and a human being; he still exists in the form of God even when he emptied himself and took on the form of a servant, and so "it is the same only-begotten Son of the Father who is both in the form of a servant and in the form of God" (*Trin.* 1.14). If we can borrow a term from Gregory Nazianzen, God and humanity in Christ "interpenetrate" one another: "Because the form of God took on the form of a servant, *both are God and both are human*. But both are God on account of God who takes on, and both are human on account of the human existence [*hominem*] that is taken on" (*Trin.* 1.14, emphasis added). And the very moment that Augustine affirms this cross-predication and cross-penetration, he specifies as well that God and human existence "become" each other in such a way that they also remain what they are and do not change their natures: God was not changed into a creature, ceasing to be God, nor did Jesus's humanity cease to be a creature in its unity with the divine. Finally, Augustine emphasizes the asymmetry involved in the incarnation, much as Gregory did. In several accounts of the exegetical rule, Augustine distinguishes between the verbs used: Christ *is* in the form of God, but he *assumed* the form of a servant (*Trin.* 1.22; 2.2, 4). In slightly different terms, "the Son of God is therefore equal to God the Father by nature, but less than him by condition [*habitu*]" (*Trin.* 1.14). In both respects Christ's divine status outweighs and guides his human status; they are neither equal with one another, nor, to be sure, does his human status overrule his divinity. Thus Christ is at the same time "equal to the Father in the form of God, while in the form of a servant he is 'the Mediator of God and man, the man Christ Jesus' " (1 Tim 2:5; *Trin.* 1.14).

In sum, Augustine establishes in book 1 that Christ's divinity and humanity, the form of God and the form of a servant, are distinct; they have come together in the same Son of God in the incarnation, even becoming or "intermingling with" each other, yet without fundamental change; and the divine predominates over the human. A further aspect of the asymmetry between Christ's divinity and humanity has a definitive effect on how Christ is known, and indeed on the very nature of faith, and in many respects this is the theme of the rest of the work.

Even though in Christ God has become human, the two are "the same" entity, and the human Jesus is all the while the only-begotten Son of God. Nevertheless, there is a fundamental difference in whether his true, divine identity is *known*—that is to say, whether or not one believes, perceives, or knows Christ's divinity is the determining factor in whether or not one has faith; for to know Christ to be the Son of God is the very nature of faith. It was this difference, Augustine says, that distinguished those who killed the Lord of glory and those who chose to follow him in faith.

Ultimately, it will be the fate of the wicked precisely not to see the form of God in Christ, but only to see the form of a servant, even as he acts as their judge in full divine authority. Yet the righteous will see God in Christ and eternally rejoice, since eternal life is, according to John's gospel, "to know you the one true God and Jesus Christ whom you have sent" (John 17:3; *Trin.* 1.28, 31). To apply Augustine's general point to the theological question at hand, the way in which one interprets the manifold witness to Christ in the Scriptures determines whether one has faith and ultimate beatitude.

With these foundations in view, we can now examine the remainder of Augustine's unitive Christology in books 4 and 13 of *The Trinity* as well as in *Christian Doctrine* and passages from the *Confessions*. As these texts bear out, the entirety of Augustine's spiritual and theological project reflects and depends on the unity of Christ.

Theophany

Augustine's first Christological theme is that of theophany. Having set himself the task of pursuing the knowledge of God as it is revealed in Scripture, Augustine devotes the next three books of *The Trinity* to God's self-revelations, or theophanies, in the Old and New Testaments. As noted in book 1, human minds are trapped in intellectual and moral weakness, so that if we are to have any hope of knowing God, God must show himself to us. Books 2 and 3 consider the theophanies in the Old Testament, including the question of whether it is only one member of the Trinity, the entire Trinity, or something else that is appearing in them. In book 4 Augustine considers the incarnation, the greatest of God's self-manifestations.

Rather than being trapped in the knowledge of earthly things, believing that we find true wisdom in them, we must instead come to appreciate our weakness by contrast with God's purity and strength—that is, we must not be "puffed up with knowledge," as Paul admonishes (1 Cor 8:1). In this way alone, Augustine writes, can we receive enlightenment from Christ the Savior. In order to reach us in our exiled condition, God has therefore been sending visions of himself since Old Testament times which seek to redirect our gaze toward him. These theophanies convey both the futility of trying to reach God by our own strength (which causes us to sink even lower) and the degree to which God loves us, which guards against despair. God's ultimate intent is for us to progress in *God's* strength, not our own, through the power of his love and the weakness of our humility. In order to accomplish this, finally and definitively the Word of God shines in the darkness of minds blinded by unbelief by becoming flesh and coming among us (*Trin.* 4.1–4).

In book 1 of *Christian Doctrine*, which was written slightly earlier than books 1–4 of *The Trinity*, Augustine expands further on the revelatory aspect of the incarnation. Here he concentrates on Christ's identity as the Wisdom of God, which suits his purpose in a work on hermeneutics and communication. Again, only God the Trinity, whose nature is unchangeable, can serve as the ultimate object of our desire and longing. In Augustine's terms, only God is to be "enjoyed" (*frui*), by which he means to "cling to something in love for its own sake," so that we attain permanent happiness (*Doctr.* 1.4–5). Moreover, the divine life by which we are meant to live—not living things, but Life itself, beyond the changeability of creation—is the Wisdom of God, by whom alone creatures come to be wise (*Doctr.* 1.8; *Conf.* 7.23). Yet, given our weak and darkened condition, we can know the divine Wisdom only if Wisdom adapts herself to our weakness, and that is exactly what has happened in the incarnation. By becoming flesh as Jesus Christ, "Wisdom deigned to adapt herself to our infirmity and offered an example of how to live in human existence [*in homine*], since we too are human" (*Doctr.* 1.11). The human existence of God's Wisdom thus reveals to us the source and model of our own life. By appearing to our carnal eyes, becoming a bodily human being, the "homeland" that we long for has made itself to be also the "way" to the homeland—our *patria* has made itself the *via*—in Jesus Christ. Even the Apostle Paul, who speaks of having already moved beyond the beginning of Christ's ways, since he no longer knows Christ according to the flesh (2 Cor 5:16) and "forgets what was beyond and strains forward to what lay ahead" (Phil 3:13–14), is nevertheless "still walking on the way" of the humanity of Christ, through whom the journey must be undertaken. When Christ says, "I am the way, the truth, and the life" (John 14:6), it is as if he were saying, "You come by me, you come to me, you abide in me." By proceeding through and always with Christ, we move beyond temporal things to eternal things in hope of being seated with him at the right hand of God the Father (*Doctr.* 1.38).[32]

In *The Trinity* and *Christian Doctrine* Augustine thus describes the incarnation in fundamentally unitive terms. Christ's humanity, which is the Way home, is the humanity *of the divine Son*, the humanity of the Divinity—not a human being existing separately alongside the Son of God, or the humanity of the hypostasis or person of the Son, placed alongside his Divinity—and in *The Trinity* 4.1–4 Christ is the strength *of God* that has made itself available to human weakness. The unity of Christ must be very tight precisely because, as earthly and finite creatures, we require a "temporal means" similar to other things we know to purify and adapt us for eternal things; we require a remedy that is halfway between sickness and health and that has affinity with both. Accordingly, the Son of God became the Son of Man "to capture our faith and draw it to himself," leading us through his humanity to the truth of his divinity. Without such a union of divinity and humanity in the one Christ, we would still be left adrift, trapped in our fixation on earthly signs. In Christ we are able actually "to have faith in temporal things" (*Trin.* 4.24) only because his temporal humanity is united with the eternal Son.[33] Augustine summarizes in similar terms: as exiles from our homeland in God, human beings strive to return from afar "by the way that [God] has laid out in the humanity of the divinity of his only Son" (*Trin.* 4.4).[34]

The Blood of a Just Man

Augustine turns next to Christ's saving sacrifice. The darkening of our minds that Augustine describes in *The Trinity* books 1–4 is not a mechanical problem, at it were, like peripheral antennae that merely need to be read-justed, with no real implication for the inner person. Rather, what clouds and traps our vision in earthly things is our sin; and conversely, our sin is to be seeking our final happiness in creatures rather than in the creator. Here Augustine bases his argument to a large extent on Romans 1, where Paul also defines primordial sin as an idolatrous focus on creatures instead of the creator and characterizes it as "ungodliness and wickedness," which mani-fests itself in covetousness, envy, murder, deceit, and so on (Rom 1:18–32). In order for us to be redeemed from our pride and wickedness two things were required: "the blood of a just man and the humility of God" (Matt 27:24; 1 John 1:7; *Trin.* 4.4). As Augustine interprets our condition, sinful human beings stand under the just condemnation of God and the evil power of the devil, in addition to suffering from debilitating ignorance. Augustine's understanding of how Christ saves us from this condition is complex and evolves over the course of his career. On the one hand, the just condemnation of the wicked could be revoked only by the sacrifice of a just and innocent person who dies voluntarily out of mercy. Christ's voluntary sacrifice on the cross thus destroys our guilt and the debt that we owed to God (*Trin.* 4.17). But this is a human sacrifice that only God can provide: "So God became a just man and intercedes with God for sinful humans," in order that we could again contemplate God (*Trin.* 4.4).

On the other hand, we were also in bondage to evil and under the power of the devil, who had full rights over humanity after it had turned from God. It is the evil character of the devil to act out of power alone, with no regard for justice. Conversely, God's power is always characterized by justice. In order to overthrow the devil, God therefore acts from justice rather than power, so that, paradoxically, it was the justice of Christ that overthrew the power of the devil, and justice proves to be more powerful than power. Similar to the reversal that occurs in a Roman court when a false accuser becomes himself culpable by killing an innocent victim who was not in his debt, the devil is obligated to release those in his debt who placed their hope in the just man. In this way Christ's death not only redeems our sin and debt to God, but it overcomes the devil and defeats his power over humankind as well (*Trin.* 13.17–19).

Here again, only a real incarnation can accomplish this. Only the divine Son of God made human could be such a pure offering for sin, since he had no faults of his own. And only God made human could truly die willingly, because he possessed the power to avoid it. Christ alone can therefore be the pure sacrifice and also the holy priest who makes the offering (*Trin.* 4.19). So the devil drove to death the very redeemer who had come down from heaven and died willingly, that is, the Son of God (*Trin.* 4.17). As Augustine explains nearer the end of *The Trinity*, Christ needed to be human in order to die, but he also needed to be God so that he would not merely lack the power not to die. Again we have a paradox: the power of divinity that lay behind Christ's life and death (which was made evident at his resurrection) made his innocent human suffering more powerful and effective than the raw power of the devil, which is ultimately impotent by comparison (*Trin.* 13.8). By becoming incarnate in Jesus Christ, the Son of God—as the primary subject and actor—has brought us from death to life: "He was made a participator in our mortality and made us participators in his divinity"[35] (*Trin.* 4.4; *En.Ps.* 52.6). Consequently, it gives believers confidence and hope to know "what great things such a great one suffered for those who did not yet believe" (*Doctr.* 1.14). Only the divine Son of God could undergo a just and righteous death, defeat the devil, and inspire hope for salvation.

The Humility of God

Augustine's reflections on God's self-revelation and Jesus's human sacrifice join together in what is arguably his favorite image for the incarnation in the first half of his career.[36] The incarnation and sufferings of such a great one represent for Augustine nothing less than "the humility of God," a phrase based on Paul's language in Philippians 2. As he argues in *The Trinity*, the only thing that can cleanse the wicked and proud is "the blood of a just man and the humility of God" (*Trin.* 4.4). Because in Christ the almighty God has submitted to human obedience and suffering and Christ died voluntarily and willingly, his death is literally an act of divine humility. Far from being compromised, the justice of God is actually perfected in his humility in Christ. So Christ needed to be human in order to die for our sins, but he also needed to be God so that he could die willingly (*Trin.* 13.18). Real humility of the sort that can overturn the power of sin and evil, in other words, is possible only if Christ is himself God made human as a single subject of existence. The humility of God in Christ is divine power actually submitting itself to human suffering and death; otherwise, God would be avoiding our broken condition rather than embracing it in justice and love, and he would have remained in a position of power alone, just like the devil.

God's humility in Christ stands in stark contrast with the pride of human beings and the devil. It is the very nature of pride, moreover, not to recognize the incarnation, and specifically the union of God and humanity in Christ. Those who are proud cannot understand how the Word of God can "take on a lower nature and suffer what is proper to that nature" while at the same time remaining unchanged in itself (*Trin.* 4.18). By contrast, faith sees in Christ that the Word of God was made human and that "the whole thing is called 'God' because of God and 'man' because of man" (*Trin.* 4.31).[37] The unity of Christ, in other words, is the very marker that distinguishes true faith from sin and pride.

Augustine's most famous description of the humility of God in the incarnation comes in book 7 of the *Confessions*. Here he speaks to God about his own pride as he made his way from Manichaeism through Platonism and finally to the catholic faith. "First you wanted to show me how you 'resist the proud and give grace to the humble' [1 Pet 5:5], and with what mercy you have shown humanity the way of humility, in that your 'Word was made flesh and dwelt among' men and women (John 1:14)" (*Conf.* 7.13). Where the Platonists taught the vision of divine greatness, they showed no awareness at all that the Son of God "humbled himself" (Phil 2:8) and became human, and so their vision amounted to nothing but "monstrous pride." The philosophers did not believe that "at the right time he—the only-begotten Son—died for the unrighteous"; Augustine's very sentence structure emphasizes that the divine Son is the subject of Paul's statement

(Rom 5:6; *Conf.* 7.14). The wisdom of the world, as Augustine encountered it in Platonist philosophers, blinds them to God's true nature, which is that he is "meek and humble in heart," as Jesus says of himself (Matt 11:29). Unable to hear this said about God, the philosophers remain lost in their foolishness (Rom 1:23; *Conf.* 7.14). Augustine further describes the pride of philosophical contemplation in *The Trinity*: it does no good to have a partial vision of God far across the sea if one is unwilling to "climb aboard the wood" of the cross; meanwhile, those who are humble will be carried by that wood to the far shore whether or not they can see it now (*Trin.* 4.20). Wisdom's adaptation of herself to our weakness is therefore not weak or foolish at all, as the pagans think, but, paradoxically, the mark of real divine strength (*Doctr.* 1.11).

In order to conquer the pride of sin and evil, Christ enacted the humility of God by becoming human and dying for our sins, while at the same time showing that he is one with God the Father, in one "person" who is made up of both God and humanity (*Trin.* 4.12). The unity of Christ *is* the humility of God, which alone can save. In conclusion to *The Trinity* book 4, Augustine defines the unity of Christ in terms remarkably similar to those of Gregory Nazianzen and parts of Gregory of Nyssa. In Christ "human existence was coupled and somehow co-mixed with the Word of God into a unity of person"[38] when the Son of God was sent into this world for our salvation (*Trin.* 4.30).

AUGUSTINE'S LATE CHRISTOLOGY: CHRIST THE MEDIATOR IN *THE CITY OF GOD*

As Augustine's Christology matured through years of biblical study, pastoral ministry, and theological controversy, the one idea that best expressed all the others is that of Christ as the "Mediator between God and humankind" (1 Tim 2:5). The idea is already in play early in Augustine's ministry, as we have seen in connection with God's revelation through the incarnate Son. As both the Way and the Homeland, Christ serves as a mediator or path to God, and he does so chiefly through his divine humility.

In *The Trinity* book 4, still a relatively early text, Augustine takes a further step in developing the idea of Christ's mediation. Here he gives the idea more specificity, first by noting that there are different kinds of mediation. Whereas Christ is the mediator of life, the devil is the mediator of death. Through false ideas, philosophy, sacrilegious rites, blasphemous acts and symbols, and the preference of power over justice, the devil brings proud human beings down to death. By contrast, the humble Christ leads obedient human beings back to life. The devil's false mediation blocks the way to higher things by instigating our pride and misguided desires. But in order to reverse the damage, Christ came as a holy mediator, to the very place where the mediator of death had taken us. Being the Lord and God, he introduced healing into the death of the flesh by the hidden and mysterious decree of his high divine justice (*Trin.* 4.13–15). In *The City of God*, which Augustine began while still writing *The Trinity*, he develops the idea further. The fundamental principle of Christ's mediation is, again, his divine-human identity. Because we were in a wretched state due to our mortality and unable to deliver ourselves, we needed a mediator who could bring us over to immortality by being both divine and human. Christ intervened in our situation by being mortal in such a way that would not remain mortal, having a "transient mortality and a permanent blessedness" (*Civ.Dei* 9.15). By coming to exist in solidarity with us, Christ the mediator transfers us from what is transient to what is permanent.

What is both essential and unique about Christ's mediation is again brought out by contrast with evil mediators. The devil and his demons can also mediate the knowledge of certain divine things, and even a kind of supernatural power, such as pagan rites and religious practices sought to procure. In this major apologetic work, Augustine aims to meet head-on the various forms of evil and all that characterizes the city of earth, which is opposed to the City of God, from their beginnings in creation and the fall through the present life of the Roman empire, to their final destinies in the age to come. Accordingly, he does not want to minimize the supernatural activities associated with pagan religion, but rather to confront them directly. Above all, Augustine wants to make crystal clear the difference between the mediation of Christ and that of the wicked angels. It is a difference in both kind and effect. Proud evil angels do indeed mediate divine knowledge, because they are immortal beings who exist in a sort of heavenly realm. Yet here lies the greatest contrast of all, and it points again to the unity of the incarnate Christ. It is not enough merely to be immortal, as Augustine noted years earlier in his critique of Platonic contemplation in the *Confessions*. Although the demons are immortal, they are also deeply wicked and bent on the exercise of power. Christ the mediator, on the other hand, is that divine being who has chosen to *become mortal*, and who does so out of love and justice. As the good, mortal mediator, Christ destroys the power of the wicked, immortal mediators through his humility and kindness. The difference is visible as well in its effects: for an evil mediator divides friends from one another, while a good mediator reconciles enemies. All of this is possible through Christ because, in his case alone, God has himself become mortal: "The blessed and blessing God became a partaker of our nature and thus offered us a shortcut to participation in his divine nature" (*Civ.Dei* 9.15). The nature of true, divine mediation, then—which is also simply the nature of God—is not to wield absolute power, but to extend oneself in love and justice to raise up those who are unable to do so themselves.

Through his reflection on divine versus demonic mediation in this, his last major work, Augustine sharpens his emphasis on the unity and corporeality of Christ even further, making it the center point of his critique of pagan religion, philosophy, and society. He zeros in on the main difference between the pagan and Christian understandings of God. Plato, for example, argues that the gods or demons will be contaminated by contact with mortal human beings, even though the later philosopher Plotinus points out that such contact is not really in question. On the contrary, Christ reveals that God's nature is just the opposite: he is the sort of God who joins himself with "our lowliness by reason of the mortal nature of his body, and yet is able to render truly divine assistance . . . through the immortal justice of his spirit," in which he simultaneously remains on high. Against the Greeks and Romans, the incarnation of Christ shows not only that God is not polluted by contact with human flesh, but that the pagan gods are hardly superior for having avoided such contact. For Augustine, there is most certainly not any ontological conflict between divinity and humanity; in fact, to imagine that there is reflects the pride and wickedness of pagan society. Rather, the unity of Christ in the incarnation shows the true divine way of justice, love, and humility (*Civ.Dei* 9.16–17).

Augustine aims his unitive Christology directly at the anti-Christian critique of Porphyry, thus carrying forward an apologetic enterprise begun by Eusebius of Caesarea. Whereas Porphyry complained that he had never found the one principle that unifies all human history, Augustine points to the single eternal principle within the Trinity (God the Father) and the single economic principle of the Word of God made flesh. In Augustine's view, Porphyry's objection to Christ's lowliness, much like that of Celsus before him, whom Origen opposed, is a typical instance of pagan pride, much like the false superiority of the demons. This is just the sort of objection that Christ shows to be ill-founded; for it is not embodiment or materiality that is evil, such that God should avoid contact with it, but rather sin. If Porphyry were a true lover of wisdom—that is, a "philosopher," as he claims to be—he would have "recognized 'Christ the Power of God and the Wisdom of God' (1 Cor 1:24) instead of shying away from his saving humility, inflated with the swollen pride of useless learning" (*Civ.Dei* 10.24). Pagan philosophy is therefore no real philosophy at all, and the only true wisdom is the Wisdom of God made human. Against the false claims of pagan philosophy stands the grace of God in Jesus Christ, for Christ is himself the supreme instance of divine grace. Rather than pretending to ascend to God, one must "see the incarnation," in which the only Son of God "took a human soul and body . . . while remaining unchangeably in his own proper being . . . and gave to human beings the spirit of his love by the mediation of human existence, so that by this love people might come to the one who was formerly so far away from them." Such an act was possible only through the humility of God, and the proper response is likewise humility and gratitude (*Civ.Dei* 10.28–29). In this late major work Augustine heightens the justice, goodness, and ontological inclusiveness of the incarnation, all based on the unity and singularity of Christ.

In response to Porphyry's search, Augustine answers that Christianity is indeed "the universal way for the liberation of the soul" and that the soul cannot be freed in any other way. The story of Jesus Christ is the history of the unifying principle that Porphyry complains he has never heard (*Civ.Dei* 10.32). Augustine then summarizes his Christology in a concise, nontechnical description: "The divine Son of God, who is himself the Truth, took human existence without abandoning his divinity, and thus established and founded this faith, so that human beings might have a path to their God through the human who was God [*per hominem Deum*]." Christ is this mediator; he is the one and only road to God, "who is himself both God and man. . . . As the goal of the journey, he is God; as the means of the journey, he is a human being" (*Civ.Dei* 11.2).

The unique and universal path that Christ is shows several things at once, Augustine explains in one of the later books of *The Trinity*. By seeing that "human nature could be conjoined with God" in order to be "one person from two substances," Christ shows, first, the sort of place that all people can occupy in God's overall design, namely, one defined by and filled with divine grace, humility, and glory. This is because Christ is, second, the preeminent example of unmerited grace—an idea that is reinforced by Augustine's unitive Christology, since Jesus's humanity has even less possibility of having merited God's favor if it did not come into existence until it was created and assumed by the Word. Third, Christ shows how far human beings had strayed from God; yet, fourth, he also shows that the obstacle of pride can be cured by God's own humility. Likewise, Christ demonstrates that God's justice and goodness conquer the devil even when the devil thought he had conquered Christ. And finally, the incarnation demonstrates perfect obedience to God and shows the reward of that obedience in the resurrection of Jesus (*Trin.* 13.22; *Enchir.* 36).

Yet one of the most important effects of the incarnation, in Augustine's mind, concerns the whole body of the faithful, much as we saw in his early *Exposition of Psalm 56*. In *The Trinity* book 4, Augustine writes that the Son of God, "who is at once the Word of God and the Mediator between God and human beings, the Son of Man," reveals God to us and intercedes for us in order that we may all be one even as Jesus and the Father are one (John 17:20). The aim of the incarnation is ultimately to bring about the union of all people in a community of love, and this holy society is visible even at the technical level of Christ's composition, through the doctrine of the *totus Christus*. Head and body, Augustine writes, make up one Christ, one "person," but not one thing—so that the unity of Christ includes his church as well. Because of who Christ is, love becomes the aim of all biblical interpretation and the purpose of "the entire temporal economy," of which the incarnation is the centerpiece (*Doctr.* 1.39–41). Only by being joined together in Christ, who is himself a single being representing the humility, justice, and love of God, can human beings know peace and be united with one another in a harmony of will, because they are "fused in the furnace of charity" and share the same love, just as the Father and Son share a single nature and will with one another (*Trin.* 4.12).

6. Cyril, Leo, and Chalcedon (451)

The fifth century marks a new period in the development of patristic Christology. A major shift occurred in this period not merely because of new circumstances that inevitably come with the passage of time, but also because the way in which theologians constructed and defended their views of Christ changed in a more fundamental sense. At the heart of this change was the reception and use of earlier "patristic" authorities. In the fourth century, theologians made both direct and indirect use of earlier sources, with the work of Origen holding a special place of sustained influence. Yet the great debt of theologians such as Gregory Nazianzen and Gregory of Nyssa to Origen went largely unseen, since authors at that time did not normally cite their sources by name. In the fifth century, however, a new sort of reception developed, in which previous church fathers—in particular a select group of fourth-century theologians focused on Athanasius and the Cappadocians—became authoritative in a new way.

Beginning especially with Cyril of Alexandria, the major fourth-century fathers came to be seen as authorities in their own right, and they were cited as such by name, often with direct quotations from their texts. As before, patristic writers remained ordered under the greater authority of the Scriptures, yet in this period they now acquired a named identity that was unmatched in previous ages. In this process of naming and receiving new authorities, moreover, the later theologians inevitably made deliberate choices of selection and prioritization. The reception of earlier authorities was thus intimately tied up with the ongoing construction of new theological arguments and positions, so that present and past had a mutually formative effect on each other. The identification of which authors and texts to cite as authorities, in other words, was a creative act on the part of the later controversialists and anthologists, and their work shaped and was shaped by the sort of material they found in the earlier sources. In this chapter we trace the complexities of the reception of earlier Christological works by two theologians who played a major role in the fifth-century controversies, Cyril of Alexandria and Leo of Rome, together with the momentous Council of Chalcedon in 451.

CYRIL OF ALEXANDRIA

It is difficult to exaggerate Cyril of Alexandria's reputation in patristic Christological tradition. Since practically his own lifetime, a wide array of theologians and church leaders have considered him the chief architect of the grand edifice of Christological orthodoxy.[1] More recently, scholars have argued that the construction of post-Chalcedonian Christology from the fifth to the eighth centuries—a body of doctrine that in turn formed the basis of many later theological positions—consists largely in the reinterpretation of Chalcedon in light of Cyril's mature thought.

Yet of course Cyril's Christology is not an original creation of the 420s and 430s. Cyril constantly invokes the authority of the earlier "holy fathers and bishops" of the church, and his honorific title as the "seal of the fathers" testifies to his debt to earlier writers. Thus far scholars have tended to assume that the most influential of Cyril's patristic sources was Athanasius, his predecessor in the see of Alexandria twice removed. Accordingly, Cyril has been seen as a key representative of a distinctly Alexandrian theological tradition.[2] At the Council of Ephesus in 431, Cyril presented a collection of patristic authorities in support of his case against the claims of Nestorius. In this patristic "florilegium," the two strongest witnesses are Athanasius and Gregory Nazianzen, each of whom occupies twice as much space as any other author, with Gregory's *First Letter to Cledonius* (*Ep.* 101) being the longest single excerpt.[3] Even apart from the council, Cyril's work amply shows that Athanasius and Gregory are in fact the greatest direct patristic influences on his thinking.

At the Council of Ephesus Cyril claims, "At an early age we studied the holy Scriptures and have been nurtured at the hands of holy and orthodox fathers" (ACO 1.1.3:13, 22:8–10). A close study of Cyril's works shows that he did indeed make a substantial, though not exhaustive, study of the fourth-century fathers in the early years of his theological development. After the outbreak of the Nestorian controversy, he regularly appeals to the authority of Scripture, the fathers, and the Council of Nicaea (*Ep.* 1.2, 4; *2Ep.Nest.* 1; *Ep.Acac.* 7). Before the Council of Ephesus, in 430 or 431, Cyril addressed two works to the imperial court, which consist largely of a series of biblical quotations, together with a few references to patristic sources.[4] He then enclosed a similar collection, along with excerpts from the writings of Nestorius, in his first letter to Celestine (*Ep.* 11.6). The florilegium presented at Ephesus in 431 was the most extensive body of explicit patristic references in Cyril's work to date. Most often these citations and quotations serve mainly to bolster his authority in the immediate ecclesiastical disputes. Cyril invokes the legacy of Athanasius, for example, mainly in texts in which Athanasius's authority would strengthen Cyril's position, as in his letters to the monks of Egypt (*Ep.* 1.4) and to John of Antioch, where Athanasius's *Letter to Epictetus* of Corinth was being debated at the time (*Ep.* 39.10–11)—a practice that helps to explain why Cyril has so often been seen as the great heir of Athanasius. If we look beyond these relatively superficial citations and collections and compare Cyril's work with that of the fourth-century fathers in detail, it becomes clear that the major influence was not in fact Athanasius, but Gregory Nazianzen. Moreover, when Cyril does make use of Athanasius, especially during the third phase of his career, when he was trying to accommodate the Antiochene position as much as possible, several elements of Athanasius's work conflict with the Gregorian foundation, much as we might expect after the analysis given in the previous chapters. The resulting complexity of Cyril's Christology not only renders his work difficult to interpret, but has introduced major difficulties into the work of theologians who sought to follow him in the post-Chalcedonian period, as we shall see in chapter 7.

In order to understand the nature and the process of Cyril's reception of earlier authorities, it is important to distinguish among several stages of his career. There are four distinct phases in which Cyril's Christology takes shape:

1. Pre-428, before Cyril's controversy with Nestorius. He begins his theological career in opposition to the Antiochene Christology of Theodore of Mopsuestia. Major works from this period include his *Commentary on John.*

2. 428–433, the Nestorian controversy. During this period Cyril refines his Christology into its sharpest form, primarily on the basis

of the work of Gregory Nazianzen and defined in clear terms against Nestorius.

3. 433–c. 438, an accommodating interlude. As he signs the Formula of Reunion in 433, in order to compromise with Antiochene theologians, Cyril integrates Athanasian elements into his Christology, which partially corroborate and partially conflict with the basic Gregorian framework.

4. c. 438–444, Cyril's mature position. During this final period, as seen in his late work *The Unity of Christ*, Cyril returns to his earlier Gregorian, anti-Antiochene position.

Cyril and Gregory Nazianzen

Already in his own lifetime, Cyril earned the reputation for making the unity of Christ the centerpiece of his theological vision. In this regard he was guided primarily by Gregory Nazianzen. Cyril's emphasis on Christ's unity was well established in his earliest works, in which he already opposed the Antiochene Christology currently being advanced by Theodore of Mopsuestia, the former student of Diodore of Tarsus (*Pasch.Hom.* 8; *Com. Jn.*).[5] In his *Commentary on John*, for example, Cyril writes that the Word, who is by nature God, came together with his flesh in unity, and "united in himself things widely opposed by nature and averse to fusion with each other" (*Com.Jn.* 1.9, 17, 18; 14.20). Yet Cyril's fuller treatment of the unity of Christ began in earnest after 428, the year that Nestorius became archbishop of Constantinople and the controversy between them ignited.

In his polemical letters and treatises from this second period, Cyril argues more specifically for a "hypostatic union" in Christ—specifically, that the Word of God united human existence to himself "in hypostasis" (καθ' ὑπόστασιν) (*2Ep.Nest.* 3–4),[6] a phrase that is difficult to translate. Consequently, all biblical texts about Christ refer to "one incarnate hypostasis of the Word" (*Ep.* 17.8). The idea of Christ's hypostatic union is Cyril's most distinctive contribution to the technical terminology of Christian theology; it reflects neither the usage of the Cappadocians nor that of Athanasius, despite the latter's discussion of the equivalence between hypostasis and *ousia* at the Council of Alexandria in 362 and Gregory of Nyssa's categorization of nature and hypostasis. In light of the metaphysical distinctions that were later made after the Council of Chalcedon, Cyril's idea of hypostatic union has often been taken to be a technically accurate definition of the union of Christ. Yet in fact Cyril's reference to Christ's "hypostatic union" is ambiguous. He is not making a technical distinction, for example, between a union in hypostasis versus in nature (or in both), as one might expect following the Chalcedonian distinction between these terms. In his *Third Letter to Nestorius*, for example, Cyril speaks of a union "in nature" (κατὰ φύσιν), or a "natural union" (ἕνωσις φυσική) (*3Ep. Nest.* 4, 5, 12 anathema 3), in addition to union "in hypostasis." It has often been supposed, on the basis of examples such as this, that hypostasis and nature simply mean the same thing for Cyril, namely, a single existent being. But this is not the case either. Instead, the phrase "hypostatic union" indicates that the Word is united with human flesh as a single hypostasis or person, not two—that the union occurs in and by the unique Son of God, so that there is one Son in the incarnation just as there is one Son apart from it; yet the meaning of "nature" is not exactly equivalent to this, since the divine nature belongs to the entire Trinity. Neither term is strictly necessary, in any event. Cyril can just as well speak of the unity or union of Christ, pure and simple, and in one text the main deficiency in Nestorius's Christology is that he fails to "confess the union" (*Ep.Eulog.* 62). The most succinct definition that Cyril gives comes directly from Gregory Nazianzen, and when he defines the term in *The Unity of Christ* Cyril notes that it "has come down to us from the holy Fathers." A union, he writes there, is "the concurrence into one reality [ἕν]" of the things being united, which in Christ are "different from one another in nature" and which are not confused with one another (*Un.Chr.* 362/18; *Ep.Eulog.* 64).

As Gregory and Augustine also had done, Cyril expresses the unity of Christ by calling him "one and the same" Son or Christ. In his *Second Letter to Nestorius*, he famously argues that Christians do not worship the man Jesus "along with" (σύν) the Word, but rather "one and the same Christ," because his body cannot be separated from the Word, as the former language suggests (*2Ep.Nest.* 6). Cyril relies on this expression throughout his career, from his earliest writings through every subsequent phase. A key statement comes in his *First Letter to Successus*, written after 434: "We confess one Son and Christ and Lord, the same one [τὸν αὐτόν] God and a human being—not someone alongside someone else, but one and the same [ἕνα καὶ τὸν αὐτόν] who is and is known to be both things" (*1Ep.Succ.* 6; see *Ep.* 41.18).[7] As in Gregory, the phrase is meant to indicate that Christ is a singular being, namely, the Son of God, who in the economy of the incarnation is both God and a human being. It signifies that there is only one Son, who is also the one incarnate Christ.

Cyril likewise makes extensive use of the body-soul comparison in his explanation of the unity of Christ. Again the *First Letter to Succensus* provides a key example: "Our view is that there are two united natures but one Christ, Son, and Lord, the Word of God become human and incarnate. If you like, we can illustrate this by the example of our own composition, which makes us human beings. For we are composed of soul and body, and we see two different natures—that of the body and that of the soul. Yet a single human being is made by a union of the two, and the composition of two natures does not turn the one person into two people; but there is a single human being made by the composition of a soul and body" (*1Ep.Succ.* 7).[8]

For Cyril, as for Gregory, Christ is thus a single Son of God—even a single nature—similar to the way in which a human being is a single, unified nature made up of two different natures (*Ep.Eulog.* 62–64).[9] Although Cyril does not use the body-soul analogy to argue that Christ is composed of two perfect things, as Gregory does, their different approaches can easily be explained by making two observations. First, Cyril's polemical situation is virtually the opposite of Gregory's in the relevant sections of *Letter* 101—he is facing Nestorian rather than Apollinarian opponents—which requires a different sort of argumentation. Second, whereas Gregory is an avid Origenist, Cyril typically avoids Origenist notions, which leaves him relatively uninterested in the role of Christ's human soul—a point to which we will return. Scholars have also debated whether for Cyril the image functions merely as an illustration of the singularity of Christ as the Word made flesh, or more specifically as a constructive analogy to indicate something of the actual relationship and workings between divinity and humanity in the Christological union.[10] It is surely both, although the image illustrates the relationship between the Word and his flesh (without being Apollinarian) to only a limited extent.

Similarly, Cyril follows Gregory in using the idea of composition to explain the union and singularity of Christ, as we saw in the *First Letter to Succensus* (*1Ep.Succ.* 7). He expands the idea in the *Second Letter to Succensus*. The union of two different natures in "one incarnate nature of the Word" results in a real singularity (τὸ ἕν) that applies not only to things that are simple, but also to things that are "brought together in a synthesis [κατὰ σύνθεσιν συνηγμένων], as in the case of a human being, which [is composed] of soul and body" (*2Ep.Succ.* 3).[11] Because the idea of composition is so ubiquitous in late-ancient Greek thought, one could point to several philosophical parallels, some of which Cyril no doubt knew, yet there should be no doubt that his major source is again Gregory Nazianzen.

The idea that became the single greatest source of controversy in Cyril's lifetime and a point of acute disagreement in the following century is his notion that, in the most basic sense, Christ possesses only one, divine nature. Here again he follows Gregory Nazianzen directly. For Cyril, as for Gregory, the notion of one nature includes the admission that God and human existence are different things without confusion, and it allows that one can also say that Christ has two natures. Nevertheless, the preferred expression of both theologians is that Christ has one nature, properly speaking. In his anti-Nestorian work, Cyril follows Gregory's habit of saying that Christ has become incarnate out of two natures, in order to indicate the sources of the singular composition of Christ. He characteristically describes "the mode of the incarnation" in this way: "Two natures have met in an unbreakable mutual union" without merging or changing into one another, and the Word became flesh "out of two natures," so that there is now "one incarnate nature of the Word of God." On the one hand, Cyril clearly affirms the presence and continuing integrity of Christ's divinity and humanity: Christ's "flesh is flesh and not Divinity, . . . and likewise the Word is God and not flesh" (*1Ep.Succ.* 6; *Ep.* 46.3). Yet, on the other hand, he resists the idea that there are two natures after the incarnation, properly speaking. In an especially paradoxical statement, he argues that "while each [element] persists and can be discerned in its natural character,[12] God reveals to us a single nature of the Son, mysteriously and inexpressibly united—as I said, incarnate" (*2Ep.Succ.* 3).[13] Cyril's most common qualification of such language is to say that Christ's divine and human natures can be perceived only theoretically, whereas in fact they have become "one thing out of the two" (εἰς ἐξ ἀμφοῖν) (*Pasch.Hom.* 8). Although the distinct characteristics of divinity and humanity persist in the incarnation, the divine and human natures cannot properly be distinguished because, like a human soul and body, they now combine to make up a single living thing (ζῷον). If they were distinguishable as two distinct natures, Cyril reasons, they would be completely isolated from one another "in mutual difference and distinctness" (*2Ep.Succ.* 5)[14]—just as the divine and human natures were apart from the incarnation. In this respect, Cyril is insisting that the confession of Christ's divine identity means that humanity and divinity must be conceived differently from how they are in cases other than the incarnation. In other words, if divinity and humanity can be conceived as two natures apart from the incarnation, then they should not be so conceived in it, without serious qualification.

In his early work Cyril does make use of two-nature constructions in describing Christ, just as Gregory and Athanasius had. In the *Commentary on John*, for example, he argues that in the incarnation "the divine Word was not transformed into the nature of flesh," nor vice versa, "for each remains what it is by nature, and Christ is one thing from the two" (*Com.Jn.* 6.54). Yet once he learns what the Antiochenes are teaching, he generally avoids such language.[15] In response to the Antiochenes' persistence, he concedes that the statement that Christ suffered in his human nature can have an orthodox meaning—it "does no damage to the principle of the mystery" of the incarnation—but he does not think their intention is so innocent (*2Ep.Succ.* 5; *Ep.Eulog.* 64). In the end he clearly believes that single-nature language better expresses who Christ is. He summarizes the point in the later work *The Unity of Christ*. On the one hand, it is imperative to recognize that neither the divine nature of the Word nor Christ's human flesh underwent any change of nature in the incarnation, as Cyril's opponents were concerned to maintain. Nevertheless, it is equally imperative to confess "that there is one Son, and that he has one nature, even when he is considered as having assumed flesh endowed with a rational soul," because he has "made the human element his own." In this way "the same one is both God and a human being." Finally, in language that will anticipate that of the Council of Chalcedon: "Divinity is one thing and humanity is another, when they are considered with regard to their respective and intrinsic beings. But in the case of Christ, they came together in a mysterious and incomprehensible union without confusion or change. The manner of this union is entirely beyond conception" (*Un.Chr.* 372–73/77). Because of their union in Christ, divinity and humanity have come together in such a way that they are one entity within the divine nature, even while each one remains in its own proper existence.

Like Gregory, Cyril's preference for single-nature language for Christ mainly reflects a strong emphasis on the predominance of the Word's divine nature over its human form. He frequently comments on the smallness of Christ's human characteristics compared with his transcendent divinity, on account of his being Lord by nature (*Ep.* 1.10).[16] Likewise, he shares Gregory's central conviction that the incarnate Christ is God in his most fundamental identity, which is less clear in Athanasius, for all his defense of the divinity of the Word (*Ep.* 1.7).[17] Against Nestorius, Cyril argues that

Christ is "truly God as the one natural Son," and he regularly appeals to Christ's title "Emmanuel" as evidence that he is "God with us" (*3Ep.Nest.* 12 anathema 5, 1; *Un.Chr.* 310/52).[18]

As for both Gregory Nazianzen and Augustine, Cyril's emphasis on the unity of Christ includes a clear commitment to the practice of single-subject biblical interpretation. Cyril's conviction that Christ is a single subject of existence lies at the heart of his response to Nestorius, whom he faults for dividing Christ into two sons, much as Gregory had accused Diodore of doing. Cyril makes his case clearly in the *Second* and *Third Letters to Nestorius*. After pointing out that the Nicene Creed speaks of a single Son, who is begotten out of God the Father and lived, died, and rose for us (*2Ep.Nest.* 3), he outlines a clear pattern of single-subject exegesis, against what he perceives as the dualist tendency of Nestorius's biblical interpretation. Christ's different statements in the gospels are spoken by only one speaker (παρ' ἑνὸς εἰρῆσθαι); they refer to a single person (πρόσωπον), namely, "the one incarnate hypostasis of the Word" (*3Ep. Nest.* 8). The principle is then ensconced in the letter's fourth anathema: sayings about Christ must not be referred to two *prosopa* or hypostases, or allocated to a man considered apart from (ἰδικῶς) the Word from God, or to the Word alone. In his later commentary on the fourth anathema, in the *Explanation of the Twelve Chapters*, Cyril explains further that all the sayings about Christ in Scripture, whether befitting God or humanity, refer to one person (πρόσωπον), the only Son of God, who was made human (*Exp.xii.cap.* 13–14). This exegetical practice is evident from Cyril's early works to his late work *The Unity of Christ*: "For there is one Son, the Word who was made human for our sake. . . . Everything refers to him, both words and deeds, the statements that are appropriate to God and those that are human" (*Un.Chr.* 448/107).[19] When he teaches that all biblical sayings about Christ refer to the same subject, Cyril reflects a deeply Gregorian principle.

Cyril, Gregory, and Athanasius

After the agreed Formula of Reunion of 433, however, Cyril adopted a different exegetical approach, which proved to be problematic when set alongside the Gregorian method. In defense of his subscription to the Formula, Cyril addressed the exegetical practice of the Easterners who signed it (*Ep.* 39.5). Sometime between 433 and 435, Cyril writes approvingly that, unlike the dualistic exegesis of Nestorius, the Easterners distinguish between biblical expressions that are either "appropriate to God" (θεοπρεπεῖς), "human" (ἀνθρωπίνας), or else common to both divine and human types; and that they were all uttered by "one and the same" Son. The first two categories (divine or human) appear in the fourth anathema and the late *Unity of Christ*; however, the third (both divine and human) is new to Cyril's work and does not recur in his final treatment of the subject. Although he is aware that this threefold scheme differs from his own practice, Cyril nevertheless considers it to be sufficiently unitive and, in the end, preservative of a single subject in Christ, so that one may distinguish (διαφοράν) the sayings without dividing (μερίζειν) Christ into two different entities (ἕτερος καὶ ἕτερος) (*Ep.Eulog.* 66).[20] Yet, by accepting the Antiochene terminology Cyril introduces a subtle but far-reaching dilemma into his doctrine. The threefold scheme differentiates the limited categories of divine, human, and common sayings from the Son of God, who utters them all, thus suggesting that the human (and possibly the common) statements do not refer to the one and only *divine* Son; in other words, it implies, as an exegetical practice, something like the later distinction between nature and hypostasis. We will return to this ambiguity in our consideration of Christ's suffering below.

Cyril's appropriation of the Easterners' approach in 433 incorporates elements of Athanasius's work into the more unitive Gregorian program. While unitive exegetical statements can be found in Athanasius's work, his most detailed and mature Christological discussion presents a different picture. Rather than referring all statements about Christ to the one, divine Son of God, either apart from or in the incarnation, as Gregory does, Athanasius distinguishes between divine and human referents, while maintaining that they belong to the same Christ, much like the approach of the Easterners in 433. In the third *Oration against the Arians* and the *Letter to Epictetus*, he argues that Christ did certain things "as God" and did others "as man," or, similarly, that some things are spoken of the Son "humanly" and others "divinely" (*C.Ar.* 1.41, 48; 3.32, 35). Athanasius describes his own approach as emphasizing the "double character" of Scripture (*C.Ar.* 3.29). Moreover, he expresses the unity of Christ in these late works through a relatively loose form of predication, saying that the flesh and its experiences are "said" to belong to the Word (*C.Ar.* 3.31–34; *Ep.Epict.* 6), by contrast with the Word's own, proper divine characteristics and actions. Like the Easterners' method in 433, Athanasius's exegetical approach suggests that Christ is a third thing, which can act either divinely or humanly, rather than being the divine

Son of God both eternally and economically. The connection between Christ's human acts and the divine nature of the Word in Athanasius's work is sufficiently ambiguous to have given several modern scholars the impression that either the Word is the subject of Christ's acts to the exclusion of any activity on the part of his humanity, or, conversely, that Christ's human experiences are remotely detached from the Word.[21] By adopting these Athanasian tendencies from the Easterners in 433, Cyril complicates his otherwise coherent practice of single-subject exegesis, which he learned from Gregory.

The clearest point of combined influence can be seen in Cyril's treatment of Christ's suffering, which is closely related to practices of Christological exegesis. Cyril's understanding of the Word's relationship to creaturely suffering in the incarnation—which he memorably calls Christ's "impassible passion" (*Schol.Inc.* 35; *Un.Chr.* 472–78/117–19)[22]—often draws heavily on Gregory Nazianzen, yet it too is complicated by certain Athanasian elements. We have already noted the strong terms with which Gregory expresses the unity of the incarnation and the depth of Christ's assumption of our broken human condition. Even as he maintains that the Son remains sovereign and unconquerable in his own divine existence, Gregory does not hesitate to confess that the Son has fully entered into and "submitted" to human suffering and death in order to save us (*Or.* 30.2). Only by a real and complete union, Gregory argues, is Christ's saving work efficacious, so that when the devil attacks Jesus in the crucifixion, he unwittingly meets with God, and death is defeated by death (*Or.* 39.13). Aware of the paradox involved, Gregory insists that God's suffering in the incarnation represents the very essence of Christianity, which he unhesitatingly expresses in theopaschite terms: Christ's suffering shows how great is God's love for us, because in him *God* has died in order to forgive our sins (*Or.* 33.14).[23] Christ is "God made passible for our sake against sin" (*Or.* 30.1),[24] and we are "saved by the passions of the impassible one" (*Or.* 30.5)[25]—passages that provide the source of Cyril's idea of impassible passion. Thus, Gregory argues that the awesome nature of the Christian faith is chiefly "to see God crucified" (*Or.* 43.64).[26] Gregory chooses to conclude his final published oration with a shocking evangelical proclamation of divine suffering: "What we needed was an incarnate God—a God put to death—so that we might live"; so "God is crucified" and "we were put to death with him" (*Or.* 45.28–29). Only because it was God who died on the cross—the Son of God made human just for this purpose—can Christ's death include the death of all humanity and his divine life make the whole creation new.

To a certain extent, Athanasius wants to say, like Gregory, that in Christ the Word has truly suffered for our salvation. In the third *Oration against the Arians* and the *Letter to Epictetus*, he argues that in Christ the Word actually became human and suffered in the flesh and bore our sins, appropriating human characteristics (ἴδια) and passions in a way that was neither imaginary nor like the Word's indwelling of the prophets (*C.Ar.* 3.30–32; *Ep.Epict.* 7). Because the Word took a corruptible and moral body and was in a body that suffered, "the properties of the body are in the incorporeal" as being attributable to him, and the creator suffered in his outraged body (*C.Ar.* 3.56; *Ep.Epict.* 10).

Yet, here again, Athanasius conceives of the incarnation in ways that mitigate against a unitive view. When he argues, for example, that Christ's body and its sufferings belong to the Word uniquely, he immediately issues the qualification that "they did not touch him according to the Divinity" (*C.Ar.* 3.32). No sooner does he say that the Word wore a body and truly suffered, than he adds the disclaimer that it was not the Word who hung on the tree but only the body (*Ep.Epict.* 2)—rather than, say, maintaining that the Word wore a body precisely so that it *could* hang on the tree. Moreover, Athanasius generally avoids the sort of theopaschite language that Gregory and, often, Cyril regard as a crucial expression of the gospel (*C.Ar.* 3.31; *Ep.Epict.* 6). He sharply contrasts the Word's divine activity through the body with the body's human passions, which are merely *attributed* to the Word (*C.Ar.* 3.32)—as if the Word's activity in Christ did not above all consist in undergoing the crucifixion. In passages such as these Athanasius reacts against his own unitive suggestions, out of a concern to protect the Word against an unseemly involvement in Christ's human passions and death, in keeping with a classical doctrine of divine impassibility.[27] Compared with Gregory's doctrine, we could say that Athanasius confuses divine and human suffering and fails to appreciate God's ability—let alone merciful nature—to assume human existence and to undergo the full depth of human suffering and death in his own divine being, in order to heal and redeem it. Thus, Athanasius stops short of asserting the Word's complete and singular assumption of human existence, despite his own better instincts.

In this regard, Athanasius's view of divine suffering is remarkably close to the later Antiochene position, particularly if we allow for Diodore's disavowal of the doctrine of two sons (BD 30–33). It is a problem for Athanasius, much as it is for the Antiochenes, to understand how the Word could become human and yet avoid being affected by creaturely passion;

consequently, there is a considerable tension on this point in his Christology.[28] In the *Letter to Epictetus*, for example, Athanasius argues that the impassible and incorporeal Word leaves Christ's body in the grave in order to go and preach to the spirits in Hades (*Ep.Epict.* 5–6). Despite his qualification that the Word left the body "without being separated from it," the suggestion that it leaves it at all runs counter to the unitive impulses of Gregory, who asserts the Word's presence and unity with human existence *especially* in the dark moments of Christ's passion and death (*Or.* 30.5; 33.14; 45.28). Athanasius's concluding statement in the letter, that "the body was not the Word, but body of the Word," like his earlier claim that Christ as a human received divine grace, rather than being transformed by natural or hypostatic union with the Word, anticipates the very sort of dualistic language that Cyril sought to expose as unorthodox (*Ep.Epict.* 6; *C.Ar.* 1.45, 48). The fact that Athanasius struggles in this way indicates how different his frame of mind is from that of Gregory, who consistently and enthusiastically affirms the Word's involvement and close contact—to the point of mixing—with Christ's human form. We might say that for Athanasius the incarnation is merely paradoxical, whereas for Gregory it is truly mysterious, in a sense that Cyril repeats.

Cyril often approaches the question of Christ's suffering and death much like Gregory, as the culmination of God's unifying embrace of human sin and brokenness (*2Ep.Succ.* 4). Yet at times he also incorporates Athanasian elements in a way that produces conflicting results. Before the Council of Ephesus, Cyril shows a generally Gregorian emphasis. In the *Second Letter to Nestorius*, after reiterating the Nicene confession that the only-begotten Son was himself made human, suffered, and rose again on the third day, Cyril discusses the hypostatic union and the real joining together of different natures in one Christ and Son, so that the divine Son underwent a fleshly birth from Mary (*2Ep.Nest.* 3.4). Thus far we are in a Gregorian framework. Then, in reply to Nestorius's typically Antiochene concern to uphold the transcendence and impassibility of God, Cyril adds several Athanasian qualifications: the Word did not suffer in his own nature, because the Divine is impassible, but it was his body (or flesh) that suffered and the impassible Word suffered only inasmuch as the impassible was "in" the suffering body (*2Ep.Nest.* 5).[29] Although he makes the point more strongly than Athanasius—by saying that the Word actually suffers through the body, rather than that such suffering is merely attributed to the Word— Cyril follows Athanasius in leaving Christ's human suffering in some sense distinct or detached from the Word's presence in the incarnation, in a way that Gregory typically resists. Yet the letter resolves in a Gregorian statement: that Christians worship "one and the same" Christ, who assumed flesh while remaining what he was before the incarnation; for which reason Mary is Theotokos (*2Ep.Nest. 6*), the technical title given to her through the Origenist-Eusebian tradition via Gregory.

Not surprisingly, the stronger *Third Letter to Nestorius* is even more clearly Gregorian. Cyril begins with a unitive position, arguing that the only-begotten Word himself underwent human birth and giving a strong defense of Christ's union against the idea of a mere conjunction (*3Ep.Nest. 3–5*). Then follows an Athanasian interlude: the Son is impassible in his own nature, suffered in the flesh and was "in" the crucified body, impassibly making the things of the flesh his own (*3Ep.Nest. 6*). Finally, in the longest section of the letter, which includes the twelve anathemas appended to the end, Cyril reasserts a solidly Gregorian perspective, into which he integrates compatible Athanasian elements. Here the crucifixion is explicitly the fleshly death of the Son of God, and the Eucharist is a participation in the very flesh of the Word. Cyril reiterates Gregory's single-subject hermeneutic, and he argues that the one and only Christ is not dual but is compounded within an inseparable unity, like a human body and soul, and that Christ is seen primarily as God even within his human limitations: he is "the only-begotten Son of God in nature" and "the Word of God himself, when he became flesh." In strongly theopaschite terms, the Word of God "underwent fleshly birth, having united humanity with himself hypostatically"; the Virgin Theotokos gave birth to "God" united with flesh; and the divine Word suffered in the flesh (*3Ep.Nest. 7–12*). Each of these points represents a key element of Gregory's unitive Christology, with a hint of Athanasian flavoring.

In the aftermath of Ephesus, however, when he is faced with Antiochene objections to the Word's suffering "in his own nature"—objections similar to Athanasius's own reservations—Cyril distances himself from Gregory's theopaschite confession and takes refuge in more equivocal expressions. He follows Athanasius directly in the *Second Letter to Successus*, forcefully arguing that, while the flesh suffered, the Word remained impassible, that we merely attribute suffering and other human characteristics to the Word, and that Christ "did not suffer as God, but did suffer as man, since his flesh suffered" (*2Ep.Succ. 2, 4*). Cyril thus abandons Gregory's radical affirmation of God's suffering in Christ in order to defend himself against the charge of theopaschitism (θεοπάθεια). In a brief coda—as if he has realized the extremity to which he has allowed himself to be pushed—Cyril abruptly returns to a Gregorian conception: Christ's sufferings do not belong to the human Jesus in any independent sense, but the Word's blood was shed for us, because (as Gregory himself might have explained) to say anything less violates "the whole rationale of the fleshly economy" and the "divine mystery" of the incarnation (*2Ep.Succ.* 4).[30]

Under the influence of such Athanasian ideas, Cyril has accommodated himself to the Antiochene position to a considerable degree[31] and thus departed from his otherwise Gregorian doctrine. By contrast, we may compare Gregory's own response to the Antiochene challenge. When he was faced with Diodore's concern to protect God's transcendence from the threat of any involvement in passible nature, Gregory instead reemphasized the central mystery of the incarnation—that God, in his mercy, did become involved in our condition precisely in order to heal it, and that God's union with human existence is the fullest revelation of the true relationship between the divine and human natures—without either succumbing to Apollinarianism or suggesting that the Word thereby underwent any change. In Gregory's mind, and in those Cyrilline texts that take their cue from him, confessing God's presence and involvement with human brokenness in the economy of Jesus Christ is by far a more appropriate evangelical doctrine than ensuring that God and humanity are kept safely apart. In the heat of the Nestorian controversy, Cyril takes the opposite approach and turns instead to Athanasius, in a way that threatened to undermine his central confession and that bequeathed to the later fathers a considerable challenge of patristic interpretation and constructive theology.

Cyril against Gregory

We may note, finally, several points of Cyril's work that are positively non-Gregorian. The most obvious is Cyril's opposition to the language of "mixture" (σύγχυσις, σύγκρασις, *1Ep.Succ.* 5; *2Ep.Succ.* 3), which Gregory found to be a compelling expression of the Christological union and which even Athanasius occasionally used. When the Antiochenes seized on these terms as telltale signs of Apollinarian confusion of the divine and human natures, Cyril conceded that the unity of Christ should not be described in terms of mixing or blending.[32] While such terms also have a Platonic and Stoic provenance, they were indeed typical Apollinarian expressions; however, in his own response to the Antiochene-Apollinarian debate, Gregory accepted them as vivid descriptors of the mysterious union of the

Word with human existence in Christ—beating Apollinarius at his own game, as it were. Yet on this point Cyril cannot sustain the Gregorian legacy; although the issues were very much the same, Cyril either lacked Gregory's resolve or appropriately judged that the polemical situation could no longer sustain the received doctrine. The Council of Chalcedon followed the same course, after which these characteristically Gregorian phrases were positively forbidden in the new theological establishment.

Equally significant is Cyril's almost total avoidance of the subject of Christ's human soul, which, in Gregory's view, plays an intermediary role between the Word and Christ's flesh. This movement away from the legacy of Origen marks an even greater divergence from Gregory, who was one of the most thoroughgoing Origenists of his age. By ignoring the structural principle of Christ's psychology, Cyril thereby neglects the full soteriological significance of Christ's assumption of a human soul, on which Gregory gives the classic treatment in *Letter* 101.32–52. Cyril is happy to grant that Christ did not lack a rational soul, in defense against charges of Apollinarianism, but he entirely overlooks Gregory's argument that Christ assumed a human mind in order to heal that part of us that most needed saving. This divergence on such an important point of soteriology has far-reaching implications for Cyril's theological anthropology, which can be related to his lingering discomfort with theopaschite language. Likewise, Cyril's lack of concern for Christ's human soul somewhat obstructed the legacy of Origenist spirituality in later Greek theology. In lieu of Gregory's more robust conception of Christ's saving work, Cyril at times settles for the residue of a weaker, Apollinarian soteriology, which emphasizes the destruction of the corruption of the flesh over the healing of the mind (*1Ep. Succ.* 9). On points such as these, the limitations of Cyril's use of Gregory's doctrine become particularly evident.

Conclusion

Cyril of Alexandria's complicated use of Gregory Nazianzen accounts for several key aspects of Cyril's work. Although he has been largely obscured by the figure of Athanasius in modern historiography, Gregory is the primary source of the deepest and most enduring aspects of Cyril's unitive Christology and exegesis. Cyril's early formation in Athanasian doctrine makes his use of Gregory all the more striking. Once he came to appreciate the power and insight of Gregory's Christology (by 428 at the latest), Cyril adopted it as the basic framework of his own thought, within which he could locate compatible motifs from Athanasius. The fundamentally Gregorian scheme of Cyril's Christology can be seen across his mature works, from the *Second Letter to Nestorius* (430) to *The Unity of Christ*, written near the end of his life (c. 438). Yet, for several years after 433 Cyril attempted to incorporate contrary elements from Athanasius and the Antiochenes, in reaction to mounting ecclesiastical pressure. As a result, he began to waver on the single-subjectivity of Christ, and he became reluctant to attribute human suffering directly to the divine Word, as he did before and after. Consequently, a number of Cyril's later works, such as the *Letters* to John of Antioch, Acacius of Scythopolis, and Successus, contain an uneasy tension on several basic points, which would demand resolution in the centuries ahead. What Gregory Nazianzen conceived as the mystery of the incarnation risked becoming, in Cyril's work, an outright inconsistency.

Cyril's indebtedness to Gregory also sheds light on the age-old question of his supposed Apollinarianism. Because Gregory's Christology has typically been regarded as dualist and anti-Apollinarian, rather than primarily unitive, Cyril has often appeared to be Apollinarian in places where he is simply being a faithful Gregorian.[33] The chief difficulty for Cyril, of course, was that, after the council of 381, Apollinarius had ended up on the losing side of the new political-ecclesiastical regime, in which the Antiochenes prevailed. The fact that Diodore occupied such a key position in the Theodosian establishment is often overlooked, yet it had enormous implications for the course of the fifth-century debates. Gregory is not only the major influence on Cyril's Christology, but he is also the source of much that has passed for Alexandrian tradition prior to Cyril. The old caricature of fourth- and fifth-century Christology as being divided between Alexandrian and Antiochene schools is no longer tenable. The streams of "orthodox" tradition ran in more than two channels.

LEO OF ROME

Bishop Leo of Rome is well known not only for his pastoral, administrative, and ecclesiastical activities, but also for the decisive role he played in the Christological debates in and around the Council of Chalcedon in 451. Leo played a major part in augmenting the authority of the bishop of Rome within the city and throughout the wider church. Taking a cue from Ambrose, he sought to combine Christianity with classical Roman civic virtue, aiming to ensure that the gospel was accessible to all citizens rather than being the purview of an elite few. Leo was also the first pope to produce a significant body of theological works. He assembled his corpus in the form of a series of sermons on major Christian feasts, which he delivered from 441 to 445, probably intending them to serve as a basic summary of Christian doctrine. In his reflections on the identity and work of Christ, Leo drew heavily on Augustine, although Hilary was a key influence as well; John Cassian, the archdeacon of Rome whom Leo commissioned to write a treatise, *On the Incarnation of Christ*, against the Nestorians in 430, also influenced how Leo came to understand various heresies.[34] Together, these influences made for a complicated mixture.

Leo echoes several of Augustine's main themes in the first set of sermons that he gave between 441 and 443. Christ's death on the cross has a saving effect because of Christ's sinlessness, which was made possible by the influence of his divinity on his humanity. Christ is also the mediator of God to humankind and the one who unites the body of Christ in himself. Leo expands as well on the meaning and effects of both Christ's death and his resurrection, and he understands Christ's entire life to be a saving example for Christians. Leo maintains the preeminence of Christ's divinity in his identity and saving work, and he discusses the interchange between Christ's divine and human natures. On each of these points the influence of Augustine can be strongly felt. Yet at the same time, a distinctly non-Augustinian strain of thought can be detected as well. Leo describes Christ's divine and human natures as corresponding with each other and acting in coordination in such a way that they appear at times to be independently acting subjects. Here we see the contrary influence of Hilary of Poitiers, whose Christology, as we have seen, is considerably more dualist than that of Augustine.

This dualist-tending strain of Leo's Christology became even more predominant thanks to Leo's response to new developments in Rome in 443. In his sermons from 443 to 445, Leo responded to a challenge of Manichaeism in the city by emphasizing Christ's humanity in a new way. In order to counter Manichean disparagement of the body and the physical world, and hence the Christological error of docetism, Leo highlights the potential for glorification that Christ's humanity (and thereby all humanity) possesses in ways that further differentiate it from Christ's divinity (*Serm.* 34.4.1), even as he tries to maintain the basic framework of Christ as the mediator between God and humanity, which produces a kind of tension. Here, too, similarities with Hilary, and by extension with Gregory of Nyssa, are more apparent.

Leo's full defense of the humanity of Christ provides the key background for his involvement in the controversy over Eutyches and his drafting (or commissioning) of his famous *Tome* of 449. The *Tome* echoes several of Leo's earlier sermons and letters, although it is possible that it was his secretary Prosper of Aquitaine who actually compiled the text, possibly with the addition of some of his own thoughts.[35] Leo pitches the work against both Eutyches, who had been accused of denying Christ's humanity by refusing to confess that Jesus has two natures in the incarnation, and Nestorius, who incurred the opposite charge of denying Christ's divinity by separating the divine Son from the human Jesus. "It is dangerous," Leo says, "to believe the Lord Jesus Christ is merely God and not human, or that he is merely human and not God" (*Tome* 5).[36] If either of these statements were true without the other, then salvation itself would be undermined. In these terms Leo presents himself as upholding Christ's divinity and humanity in a balanced and impartial manner.

Yet despite the balance of such statements, Leo's chief concern is plainly to lobby for Christ's full humanity against Eutyches, who is being opposed by Flavian of Constantinople, an approach that reflects Leo's own interests prior to the Constantinopolitan debate.[37] The *Tome*'s main argument against Eutyches shows the same uneasy combination of unitive and dualist strains that existed in Leo's work before 445. For several paragraphs Leo responds to Eutyches by presenting a typically unitive Augustinian Christology. Eutyches fails to understand "the incarnation of the Word of God," and he has misinterpreted not only the Scriptures but the creed as well,[38] which shows a clear single-subjectivity. Leo proceeds to define Christ in a clearly unitive fashion. He is the eternal Son of God, who is eternally born from God the Father and also born from Mary in time. The same divine Son took on himself human nature, making it his own, and he was "neither contaminated by sin nor detained by death" (*Tome* 2). Even when Leo speaks of both natures coming together "in a single person," which is in itself ambiguous, he specifies that it was the divinity that served as the operative and unifying agent: "lowliness is assumed by majesty, weakness by power, mortality by eternity." Christ is therefore "one and the same 'Mediator between God and humankind'" (1 Tim 2:5), and Leo can declare that in Jesus "God himself was born" as a human being (*Tome* 3),[39] and "the invisible God did not disdain to become passible"[40] in a "union" that is in every way real (*Tome* 4). Such terms could hardly be more unitive, and they accord perfectly with the doctrine of Gregory Nazianzen, Augustine, and Cyril.

Nevertheless, the *Tome* contains more troublesome passages as well, which caused the Easterners to receive the document with such fury at the Council of Ephesus in 449. As he moves to explain that Christ's divinity and humanity are each preserved in the union (as Gregory, Augustine, and Cyril also did), Leo begins to speak of Christ as a combination of two acting subjects. Echoing Paul's language of the "form of God" and the "form of a servant" in Philippians 2, Leo argues that "each form does what is proper to it in communion with the other: the Word performing what belongs to the Word and the flesh carrying out what belongs to flesh" (*Tome* 4).[41] As he envisions the divine Son doing certain things and the human Jesus doing others, albeit in communion with the other nature, Leo has moved from a unitive to a dualist scheme. For his part, Augustine repeatedly insists that Christ *remains* in the form of God when he assumes the form of a servant, for reasons that are fundamental to salvation, so that the form of God does *all* of Christ's acts, some purely divinely or eternally and others economically, just as Gregory and Cyril had also held. Hilary of Poitiers, however, often divides the two forms exegetically and in terms of Christ's action, as we have seen, and here Leo has obviously aligned himself with the latter. He shows a similar tendency in the following section when he discusses the *communicatio idiomatum*. Unlike his bold opening statements of divine birth and suffering, Leo now issues qualifications to the effect that the divine Son is merely "said to be crucified" (for example, in 1 Cor 2:8) but is not in fact killed "in his actual divinity," as if mortality has not really been "taken up by eternity" after all (*Tome* 5).

It is from this very different trajectory, finally, that Leo cannot countenance Eutyches's view that Christ was incarnated "out of two natures" but now exists only "in one nature." Even if Eutyches's preference for a single-nature Christology is supported by the similar custom of both Gregory and Cyril, he has obviously adopted a novel, extreme position by refusing to confess that there is also an orthodox sense in which Christ now exists in two natures, as Gregory and Cyril happily conceded. Yet, for his part, Leo adopts the equally extreme, opposite position. He denies that a single-nature Christology can have any orthodox sense, calling such a view absurd, perverse, and blasphemous (*Tome* 6). At this point he is treading on the unitive Greek tradition that ran from Eusebius to Gregory to Cyril, as well as the Latin precedents of Ambrose and Augustine. It is no wonder that Leo's attempt at reconciliation blew up in his face.

When he saw the reaction that the *Tome* elicited, Leo sought to remedy the situation over the next few years, particularly by clarifying his opposition to Nestorius. Leo's most significant attempt at damage control came in his *Letter* 124 written in 453 to certain monks in Palestine who were discontented with his previous teaching.[42] Here Leo sought to clarify what he really meant, as it were, in the *Tome*, while at the same time defending the original text. He pleads difficulties with understanding the Christological terms of the Greek language, which he did not speak, and some of the subtleties of the issues themselves (*Ep.* 124.159). Yet, while he takes care to reiterate his opposition to Nestorius, his Christological position remains essentially the same. For teaching Christ's one nature in the incarnation, Eutyches is to be anathematized because he "denies the reality of [Christ's] human flesh and soul" after the fashion of Apollinarius (*Ep.* 124.159–60)—a view that neither Eutyches nor Apollinarius held. In fact, Leo has retreated even further from any realistic sense of divine suffering in Christ. In the end, he locates the unity of Christ in Christ's "person" in a way that is distinguished from the divine nature. He conceives of Christ's unity as a unity *of* two natures in or by his *persona*, so that the chief unifying effect of the divine nature, such as one finds in Augustine or Cyril, is no longer in view. Leo's overriding emphasis is on differentiating Christ's divine and human actions, and the divine and human essences are each regarded as having their own actions, even though they are accomplished in common with one another (*Ep.* 124.161). In this key respect, Leo's Christology is ultimately far more dualist than that of Augustine.[43]

Because of its official character as a missive from the pope, and its eventual inclusion among the authoritative documents at the Council of Chalcedon, Leo's *Tome* came to represent his most definitive contribution to the Christological debates. As a result, Leo's work introduced a notably dualizing sort of Christology into the later Western church, which served to reinforce similar tendencies in the soon to be authoritative Definition of the Council of Chalcedon.

THE COUNCIL OF CHALCEDON (451)

The Definition of the Council of Chalcedon has long stood as a definitive Christological statement, second only to the Nicene Creed, for many though by no means all churches, and it functions as such for many Eastern and Western constructive theologians. Yet of all the seven "ecumenical councils," Chalcedon is notorious for the tensions, intrigues, and exertion of imperial and military pressures that marked its proceedings. In its inception, the council was designed to resolve acute debates that had occupied the Eastern church for almost twenty-five years. Yet, as many scholars have observed, the supposed solution of Chalcedon created far more problems than it solved, both for the understanding of Christ and for the unity of the church, producing nothing less than a major schism among the Eastern churches that persists to this day and reinforcing certain Christological differences between East and West. These tensions are embedded in the council's Christological Definition.

As we have now seen in great detail, disagreements about the identity of Christ—and thus about the Christian faith—including especially those about his unity and duality, are not uniquely fifth-century concerns, as they are often imagined. In formal terms they date to the fourth century, with deep roots in the work of Origen and faint precedents in even earlier theologians— all fueled by the ongoing interpretation of Scripture in the church's liturgical, ascetical, and theological life. The influential doctrine of Cyril, moreover, is fraught with tensions that derive from his complex appropriation of fourth-century authorities. Cyril was hardly the first to oppose the Christology of the Antiochene tradition that (as far as the historical record reveals) originally stemmed from Diodore of Tarsus. He adopted—or at the very least found great precedent to adopt—the anti-Antiochene stance of Gregory Nazianzen at an early point in his theological career, so that we find him already arguing against Diodore and Theodore in his earliest works (pre-428).

These long-standing disagreements over the respective unity and duality of Christ escalated into an acute international controversy in the years after 428, when the Syrian monk Nestorius became archbishop of Constantinople. When word spread that Nestorius had denounced the title Theotokos for the Virgin Mary, Archbishop Cyril of Alexandria reacted vehemently, for both doctrinal and political reasons (in order to reassert the prerogative of Alexandria over the new patriarchate of Constantinople), by initiating a letter campaign against Nestorius. Nestorius was condemned at the Council of Ephesus in 431, causing an equally strong reaction on the part of the Antiochene church, which reasserted itself over the next few years, leading to the Formula of Reunion in 433, through which Cyril offered certain compromises to the Antiochenes, thus initiating the complicated, middle phase of his work that we have examined. After Cyril's death in 444, his successor, Dioscorus, renewed the campaign to vindicate Cyril's unitive

Christology against the Antiochenes. The crucial events that led to the Council of Chalcedon began in 448 in Constantinople. The new archbishop of Constantinople and an Antiochene sympathizer, Flavian, held a local synod that excommunicated the esteemed priest Eutyches, who was the head of a monastery in Constantinople, a follower of Cyril's doctrine, and an ally of Dioscorus, for denying that there are two natures in Christ after their union in the incarnation. Under the leadership of Dioscorus of Alexandria, a second Council of Ephesus in 449 sought to settle the matter against the Antiochenes once and for all. It reversed the charges against Eutyches and instead deposed Flavian, in addition to Domnus of Antioch, Theodoret of Cyrus, Ibas of Edessa, and other Syrian bishops. Meanwhile, Leo of Rome had sent his *Tome* to the council in support of the condemnation of Eutyches, giving Roman support for the Antiochenes and the actions of Flavian of Constantinople; the 449 council refused to allow Leo's letter to be read. The Eastern emperor, Theodosius II, confirmed the council's decisions against the Antiochenes, giving Dioscorus and those sympathetic with the legacy of Cyril the appearance of victory at last. However, the Western emperor, Valentinian III, rejected the recent council in Ephesus in support of Leo, leaving the Eastern and Western churches in schism and the apparent settlement of 449 deeply frustrated.

The tide turned when Theodosius II died in 449 and was succeeded by Emperor Marcian, whose consort, Pulcheria, was a friend and correspondent of Bishop Leo of Rome. Showing greater favor to the views of Rome, Marcian deposed Eutyches (this time permanently) and began the process of restoring the bishops condemned at Ephesus in 449; their full reinstatement would require another church council. In order to resolve the bitter dispute, Marcian accordingly convened the so-called fourth ecumenical council in 451. Leo opposed the gathering, believing that the bishops should signal their unity by signing his *Tome*; yet the emperor had already called the meeting before he learned of Leo's views. It was a massive assembly, with between three hundred and four hundred bishops present, all Eastern except two from Africa plus two papal legates, and a host of government officials and military guard. The council condemned Eutyches and, in its fifth and sixth sessions, produced its famous Definition of faith.

Before we examine the council's Definition, it is important to appreciate the bishops' understanding of their doctrinal work and the methods by which they approached it. The direction of the council is made clear in its early sessions. Immediately, Dioscorus was tried and deposed, with five other bishops, for the actions of the Council of Ephesus (449). The second notable event was the reception of Leo's *Tome*. When the authoritative documents that were to be the basis of the council's work were read out, the only one that aroused protest was the *Tome*. Some bishops attempted to argue that Leo is in essential agreement with Cyril by producing quotations from Cyril's works—which would not be entirely impossible, given the equivocation on Cyril's part during his middle period—though, notably, not from his clearest Christological statements such as the *Third Letter to Nestorius* with its twelve anathemas or *The Unity of Christ*. Bishops who wanted to compare the *Tome* with Cyril's *Third Letter* were actually prohibited from doing so, and those who sought the rehabilitation of Dioscorus were ignored. At this point the supporters of Dioscorus probably absented themselves from the meetings, thus threatening to void the council's claim to ecumenical status. In order to avoid such a rupture, the third session included a formal trial of Dioscorus by the bishops alone. Probably knowing that the outcome was already assured, Dioscorus absented himself from the proceedings so as not to disparage the doctrinal cause, and only half of the bishops in residence actually attended the session. The only charges presented were dubious financial ones, and Dioscorus was condemned mainly for nonattendance. The fourth session then declared Leo's *Tome* to be in agreement with Cyril's *Second Letter to Nestorius*, in a further attempt to co-opt Cyril for the government's pro-Antiochene and pro-Roman agenda.[44] The reinstatement of the five bishops other than Dioscorus who had been deposed in the first session was then made dependent on their signing Leo's *Tome*; at this cost the full complement of bishops (minus Dioscorus) was reinstated, and the course of the council was restored. This was the last session that any Egyptian bishops attended, and they refused to sign the *Tome*, for fear of their lives on their return home. By the time the bishops undertook to craft a doctrinal definition in the fifth session, then, the council's prevailing agenda was clear: to rectify the situation enacted at Ephesus in 449, which favored the Christology of Cyril and those who opposed two-nature doctrine, by giving precedence to Antiochene views and the dualist-tending Christology advanced by Leo of Rome.

The council's Definition likewise shows a distinct method of approach. The bishops declare that they speak by the grace of God, on the summons of the emperors, and in the interest of the peace of the church, which Christ himself commanded (John 14:27). Next they make an important set of pronouncements about what the Christological Definition is not: it is not meant to be a new creed or confession of faith. The bishops' first point, then, is that they intend to be thoroughly traditional. In their deliberations they claim to have "renewed the unerring faith of the Fathers," and they reaffirm the preeminence of the creeds of Nicaea and Constantinople, reproducing each one in full (*Chalc.Def.* 126/83).[45] The bishops further define the purpose of the Definition as follows. On the one hand, the Nicene Creed is a sufficient statement of faith concerning the Father, Son, and Holy Spirit as well as the incarnation, and "this wise and saving creed" remains the fundamental doctrinal statement (below Scripture). Yet, on the other hand, there have been significant disagreements about the meaning of the faith thus defined, namely, the errors of Nestorius and Eutyches (*Chalc.Def.* 127/84). It is significant that the council considers the present Christological debate a disagreement about *Nicaea*—a claim that is entirely accurate. The purpose of the Chalcedonian Definition is specifically to resolve problems that have arisen in the interpretation of the Nicene faith—problems that were hardly new to the fifth century, as we saw in great detail in chapters 1–3. Accordingly, the Definition is designed to exclude certain Christological errors, and, in doing so, it is an act of reception and reinterpretation of the faith confessed at Nicaea in a way that constitutes tradition-making and ongoing theological construction. It is not the case, therefore, that the faith in the Trinity was settled at the Council of Constantinople in 381, as it has often been imagined, and that the Christological debates that followed were intramural disagreements between parties who otherwise agreed on the Nicene faith. Rather, the fifth-century debates are a continuation of many of the same issues that occupied theologians throughout the fourth century, and Cyril's work itself preserves some of those tensions in what is now the most authoritative doctrinal program.

The way that the council defines the errors of Nestorius and Eutyches immediately shows the perspective that the full document seeks to advance. The error of Nestorius is that some have denied "the mystery of the Lord's economy," that is, the real incarnation of the divine Son, and accordingly they have refused to call Mary Theotokos. This is a fair description of Nestorius's doctrine, as far as it goes. The error of Eutyches is that he confuses Christ's flesh and his divinity by "mindlessly imagining that there is one nature of the flesh and the Divinity," which includes employing the notion of "mixture" (κρᾶσις), and also by believing that "the divine nature of the Only-begotten is passible" (*Chalc.Def.* 127/84). Here we have a case of misrepresentation, even granting the brevity and the bare terms of the Definition. While it is true that Eutyches advances a single-nature Christology, it is not true that in doing so he confuses Christ's divinity and humanity. It would have been a more accurate objection to fault Eutyches for insisting that *only* a single-nature Christology is adequate, that is, for denying that there is an orthodox sense of two-nature language, which Gregory Nazianzen, Augustine, and Cyril had all allowed (and which Augustine preferred). But it would also have been a more ecumenical gesture on the council's part had it allowed that there is an orthodox sense of single-nature Christology as well. Moreover, Gregory, Cyril, and Augustine all happily employed the notion of mixture without at all meaning that Christ's divinity or humanity fundamentally changed its nature, and all three vigorously affirmed the suffering of God in the incarnation as being central to Christian salvation.

Accordingly, the council excludes from the priesthood "those who dare to say that the divinity of the Only-begotten is passible," opposes the notion of mixture, and anathematizes single-nature Christology (*Chalc. Def.* 129/86). On these terms, Gregory, Cyril, and Augustine were all evidently unorthodox. Against Nestorius, the council refutes the idea that there are two sons, a point on which Nestorius himself agrees. In its initial definition of the problem and replies to it, the Definition thus betrays a clear Antiochene bias, which was reinforced, as we now know, by the input of Leo of Rome.[46] This bias can be seen as well in the new documents that it deems authoritative, in addition to the councils of Nicaea, Constantinople, and Ephesus (431): namely, Cyril's *Second Letter to Nestorius*, his *Letter* to John of Antioch following the synod of 433, which includes the Formula of Reunion, and Leo's *Tome*. The clearer statement of Cyril's doctrine in his *Third Letter* has been excluded; he has been represented at his most "Antiochene" moment in the *Letter to John of Antioch*; to which is added the dualist character of Leo's *Tome*.

After these initial exclusions and disclaimers, the bishops then give their famous definition of Christ in a single, succinct paragraph:

> Therefore, following the holy fathers, we all in unison teach the confession of one and the same Son, our Lord Jesus Christ, the same perfect in Divinity and the same perfect in humanity, the same truly God and truly human,[47] of a rational soul and body, consubstantial [*homoousion*] with the Father as regards his Divinity, and the same consubstantial with us as regards his humanity, like us in all things except sin, begotten from the Father before the ages as

regards his Divinity, and the same in the last days [born] for us and
for our salvation from Mary the Virgin, the Theotokos, as regards
his humanity—one and the same Christ, Son, Lord, Only-begotten,
acknowledged in two natures without confusion, change, division,
or separation: the difference in the natures being at no point
destroyed through the union, but rather the property of each nature
being preserved and coming together into one person [*prosopon*]
and one hypostasis; not parted or divided into two persons, but one
and the same Son, Only-begotten God, Word, Lord, Jesus Christ,
just as the prophets taught about him from the beginning and Jesus
Christ himself instructed us and the symbol of the fathers has
handed down to us. (*Chalc.Def.* 129/86)

The key paragraph of the Definition begins with the words "one and the
same Son," which are a familiar element of the unitive tradition of Gregory
Nazianzen and Cyril of Alexandria. Yet unlike the typical narrative
approach of those theologians, or even that of the Nicene Creed, which the
council stringently aims to uphold, the council does not define Christ
primarily as the divine Son of God, who in the divine economy assumed
human existence (or nature) for our salvation. Instead, right from the
beginning of the technical definition, Chalcedon makes its focus to be
the incarnate Lord, who is to be conceived in a balanced way as being
both divine and human.[48] Accordingly, the Definition proceeds to describe
Christ in a series of balanced terms for divinity and humanity, which
could suggest that he is equally composed of each, or at least should
be equally regarded as such: perfect in divinity, perfect in humanity; truly
God and truly human; consubstantial with the Father in divinity and
consubstantial with human beings in humanity. This parallelism is then
reiterated in the most explosive phrase in the Definition: Christ is to be
"acknowledged *in* two natures."[49] From the beginning of the statement
through to this point, the imperial agenda has clearly prevailed: this
particular phrase was in fact added in last-minute deliberations at the behest
of the emperor and the Roman delegates, in order to make clear the
continuing duality in Christ, echoing the "home synod" of Constantinople
(449), at which Flavian had Eutyches condemned, as well as the *Tome
of Leo.*[50] Here again, Christ's identity is understood in a dual, parallel
sense, with no indication of the infinite difference between the divine and
human natures, and hence Christ's fundamental identity as the divine Son—
both of which were basic points of Gregory's, Cyril's, and even Augustine's

Christologies. It is certainly possible for a committed Cyrilline or Augustinian to find an orthodox sense in such a statement, but only if the deeper theological issues embedded in their unitive doctrines are assumed.

In the most famous series of adverbs in all of Christian tradition, the Definition next codifies its balanced approach to Christ by qualifying the union of God and humanity. Believers are to acknowledge Christ in two natures "without confusion, change, division, or separation."[51] This series of qualifications is relatively innocuous, as far as it goes: both Antiochenes and Cyrillians maintained that the incarnation did not cancel either the divinity or the humanity of the Son, nor did it leave them radically separated from one another, as if nothing had occurred to bring them together. Much more depends on larger structural questions and whatever further qualifications one makes of these terms, as well as the following comment that the incarnation does not threaten to remove the unique characteristics of each nature. The final qualification, however—that these characteristics "come together into one *prosopon* and one hypostasis"—has led to perhaps more confusion than any conciliar phrase since the Nicene *homoousion*. Over the next three centuries, and, in many ways, up to the present day, this phrase has been taken as indicating the metaphysical underpinning of the whole Definition and of the orthodox understanding of the Trinity in many circles. The notion that Christ consists of two natures that join together "into" (εἰς) a single hypostasis leaves it unclear what exactly is the basic building block of Christ, as it were. On the face of it, the binding element appears to be the hypostasis or *prosopon*, which takes into itself or contains both divinity and humanity; but such a notion is entirely foreign to the language of Nicaea and to the doctrine of most of the theologians we have examined. The implications of this formulation led to considerable debate and the need for further constructive argumentation in the succeeding centuries, which we will examine in the next chapter. To be sure, the idea that Christ is a single hypostasis is native to Cyril's Christology, as we have noted, but the way in which the Definition speaks of two natures being united in (or into) one hypostasis is distinctly non-Cyrilline.

The only phrase guaranteed to irritate most Antiochenes is the confession that Mary is Theotokos, a term that Diodore, Theodore, and Nestorius all resisted but which one could hardly imagine any council denying if it hoped to seek unity. Even the otherwise unitive suggestion that Christ underwent two births is so heavily qualified that an Antiochene could probably stomach it. Christ's birth from the Father is "with respect to divinity" (κατὰ τὴν θεότητα) while his birth from Mary is "with respect to humanity" (κατὰ τὴν ἀνθρωπότητα), a qualification that greatly waters down the meaning of "Theotokos" because it leaves room for denying that it was the *divine* Son who was born from Mary "with respect to humanity." Aside from the term "Theotokos," there is really nothing in the Chalcedonian Definition to mitigate a fundamentally Antiochene Christology based in the tradition of Diodore. The token anti-Apollinarian statement that Christ has a rational soul would again please the Antiochenes; yet, notably, there is no refutation of the dual-subject exegesis that became the hallmark of Antiochene Christology.

In sum, the council defines Christ in terms that are hardly representative of a Gregorian, Augustinian, or Cyrilline position, or even the Nicene Creed, despite its claims to the contrary. The Chalcedonian Definition is a clear statement of Antiochene and Leonine (but not Augustinian) two-nature Christology enforced under government pressure, which left the basic identity of Christ and the nature of the union disastrously ambiguous from the point of view of the more unitive traditions.[52] It is no wonder that Nestorius reportedly felt vindicated by the result. Many have claimed that the council represented the doctrine of Cyril with a moderate degree of faithfulness. Yet, because much of the work of Cyril is itself complicated by the dualizing influence of Athanasius, who unsurprisingly came to be well regarded in Antiochene tradition,[53] and the council explicitly rejected the clearer standard of Cyril's *Third Letter to Nestorius* with the twelve anathemas, adherence to Cyril in name or even in certain quotable passages is not the gold standard that it appears to be.

In the session following the adoption of the Definition, Emperor Marcian compared himself to the great Constantine and congratulated himself for achieving the unity of the church through unity of doctrine. But this achievement almost immediately proved to be a chimera, as we can detect in the fact that Marcian threatened punishment of any who disagreed with the council. Even those who later sought to reinterpret Chalcedon in ways that would bring it more closely in line with Cyril's thought faced an unexpected set of obstacles. For this reason the tensions we have been tracing in this chapter persisted in the patristic traditions that sought to ally themselves with Chalcedon and its successor councils. To that story we must now turn.

7. Post-Chalcedonian Christology

It has long been customary in some circles to think of the Council of Chalcedon as the great watershed in the definition of Christological ortho-doxy. In fact, the council of 451 led to even greater divisions among churches that based themselves on roughly the same group of traditional authorities, and in terms of Christology it arguably brought more problems than solutions, for reasons that we have just discussed. In reaction to the council's dualizing pronouncements, the churches of the East ruptured into a formal schism between Chalcedonian and non-Chalcedonian bodies that still exists today. Far from being the end, or even the climax, of patristic Christological developments, the decrees of Chalcedon initiated a series of intensive debates and constructive theological work that lasted for almost four more centuries.

The complexities inherent in the fourth-century Christological tradi-tions, as they were received and reinterpreted by Cyril, Leo, and the Council of Chalcedon in the fifth century, passed on into this later period of Christological work. Just as theologians worked to define the Nicene faith well beyond the Council of Constantinople of 381, so too this process of reception and redefinition continued until the end of the patristic age. In this final chapter, we trace the course of this mixed stream of traditions as it ran through the post-Chalcedonian period, concentrating on the Byzantine Chalcedonian tradition that included the Second and Third Councils of Constantinople and culminated in the work of John of Damascus in the eighth century, just as the iconoclastic controversy was getting under way.

LEONTIUS OF BYZANTIUM

The Council of Chalcedon neither intended nor explicitly taught the categorical distinction between nature and hypostasis for which it is often credited. Yet the terms of the Definition did express an Antiochene-leaning doctrine of Christ, and the terms "nature" and "hypostasis" (and "person") do lend themselves to a certain understanding of the metaphysical construction of Christ, if one is inclined to read them that way. The person who did more to crystallize and systematically explain these metaphysical implications is a figure little known to most modern theologians and churchgoers—Leontius of Byzantium. A scholar-monk probably from Palestine, Leontius defended the Chalcedonian position in theological controversies in Constantinople during the 530s and 540s. He articulated his main doctrinal position in works against anti-Chalcedonian theologians of the "miaphysite" group associated with Severus of Antioch (theologians who continued to assert Jesus's single, divine nature), "aphthartodocetists" (those who believe that Jesus's humanity was incorruptible from the beginning) both within and outside the Chalcedonian party, and so-called Nestorians. Significantly, Leontius describes himself as having once been an Antiochene theologian or sympathizer himself.

Leontius takes as his starting point the balanced, two-nature scheme of Chalcedon and expands it into a full-blown Christological metaphysic that has since come to be regarded as the heart of Chalcedonian Christology, and, for some, the central logic of fourth-century Nicene Trinitarian orthodoxy. The fabled "Cappadocian solution" to the Trinity, which categorically distinguishes between nature and hypostasis and thus solves intractable problems of Trinitarian metaphysics, is largely the invention and retrojection of Leontius of Byzantium. Leontius himself connects what he is doing in Chalcedonian Christology with language used earlier to discuss the Trinity. He refers to specific passages in fourth-century theologians to prove that he is simply extending and reapplying their thought, when in fact he is reinterpreting them in sometimes drastic ways in order to defend the Chalcedonian project as he conceives it. Leontius's new synthesis is often called Strict Chalcedonianism. Few times in Christian history has so obscure a figure accomplished such groundbreaking theological work.

The centerpiece of Leontius's Christology is the distinction between the Chalcedonian terms "nature" or "essence" and "hypostasis" or "*prosopon*" (*C.Nest.Eut.* 1273A). Like Pope Leo and Chalcedon, Leontius is concerned to defend Christ's divinity and humanity in a balanced and reasonable way. In this light he faults Nestorius and Eutyches for committing equal and opposite errors—Nestorius for denying the divinity and Eutyches for denying the humanity of the Savior—and each amounts to a denial of the incarnation (they are "opposite kinds of docetism," *C.Nest. Eut.* 1276A). As we have already noted, this characterization of Eutyches—and, we may add, of Leontius's miaphysite opponents—is hardly accurate, yet as many polemicists have done over the centuries, Leontius claims the middle ground of truth against these two erroneous extremes in a "common struggle against both parties" (*C.Nest.Eut.* 1276D). In terms of its immediate polemic, the argument of *Against the Nestorians and Eutychians* is aimed at the monophysites, although Leontius intends the overall metaphysic represented there to speak against Nestorians too.

Early in the work Leontius makes a point that became a lasting contribution to understanding the Christological union, and one that transcends his own particular argument against the monophysites. He reports an objection to the Chalcedonian doctrine that goes as follows. Since natures are always hypostasized (there are no nonhypostatic natures), then if Christ were to have two natures, he must also have two hypostases; which means that two-nature Christology is necessarily a two-son Christology, that is, Nestorian. Yet since even Chalcedon rejected Nestorianism, it must be acknowledged that the one Christ has only one nature (*C.Nest.Eut.* 1276D–77A). In reply, Leontius acknowledges that all natures are hypostasized, but he makes the additional point that they need not all have different hypostases, and that it is possible for a given hypostasis to serve for more than one nature. It is perfectly logical to hold that the one Christ provides the hypostasis for both his divine and his human natures; therefore, two-nature Christology is perfectly compatible with the unity of Christ and need not imply Nestorianism. The argument that two natures would require that Christ also possesses two hypostases is an additional point that has been produced by monophysite polemics against Nestorianism. As we have seen, Gregory, Cyril, and Augustine all countenanced two-nature language without drawing this conclusion. In this respect, Leontius's denial of the logic presented by his interlocutor could be received as a welcome corrective in the debate, which the earlier unitive theologians, including Cyril of Alexandria, would have wanted to make: of course the divine Son can take on human nature and become a complete human being without multiplying himself into two sons or hypostases. This is close to the idea that would later be called "enhypostasization," although Leontius does not develop it as such—that the hypostasis of the Son of God serves also as the hypostasis of the incarnate Christ—and that has assumed different versions in modern systematic theology.[1]

Yet Leontius's concerns run much deeper than this initial point. In a broader scope, he is concerned to articulate what we might call a thorough-going nature metaphysic. While he agrees that natures are necessarily hypostasized, he is chiefly concerned to argue that Christ's humanity exists together with his divinity as a "nature" and nothing less. It is not enough to say that in Christ the divine Son has assumed human existence while remaining predominantly a divine nature, and to specify that the incarnate, divine Son is fully human in every way. One must speak of Christ as possessing a human nature or essence, "a second nature alongside that of the Logos" (*C.Nest.Eut.* 1277A). Leontius's characteristic approach is to create a categorical distinction between nature and hypostasis to explain what he takes to be the sense of Chalcedonian orthodoxy. The hypostatic character of every nature (*to enhypostaton*), he argues, is not the same thing as the nature itself; that is, there is a fundamental difference between nature and hypostasis.

Leontius gives two different definitions of this distinction. Both represent the balanced nature metaphysic, although one can be seen as more compatible with fourth-century norms of Trinitarian theology and Christology than the other. In one way of thinking, Leontius defines the distinction thus: a nature is a general category, while a hypostasis is an individual, existing thing. A nature has the rationale of a genus or form, compared with which a hypostasis is the particular thing that exists as an instance or example of that genus (*C.Nest.Eut.* 1277A). In this sense we can speak of human nature in general on the one hand, and individual humans like Peter, Paul, and James on the other. Therefore, a hypostasis "exists in itself," whereas a nature can exist only as a hypostasis.[2] In this regard, every hypostasis (every individual) is itself *also* a nature; but the reverse is not also true, for a nature as such is not a hypostasis, even though all natures are hypostatic (*C.Nest.Eut.* 1280A).[3] If we apply this definition to the Trinity and the person of Christ as they were treated by the major fourth-century theologians, it makes sense up to a point. Athanasius or Gregory Nazianzen would certainly agree that the divine nature exists only as the Father, Son, and Holy Spirit—that there is no divine nature apart from the three hypostases of the Trinity[4]—and they would also agree that the Son of God is a personal or hypostatic instance of the divine nature. Yet the liability of the definition, even thus far, is that it suggests a generic theory of the Trinity: that the Father, Son, and Holy Spirit are each instances or individuals of a common category of divine nature, with no necessary definition or "root" in their relations of origin. And this view of the Trinity Athanasius, Basil, Gregory, and Origen firmly rejected, Gregory of Nyssa being an exception.

Even greater problems arise, however, with Leontius's second definition of hypostasis and nature. (The two definitions are often mixed together in his argumentation, but they can nevertheless be distinguished fairly clearly.) Here a nature is a universal thing (a καθολικὸν πρᾶγμα), while a hypostasis is what distinguishes the particular (το ἴδιον) from what is common (τὸ κοινόν) (*C.Nest.Eut.* 1280A). To use the human comparison again, the hypostasis in this case would not be Peter himself, but whatever characteristics Peter possesses that distinguish him from Paul and other humans. On the former definition (hypostasis as individual thing), the hypostasis is an individual thing itself, which is an instance or example *of a nature* and is thus also itself a nature, but in the second definition— hypostasis as what is distinct from the common nature and/or from other hypostases of the same nature (*C.Nest.Eut.* 1280A)—the hypostasis does not include the common nature.[5] According to the first definition, we would want to say that a hypostasis is distinguishable as an individual *not* only by its distinctive characteristics (*C.Nest.Eut.* 1277D), but by how the individual exists as a nature as well. What makes Peter the individual that he is, in other words, includes the fact that he is human, not merely the ways in which he is different from other humans.

In the second definition, the meaning of hypostasis has thus shifted from an individual thing that is also a nature to a principle of individuation as such. That this is the dominant meaning of hypostasis in Leontius's mind can be seen most clearly in his explanation of Christological exegesis and the *communicatio idiomatum*. In Leontius's view, when the Scriptures call the Word by human titles, or the human Jesus by divine titles, they are referring to the whole by means of the part (or sometimes the part by the whole). Both divine and human statements, which ostensively denote the respective nature (for example, human statements seem to refer to the human nature), refer ultimately to the hypostasis, and in this way the unity of Christ is preserved in biblical interpretation. "We contemplate the *communicatio idiomatum* in the one hypostasis," even as the particular characteristics of each nature are preserved (*C.Nest.Eut.* 1289C). In other words, the universal genus (either the divine or human nature) is predicated of the individual (the hypostasis), so that the hypostasis is the actual referent of both divine and human things (*C.Nest.Eut.* 1289D). In his treatment of the question, Leontius says that he is following "the logicians"; he is trying to explain Christological exegesis in terms of received philosophical logic (*C.Nest.Eut.* 1289D–92A).[6] Yet he is also repeating the Antiochenes' "third position" of the Formula of Reunion of 433, which Cyril also accepted in his letter to John of Antioch (with considerable internal difficulties, as we have seen). Leontius's exegetical approach is not strictly a two-subject method such as Diodore practiced, at least not always;[7] though neither is it the single-subject method of Gregory, Augustine, and Cyril, for whom the referent of all statements is the divine Son, who not only is both hypostasis and divine nature and is therefore *always* divine (closer to Leontius's first definition), but also derives his identity from God the Father in a way that Leontius generally ignores.

That Leontius conceives of hypostasis as a principle of individuation per se—an instantiator of a nature, or a container in which a nature comes to exist, as it were—is evident as well from his application of the terms to the intra-Trinitarian relationships. In view of the fact that the Son is both identical to God the Father and also distinct from him (as most theologians in view here would agree), Leontius applies the term "nature" only to the relationship by which the Son is identical with the Father, while hypostasis refers to the way in which the Son is different from the Father (the fact of being begotten), including the fact that he is called "Son" at all, as a distinct hypostasis that arises from his generation from the Father (*C.Nest.Eut.* 1288A–B). Nature thus refers to sameness; hypostasis refers to distinctness as indicated by the title "Son."

Yet, if we compare this scheme with the fourth-century authorities examined above, Leontius has deeply confused matters in the Trinity. For both Gregory Nazianzen and Athanasius, Christ's identity as Son of God signifies *both* his equality with God the Father and his distinctness from him. As nearly every student of fourth-century theology knows, it was a fundamental point of pro-Nicene theology, nearly across the board, to argue that the Son's generation from the Father is what makes him *God*, that is, sharing the same divine nature with the Father, as well as distinct, much as Origen also had posited. Through his definition of nature and hypostasis, Leontius has parceled out the logic of sameness and difference in the Trinity in a way that is unrecognizable in any fourth-century authority, except perhaps Gregory of Nyssa. When Leontius writes that Christ is a connecting link between humans and God the Father (*C.Nest.Eut.* 1288C), he does not mean the same thing that Augustine does by Christ as mediator; for in the latter case Christ is mediator as the divine Son made human: he mediates primarily from God's side. For Leontius the connection is of the two natures within the "hypostasis" as a kind of neutral space, rather than in and by the Son of God, who is both divine nature and hypostasis (or hypostasized Divinity, as Leontius recognizes to a limited extent). According to Gregory Nazianzen and Augustine (and possibly Athanasius and Basil), in the Trinity the hypostases (the Father, Son, and Holy Spirit as individuals) *are indeed* the divine nature, and the divine nature *is* the Father, Son, and Holy Spirit and nothing other than them. Leontius's distinction between nature and hypostasis therefore does not comport with earlier pro-Nicene doctrines of the Trinity, as he claims it does, any more than it represents basic pro-Nicene Christology.

A further complicating aspect of Leontius's doctrine that particularly highlights his Antiochene provenance is his emphasis on theological precision and exactness over ordinary Christian speech. In one passage he argues that Christ is a connection of extremes or "parts," which together comprise the *prosopon* or hypostasis of Christ. He then comments that the problem with one-nature Christology is that it ignores the parts and is for that reason "imprecise" (*C.Nest.Eut.* 1288C–89B). Later in the same work, he voices the same concern for precision. He argues that the very term "Christ" is not a commonly recognized name among Christians like "human being" is among people, but is rather "a technical and scientific name," the truth of which is known only to those who are "wise in the things of God" (*C.Nest.Eut.* 1296A–B). Because the simple and concise language of the gospel does not speak clearly of the division of Christ's parts (the human and divine natures), it falls to those able to employ "critical speculation and a kind of technical language that is strange to most people and hard to grasp" in order to discern "the manner of the union" in Christ (*C.Nest.Eut.* 1297B–C). In other words, ordinary believers are bound to have blurry and substandard Christologies, unless they are fortunate enough to consult theological experts like Leontius. On this view of theological language and method, we are very far indeed from Athanasius, Gregory Nazianzen, Augustine, Cyril, and even the ever-inquisitive Origen, all of whom regarded the simple language of the apostolic faith to be the foundation and the constant norm for all higher theological speculation. Leontius's specialist approach to theological language, which appears to be philosophically motivated, was well known in the Antiochene theological tradition, and Gregory of Nyssa tends to take a similar approach.

Leontius's Chalcedonian nature metaphysic therefore stands in a highly problematic relationship to the standard earlier authorities, from Athanasius to Cyril. At the same time, he knows full well that he must justify himself on the basis of those very authorities. At the end of *Against the Nestorians and Eutychians*, Leontius appended a collection (a florilegium) of eighty-eight quotations from patristic witnesses to justify his position. He is quite explicit in the preface to the collection that he has quoted only passages that speak in the terms that he has just argued for: texts that speak only of natures "in which" and "through which" Christ exists, and of "natures" and "substances" in the plural. He has deliberately and admittedly excluded all single-nature expressions, including those that speak of two natures "out of which" or "from which" Christ was composed (*C.Nest.Eut.* 1308C). Even if someone were to produce contrasting passages from the same authors, Leontius would refuse to accept them as meaning anything other than what he himself means, that is, a Chalcedonian Christology based on the difference between nature and hypostasis. The collection of texts that Leontius presents fulfills his purposes only if one places great trust in his authority as an editor.[8]

The collection begins with several excerpts from Basil that seem unquestionably to validate Leontius's metaphysic.[9] In these texts Basil speaks in similar terms of the difference between the general and the particular, and he occasionally uses the language of hypostasis and (unsurprisingly) of being and nature. With no knowledge of Basil's work on its own terms, the reader may well believe that Leontius is faithfully representing the great Cappadocian. Yet those who do have such knowledge will realize that in these passages Basil is making *grammatical* rather than metaphysical distinctions; that he does so in varied ways in different texts; and that he does not base his Trinitarian theology or his Christology on the kind of system that Leontius has laid out. Three passages from Gregory Nazianzen follow the opening four from Basil, and these are similar in character. They are even less supportive of Leontius's program when read in their own contexts, yet Leontius has found one in which Gregory speaks of "three hypostases or *prosopa*, or whatever you want to call them" (*Or.* 42.16). Ironically, Leontius has failed to suppress Gregory's equivocating remark at the end of the passage—"Let those who quarrel about these things not disgrace themselves!"—which shows how unconcerned Gregory is with the sort of metaphysical constructions that Leontius makes so central. Likewise, a passage quoted from Gregory's *Letter* 101 includes the term "mixture" that the Antiochenes and Chalcedon have forbidden and which supports the unitive Christology that Leontius opposes. Unaware of these ironies, Leontius places these excerpts from Basil and Gregory at the head of the collection in hopes that the reader will understand them as he does.

The rest of the collection is a mixture of texts that speak of the consubstantiality of the Trinity, the two natures and doubleness of Christ, and Christ's divinity and humanity in multiple ways, which of course can be found in many authors.[10] Significantly, the collection closes with twenty-three quotations from Cyril,[11] by far the largest concentration by any individual author. This editorial choice shows the great authority that Cyril still possesses: whatever one may teach, it must be made to agree with Cyril if it has any hope of being regarded as orthodox. Not surprisingly, the passages that Leontius excerpts from Cyril contain a high representation of texts in which he has incorporated Athanasian elements, such as the *Letters* written between 433 and 435, and others in which Cyril happily employs two-nature expressions, while he excludes any that would show the deeper stream of Cyril's unitive Christology. Moreover, Cyril's case highlights the inherent complications that we have seen among the earlier authorities themselves. Athanasius and Basil, for example, happen to be more dualist in their Christologies than Gregory and Cyril were, which adds a further layer of complexity to the kind of authority that Leontius is representing, despite appearances of unified support.

In his florilegium Leontius not only claims to have discerned the singular mind of the fathers, but to have divine sanction in doing so. "For to attempt to lead the [great] theologians to oppose each other, and to say they have been in conflict among themselves, is not an assault against us but against their reputation, . . . and even against the authority of the Holy Spirit and of Christ." Whoever does not accept the fathers as Leontius presents them is guilty of "resisting the command of God" (*C.Nest.Eut.* 1308D). The selectivity, bias, and presumed power of the collection could hardly be more evident. Through his theological argumentation and his anthologizing of earlier writers, Leontius greatly affected how later theologians have read and understood the patristic authorities, both in the subsequent centuries and in the modern period.

CONSTANTINOPLE II (553)

With the Second Council of Constantinople, the fifth ecumenical council, we see some movement away from the Strict Chalcedonianism of Leontius back toward the more unitive Christology of Cyril, who continued to command normative status for many, and so to the doctrine of both Gregory Nazianzen and Augustine. This movement was partly due to continuing pressure around the Eastern church to include single-nature views within the orthodox fold, as well as the personal influence of Emperor Justinian, who wanted to make peace with committed miaphysite groups.

The focus of the council and its immediate cause was a continuing dispute over the works of three figures—the so-called Three Chapters— Theodore of Mopsuestia, Theodoret of Cyrus, and Ibas of Edessa. For brevity's sake, we will refer to them together as "Antiochenes" because of their clear theological provenance. The Council of Chalcedon had accepted all three bishops, yet a wide range of Miaphysites felt that they could no longer be countenanced. Justinian condemned the Three Chapters twice, in 543–44 and 551, and both times he met with resistance from Vigilius of Rome, who was concerned to defend the decrees of Chalcedon. Vigilius eventually issued a *Iudicatum*, which condemned the Three Chapters but upheld Chalcedon, although he was opposed by certain Western bishops, especially in Africa. Justinian eventually convened a council in Constantinople to deal definitively with the matter; Vigilius had hoped it would be in Italy or Sicily. Because the meeting was composed mostly of Easterners, Vigilius refused to attend.[12] He drafted a *Constitution* that condemned sixty propositions of Theodore but refused to anathematize him because he was dead; he also refused to condemn Theodoret or Ibas, since Chalcedon had explicitly vindicated them. The *Constitution* was signed by sixteen bishops: eleven Westerners, two from Illyricum, and three from Asia Minor. After the Council of Constantinople, Vigilius weighed its decisions for six months and finally accepted them, giving the council binding force in both the East and West, although he remained loyal to Chalcedon in the end. In a second *Constitution* he tried to reconcile the council of 553 with that of 451.

In both its decrees and anathemas,[13] the council points in several ways to Christ's identity as the divine Son who has become human in the economy, much as Nicaea and the fourth-century fathers had declared, and it faults the Antiochenes for not recognizing this fact and making it paramount. Christ is "the only-begotten as a human being, and the Word of God who was made flesh of Mary and therefore had two births (2Const. 14, 27 anathema 2). By contrast, the Antiochenes have failed to recognize the "name" of Christ as the only-begotten Son of God (2Const. 1, 12). Structurally, the council also signals a difference from the balanced nature metaphysic championed by Leontius. When it argues that the Christ who worked miracles yet also suffered is one individual (*allos*) and "one and the same"—both unitive terms taken from Gregory Nazianzen—it identifies that single individual as the Word of God: that is, a primarily divine subject who has been made flesh, not a compound or a hypostasis that contains both natures. Both Christ's divine acts and his human suffering belong to "the same one," the Word of God. The one hypostasis who is the Lord Jesus Christ is clearly defined to be "one of the holy Trinity," and the council offers the highly unitive confession that "one of the Trinity was crucified in the flesh." Where the council employs single-nature language, however, as in the phrase "one nature of God the Word made flesh," it insists that it must agree with the doctrine of Chalcedon, in particular the idea that Christ is a union of divine and human natures *by hypostasis* (2Const. 27 anathemas 3–4, 8–10). Although the council claims to base itself on the authority of earlier theologians and councils,[14] it also carries forward the complicated tensions involved in how that legacy is read, much as we saw in Leontius. At the same time that it makes concessions to Miaphysites and condemns the Three Chapters, the council nevertheless repeats a Leontine-Chalcedonian metaphysic together with new expressions such as "one of the Trinity was crucified in the flesh."

MAXIMUS CONFESSOR

Arguably the greatest theologian of the post-Chalcedonian period, Maximus Confessor further synthesized the unitive traditions of Gregory and Cyril with the reigning Chalcedonian program. The monk Maximus was a versatile and wide-ranging teacher of Christian prayer, liturgy, and dogmatic theology. During the first fifteen years or so of his theological work, he closely studied patristic sources, including Pseudo-Dionysius, who significantly influenced his thought, and above all Gregory Nazianzen, whom Maximus regarded as the greatest of the fathers. His early *Questions and Doubts* (c. 624–626) shows a strong preoccupation with Gregory's work, citing him frequently on matters of biblical hermeneutics and the Christian life. In the following decade Maximus produced a set of *Ambigua* (numbers 1–5, from c. 634), which concentrates on solving conundrums in Gregory's texts. Yet just as interesting as Maximus's early devotion to Gregory are the ways in which he misinterprets Gregory at the same time. In both texts he misreads a key passage on the Trinity. Where Gregory conceives of the Trinity as a monad moving to a dyad and ending in a triad (*Or.* 23.8), Maximus resists the passage's theological meaning and argues instead that Gregory is referring to creation (*Quaest.* 105; *Ambig.* 1). In the *Ambigua* Maximus also begins to use Gregory for Christological purposes, and it is at this point that his own, prior Chalcedonian commitments come into sharpest focus. In *Ambig.* 2–3 Maximus takes up Gregory's unitive rule of biblical interpretation, as expressed in *Oration* 28.18–19, yet he interprets it in a Leontine, Strict Chalcedonian sense, emphasizing the *ousia*–hypostasis distinction and—most pronounced of all—explicitly denying the divine suffering that Gregory had so strongly championed.[15] In the fourth of the *Ambigua* Maximus gives a definition of the hypostatic union of Christ that again reflects Leontius's Chalcedonianism, conceiving of Christ as a kind of third thing,[16] rather than the Son of God made flesh, as Gregory would have it. Maximus thus begins his theological career as a committed Strict Chalcedonian, even though he will later shift in a more unitive, "Neo-Chalcedonian" direction.[17]

By 642 Maximus began to take part in the widespread controversy over the question of whether Christ has one or two natural activities and wills. The official orthodoxy of the day, meant to be a compromise between Miaphysites and Chalcedonians, was the Monenergist and eventually Monothelite position: that even though Christ may have two natures, he nevertheless functions as a single being and therefore has only one proper activity and one will. Maximus took up the defense of Christ's natural human activity and will, alongside the divine activity and will, and committed himself to opposing the Monothelite program. Various patristic figures are credited with defending Christ's full humanity; the one who did so most thoroughly was Maximus. The most important works for understanding Maximus's Christology are his *Tome to Marinus* (*Opuscule* 7) and *Dialog with Pyrrhus*, both from the later polemical period, which we will supplement with other texts as well.

The Monothelite debate presents a challenge similar to the one Leontius faced against monophysitism, at least in principle: namely, how to articulate what Maximus calls the "duality" of Christ—the belief that he possesses a fully human will and activity in addition to being the divine Son of God—without jeopardizing his unity. Given Maximus's allegiance to Chalcedon and Leontius's strong influence on him, it is all the more striking that he moves as far in a unitive direction as he does. The reason for this, however, is not surprising: for Maximus continued to read Gregory Nazianzen, as well as Cyril, during the intervening years, and he came to accept more fully the unitive formulations of the Second Council of Constantinople. The final result is not without its compromises, but the achievement is remarkable nevertheless.

In the *Tome to Marinus* Maximus begins with a recognizably Chalcedonian declaration of intent: "the knowledge of [Christ's] Divinity and the truth of his humanity has been revealed to all" by the voice of the fathers, that is, by the council of 451 together with the other witnesses that have been assembled since then. Yet Maximus proceeds straightaway to summarize the received faith in a unitive confession: "The only-begotten Son, one of the holy and consubstantial Trinity, who is perfect God by nature, has become a perfect human being in accordance with his will, by truly assuming flesh that is consubstantial with us and endowed with a rational soul and mind from the holy Theotokos and ever-Virgin. He united it properly and inseparably to himself in accordance with the hypostasis, being one with it right from the beginning. . . . Remaining God and consubstantial with the Father, when he became flesh, he became double, so that being double by nature, he had kinship by nature with both extremes, and preserved the natural difference of his own parts each from the other" (*Opusc.* 7, 73B–C). Like Gregory, Cyril, and the faith of Nicaea, Maximus bases himself not in the balanced metaphysics embodied in Chalcedon, but in a narrative Christology focused on the being and action of the divine Son of God. The subject of the long sentence above is the only-begotten Son, "one of the holy Trinity," as Constantinople II declared, and it is he who becomes fully human, uniting a human nature to himself, so that Mary is truly Theotokos, the Mother of God. Accordingly, the divine Son is the primary agent of the union: he united his humanity to himself in a hypostatic union, while remaining God as he has always been. This is a very different sort of statement than virtually anything we find in Leontius or the Chalcedonian Definition (apart from its quotations of Nicaea and Constantinople I). Finally, the Son of God himself "became double" in the incarnation, and double "by nature," not merely by virtue of the fact that his hypostasis joins together two natures; the union, in other words, comes from the divine side and involves both natures in one another, as Gregory had taught in terms of their "perichoresis" or mutual interpenetration.

Moreover, Maximus continues, the natural difference between the two natures and their distinctive properties are preserved by the Word (*Opusc.* 7, 73C);[18] the divine initiative remains foremost even in establishing the integrity of Christ's fully functioning humanity. Maximus adds the extremely interesting comment that if the Word did not preserve the distinctive properties of both natures, that would be a shortcoming in his divinity (*Opusc.* 7, 73D)—that it is truly godlike and divine for the Word to sustain Jesus's humanity. In his *Dialog with Pyrrhus*, Maximus articulates his position similarly, basing himself in the single-subject language of Gregory Nazianzen and Nicaea: *God* is the cause of the natural harmony between Christ's divine and human wills, so that there is no conflict between them (*Pyrrh.* 291A). Christ is the superessential Word of God who has come to exist in a human way and gives his humanity the very power to exist (*Pyrrh.* 297B). Maximus's clarification of the interrelation between the divine and human natures in Christ—the fact that they are not only compatible, but necessarily go together—is perhaps his greatest theological achievement, and in this regard he is theologically and spiritually very close to Augustine, although it is unlikely that he was influenced by the bishop of Hippo.[19] We will discuss Maximus's achievement with special attention to Jesus's human will.

Against those who deny Jesus's human will and operation, Maximus voices a traditional soteriological concern. As Gregory Nazianzen argued in his *First Letter to Cledonius*, Christ must have a real and functioning human mind, soul, and body in order for us to be saved, for "what was not assumed has not been healed" (*Opusc.* 7, 76D). Again following Gregory (here more than Cyril),[20] Maximus argues further that the Son's assumption of a full human nature serves to heal and divinize it rather than to diminish or eradicate it (*Opusc.* 7, 77C). On the basis of this affirmation of Jesus's full humanity, Maximus gives an ingenious and famous explanation of how Christ can possess the divine will and also a fully functioning human will while still being defined primarily as the divine Son of God. In particular, he explains how it is that Jesus can speak of doing the will of God (or his Father) *instead of* his own, as in the Garden of Gethsemane.

Jesus's human will and his divine will work together in this way. The divine Son wills all that Christ does: the entire work of the incarnation is God's. He is "the one who wills" (ὁ θέλων) and the ultimate subject of all Christ's works. As a fully human being, however, Jesus has a natural human will (τὸ θέλημα) that makes real human choices—above all, whether to follow and obey the divine will or not. Third, the object of Christ's willing (τὸ θελετόν)—its purpose, objective, or aim—is shared by Jesus as a human and as God, so that Jesus humanly chooses to will the same thing that he as God wills, in terms of outcome. Accordingly, there is, finally, the "manner" in which Jesus wills as a human being (τὸ πῶς θέλειν), namely, whether he does follow the divine will or not (*Pyrrh.* 293A). By distinguishing among these different aspects of willing, Maximus is able to explain how the divine Son is the ultimate subject of all of Jesus's deeds, as the one who wills, and yet how Jesus operates as a full human being with a will that is human in its natural functioning, but which, in his case alone, nevertheless freely and constantly chooses to have the same objective that he as God wills, and which is thus, in its manner of willing, a "divinely" functioning human will, by virtue of his perfect obedience.

As evidence for this view, Maximus cites approvingly an unidentified text of Cyril's which states that Christ "revealed one co-natural activity through both [natures]."[21] Maximus tellingly comments, "There *is* one activity of the divinity both without flesh and with flesh," and the one activity of the divine Son does not cancel out, as it were, Christ's natural human activity, which is different from his divine activity, just as a creature differs from the creator. Yet through both sorts of activities "the divine activity was made known." For "the same one" (the divine Son) was God by nature and was also "active as a human being" (*Pyrrh.* 344B–D). The same approach enables Maximus also to accommodate the famous saying of Pseudo-Dionysius, the pseudonymous author being most likely a Miaphysite from the circle of Severus of Antioch, Leontius's opponent. Dionysius's statement that Christ possessed a single "theandric activity"[22] naturally played into the hands of Monenergists and Monothelites; yet the reputed associate of St. Paul carried enormous authority, and it was advantageous to incorporate his teaching in the orthodox fold. So Maximus explains that the phrase refers to both natures periphrastically, in a way similar to the Cyrilline text (*Pyrrh.* 384C–D). As he writes elsewhere, the Son of God wills divine things together with the Father who begot him, and he also wills naturally human things (*Opusc.* 7, 77C–80A). By maintaining the single-subjectivity of Christ, Maximus makes room for the concerns of the miaphysite tradition that Chalcedon and Leontius had vehemently excluded.

The crucial test for the question of Christ's human will comes in his struggle in the Garden of Gethsemane, and here Maximus shows the full capability of his analytic scheme. When Christ prays to the Father to be spared the cup of his impending death (Matt 26:39), this shows (1) that he has a real human will and (2) that it is not opposed to the divine will (which would violate the Christological principle of single-subjectivity). It is perfectly natural, Maximus argues, to fear death, just as it is natural to hunger and thirst. Such experiences are part of being human, and they are not sinful. There are ways in which human appetites and fear can be sinful and "against our nature," but they need not be (*Pyrrh.* 297C). There is therefore no need to explain away Jesus's human fear, either by interpreting his statement to mean that he does not have a human will at all ("not my will" referring to the faculty itself), or by dividing Christ into two independently existing subjects. Yet the fact that Jesus decides not to follow his natural human desire to avoid death, but instead to follow God's will for him to die on the cross, ultimately shows the divine quality of his human willing, and that his human will has been divinized by the divine will, "since it is eternally moved and shaped by it and in accordance with it" (*Opusc.* 7, 80D; 81D–84A).

Maximus's analysis of Jesus's agony in the garden clearly shows that he has followed Gregory Nazianzen to a significant degree. The doctrine of two wills operating together within a single, divine subject was articulated by Gregory before the close of the fourth century. Accordingly, Maximus quotes the statement of "the great Theologian" in the fourth *Theological Oration*, that "the willing of [Christ] is not opposed [to God], but has been completely divinized" (*Or.* 30.13; Maximus, *Opusc.* 7, 81C)—a passage that will also be quoted at the Third Council of Constantinople. We may note as well that on this point Maximus disagrees with Gregory of Nyssa, for whom Jesus's humanity is not divinized until after his resurrection. The fact that Jesus's human will perfectly follows the will of God (in terms of its object) and thus wills divinely (in its manner) marks the key difference between his human will and ours. While Jesus makes real moral choices and must choose to obey God, there is another sense in which, by virtue of his identity as the Son of God made human, his human will lacks the quality of unfaithfulness that all other human beings possess. Jesus is truly tempted to sin, but he is not under the power of sin like we are, and so his will is not divided between good and evil, or in any other way. In Maximus's terms, Jesus's will is not "gnomic," wandering or subject to wavering human opinion. The gnomic quality of our wills subject to sin, and the non-gnomic quality of Jesus's obedient will, belongs to the manner of willing; it is not a mark of our nature itself. Jesus possesses the same natural human will that we do, only he uses it in a divine manner and we do not. In making this distinction Maximus has thereby preserved the ontological integrity of human nature after the fall, among the other points we are considering here. Yet, unlike us, Jesus was in fact "good by nature, because he subsisted divinely" on account of being the Son of God, which of course no other human being is (*Pyrrh.* 308B–9B). The full and natural operation of Jesus's human will therefore ultimately depends on his *divine* identity, and his divinity and humanity preserve and fulfill the integrity of each other precisely through the unity of Christ and the transformative process of divinization.

One of the side effects of Maximus's Christology is to exalt the natural integrity of creation. As the centerpoint of creation and of the economy of salvation, the incarnation of Christ shows preeminently how the being and activity of God support and fulfill the natural existence of creatures. Here again Maximus's main source and guide is Gregory Nazianzen.[23] In the first place, the full presence and operation of God are perfectly compatible with natural creaturely functioning, as Gregory had argued. Yet, even more, the presence and will of God uniquely fulfill creaturely nature through what Gregory termed divinization. In other words, Maximus is thoroughly opposed to the idea that the incarnation (or any of God's acts) poses an ontological conflict with creatures. God does not conflict with the natural, for he is the one who created it. Maximus explains: "Nothing that is natural, and certainly no nature itself, would ever resist the cause of nature, nor would the intention [*gnome*], or anything that belongs to the intention, if it agreed with the inner rationale [*logos*] of nature." To suggest otherwise would mean that God has "introduced war naturally into the realm of being and raised up insurrection against himself and strife among all that exists;" whereas, in truth, "nothing natural is opposed to God" (*Opusc.* 7, 80A). For this reason Maximus opposes the characterization of human activity as passivity, when compared with the supreme activity of God; it is Pyrrhus who raises this objection in Maximus's own time, yet we have also seen that it was the view of Athanasius as well, who similarly downplayed the natural status of creation in order to elevate the sovereignty of God. Maximus recognizes the liability of such a view, that it artificially degrades humanity in order to make God seem good, which is both unnecessary and false

(*Pyrrh.* 349B–52A). For Maximus, sin is neither a part of nature nor something natural, which can oppose the divine nature ontologically; rather, sin is a perversion of nature (*Opusc.* 7, 80B). Here again we have a striking correspondence with the thought of Augustine, whose concept of evil as the privation of the good is very similar, and which is likewise designed to preserve the substantial integrity of the created world (in his case, against Manicheans).[24] In this regard, Maximus articulates better than anyone since Gregory Nazianzen and Augustine the way in which God and human existence mutually fulfill each other. Of all the theologians we are considering in this book, it is not the Antiochenes, but Maximus Confessor, the disciple of Gregory Nazianzen and Cyril, who truly upholds the integrity of Christ's humanity and creaturely nature in general.

The heart of Maximus's Christology runs in this way, and it is in deep agreement with the preceding unitive traditions. Yet, as we have noted, he is also beholden to Chalcedon, and so contrasting elements run throughout his work. He occasionally echoes the second Leontine definition of hypostasis: for example, when he writes to Marinus that the Word is different from God the Father in his hypostatic characteristics (*Opusc.* 7, 85B);[25] in balanced statements of difference and union; and above all in his interest in "keeping the Word unharmed," as if the experience of creatures threatened to overwhelm it (*Opusc.* 7, 84A–B, 88B).[26] Such expressions run right against the natural compatibility we have just been discussing. Nevertheless, the Gregorian and Cyrilline undercurrent in Maximus is strong indeed, and it flows through him into the sixth ecumenical council as the great synthesis of John of Damascus.

CONSTANTINOPLE III (680–681)

During the last decade of his life Maximus endured arrest, exile, and several trials. In 662 he was tragically mutilated, and died soon thereafter, for his defense of Christ's human will against the Monothelites, a sacrifice that earned him the honor of being a confessor of the faith. Just a few years before this period, in 649, a Roman council meeting at the Lateran formally condemned Monothelitism; Maximus wrote a large part of the Lateran doctrinal definition, just as he had secured similar condemnations at several synods in Africa.

Despite his persecution, Maximus's doctrine of Christ's two wills was eventually ratified in another "ecumenical" council nearly twenty years after his death. In 680 Emperor Constantine IV called a council to bring an end to the Monothelite controversy. The previous spring, Pope Agatho had held a synod of 125 Italian bishops in Rome that upheld the doctrine of Christ's two wills, and in the following autumn papal delegates advanced the same agenda at the Third Council of Constantinople. Composed mainly of the patriarchates of Constantinople and Antioch, together with the papal legates, the council immediately declared itself an ecumenical council, and the emperor himself presided over the first eleven of eighteen sessions. In the eleventh session the council adopted Agatho's position, which derived from Maximus. Its decisions were signed by the emperor, 174 bishops, and the new Pope Leo II. The pope had the acts immediately translated into Latin and signed by all bishops of the West, and the emperor promulgated them throughout the empire, giving the council a nearly universal scope.

The council's exposition of the faith attempts to hold Maximus's doctrine of the single subjectivity and two wills of Christ together with a strong reaffirmation of Chalcedon. Like the previous council, Constantinople III begins with traditional Nicene language, defining Christ first as "the only Son and Word of God the Father, who became a human being like us in all things except sin," and it preserves the definition that the incarnate Christ is "one of the holy, consubstantial, and live-giving Trinity" who was born from the Father divinely and also from Mary the Theotokos (*3Const.* 768/124). To these initial statements it then adds several parallel, Chalcedonian phrases, and it repeats the Chalcedonian definition of "one and the same Christ" (rather than Son), who is "acknowledged in two natures without confusion, change, separation, or division." Third, it reproduces Leontius's "container" idea of hypostasis as that into which Christ's two natures "come together" (*3Const.* 774–76/127–28).

The council's doctrine of two wills follows Maximus fairly closely. Christ has two natural wills and energies without division, change, partition, or confusion (in Chalcedonian terms), yet it is the divine will that leads his human will.[27] Moreover, in a striking phrase, it defines Christ's human will as being "proper" (*idion*) to the Word of God, on the basis of John 6:38 ("not my own will, but the will of him who sent me"). It reiterates Maximus's cardinal principle that the presence of the divine Son does not destroy his human will but preserves it, giving the same quotation from Gregory Nazianzen that Maximus had used (*Or.* 30.12). Here the single acting agent is clearly the divine Son. Christ's two natural energies are then also affirmed, this time on the basis of Leo's *Tome* and a quotation reputedly from Cyril.

Finally, the council reiterates the combination of single-subject language ("one of the holy Trinity") and Chalcedonian adverbs ("without confusion or distinction"), followed by the second Leontine sense of hypostasis, "from which" Christ's miracles and sufferings both shine forth, which is an ultimately divisive notion. The council thus condemns the doctrines of Monenergism and Monothelitism via the theology of Maximus on the one hand, while upholding Chalcedon even more strongly than Maximus had, even to the point of repeating the same list of authoritative documents: Leo's *Tome* and Cyril's letters against Nestorius and the Eastern bishops (*3 Const.* 772–76/126–27). In this regard, the council exacerbated the tensions latent in Maximus's work and, thanks to its universal scope, forwarded those tensions into the Christology of the Eastern and Western Middle Ages.

JOHN OF DAMASCUS

John of Damascus is often regarded as the last of the great fathers and the one who most adeptly synthesized the patristic achievement. Having served in the court of the Islamic caliph in Damascus, John later became a monk. Among his other activities, he became seriously engaged in Christian-Muslim apologetics, and he defended the veneration of icons against iconoclasm, which earned him the approval of the seventh ecumenical council at Nicaea in 787. His greatest theological work was a three-part summary of Christian doctrine, the *Fount of Knowledge*.

In the third and most famous part of this work, titled *An Exposition of the Faith* (also known as *The Orthodox Faith*), John brought together much earlier patristic teaching, and it became a major influence in the later Eastern and Western churches. *The Orthodox Faith*, John's main Christological work, is in effect a quasi-florilegium.[28] The work exemplifies in a particularly concrete way the sort of selection and prioritization of earlier authorities that reflect one's own theological position at least as much as they exhibit the fathers themselves. John's use of earlier sources, and hence the nature of his own doctrine, is different from Maximus's in two key respects. First, he begins his study not with Gregory Nazianzen, as Maximus did, but as a committed Chalcedonian who samples the fathers from that standpoint. Second, John relies quite heavily on Leontius of Byzantium, which makes him in the end more of a Strict Chalcedonian, closer to the old Antiochene doctrine and further from Gregory and Cyril, than Maximus was.[29] Throughout books 3 and 4 of *The Orthodox Faith*, John assembles various quotations and arguments from the fathers against heretical Christological positions. In the first two chapters, however, he gives an introductory presentation of his own Christology,[30] which stands in an interesting relationship to the patristic material that follows.

The most notable aspect of John's treatment of the incarnation, or "the divine economy," as the first chapter of book 3 is subtitled,[31] is how he describes the entire saving process as the work of God. John narrates the history of salvation, following primarily the account of Gregory Nazianzen in *Oration* 38.13. When humankind forfeited the grace and knowledge of God and incurred death and corruption, the compassionate God nevertheless did not abandon us, but schooled and exhorted us through the various events of the Old Covenant, and especially the law and the prophets. Yet because we remained under the destructive power of sin, we needed a redeemer who was himself not liable to the death of sin, and we needed to be taught again the way of virtue by human example. In response, therefore, "the Creator and Lord himself took up the struggle on behalf of his own creation and became a teacher in deed" (*Exp.Fid.* 45). The incarnation of Christ is God's own struggle with sin and death in human form on our behalf. This initial narration includes a passage from Gregory of Nyssa's *Catechetical Oration* on how Christ fulfills both God's justice and goodness (*Cat.Or.* 56–61), together with another echo of Gregory Nazianzen on the salvation of like by like (*Or.* 39.13; *Ep.* 101.32, 50–55).

John then gives his own confessional statement, which makes even clearer Christ's primarily divine identity within a unitive, single-subject scheme. The only-begotten Son and Word of God and God (John gives a lengthy list of divine titles) descended to earth while still remaining divine, in an "ineffable and incomprehensible condescension." The one who was perfect God became perfect man and accomplished "the only 'new thing under the sun'" (Eccl 1:9), an allusion to Gregory Nazianzen's idea of the new commingling of God and humanity in Christ (*Or.* 39.13), which was one of Maximus's favorite patristic passages.[32] "For what is greater than for God to become human?" John asks. Therefore the Word became flesh from Mary the Theotokos. It is the Word of God, then, who is "the Mediator between God and human beings" (1 Tim 2:5), as in Augustine, and it is the same Word of God who was conceived and born of Mary and who became obedient to the Father as a model for our salvation (*Exp.Fid.* 45). Again, there is no trace thus far of anything but a unitive Christology in the mold of Gregory, Augustine, and Cyril.

As he continues the narrative of salvation, John focuses on Christ's incarnation in the second chapter, which is subtitled "On the manner of the coming together [σύλληψις] of the Word of God and his divine flesh." At this point the unitive force of John's exposition becomes clearer. He begins with the annunciation of Gabriel to Mary, as recounted in Luke 1:28–38. He highlights the meaning of Jesus's name as Savior and the fact that the child to be born will be called "the Son of God." In the commentary that follows, John accentuates Christ's divine identity in several ways. The angel, he says, purified Mary (in another reference to Gregory Nazianzen, *Or.* 38.13) and gave her the ability "to receive the divinity of the Word and give birth." John then describes Christ's identity in the following way. "The subsistent Wisdom and Power of God Most High, the Son of God who is consubstantial with the Father," overshadowed Mary and "put together for himself" a human body from Mary's pure blood. The birth of Jesus was thus the action of God: it was the incarnation of the Son and a creation by the Holy Spirit, not a regular human birth or a gradual incarnation, as Gregory likewise taught (*Or.* 29). He then describes the incarnation in technical terms that are more Gregorian or Cyrilline than they are Chalcedonian: "The Word of God himself served as hypostasis for the flesh," a phrase that comes from the anti-Antiochene (and *pre*-Chalcedonian) *Tome* of Proclus of Constantinople.[33] In contrast with the language of Chalcedon and the second definition of Leontius of Byzantium, John here views the divine Son and Word of God as the individuating principle of the incarnate Christ, not as a hypostasis distinct from the divine nature. Christ's flesh has no subsistence on its own (again from Proclus); it does not exist at all apart from being hypostasized by the Word of God, as Leontius would also agree. The incarnation of Christ was the coming of the Word of God "in his own hypostasis" to dwell in Mary's womb and to cause human flesh also to subsist, or to be hypostasized. By taking intelligent human flesh from Mary, "the very Word became hypostasis to the body" of Christ (*Exp.Fid.* 46). The human body of Jesus is therefore "the body of God the Word," and through the hypostatic union, Jesus's human body has its existence in the Word, even as both natures are preserved in their integrity. Even though Jesus's humanity is divinized, as most now believe, it is nevertheless important to maintain that, in the first instance, it was *God* who became human, not a human being becoming God, much as Gregory Nazianzen argued in *Letter* 101 (*Exp.Fid.* 46). John's opening Christological confession is highly unitive, and it accords very well with the language of Nicaea and the doctrine of Gregory Nazianzen, Augustine, and Cyril of Alexandria.

The unitive nature of John's opening confession makes the rest of the work all the more striking. For like Maximus, John of Damascus is committed to a Chalcedonian program—only in John's case he remains loyal to Strict Chalcedonian metaphysics, whereas Maximus found his way to the unitive doctrine of Gregory and Cyril. In the chapters that follow, John strives to make the unitive Christology that he has found in Gregory Nazianzen and others accord with the logic of Chalcedon. Yet he is beholden to the Strict Chalcedonian logic of Leontius far more than Maximus was, and for this reason his Christology—which was for many later theologians the "final" patristic synthesis—is even more fraught with tension.

Several examples will suffice to show the Chalcedonian character of John's argumentation. Just after beginning with a strong emphasis on the unity and single subjectivity of Christ, John qualifies himself in a Chalcedonian direction, arguing that the two natures do not change even as they are compounded with one another. In book 3, chapter 3 he runs through several expressions of the parallel nature metaphysic that we saw in Leontius, and makes his way immediately to Leontius's dualizing second definition of hypostasis. John quotes Leontius directly: "The reason for the heretics' error is their saying that nature and hypostasis are the same thing" (*Exp.Fid.* 47). The radical distinction between nature and hypostasis recurs several times throughout book 3 (*Exp.Fid.* 50, 51), including the startling statement, "We have never heard that the Divinity was made human or was incarnate or put on human nature" (*Exp.Fid.* 55). Leontius's more inclusive, first definition occasionally appears as well (*Exp.Fid.* 48, 50). Similarly, John accepts Leontius's definition of Christ's union as being "hypostatic" rather than according to nature, so that he is "one composite hypostasis" (*Exp.Fid.* 47). To say that Christ's union was "essential" (οὐσιώδη), then, means only that it was real and not imaginary, not that the union took place in and through the divine Son, who is himself the divine nature begotten from God the Father, as Gregory Nazianzen meant by union "according to essence" (κατὰ τὴν οὐσίαν, *Ep.* 101.22). In this way John has shifted from defining Christ's hypostasis as the Son of God, in the doctrinal summary above, to defining hypostasis as something other than the Son's divine nature, in the Strict Chalcedonian mode. From here naturally follows a quotation from Leo's *Tome* that points to the divine and human natures each showing forth from Christ's miracles and sufferings, respectively (*Exp.Fid.* 47). Where Maximus had said that *both* sorts of events show Christ's divinity (the latter doing so humanly), John has retreated to a more purely Chalcedonian position.

Even as John begins again with unitive language (the Word makes all human things his own),[34] he enforces the Chalcedonian logic, so that "one and the same" Christ who does both human and divine things is again a kind of third thing: "he who 'with each form cooperating with the other performs' both divine and human acts," quoting another passage of Leo, taken from the anthology *Doctrina Patrum* (*Ep.* 28.14). In this view, the one who does things according to the form of a servant (that is, humanly) is not also himself still in the form of God (that is, divine); the human Jesus is not divine *in* his humanity, as Gregory, Augustine, Cyril, and Maximus had each insisted he was. Following the same dualist logic, John is likewise eager to deny that Christ's divine nature suffered (*Exp.Fid.* 47). He goes so far as to say that "we have never heard up to now that the nature of the Word suffered in the flesh" (*Exp.Fid.* 55)—a statement that is bound to strain the credulity of anyone in a Cyrilline tradition—and he does not want there to be any talk of God suffering "in the flesh," as even Athanasius was willing to do (*Exp.Fid.* 48, 50, 70). John's understanding of Christological exegesis likewise follows that of Leontius: both divine and human statements refer to the hypostasis, so that there is no true cross-predication from the divinity to the humanity or vice versa: "we never speak of uncreated flesh or humanity" (*Exp.Fid.* 48). John's resistance to the *communicatio idiomatum* approaches the vigor of Diodore's, and he is quite far indeed from the single-subject approach of Gregory or Cyril.

Perhaps the most glaring Chalcedonian accommodation is the way in which John merges Maximus's unitive defense of Christ's two natural wills and operations with the older, Strict Chalcedonian metaphysic of Leontius (*Exp.Fid.* 58–59). On most points John represents Maximus faithfully and well, with one important exception. Whereas for Maximus the ultimate agent of all of Christ's divine and human acts is very clearly the *divine* Son of God, John has omitted Maximus's discussion of the single-subjectivity of the divine Son from his excerpts—because he wants to shift the idea in a Chalcedonian direction. For John of Damascus, the ultimate agent of Christ's divine and human acts is in fact the Leontine distinct hypostasis, an idea reinforced once again by reference to Leo's *Tome* (*Exp.Fid.* 59). In the text that John gives us, the singularity of Christ's double willing is preserved mainly by the mutual characterization of the divine and human actions themselves, not by the divine Son of God (who is both nature and hypostasis). Through his rereading of the earlier tradition, John causes Maximus to appear more Strictly Chalcedonian than he was.

In the end, John of Damascus produced a Christology that is fraught with even more tension than Maximus's. Like Leontius, he claims to be presenting the unified, collective teaching of the great fathers, but his collection is deliberately skewed in a Strict Chalcedonian direction. John's famous synthesis of patristic thought is neither a catalog of undifferentiated sources nor a neutral representation of an unblemished Christological tradition, as many later readers took it to be. At the end of the patristic age, the unity of Christ, which theologians such as Gregory Nazianzen, Augustine, and, for the most part, Cyril and Maximus Confessor had championed, stands in an uneasy tension with the contravening forces of dualist Christology. Such is the complex and unstable nature of the patristic tradition that many later theologians and church bodies have considered normative.

Epilogue

It can be tempting in theological, historical, and ecclesiastical work, when faced with great complexity and conflict, to throw one's hands up in exasperation. One of the chief aims of this book has been to urge that we must do just the reverse—that in order to understand patristic theological tradition, it is crucial that we acknowledge both the conflicts and the continuities wherever they may exist. The pressure either to overstate the fragmenting effects of disagreement or to gloss over real problems in the name of an easier solution can be considerable. But there is no other way of making true progress in scholarly work, theological enquiry, church procedure—or indeed the good life. As Augustine writes about the work of Christian teaching, it is just as important to undo falsehood and error as it is to discover and teach the truth (*Doctr.* 4.6). The two must go hand in hand.

In the argument presented here, I hope to have shown the pervasive influence of Origen over the whole period, as well as both the resources and the liabilities that exist in his work. Recovering Eusebius as a major Christological authority and decentering Athanasius in the grand picture of fourth-century orthodoxy should go far toward reorienting our understanding of how the high-patristic traditions actually developed. The same can be expected from a new consideration of the differences that exist among the fabled Cappadocians, which had a great impact on the post-Chalcedonian situation. And the great compromises and the resulting theological tensions that were required in order to maintain Chalcedonian orthodoxy have likewise affected later theological constructions, even to the present day. Yet we have also seen the unity of Christ running persistently through the works of several major theologians, from Eusebius and Gregory Nazianzen through Cyril to Maximus Confessor, with a strong affirmation by Augustine, guided by the example of Ambrose, who had studied with the Greeks himself.

With this tradition more clearly in view, we are in a position to note, finally, how unitive patristic Christology can serve as a valuable ecumenical resource. To those who have been looking for a bridge between the Eastern and Western churches, I would suggest that it exists here, in the Christology of the magisterial Greek and Latin fathers, rather than in an attempted rapprochement among their respective Trinitarian doctrines, where Augustine was the first to admit the tenuous nature of his work. When it came to the unitive confession of Christ as the divine Son of God made human, however, he was absolutely confident, deeply humbled, and supremely hopeful. Here, we might say, is the orthodox and catholic faith shared across the great church.

Notes

CHAPTER I. ORIGEN OF ALEXANDRIA

1. Bagnall and Rathbone, *Egypt*, 51–52.
2. Fuks, "Aspects of the Jewish Revolt," 98–104; Eusebius, *H.E.* 4.2; see also Mélèze-Modrzejewski, *Jews of Egypt*.
3. Layton, "The Significance of Basilides"; Roberts, *Manuscript, Society, and Belief*; Pearson, "Earliest Christianity," and *Gnosticism and Christianity*, 12–19, 82–99; Heine, *Origen*, 1–82. No second-century Christian author mentions Mark in connection with the Alexandrian church, nor is there any evidence that Mark's cousin Barnabas was involved in early Alexandrian mission, as related in the pseudo-Clementine *Hom.* 1.8.3–15.9. Given what we know of Philo's Judaism, it is unlikely that Jewish Christianity before the destruction of the Jewish community in 117 was radically different from the Christianity that emerges by the year 180, *pace* Mélèze-Modrzejewski, *Jews of Egypt*, 227–30. On the relative independence of Christian teachers in the second century, see Bardy, "*Aux origines de l'ecole d'Alexandrie*"; Jakab, *Ecclesia alexandrina*, 91–106.
4. Clement's presbyterate is suggested by a letter from Bishop Alexander of Jerusalem recorded by Eusebius (*H.E.* 6.11.6). Nautin, *Lettres*, 114–18; and Pearson, "Egypt," 339, 342. For an alternative view in favor of an official church school before Demetrius, cf. van den Hoek, "Catechetical School." A high regard for the Jerusalem church exists in the *Kerygma Petri* and the *Gospel of the Hebrews*; ascetical Greek-speaking Christianity can be discerned in the *Gospel of the Egyptians*, which shows interesting similarities with the (real or imagined) Jewish *therapeutae* described by Philo (*Contemp. Life*); an apocalyptic orientation appears in the *Epistle to Barnabas* and the Alexandrian Christian Sibylline writings; and Clement polemicizes against Marcionite tendencies in *Strom.* 3.3.12. See Dorival, "Les débuts," 171; and van den Broek, "Juden und Christen." On the practice of selecting one of the presbyters to serve as supervisor-bishop, see Jerome, *Ep.* 146.1.
5. The pioneering modern study of Origen's life is Nautin, *Origène*. Our main ancient source, Eusebius's *H.E.* book 6, has both assets and liabilities. If

Eusebius shows some personal bias to defend Origen against criticisms in the early fourth century, he had the great benefit of direct access to Origen's works and correspondence in what remained of Origen's library in Caesarea. Among Eusebius's sources was an autobiographical letter in which Origen answered certain accusations following his move to Caesarea (see *H.E.* 6.19.12–14) and which may be the same document that Jerome reports Origen sent to Pontianus of Rome in order to defend himself against charges of irregular ordination and unorthodox doctrine by Demetrius of Alexandria (Jerome, *Ep.* 84.9). On the Greek versus native Egyptian character of Origen's family, see Heine, *Origen*, 20. On Origen's Greek education, see Runia, "Origen and Hellenism"; Neuschäfer, *Origenes als Philologe* (on Alexandrian grammar); and Heine's introduction to Origen, *Com.Jn.* 3–12, which argues that Origen's methods of biblical commentary drew heavily on the practices of the Alexandrian philosophical schools. Origen's father's name is sometimes disputed; on his mother's doubtful Roman citizenship, see McGuckin, "Life of Origen," 3.

6. Even if Eusebius's account is exaggerated—we read of sleepless nights, poverty, celibacy, prayer, and fasting (see *H.E.* 6.3.9–13)—it is clear from everything we know about Origen that something to this effect was the case. Eusebius's story that Origen had himself castrated in order to preserve his chastity and to avoid any untoward suspicions in his work with students of both sexes is highly unlikely.

7. Among the difficulties in identifying Origen's teacher with the Platonist Ammonius Saccas is the fact that an Aristotelian Ammonius was even more popular at the time, among several others by the same name. Edwards, "Ammonius, Teacher of Origen," 169–81. A further difficulty is the likelihood that Ammonius Saccas may have begun teaching in Alexandria shortly before Origen's departure, in which case Origen would have heard only a few lectures by him anyway. Heine, *Origen*, 24–25. For a defense of Ammonius Saccas, cf. Trigg, *Origen*, 12. On Origen's overriding Platonism, see Trigg, *Origen*, 66–76; and Heine, *Origen*, 63–64.

8. The date of Origen's move to Palestine comes from preferring Eusebius, *H.E.* 6.26 (the tenth year of Alexander Severus) over 6.23.3–4 (the eighth year of Pope Urban and his succession by Pontian). A rare glimpse of the Alexandria-Caesarea transition comes in Origen's *Com.Jn.* 6.8–11. According to Eusebius, Demetrius was "subject to human feelings" about Origen (*H.E.* 6.8.4). At the time of Origen's first visit to Palestine, around 215, the local bishops invited him to teach in their churches while he was still a layman. This gesture enraged Demetrius, who sent letters to the bishops denouncing their actions as uncanonical (*H.E.* 6.19.16–19). At the same time that Origen

was establishing himself as a notable Christian teacher, Demetrius was in the process of consolidating his authority as bishop and expanding his pastoral supervision over other areas of Egypt. Demetrius appointed three additional bishops for the first time; his successor Heraclas appointed an additional twenty, according to the tenth-century patriarch Eutychius (PG 111.982). Davis, *Early Coptic Papacy*, 21–26. On account of this work, Demetrius was later regarded as the "second founder of the church of Alexandria" and "founder of the church of Egypt." Telfer, "Episcopal Succession," 2. The simultaneous ascent of two such strong men may well have placed them on a collision course.

9. Fragments of Origen's defense are preserved in Rufinus's *Falsif.* 6–8 and Jerome's *C.Ruf.* 2.18–19. In a fragment of book 5 of Origen's *Com.Jn.* (written in Alexandria) preserved in the *Philokalia*, Origen speaks of those who say that he has written too much. In a letter to Fabian of Rome, Origen similarly defends his teaching by saying that his patron Ambrose had published certain (presumably experimental) texts that he had meant to keep private (Jerome, *Ep.* 84.10). Jerome also refers to many who accuse Origen of heterodoxy, although no synod of Rome did (*Ep.* 33.5).

10. Our knowledge of Origen's ordination by Theoctistus relies on Photius's report (*Bibl.* 118) over Eusebius, *H.E.* 6.23.4; Crouzel, *Origen*, 18. On the purpose of Origen's school in Caesarea, see McGuckin, "Life of Origen," 13–16. Eusebius reportedly gave a full account of the ecclesiastical procedures against Origen in the now lost second book of the *Defense of Origen* that he helped Pamphilus complete (*H.E.* 6.23.4). According to Photius (*Bibl.* 118), a synod of bishops in Alexandria deposed Origen, declaring him ineligible to exercise his priesthood there. Some have speculated that Clement left Alexandria for similar reasons of conflict between his educational work and the church's official authority. See Nautin, *Lettres*, 18, 140; Pearson, "Egypt," 342.

11. As can be seen in his *Hom.Endor* (1 Sam 28:3–25). Socrates reports that Origen preached every Wednesday and Friday (*H.E.* 5.22), and we can assume certain Sundays as well.

12. If we prefer Eusebius's report of Origen's age (*H.E.* 7.1) over his identification of the ruler at the time of his death.

13. Writing from Origen's library in Palestine, Eusebius lists just under two thousand volumes, according to Jerome (*C.Ruf.* 2.22). Jerome's own list of eight hundred (*Ep.* 33) may have been reduced over time by medieval copyists. McGuckin, "The Scholarly Works of Origen," 27.

14. Heine, *Origen*, vii, 85, and passim.

15. Nine of the original thirty-two books of *Com.Jn.* survive in Greek, making those sections particularly valuable. The first book covers only John 1:1, and

when Origen reached John 13:33, he gave up the work. Also important are the remaining eight Greek books of *Com.Mt.*, written late in Origen's career (244 or later): books 10–17, on Matt 13:36–22:33, survive from the original twenty-five books, in addition to a homiletical Latin adaptation of most of the commentary dating from the fifth or sixth century. The Greek text of Origen's *Com.Rom.*, which he wrote probably before the Matthew commentary, exists now only in fragments, although we possess Rufinus's complete Latin translation; scholars debate the extent to which Rufinus compressed or paraphrased this work. Also written before the Matthew commentary, in Athens and Caesarea, was Origen's monumental *Com.Song*, which we have only in Rufinus's Latin translation of the first four of ten original books. The work seeks to show how the Song of Songs makes sense as part of a Christian canon of Scripture. This commentary is the first sustained Christian work on the mystical union of the soul with God, and it became greatly influential on later spiritual and ascetic literature. Jerome, who knew the whole work, praised Origen for excelling even himself on this occasion. The rest of Origen's commentaries are either lost or greatly fragmented: we know of works on Genesis, 1–2 Kings, the Psalms, Isaiah, Lamentations, Ezekiel, the minor Prophets, Luke, Acts, Galatians, Ephesians, Philippians, Colossians, Thessalonians, Hebrews, Titus, and Philemon, but nothing on Mark, the Catholic Epistles, or Revelation. Jerome valued Origen's biblical interpretation so highly (before he turned against him) that his own commentaries on Galatians, Ephesians, Titus, and Philemon were nearly copies of Origen's on the same. During his time in Caesarea, Origen preached what must have been hundreds of sermons on biblical texts, covering most if not all of the Scriptures. Only 279 homilies now survive, the only Greek texts being twenty homilies on Jeremiah and a sermon on the Witch of Endor (1 Sam 28), plus fragments of homilies on Matthew and Luke. Fortunately, we do have several sets of homilies in Latin translation: on Genesis, Exodus, Leviticus, Numbers, Joshua, Judges, and Psalms 36–38 translated by Rufinus; on the Song of Songs, Jeremiah, Ezekiel, Luke, and (it appears) the Psalms, translated by Jerome; plus an abbreviated Latin version of a set on Job translated by Hilary of Poitiers and sets on 1 Samuel 1–2 and fragments on 1–2 Samuel, 1–2 Kings, 1 Corinthians, and Hebrews of uncertain translator. Only a few of Origen's many notes on the Bible (*scholia* or *excerpta*) remain, in sections of Pamphilus's *Apology* and the *Philokalia* compiled by Basil of Caesarea and Gregory of Nazianzus, and in fragmentary form in collections of such notes made centuries later (the patristic *catenae*). As an aid to his work of interpretation, Origen also produced the *Hexapla*, a massive, six-columned version of the Old Testament, containing the Hebrew text, a

Greek transliteration of the Hebrew, and four Greek translations: the Septuagint plus three other translations, with two or three other versions sometimes added, in the case of the Psalms. The Septuagint version printed in Origen's *Hexapla* was the basis of the church's Old Testament text in many places; for example, it provided the master copy for the fifty Bibles that Emperor Constantine commissioned Eusebius to produce for his newly built churches in the early fourth century. On the *Hexapla*, see esp. Nautin, *Origène*, 303–61, and Grafton and Williams, *Christianity and the Transformation of the Book*.

16. "Only those things which differ in no way from ecclesiastical and apostolic tradition are to be accepted as truth."

17. The complete text of *Princ.* exists only in a Latin translation by Rufinus (another by Jerome has been lost), although we have the Greek text of several sections from the *Philocalia* and (more dubiously) the sixth-century edicts of Emperor Justinian, plus fragments from other sources. On the meaning of ἀρχαί, see Trigg, *Origen*, 18; on Origen's intent to produce a system of scientific knowledge, Daley, "Origen's 'De Principiis.'"

18. He gives a shorter summary near the end as well, at *Princ.* 4.2.7. On the earliest examples of the rule of faith, see Hanson, *Tradition*, 75–129.

19. What Rowan Williams calls the "uneasy relationship between the two controlling factors in Origen's thought: the given constraints of scriptural metaphor and the assumptions of Platonic cosmology" (*Arius*, 140); see also Grillmeier, *Das Konzil von Chalkedon*, 1.64. On Origen's several differences from Plato, see Edwards, *Origen against Plato*, esp. 74: "Origen's Son of God . . . is not the god of any Platonist." Trigg provides a convenient list of Platonic ideas in Origen's thought, including God's absolute transcendence and incorporeality and the human ideal of likeness to God via intellectual discipline (both taught by the Alexandrian Platonist Eudorus), the distinction between simple believers and a spiritual elite, the spiritualization of external religious rites, and a real sense of divine providence coupled with human freedom (reemphasized by Antiochus of Ascalon), remedial divine punishment and dualist allegorizing of traditional texts (which can be seen in Plutarch), and the overall attempt to find a coherent, rational understanding of God's purposes as a whole, *sub specie aeternitatis*. Significantly, Platonism could serve as a powerful antidote to Gnosticism, as we see also in Plotinus and in the similar role it played in Augustine's repudiation of Manichaean dualism. The often-cited parallel with Numenius's view that the transcendent first God reveals himself through a second God is more complicated, since Numenius used the Bible as a source. See also Trigg, *Origen*, 95–96 on the Platonic and Stoic background of Origen's treatment of the Father, Son, and Holy Spirit in *Princ.*

Pythagorean elements include the idea of God as a unity toward which we must move from our fragmented multiplicity; see *Hom.1Kg* 1.4; Clement, *Strom.* 4.151.3; and Bostock, "Origen and the Pythagoreanism." On Origen's philosophical eclecticism, see the report of Gregory Thaumaturgus's *Addr.* 13, and Heine, *Origen*.

20. Runia, *Philo*, 157–83. Lorenz also suggests that there are parallels with the incarnational mythology of Alexandrian Judaism, in terms of angelic spirits who descend to occupy mortal bodies (*Arius Iudaizans?*, 211–19, 223–24, echoed in Williams, *Arius*, 146). On Clement, see Pearson, *Gnosticism and Christianity*, 342.

21. On the difference between spiritual bodies and flesh-and-blood physical bodies, see *Princ.* 1.7.5; 2.10.1; 3.6.4–9; *Hom.Gen.* 1.13; *Hom.Jer.* 1.10; and Jacobsen, "Origen on the Human Body."

22. See Plato, *Symp.* 219a; *Soph.* 254a; *Rep.* 519b; *Phaed.* 99e.

23. Origen has notably rendered the passage according to his cosmological argument. 1 John 1:1 reads literally, "We declare to you . . . what we have looked at and touched with our hands *concerning* the Word of life" (emphasis added).

24. Thus Origen rejects another option, namely, the Stoic idea that all knowledge is based on sense perception. Even though Origen maintains that the soul's ascent is not achievable through reason alone or through Platonic recollection, "the framework of Origen's conception of how we come to a knowledge of God is Platonic." See Widdicombe, *The Fatherhood of God*, 44–49, comparing *C.Cels.* 7.46 with Plato, *Symp.* 211c.

25. See also *Com.Jn.* 2.188; 10.109; 13.41, 99.

26. See Edwards, *Catholicity and Heresy*, 95. In *Com.Jn.* 28.95 Origen applies the body-spirit dichotomy in a rather harsh way to the Jews.

27. On the subtleties of Origen's view of the body and its transformation to incorporeality, see Bostock, "Quality and Corporeity," 334: "The 'spiritual body' is in fact the end term of a movement from potential to actual being. The flesh of the physical body, in which the germ of the spiritual body resides, acts as the initial term of this movement," citing *Princ.* 3.6.5. On the variety of possible meanings of dualism, see O'Cleirigh, "The Dualism of Origen," 349nn2–3.

28. See also *Princ.* 1.3.1; 2.6.1; *C.Cels.* 6.47–48.

29. Edwards, *Catholicity and Heresy*, 79. For many years Henri Crouzel championed Origen's high regard for the divinity of Christ against the received consensus to the contrary (e.g., Crouzel, *Origen*, 188).

30. *mansit quod erat, deus*. See also *Com.Jn.* 20.155: the Father remains in the Son and the Son in the Father, even when the Son emptied himself during the incarnation.

31. See also *Com.Jn.* 1.111.
32. See also *Com.Jn.* 13.76.
33. The Father and Son are δύο τῇ ὑποστάσει πράγματα, literally "two things with respect to their hypostasis." See also *Princ.* 1.4.3: there are "three powers within God, which are God"; *Com.Jn.* 1.291: the Word has its own proper individuality (ἰδίαν περιγραφήν) and lives in itself (καθ᾽ ἑαυτόν); 2.75; and Gregory of Nazianzus, *Or.* 15.1. Origen makes this theme a major point in his examination of the Arabian bishop Heraclides as well: Jesus Christ, who was God (*theos*) before he became human, was also "God distinct from this God [the Father] in whose form he was" (ἕτερος θεὸς παρὰ τοῦτον τὸν θεὸν οὗ "ἐν μορφῇ ὑπῆρχεν" αὐτός, *Heracl.* 4). See Phil 2:6: although Christ "existed in the form of God [ἐν μορφῇ θεοῦ ὑπάρχων], he did not regard being equal to God [τὸ εἶναι ἴσα θεῷ] as something to be grasped, but emptied himself, taking the form of a slave, was born [γενόμενος] in human likeness." On Origen's criticism of Word-only Christology, see also *Com.Jn.* 1.266. Significant for later debates, in *Com.Jn.* 2.207 Origen writes that the prophets spoke in advance of the Son, not the Word, as the one who would be incarnate. On Origen's contemporary opponents in this regard, see Blanc, SC 120bis, 134n3; and Heine, *Origen*, 95.
34. Crouzel, SC 235.33n6.
35. In the New Testament ὁ θεός refers to the Father at John 1:1, 8:42, 16:28; and 2 Cor 13:13.
36. *substantialiter subsistentem*, i.e., essentially (or substantially) hypostasized. See also *Princ.* 1.2.13; 1.6.2; 1.8.3; *Hom.1Sam.* 1.11; *Hom.Num.* 11.8; *C.Cels.* 6.44.
37. See also *Com.Jn.* 2.76; *Hom.Jer.* 9.4. The term *monogenes* thus also indicates Christ's uniqueness: that he is the only Son by nature and the very Wisdom of God.
38. A statement that some scholars argue Rufinus must have added.
39. Similarly, Origen repeatedly comments that the Son (like the Father and Holy Spirit) is uniquely singular, or "one." See also *Com.Jn.* 1.119–41; 196–97, 200.
40. γίνονται ἐν δύο θεοί. Origen's use of the phrase "second god" should be regarded as an improvisational argument in its immediate context. Edwards, *Catholicity and Heresy*, 81n11; see also *C.Cels.* 5.39; 6.61; 7.57.
41. Jerome's accusation that "in the first volume [of *First Principles*] he said that Christ the Son of God was not begotten but made" (*in primo uolumine Christum filium dei non natum esse sed factum, Ep.* 124.2), and, by implication, that Rufinus has altered Origen's original in passages such as this to make it sound more orthodox, clearly reflects Jerome's own biases and tells us little about Origen's text. Origen happily uses each of the possible terms "beget"

(γεννάω), "create" (κτίζω), and "come to be" (γίγνομαι) to refer to the Son's generation (*C.Cels.* 6.17). Such a sharp distinction between begetting and creating makes sense only within the artificial framework established by Athanasius in the fourth century, to which Jerome was loyal. It does not matter at all for Origen's meaning whether the original read *natus* (from γεννάω) or *factus* (from γίγνομαι or κτίζω)—and it is even possible that the former is more likely, given the terms used in John 1 and Col 1:16. The difference of terms similarly gave Pamphilus no trouble: see *Apol.* 1, 550c.

42. For example, Christ is "the true light that enlightens everyone who comes into the world" (John 1:9), "the brightness of God's glory" (Heb 1:3), and "the brightness of the eternal light" (Wis 7:26). Light is of course one of the most universal images for the divine, appearing not only in the Bible and the Greek philosophers, but in other philosophical-religious systems as well.

43. See also *Princ.* 4.4.1: the Father, Son, and Holy Spirit "transcend all time and all ages and all eternity." As Edwards notes (*Catholicity and Heresy*, 83–84), the eternity of the Son's generation also ensures that it is not contingent. Origen also held that God's activity of creation is eternal as well, and it is often thought that the eternity of creation compromises the uniqueness of the Son's divinity or relation to the Father. On the contrary, the Father-Son relation is clearly prior to and more fundamental than creation in Origen's cosmology, since it is through the Son that God creates and exercises almighty power over the cosmos; see, e.g., *Princ.* 1.2.10; and Widdicombe, *Fatherhood of God*, 75. Moreover, the eternity of creation refers to Wisdom's containing the intelligible "forms and descriptions" of what would be created in time (*Princ.* 1.4.4; see 1.2.2; *Com.Jn.* 1.22), whereas created intellects are changeable, and their power of subsisting is not eternal but is made by the goodness of God (*Princ.* 2.9.2). Daley, *God Visible*.

44. See also *Com.Jn.* 1.204; 2.8–9, 36; *Hom.Jer.* 9.4.

45. See also *Princ.* 4.frag *apud* Athanasius *Decr.* 27.

46. See also *C.Cels.* 5.39; 6.47; *Heracl.* 3–4.

47. That is, it is unthinkable that the Son could be divine but *not* know the Father. Origen's phrasing in this passage has confused many readers: the Son would not be God "if he were not with God, and he would not remain God if he did not continue in unceasing contemplation of the depth of the Father." Origen is not suggesting that the Son *could* possibly cease from contemplating the Father and thereby become something less than God. Rather, he is merely stating an impossible conditional, for in his view the Son is immutable. See the commentary of Blanc, SC 120bis, 224n1.

48. This observation holds despite statements such as the following: "The Savior and the Holy Spirit transcend all created beings, not by comparison, but by

their exceeding pre-eminence. The Father exceeds the Savior by as much as, or even more than, the Savior himself and the Holy Spirit exceed the rest" (*Com.Jn.* 13.151). Here Origen is merely using two senses of greatness at the same time, as several orthodox theologians will also do later. His reason for emphasizing the Father's superiority may well be an attempt to counter Gnostic or Marcionite suggestions that the Son and his newly revealed Father are superior to the God of the Old Testament. By contrast, Origen makes the reverse statement in *Com.Mt.*, written several years later in Caesarea, when he was further removed from Marcionite troubles in Rome and Gnostic challenges in Alexandria: that the Son transcends creatures by much more than the Father transcends the Son (*Com.Mt.* 15.10).

49. Williams, *Arius*, 142.

50. The difference of conceptualization runs both ways: bolder statements such as "nothing in the Trinity can be called greater or less, for there is only one fount of deity" (*Princ.* 1.3.7), for example, may well be additions by Rufinus.

51. The appearance of *homoousios* in Pamphilus's extract may well be authentic; if so, it is a rare, ad hoc formulation on Origen's part to express community of nature between the Father and Son. Moreover, the extract from *Commmentary on Hebrews* may have been cited as evidence against Origen, on account of its modalist or Gnostic connotations, which may explain its presence in Pamphilus's *Apology*. Edwards, *Catholicity and Heresy*, 84–85, against the supposition of Hanson, "Did Origen Apply the Word Homoousios?," that the word is a later interpolation.

52. δύο τῇ ὑποστάσει πράγματα, ἓν δὲ τῇ ὁμονοίᾳ καὶ τῇ συμφωνίᾳ καὶ τῇ ταυτότητι τοῦ βουλήματος.

53. Literally, "how 'the Word was in the beginning,'" *Com.Jn.* 2.1.

54. See also *Com.Jn.* 6.222–24, 298–99; 10.21–22; and *Princ.* 1.2.1: *Nec tamen alius est primogenitus per naturam quam sapientia, sed unus atque idem est*, which Origen signals at the beginning of his discussion of the Son's various titles.

55. It is possible that Origen learned this scheme of different kinds of divine simplicity from Clement: see Radde-Gallwitz, *Basil of Caesarea*, 65. For Clement, the Son is describable because he is a complex unity, whereas the Father is indescribable, being a simple unity (*Strom.* 4.25.156).

56. Crouzel, *Théologie de l'Image*, and Harl, *Origène*. The idea derives chiefly from Col 1:15 (Christ is "the image of the invisible God"), Heb 1:3 (the Son is "the express image of [God's] hypostasis"), with reinforcement from similar motifs such as the Logos terminology of John's gospel and the figure of Wisdom.

57. The Latin text of *Princ.* contains the following explanation of the Adam-Seth comparison: the Son is the sort of an image that "preserves the unity of

nature and substance (*naturae ac substantiae unitatem*) common to a father and son." Even if this statement is an insertion by Rufinus (which it may well be), it expresses Origen's meaning faithfully enough, if it is not overinterpreted to indicate Athanasian consubstantiality. Origen expresses the common divinity and sameness of nature (if not sameness of *ousia*) shared by the Father and the Son in several other passages. On this passage, see Crouzel, *Théologie de l'Image*, 106–7, and Hanson, "Did Origen Apply the Word Homoousios?"

58. For example, *Com.Jn.* 6.294–95; 13.151, 228–29; *C.Cels.* 5.11. Origen's statement that only the Father is goodness-in-itself (*autoagathos*), although the Son is *auto*-everything else (*C.Cels.* 3.41, 6.47; *Com.Jn.* 6.38, 12.347), merely indicates the Father's role as source of the divinity and divine goodness; whereas the Son's goodness derives from the Father. See also *Com.Jn.* 13.152–53: the transcendent Son is nevertheless incomparable to the Father; "for he is an image of the goodness and brightness, not of God, but of God's glory and of his eternal light; and he is a vapor, not of the Father, but of his power; and he is a pure emanation of God's almighty glory, and an unspotted mirror of his activity."

59. For example, the Greek fragment from Jerome *Ep.* 124.2 printed in *Princ.* 1.2.13, which says that the Son is not exactly (ἀπαράλλακτος) as good as the Father because he is merely the image of the Father's goodness. See Crouzel, *Origen*, SC 253.55, on Jerome's and Justinian's distortions.

60. Accepting the authenticity of Rufinus's translation, with Crouzel (SC 253.43n41) and against Koetschau, Jerome, and Theophilus. On the Son as Truth, see also *Com.Jn.* 6.38; *C.Cels.* 3.41; on the Word in the Old Testament, see Widdicombe, *Fatherhood of God*, 105–6.

61. See Col 1:15 and *Princ.* 2.6.3; 4.4.1 (*apud* Athanasius, *Decr.* 27).

62. Note that here Origen uses the comparison of artificial images for the Son, which he said earlier was more appropriate to human beings made in the image of the image (*Princ.* 1.2.6).

63. Jerome slanderously accuses Origen of using this illustration to compare the Father and the Son (with the Son being grossly inferior to the Father); though any reader who has been following Origen's argument can recognize that this is impossible (*contra* the indecision of Crouzel, SC 253.47, and Harl's equivocation in *Origène*, 115). Origen consistently avoids describing God the Father as an image of any sort—indeed, the Father is entirely beyond description—and he has by now solidly established the Son's identity as the eternal, invisible image of God, apart from the incarnation. Whether or not Rufinus has added the explicit reference to Christ's self-emptying in Phil 2 (the first such reference in the chapter) in order to clarify the comparison, it matters little for the overall argument; such an addition would only serve to

refute Jerome. Even if one were to hold that the invisible statue is the Father, Origen nowhere indicates that the Son in himself is only as small as the world; in fact, he goes to great exertions to distinguish the invisible Word that fills and transcends the whole world from the man Jesus, as we shall see.

64. See also *Com.Mt.* 10.6. Trigg aptly comments: "The problem which was for [non-Christian Platonists] the central objection to Christian doctrine was for [Origen] the central issue to be resolved. In resolving it, Origen, as elsewhere, made the fullest use of his philosophical background" (*Origin*, 100); see also Harl, *Origène*, 201. One could argue that, in Pauline terms (see 1 Cor 1:23), Origen perfectly represents the Greek rationalist position for which the incarnation *is* a scandal. This philosophical approach to the incarnation will be reiterated by Kierkegaard's pseudonym Johannes Climacus, for whom the incarnation was also a great paradox, precisely on philosophical terms.

65. See also *Com.Jn.* 19.6–11; 20.268–75; 32.188. On the difficulty of knowing Christ truly, see also Harl, *Origène*, 172–73.

66. At the end of *Princ.* 2.6.2, Origen concludes that his task is to state concisely the content of the faith in "suppositions," rather than attempting to prove anything about it by human reasoning (*humanae rationis*) or aiming to present it in "clear affirmations." See also *C.Cels.* 1.66: it is a private matter for believers only to discuss in detail Christ's composite condition or the elements from which the incarnate Jesus was made (so far as it can be explained, we are to presume).

67. It is unclear whether Origen believed in the temporal preexistence of souls as his later enemies accused him of doing, and it is quite possible that his views on the matter are not at all radical when compared with various catholic authors as late as Augustine. Here he is referring simply to Jesus's love, contemplation, and virtue, which united him to the Word in his own created lifetime. The phrase in question should read "from the beginning of *his* creation," not "from the beginning of the creation." In any event, Origen clearly believes that Jesus's soul was created directly by the hand of God, after which it was joined with his body. For an illuminating discussion of the issues, see Edwards, *Origen against Plato*, 89–94.

68. See also *Com.Jn.* 32.225. Origen's insistence that the Son assumed a human soul as well as a body may indicate that there were some who considered the presence of both the Word and a human soul in Jesus mutually exclusive even in the early third century, just as there were in the fourth. Early affirmations of the full humanity of Christ can also be found in Irenaeus *Haer.* 5.1.1, and Tertullian, *Flesh* 10.1.

69. Origen sometimes speaks of Jesus's soul (*Com.Jn.* 20.162; *C.Cels.* 4.18) and at other times of the Word (*Princ.* 1.2.8; 2.6.1; 3.5.6; 4.2.7) as emptying itself to

become human. In his view it is Christ, however, not the Son who is composite; as we shall see, Origen is concerned to preserve the integrity of the divine nature against any notion of mixture with Christ's humanity.

70. See also *Princ.* 4.4.4. The idea that Jesus's moral purity is a precondition for his union with the Word can also be observed in Origen's *Com.Song*, which is striking given the unitive themes in that biblical book. See Jacobsen, "Christology in the Homilies," 639–42.

71. See also *Heracl.* 5; *C.Cels.* 6.44; *Hom.Num.* 11.8; and Crouzel, *Origen*, 179n27, and SC 253.182n35. Crouzel sees here a virtual statement of hypostatic union, which is surely going too far; on which see below.

72. See also *C.Cels.* 1.66: "I am the way" refers to the divinity; "kill me, a man" to the human body; *Com.Rom.* 1.6.2; and the final chapter of *Princ.*

73. This passage is supplied by a Greek fragment from Theophilus of Alexandria (*Pasch.Ep.* 16, *apud* Theodoret, *Dial.* 2.4), which was also translated by Jerome in *Ep.* 98. See also *C.Cels.* 2.18 on Jesus's foreknowledge "as God." As in other such instances, Origen apparently believes not only that the Word can speak for itself with a human voice, apart from the physical apparatus of the incarnate Jesus (in Old Testament theophanies, e.g.), but also that it did so *through* the mouth of Jesus, yet without these words being also the human speech of Jesus!

74. Just earlier, in *Com.Jn.* 32.354, Origen adds that Christ's suffering on the cross was not "without God" (as Origen's version of Heb 2:9 reads) in the way he goes on to explain.

75. See also *Princ.* 1.2.8: Christ's self-emptying serves to show us the fullness of the divinity (Col 2:9), as the illustration of the large and small statues describes.

76. Origen also speaks several times of Christ's "economy of suffering"; e.g., *Com.Jn.* 32.354; *Com.Mt.* 12.17, 19.

77. ἄλλος δή που ὁ περὶ τούτου καὶ τῆς οὐσίας αὐτοῦ λόγος ἐστὶ παρὰ τὸν περὶ τοῦ νοουμένου κατὰ τὸν Ἰησοῦν ἀνθρώπου.

78. See also *C.Cels.* 2.42: because Jesus was a human being, his suffering causes no difficulty for the faith.

79. See also *Com.Jn.* 4.6: it is impossible for God to have human feelings or to express them. The most that one can say, in terms of the *communicatio idiomatum*, is that it is "as if" the Word died on the cross, because in reality it did not; and *Princ.* 4.4.4, *apud* Theophilus, *Pasch.Ep.* 2.16.

80. For similar assessments, see Lieske, *Theologie der Logos-Mystik*, 140, 154; Kelber, *Logoslehre*, 262; and Rowe, *Origen's Doctrine of Subordination*, 143.

81. Origen is aware of the textual variant in this verse, and he prefers "apart from God" over "by the grace of God." Yet in either case his interpretation is that noted here; see also *Com.Jn.* 1.255–56.

82. Lyman, *Christology and Cosmology*, 79.

83. For "mingle," see also *Princ.* 2.6.3. Van den Hoek, "Origen's Role," argues that Origen applied the language of mixing and mingling (*anakrisis* and similar words) to the incarnation in a way that was new in Alexandrian tradition.

84. On the prior existence of Jesus's soul, see also *C.Cels.* 2.9.73: "that which was formerly a composite being" (τό ποτε σύνθετον) is now divinely one with the Logos; and *Com.Jn.* 20.162.

85. A similar conclusion is drawn by Refoulé, "La christologie d'Evagre et l'origénisme," 262n3–4; see also Lyman, *Christology and Cosmology*, 75. *Pace* Crouzel, who maintains that Origen asserts the equivalent of the later hypostatic union but merely "lacks adequate technical expressions capable of rendering the union of Christ and his soul without excessive confusion," and specifically "a clear conception of personality" (SC 253.176–77nn21–22, 179n27; see also *Théologie de l'Image*, 135). This is patently false; the only "category" Origen would have needed is the Son of God. The questionable evidence of Socrates (*H.E.* 7.32) that Origen may have called Mary "Theotokos" (normally a unitive term) in a passage of *Com.Rom.* book 1 that is no longer present in Rufinus's translation is irrelevant, in the same way that other unitive terms are mitigated by Origen's wider Christological argumentation.

86. The sexual union of Adam and Eve is a "mystery" of knowledge, following the language of Genesis and Paul (Gen 4:1; 1 Cor 6:16–17).

87. See also *Com.Jn.* 1.200: those who are ruled by the divine nature of the Son and by reason (λόγος) contemplate things that are beyond bodily existence (τὰ ἔξω σωμάτων), which Paul calls invisible and unseen (Col 1:16; Rom 1:20; 2 Cor 4:8), and have discovered the rational principle (λόγος) of sensible things, through which they glorify the one who created them—and were themselves also created by the Word (λόγος) apart from every sensible object.

88. Harl's insightful analysis of the stages of Christian development that Origen indicates in these terms (*Origène*, 258–63) nevertheless overlooks the Christological dualism involved.

89. Edwards, *Catholicity and Heresy*, 95–96; see Jacobsen, "Origen on the Human Body," 651, with references for and against the notion that we will lack bodies in the resurrection.

90. As Harl observes, for God to become known through his incarnate Son, "the instrument of revelation is a human being who dwells in the Word of God" (*Origène*, 259).

91. See also *Hom.Lev.* 12.3; *Hom.Jer.* 14.10; and Lyman, *Christology and Cosmology*: Origen's remarks on Jesus's soul "reveal the depth of his fundamental concern for human freedom and progress" (76).

92. Faith alone suffices for salvation, but Origen exhorts people not to remain in simple faith, but to progress to knowledge: *Princ.* 3.5.8; *C.Cels.* 6.13; *Com. Rom.* 3.9; 9.38; *Heracl.* 19; SC 253.184n40. Origen calls the law also "the shadow of Christ" (see Heb 8:5), and also our life on earth (Job 8:9). For more on the Old Testament and the law as shadow, see SC 253.185n43.

93. Daley, *God Visible*; see also Heine, "Epinoiai."

94. On the philosophical character of Origen's opposition to God's suffering in Christ, see Edwards, *Origen against Plato*, 56–57, and Kannengiesser's observation that although Origen was driven by the traditional confession of the faith, he "ended by projecting the incarnational mystery on the screen of a metaphysical imagination characteristic of a genuinely Alexandrian mind-set" ("Christ/ Christology," 25–26). On the exegetical aspect of this position, see Dively-Lauro, "Anthropological Context," 623n48: in Origen's view, the Platonists are right about the goal of existence, but they lack the means to achieve it. For Christians, the means come through the psychic sense of Scripture, which is not merely a call to virtue but to the imitation of Christ, which gives a Christian character to the philosophical quest.

95. Daley, "'One Thing and Another,'" 17–46.

96. Williams, "Origen between Orthodoxy and Heresy."

CHAPTER 2. EUSEBIUS OF CAESAREA

1. For example, Simonetti, *La Crisi Ariana*; Hanson, *Search for the Christian Doctrine of God*; Ayres, *Nicaea and Its Legacy*; Behr, *The Nicene Faith*.

2. See also *Mart.Pal.* 11.1–3; Jerome, *Vir.Ill.* 75.

3. *H.E.* 7.32.25; 8.13.6; *Mart.Pal.* 7.4–6; 11.2–3; 14. On the fate of the library, see Carriker, *The Library of Eusebius*. Eusebius wrote a *Life of Pamphilus*, which is now lost. On Jerome's eventual turn against Origen, and the ensuing Origenist controversy of the fifth century, see Clark, *The Origenist Controversy*.

4. Marcellus later accused Paulinus of Tyre of the same thing (Eusebius, *C.Marcel.*, 1.1.22), as Jerome did his Origenist enemies (*Ep.* 84.9); SC 464.37n1; Sheck, FC 120.40n25.

5. The authenticity of Pamphilus's excerpt is corroborated by Jerome's *Com. Tit.* (PL 26:596–98), which reproduces the same argument.

6. Origen bases his general antiheretical stance as well on Paul's statement in 1 Cor 11:19, "It is necessary that there be heresies, in order that those who are approved might become known among you," and Gal 5:19–21, where heresies are listed among the works of the flesh.

7. For example, Eustathius praises the deceased Methodius in *The Witch of Endor*, which he dedicated to Eutropius. Parvis, *Marcellus of Ancyra*, 57.

8. Edwards, *Origen against Plato*; on Pamphilus's reply to the criticisms of Origen, see Edwards, *Catholicity and Heresy*, 80–87, and Williams, "*Damnosa Haereditas*."

9. For example, the Second Council of Nicaea in 787 erroneously cited Eusebius as an iconoclast: see Murray, "Art and the Early Church," 335–36, and Jensen, *Face to Face*, 23–26; while modern historians such as Burckhardt (*Die Zeit Constantins des Grossen*) and Schwartz (*Kaiser Constantin*) misconstrued church-state relations in the fourth century in even broader terms.

10. The *Theoph.* is difficult to date as well. A safe range is between 325 (after the Council of Nicaea and the completion of the *Proof*) and 335 (the date of the Holy Sepulcher oration). Barnes, *Constantine and Eusebius*, 187 and n177.

11. Parvis, *Marcellus of Ancyra*, 38–39 and passim.

12. For the connections between Eusebius's Christology and later orthodox tradition, see Beeley, "Eusebius Contra Marcellum."

13. Even if the final edition comes from c. 325–326 (Barnes, *Constantine and Eusebius*), most of the text through *H.E.* 10.7 predates it.

14. Barnes, *Constantine and Eusebius*, 128.

15. Ibid., 141–43.

16. On Eusebius's sources, see Grant, *Eusebius as Church Historian*, 41–43, and Carriker, *The Library of Eusebius*.

17. Barnes, *Constantine and Eusebius*, 126, with Sirinelli and Harl. Studies that concentrate on *Prep.* and *Proof* include Wallace-Hadrill, *Eusebius of Caesarea*; Lyman, *Christology and Cosmology*, 106–23; and Strutwolf, *Trinitätstheologie*.

18. Porphyry's attack followed an earlier work, *On Philosophy from Oracles*, in which he had proposed an integration of Christianity into the fabric of Greco-Roman culture. For some reason, he dropped the irenic approach and turned to violence instead. See Barnes, *Constantine and Eusebius*, 21–22, 174–78, with further bibliography.

19. John Henry Newman, e.g., faults Eusebius—whom he initially recognizes for being essentially orthodox—with "corrupting the simplicity of the Gospel with an Eclectic spirit" (*The Arians*, 270).

20. Although these books were probably also edited during later revisions, they do not show the degree of wholesale rewriting that likely occurred with book 1.

21. As a result of Pliny's intervention, Trajan decreed that Christians were not to be pursued actively, which relaxed the threat of persecution (*H.E.* 3.33.2).

22. The text quoted speaks only of Theodotus the Cobbler. *H.E.* 7.30.16–17 implies that Artemon was still alive when Paul of Samosata was condemned in 268, which seems later than the early-third-century dating suggested in book 5 and the *Little Labyrinth*. Theodoret ascribed the work to Origen; Eusebius plainly thinks otherwise. Its authorship has not been conclusively identified.

23. See also *H.E.* 3.28 against the Ebionites, and 4.15 on Christ's eternal high priesthood.

24. See also *H.E.* 2.3.2; 2.24.1.

25. There is some question about how old the preface is, whether it belongs to the first edition or was inserted during a later revision. In any event, it is clearly abridged from a larger body of knowledge or a longer work (1.2.16; 14.1; 2.pref.1); Eusebius makes reference to his earlier *Prophetic Extracts* and possibly to the *Proof of the Gospel* (*H.E.* 1.2.27).

26. Eusebius's key methodological term "theology" is regularly omitted in English translations, which render it simply as "divinity."

27. *Pace* Bardy (SC 358.5n7), who cites Gregory of Nazianzus, *Or.* 38.8, in the same connection.

28. See also *Proof* 2.3.86: the economy is "mystical" and the teachings concerning it are "very secret."

29. In book 5 Eusebius writes that book 4 covered the two ways of viewing Jesus Christ, the first above nature (theology) and the second closer to us, the incarnation (economy). Accordingly, his argument will now proceed in that order, to show from the prophets the "theology" about him in the gospels (*Proof* 5.1.pref). See also *Proof* 1.pref.3–4; 3.pref; 4.1.144, 17.200.

30. διττοῦ δὲ ὄντος τοῦ κατ' αὐτὸν τρόπου. See also *Proof* 4.1: the account of our Lord is of two kinds; *Proof* 5.pref; and *Proof* 6.15: Christ was "'known between two lives' [Hab 3:2, LXX], one life according to God [κατὰ θεόν] and the other according to human existence [κατὰ ἄνθτωπον], the one mortal, the other eternal; the Lord experienced both."

31. τὸν ἡμῖν ἄνθρωπον ὁμοιοπαθῆ. Eusebius's phrase that Christ is "conceived as God" (θεὸς ἐπινοεῖται) echoes Origen's term for a theological title of Christ (ἐπίνοια), the sense of which is similar to "theology" above. See also *H.E.* 1.2.6: Abraham and the other righteous of old imagined Christ by the pure eyes of διάνοια.

32. "The history concerning him" (ἡ κατ' αὐτὸν ἱστορία) echoes the earlier phrase "his manner of existence" (τοῦ κατ' αὐτὸν τρόπου), indicating that the story of the incarnation and the church parallels the nature of Christ's own being.

33. ἄνθρωπος ὁμοῦ καὶ θεός. See also *H.E.* 1.2.23; 1.3.7: "the divine [θεῖος] Word who rules all things."

34. Weber, *APXH*, likewise holds that Eusebius's argument for Christ's divinity conforms more closely with pre-Nicene orthodoxy than the positions of Marcellus and Athanasius, who are by contrast the real innovators.

35. Here Eusebius contrasts the Son as "begotten" (γεννητός) versus all other creatures, which are "originate beings" (γενήτα), in an interesting anticipation of Athanasius's later distinction.

36. Although the verse reads ὁ θεὸς τοῦ πατρός, Eusebius does not take it to signify God the Father, probably because here, ὁ θεός is a demonstrative

adjectival construction, as opposed to the name standing alone as a unique title; see also *Proof* 1.5.10. Most other Old Testament texts in which Christ is called ὁ θεὸς, such as Ps 65:6–7 (*H.E.* 1.3.14), are vocative constructions, not nominative titles, in keeping with the normal usage in the Septuagint and the New Testament, including Thomas's confession of faith in John 20:28 (inarticular vocatives being rare). Connybeare and Stock, *Grammar of Septuagint Greek*, §50.

37. Strong statements include Opitz, "Euseb von Caesarea als Theologe," 1–19; Ricken, "Nikaia," 340; and Wallace-Hadrill, *Eusebius of Caesarea*, 120. Cf., however, the trenchant critique of this view by Lyman, *Christology and Cosmology*, 107–17, which points out that such estimations have strangely ignored the origins of Eusebius's view in Scripture, as well as his apologetic genre and motives in the works under consideration.

38. μιᾶς ἐπ' ἀμφοῖν κατὰ τὸ παράδειγμα τῆς θεότητος ἐπινοουμένης.

39. Although he refers to it, Eusebius does not appear to have studied closely the *Refutatio omnium haeresium* ascribed to Hippolytus, which describes the doctrinal error of Sabellius. Barnes, *Constantine and Eusebius*, 135.

40. The Word's saving self-manifestation in fact begins in the theophanies of the Old Testament, even though it was not a full initiation into divine knowledge (*H.E.* 1.2.6–13, 21–22; *Theoph.* 2.85).

41. For a similar judgment, see Barnes, *Constantine and Eusebius*, 182.

42. As the case against Marcellus, see Vinzent, *Markell von Ankyra*, xix, pointing to Eusebius, *C.Marcel.* 2.4.29; and Parvis, *Marcellus of Ancyra*, 129; as a self-justification, Barnes, *Constantine and Eusebius*, 264.

43. Eusebius directly follows Origen, e.g., in his interpretation of most of the texts cited in the *H.E.* preface.

44. Marcellus is led astray from "the reading that is close to hand" (τῆς προχείρου λέξεως) and is "ignorant of the mere *historia*."

45. J. P. Lightfoot concurs, allowing that Eusebius's words of rebuke are "justly severe" ("Eusebius of Caesarea," 341).

46. Directly in *E.Th.* 1.19–20 and book 3; indirectly throughout book 2.

47. Eusebius always quotes the verse in this truncated form, omitting the phrases "for whom we exist" and "through whom we exist." His reading is not listed among the textual variants in the Nestle-Aland New Testament.

48. Eusebius refers to 1 Cor 8:6 in *Theoph.* 1.21; *L.C.* 12.1; *C.Marcel.* 2.2; and *E.Th.* 2.2, 14, 18 as well. In Origen's *Com.Rom.* 8.12, 1 Cor 8:6 helps to establish "the mystery of the Trinity"; elsewhere Origen appeals to the verse to argue against the doctrine of two sons (*Com.Rom.* 7.11); see also *C.Cels.* 8.4.

49. See, e.g., Eusebius's exegesis of Gal 1:1 and 4:4 against Marcellus (*E.Th.* 1.1), and of Colossians 1:15, 18 (*E.Th.* 2.2).

50. Eusebius's immanent exegesis of Prov 8 follows Origen's directly: see *Princ.* 1.2.1; 1.4.4; 4.4.1. Here Eusebius expands the interpretation he gave initially at *H.E.* 1.2.14–15.

51. Following an earlier treatment in *C.Marcel.* 2.3; see also *E.Th.* 1.10, 20.xxii.

52. See Rom 16:25; Eph 3:3–4, 9; Col 1:26–27, 2:2.

53. See also *H.E.* 1.3.3, 13; 1.4.3; 3.24.3, 13; 3.37.3; 6.2.11; 6.29.4; 10.1.3, 3.3, 4.66.

54. From *Ec.Proph.* (26.51; 51.26; 68.20; 127.23) through many instances in the apologetic works, to the late anti-Marcellan works (*C.Marcel.* 1.2; 2.1; *H.E.* 1.20; 2.20), with the highest concentration in the *Com.Ps.*

55. On which, see Beeley, *Gregory of Nazianzus*, chap. 3.

56. Athanasius mentions the Spirit only three times, e.g., in the dual work *C.Gent.–Inc.*, twice to report that the Spirit says something in Scripture (*C.Gent.* 7.29; 14.11) and the third time in the closing doxology (*Inc.* 57).

57. Important similar expressions occur in Luke 1:70; John 9.32; 1 Cor 2:7; 2 Cor 9:9, among many examples.

58. A similar conclusion is reached in Ramelli and Konstan, *Terms for Eternity*, 142–57.

59. Lightfoot aptly notes, "This priority is not necessarily intended to be temporal, and in such a case the meaning of the writer must be interpreted by his language in other passages" ("Eusebius of Caesarea," 347). Other helpful attempts to revolve the problem include Berkhof, *Theologie des Eusebius*, 71–75, and Lienhard, *Contra Marcellum*, 116–17.

60. Parvis, *Marcellus of Ancyra*, 59–60.

61. Eger, "Kaiser und Kirche"; cited in Daley, *Hope of the Early Church*, 78n8.

62. See *H.E.* 2.25.1 (Nero is declared an "enemy of the worship of God"); 3.28.4–5 (Dionysius of Alexandria critiquing the chiliastic view of Cerinthus); 3.39.12–13 (Eusebius criticizes Papias for his chiliastic views); 5.pref.3–4 (Christians fight peaceful wars, rather than violent wars for country and possessions); 7.24.6 (again against chiliasm).

63. See also the letter by King Abgar to Jesus—and Jesus's reply!—reproduced at *H.E.* 1.13.6–10.

64. The full scope of Eusebius's treatment of persecution makes it unlikely that the original core of the work, books 2–7, was written before 303, during times of relative peace and success.

65. Cf. 17.3, where the persecutors are simply evil, and the people bear no responsibility. This statement is not surprising, however, considering that Constantine, the great deliverer, was present in the congregation at the Holy Sepulcher.

66. On the ambiguity of the phrase, see Drake, *In Praise of Constantine*, 173n5; on the confiscation of temple treasures, Barnes, *Constantine and Eusebius*, 248.

67. *Pace* the extreme view of Van Dam that Eusebius's desire to curry Constantine's favor fueled his subordinationist theology (*Roman Revolution of Constantine*, 284) and that Eusebius "essentially equat[ed] Constantine with Jesus Christ" (ibid., 318; see also 291, 312).

68. Barnes, *Constantine and Eusebius*, 249; Lyman, *Christology and Cosmology*, 83.

69. On Libanius, Praxagoras, and Julian, see Barnes, *Constantine and Eusebius*, 272–73.

CHAPTER 3. NICAEA (325) AND ATHANASIUS OF ALEXANDRIA

1. Davis, *Early Coptic Papacy*, 27, 133, on Alexandrian bishops deriving from the catechetical school; Vivian, *Saint Peter of Alexandria*, 88–89n3, 113–16, on Theognostus, Pierius, and Peter. Although Photius's censure supports the Origenist character of Theonas and Pierius, his detailed descriptions should not be trusted. Peter's moderate Origenism has been suspected since at least the work of Harnack.

2. Wiles, *Archetypal Heresy*. On the constructed nature of the Arian "heresy" and the current state of scholarship on the Arian crisis, see Lyman, "Topography of Heresy," and "Arius and Arians," with further bibliography.

3. Philostorgius writes that Arius was a candidate for bishop alongside Alexander (*H.E.* 1.3). Although Philostorgius is generally biased toward Arius, the anti-Arian Theodoret gives a corroborating report that Arius and Alexander were already rivals at the time of Alexander's election. See Parvis, *Marcellus of Ancyra*, 73.

4. Haas has suggested that he may have been a known ascetic as well (*Alexandria in Late Antiquity*, 272); cf. Lyman, "Arius and Arians."

5. See esp. Williams, *Arius*, 48–66; and Löhr, "Arius Reconsidered (Part 1)," 533–60. Löhr aptly comments, "it may be forever impossible to work out exactly what happened in the first period of the Arian controversy before the council of Nicaea" (543).

6. Arius and his associates found exile in Palestine, where a church council led by Paulinus of Tyre, Eusebius of Caesarea, and Patrophilus of Scythopolis had granted them the right to gather as a church (Urk. 10).

7. Most of the remaining fragments of the *Thalia* come from two treatises by Athanasius (*C.Ar.* 1.5; *Syn.* 15); the latter is generally considered more secure. The Palestinian location also comes from Athanasius (*Syn.* 15).

8. Löhr, 121–22. Thomas Böhm notes the biblical origin of the predicates that Arius applies to God in this opening statement (*Christologie des Arius*, 123–24).

9. The fact that the language of priority refers to causality and not temporal sequence is clear from Urk. 1.5: before (πρίν) the Son was begotten, created, ordained, founded, he was not; *for he was not unbegotten*. This is probably also the sense of Arius's statement that the Son "did not exist prior to his begetting" by the Father (Urk. 6.4): that the Son has no existence apart from being timelessly begotten by the Father, on whom he depends entirely for his existence. Löhr comments, "According to Arius the Father is prior to the Son, but not in any temporal manner" ("Arius Reconsidered [Part 2]," 131).

10. Hence Arius appears to have taken Alexander's notion that the Son exists "in relation to" the Father in the same sense, as a parallel or peerlike relation as opposed to a relation of causality. Philosophical discussions of relation (τὰ πρός τι) include Aristotle, *Cat.* 7b15, and, closer to Arius, Sextus Empiricus *Pyrr.* 3.26–32, which discusses the question of whether a cause is prior to, contemporary with, or after its effect. Supporting evidence for Arius's report that Alexander claimed "the Son exists unbegottenly [ἀγεννήτως] with God" (Urk. 1.2) can be found in Alexander, *Phil.* 12. Here Alexander may simply be making the same sort of qualification that we saw in Origen, that the Son's begetting is unlike the begetting of animals, which involves material division.

11. See Löhr, "Arius Reconsidered (Part 2)," 132.

12. πρὸ χρόνων καὶ πρὸ αἰωνίων, ἀχρόνως.

13. Stead, "The Word 'from nothing,'" 675, speculates that it may in fact be Marcellus himself.

14. See also *Thal.Frag.* 1, 16 (the Son as Wisdom), 17/18 (the Son's *epinoiai*).

15. For Origen the Son is *auto*-everything that the Father is except *auto-agathos*. By contrast, Athanasius applies to the Word all *auto*-statements that apply to the Father (e.g., *C.Gent.* 46).

16. Stead goes so far as to argue that Arius's attribution of *ex ouk onton* to the Son merely excludes Aristotle's material cause, but not the efficient, formal, or final causes of the Son's generation ("The Word 'from nothing,'" 682). Williams suggests that Arius is not claiming the phrase as his own, but merely admits that, in a certain sense, it is a necessary corollary of his position (*Arius*, 309n17).

17. The fact that Arius nevertheless calls the Son "only-begotten God" (*Frag.* 14/15; see also 21: mighty God) does not in itself mitigate against the subordinationism outlined here, since John's gospel makes both terms ("only-begotten" and "God") necessary descriptors of the preincarnate Son, whatever one takes them to mean.

18. In his landmark study, Williams observes that Arius is not directly dependent on Origen but takes the Alexandrian tradition in a more archaic direction

(*Arius*, 147), while briefly suggesting that Arius resembles the apophatic tradition of Philo, Clement, and heterodox Gnosticism (131). Both points build on the earlier claim of Lorenz that Arius echoes Judeo-Hellenistic Wisdom speculation through a teacher like Clement (*Arius Iudaizans*, 122). My argument for the apophatic basis of Arius's theology is corroborated more recently by Löhr, "Arius Reconsidered (Part 2)," 146–47.

19. Argued by Stead and concurred with by Parvis, *Marcellus of Ancyra*.

20. For the dating, sequence, and possible distribution strategy of Alexander's letters, see Parvis, *Marcellus of Ancyra*, 69–72; in support of the Athanasian authorship of *Henos somatos*, ibid., following Stead, "The Word 'from nothing,'" and Barnes, *Constantine and Eusebius*, 16.

21. Pamphilus upholds generation by will as indicating common nature and the Son's source in the Father (*Apol.* 102–6).

22. While there is some similarity between especially the first point and Origen's understanding of Christ's human soul, there is no evidence that Arius held these views about the preincarnate Son, *pace* Lorenz.

23. For the hypothesis that Constantine moved a council planned for Ancyra, see Parvis, *Marcellus of Ancyra*; on Licinius's ban, Eusebius, *V.Const.*, 1.51.1; on Constantine's expectations, Socrates, *H.E.* 8.

24. Edwards, "First Council of Nicaea," 552; and *Catholicity and Heresy*, chap. 5.

25. Canon 6 upholds the sole authority of a metropolitan bishop in his province, and Socrates further reports the settlement with the Meletians (*H.E.* 1.9). For the further enactments of the council, see Edwards, "First Council of Nicaea," 559–60.

26. On the rationale for considering Eusebius as the source, together with rival theories, see Vinzent, "Die Entstehung," 195–96; and Parvis, *Marcellus of Ancyra*, 85–86.

27. Translated from the Greek text in Dossetti, *Il simbolo di Nicea*, 226f.

28. Arius's statement that "before [the Son] was begotten he was not" in his letter to Alexander merely denies that the Son began as a latent quality or being within the Father before he was generated as a distinct hypostasis. The statement that the Son was "begotten, not made" echoes phrasing in Athanasius's *Henos somatos*, which was reproduced in the Antiochene confession of 324. Notably, the term "created" or "creature" is not prohibited in the creed, and several ancient witnesses to the council, such as Hilary of Poitiers (*Adv. Valent. Ursac.* 1.9), Basil of Caesarea (*Ep.* 125), and Cyril of Alexandria (*3Ep.Nest.*), lack an anathema against the term. "Created" does appear in Athanasius's *Ep.Jov.* 3 and in the quotation of Eusebius of Caesarea's letter in the appendix of Athanasius's *Syn.* as well as Socrates's transcript of the same (*H.E.* 1.8), which shows knowledge of Athanasius's work. Edwards, "First Council of

Nicaea," 564n49. Given that Athanasius is a conspicuously rare witness to the term, it is probable that he himself inserted it. Following Origen, Eusebius of Caesarea argued that its meaning in the Bible is equivocal.

29. A use that Eusebius defends in his *Letter to Euphration of Balanea* (Urk. 3).

30. See Parvis, *Marcellus of Ancyra*, 87.

31. Athanasius later reported that the *homoousion* was the only remaining means that Alexander had to force the question. Philostorgius, who is even less trustworthy than Athanasius, reports that Ossius and Alexander introduced it (*H.E.* 1.7).

32. A tendency that would be reinforced only by the removal of the phrases "only-begotten Son," "first-born of all creation," and "before the ages" and the omission of the explanation about the distinct substance of the three persons, contained in Eusebius's creed, if it was in fact the template used. The alteration of "Word" to "Son" and the omission of "one" from the article on the Spirit are unremarkable.

33. On the tumultuous politicking of Athanasius's career, Barnes, *Athanasius and Constantius*, remains indispensable.

34. On Athanasius's efforts to control the monastic communities, see Brakke, *Athanasius and the Politics of Asceticism*; on his lack of great theological acumen, Lyman, *Christology and Cosmology*, 128.

35. The original title of the first work may have been either *Against Idols* (κατὰ εἰδώλων) or *Against the Pagans* (κατὰ Ἑλλήνων); both are found in early witnesses. The full title of the second work is *On the Incarnation of the Word and His Manifestation to Us through the Body*. Athanasius, *C.Gent.* and *Inc.*, ed. Thomson, xx–xxi. For the debates surrounding the dating of the work, see Anatolios, *Athanasius*, 26–30, who argues compellingly for the range 328–335. It is possible that Athanasius wrote the work as early as 325, when he was still a young deacon, depending on how much theological authority one thinks Alexander granted him. Before 335 Athanasius would have had access to the Alexandrian church library, where he might have found Eusebius's apologetic works, which provide important source material. More puzzling is the absence of any reference to Eusebius's *H.E.*

36. At the outset Athanasius calls the dual work an exposition of but "a little of the faith concerning Christ" (*C.Gent.* 1), and near the end he writes that he has given "the rudiments and paradigm of the faith concerning Christ and his divine epiphany to us," adding that the Scriptures will show these points more completely (*Inc.* 56). The incarnation is the paradigm of the faith in the sense of being its central and most important part. For the view that it is a catechetical work, cf. Kannengiesser, SC 199.55; Pettersen, "Reconsideration," 1037; and Anatolios, *Athanasius*, 29–30.

37. See Athanasius, *C.Gent.* and *Inc.*, ed. Thomson, xiii–xiv; and Heil, "Athanasius als Apologet des Christentums," 159–87, who highlights the unique character of the work as such within Athanasius's corpus. The work is addressed to an anonymous Christian ("friend," *Makarie, Philochriste*), and its apologetic argument is meant to give him confidence that he has placed his trust in the truth rather than a lie by knowing Christ—that knowledge of and faith in Christ is the *most* honorable thing of all.

38. Barnes, *Athanasius and Constantius.*

39. On the pervasive influence of Eusebius's *Theophany*, see Athanasius, *C.Gent.* and *Inc.*, ed. Thomson, xxii, and Strutwolf, *Trinitätstheologie.*

40. See Anatolios, *Athanasius*, 28.

41. Against the slander of the Jews and the mockery of Greeks, Athanasius's exposition of the humanization of the Word aims to make the apparent degradation of the cross arouse even greater piety (*Inc.* 1).

42. Athanasius's Logos Christology frames the work (*C.Gent.* 1; *Inc.* 57) and runs consistently throughout it. By contrast, each time he takes up the idea of divine sonship, either the Word is the operative category being employed or else the passage resolves into the idea of the Word: see *C.Gent.* 46; *Inc.* 9–10, 14–16, 19, 32, 48. Exceptions such as the closing doxology in *Inc.* 57 show the traditional pressure of Son language, and they only prove the rule that the Logos idea dominates the work.

43. See *Inc.* 11.

44. See also *Inc.* 19, 55.

45. For example, *C.Gent.* 33, 40, 47; see also *Inc.* 13, 47.

46. Thus Athanasius also follows Origen in resisting the paradoxical affirmations found in second-century Christian literature, such as the invisible is seen, the impassible suffers, the immortal dies; Young, "Monotheism and Christology."

47. See Athanasius, *C.Gent.* and *Inc.*, ed. Thomson, 175n5, and Grillmeier, *Das Konzil*, 193 and 210.

48. See *Inc.* 19.

49. See *Inc.* 9.

50. See *Inc.* 5.

51. Athanasius's cosmological dualism is most evident in *C.Gent.* esp. 2–3, 9, 32.

52. See *C.Gent.* 7, 35.

53. See Barnes, *Athanasius and Constantius*, 11, 40, 64; Athanasius, *C.Gent.* and *Inc.*, ed. Thomson, xxiii–xxiv and passim.

54. On which see Lyman, *Christology and Cosmology.*

55. Parvis, *Marcellus of Ancyra*, 50. For exegetical evidence of Athanasius's borrowing from Marcellus, see Parvis, "The Exegetical Relationship."

56. The full list includes Marcion, Valentinus, Basilides, Mani, Simon Magus, the Phrygians (Montanists), Novatus, and Meletius. *C.Ar.* 1.3; 56. Athanasius opposes the psilanthropism and adoptionism of Paul of Samosata in 1.38 and 2.13. He opposes Sabellius only rarely, and possibly only in a passage added at a later date (3.36: Christ is not the Father but Word and Son of the Father, plus an immanent reading of Jesus's receiving things from the Father; but see also 2.38: the Word truly subsists and not just in name, which may simply be stock Origenism).

57. See also *C.Ar.* 2.70: the Arians are particularly bad because they deny Christ's divinity, whereas the Gnostics merely deny his humanity (and the divinity of the Father); the same point is made more vaguely in the *Henos somatos* (Urk. 4b.16). Athanasius's attempt to locate the Arians in connection with earlier heretics is mixed. On the one hand, he argues, their claim that Christ is a creature made from nothing, yet who can make other creatures, reflects the demiurge of Valentinus, Marcion, Basilides, and possibly the Manichees (*C.Ar.* 2.21, 39).

58. Madmen, "Ariomaniacs," *C.Ar.* 1.4 and passim; spawn of the devil, 1.8, 10; 3.1; comparable to Jews, 1.2, 4, 8; 3.16, 27; similar to women, 1.4, 22, 23, 28; 2.69; deserving of hatred, 1.7.

59. Image and form of the divinity, *C.Ar.* 1.20; character, 1.22; form and appearance (ἡ μορφὴ καὶ τὸ εἶδος), 3.5; exact image (ἀπαράλλακτος εἰκών), 1.26 (and also proper to the Father's essence); 2.33; 3.11; see also 3.5, 36: exact likeness. Eusebius likewise argues that the Son is the "exact image" of the Father, that he is "most like" (*homoiotatos*) the Father, and that the Father is the Son's "own" or "proper" (*idios*) Father (*E.Th.* 1.4).

60. These Origenist terms appear throughout *C.Ar.*; see, e.g., 1.5 (image, Word, Wisdom); 9 (Wisdom, Word, Power); 16 (Wisdom, brightness, image); 19 (offspring [*gennema*], Wisdom, Word); 2.62 (only-begotten Son, Word, Wisdom).

61. See Lyman, *Christology and Cosmology*, 132: "[Athanasius's] ontological presumptions were translated directly into statements of faith."

62. See *C.Ar.* 1.19.

63. See also *C.Ar.* 3.5.

64. The rarity of any reference to Nicaea in *C.Ar.* has long been noted. It indicates that Athanasius has obviously not yet centered his attention on the council as the universal standard of the faith.

65. On Athanasius's analysis of the language of fatherhood and sonship, see esp. Widdicombe, *Fatherhood of God*, part III.

66. Though he makes some concession for the traditional language in 3.58, as long as it doesn't come from the heretics—perhaps trying to make room for Origen.

67. Athanasius produces seven biblical citations: Matt 3:17; Ps 44/45.2; John 1:1; Ps 35/36:10; Heb 1:3; Phil 2:6; Col 1:15. Only four of these contain a verb for being (*einai* or *huparchein*), and none of them contains any substantive for being or existence whatsoever. His desperation is plain.

68. Athanasius's treatment of Prov 8 occupies roughly one-third of the entire set of *C.Ar.* (2.12–82), which is six times the length of any other section devoted to a particular biblical passage.

69. Note also the automatic or general quality of salvation: *C.Ar.* 1.50. An important corollary of Athanasius's vision of Christ—that he appears to us as a human being but shows himself to be God from his works (see *C.Ar.* 2.8)—is that he makes no distinction between the faulty vision of Christ's flesh before his crucifixion and the correct vision of it after the resurrection, which is a vision of the Son of God *in his risen flesh*.

70. See also *Decr.* 6, *C.Ar.* 1.5; *Ep.Epict.* 12. Additional new language includes "one Divinity in the Triad" (*C.Ar.* 1.2, 16; 3.6).

71. The work also confirms Athanasius's Logos-flesh model: Christ is "the Word of God in a human body" (*Dion.* 8). And it contains the interesting phrase that the Monad expands invisibly into a Triad and the Triad gathers together into a Monad (*Dion.* 17).

72. Further discussion of these groups can be found in the next chapter.

73. Richard, "Saint Athanase," likewise argues that Jesus lacked a human mind or soul in Athanasius's Christology; see also Kelly, *Early Christian Doctrines*, 288–89.

74. *Pace* Martin's view that the groups here are extreme Apollinarians. Many in the mid-fourth century thought that Christ had no human soul.

75. ἄνθρωπον αὐτὸν λέγων, ὡς ἄλλον ὄντα παρὰ τὸν Θεὸν Λόγον.

76. See also *Ep.Adelph.* 3: the leper "worshipped the God who was in the body"; 6–7: "we worship the Creator clothed with a created body," as when Israel worshipped the Lord in the temple.

77. Jasper and Cumming, *Prayers of the Eucharist*, 52.

78. Some of these elements can be seen in the Egyptian Anaphora of St. Basil as well, which is a West Syrian prayer that shows Egyptian influence. The Boharic and Coptic translations that have come down to us may represent a late-third-century version (Jasper and Cumming, *Prayers of the Eucharist*, 67–68). Origenist-type elements here include a Son Christology, the temporal language "before the ages" (rather than Athanasian pure eternity), an antimonarchian pluralism in prayer structure, and the emphasis on the Father, Son, and Spirit as each being "one." There is no Logos doctrine.

79. One mention of a reasonable (*logike*) sacrifice in the Strasbourg papyrus (Jasper and Cumming, *Prayers of the Eucharist*, 53) is a reference to Rom 12:1

and a statement that the eucharistic sacrifice is bloodless—not a Christological statement.

80. Johnson, *Prayers of Sarapion*, 233–53.

81. Jasper and Cumming, *Prayers of the Eucharist*, 79.

82. What Lyman calls "the essential instability of the human body" in Athanasius's view (*Christology and Cosmology*, 143).

83. Brakke notes the crucially ascetic character of Athanasius's Christology, "which places the proper control of the body and its passions at the centre of the human plight" ("Athanasius," 1122).

84. An interesting piece of evidence for the Nicene-Athanasian confusion is Rufinus's translation of Origen, which sometimes changes things for the worse in an attempt to improve them: e.g., *Princ.* 1.2.6, reversing image and truth (p. 20n1).

CHAPTER 4. GREGORY OF NAZIANZUS, GREGORY OF NYSSA,
AND CONSTANTINOPLE (381)

1. Mansi, *Sacrorum Conciliorum*, 2.1308c; Hahn, *Bibliotek der Symbole*, §153.

2. Hahn, *Bibliotek der Symbole*, §154.

3. See Beeley, *Gregory of Nazianzus*, 277–84, on the lack of Athanasian influence on Gregory Nazianzen, and 309–16 on the Eusebian tradition that fostered Cappadocian theology.

4. Hahn, *Bibliotek der Symbole*, §160, anathemas 6–7.

5. Ibid., §163.

6. On heterousian doctrine, see further Beeley, *Gregory of Nazianzus*, 21–24, 91–93; Behr, *The Nicene Faith*, 267–82; Ayres, *Nicaea and Its Legacy*, 144–49, and Vaggione, *Eunomius of Cyzicus*, chap. 5.

7. On which, see esp. Ayres, *Nicaea and Its Legacy*.

8. For a more detailed account of the debate, see Beeley, "Early Christological Controversy."

9. See also Damasus, *Il. sane* 83.

10. See also *Conf.Faith* 11, 28, 30; *Frag.* 22, 28, 41, 72, 129, all of which speak in terms of the Word plus human flesh. Apollinarius also denotes a three-part anthropology in *Frag.* 22, 25, 89, 91.

11. See *Conf.Faith; Union* 7–10, with exegetical examples.

12. See *Union* 5; *Frag.* 123, 129.

13. For an account of the passages in question and the accusations by Gregory Nazianzen and Gregory of Nyssa, see Beeley, "Early Christological Controversy."

14. See, e.g., *Union* 1, 13.

15. Julian's disparaging *Ep.* 55 makes reference to Athens. Basil, *Ep.* 135.1, describes the florid style of one of Diodore's texts. Jerome, *Vir.Ill.* 91,

reports that Diodore studied biblical interpretation under Eusebius of Emessa (bishop 341 to before 359). It is also possible that Diodore publicly opposed the diaconal ordination of the heterousian theologian Aetius in 346, although the source of this account is Theodoret (*H.E.* 2.24.6–8), who is too favorable to the Antiochene tradition of Diodore to be trusted entirely without corroborating accounts.

16. Basil, *Ep.* 99.3.

17. For evidence that such an agreement existed between Meletius and Paulinus, see Beeley, *Gregory of Nazianzus*, 47 and n153.

18. See Field, *On the Communion*, 183.

19. Unfortunately, Diodore's *Com.Ps.* 1–51 is relatively unilluminating for our purposes.

20. BD 27, 30; see also SD 9. Diodore also speaks of Jesus as being "worthy" of the Word: SD 1; BD 15.

21. BD 6; SD 11. For further exegetical examples, see Beeley, "Early Christological Controversy," 14–15.

22. See Greer, "The Antiochene Christology," 335.

23. See Beeley, *Gregory of Nazianzus*, for Gregory's overall theological achievement, and "Cyril of Alexandria," for his influence on Cyril.

24. For further details, see Beeley, "Early Christological Controversy," 20–23.

25. Although they are often considered anti-Apollinarian works, Gregory's late epistles are in fact oriented primarily against the Antiochene Christology of Diodore; see Beeley, "Early Christological Controversy." For a more detailed analysis of each of these four texts, see Beeley, *Gregory of Nazianzus*, chap. 3 and esp. 122–37.

26. θέωσις, from θεοῦν. Earlier writers such as Origen and Athanasius had spoken in different terms of "making divine" (θεοποιεῖν, θεοποίησις) and "divinizing" (θεοῦν).

27. See also *Or.* 2.23–24.

28. See also *Or.* 1.5; 29.19; 38.13.

29. Literally, "becoming a human being who is God on earth" (γενόμενος ἄνθρωπος ὁ κάτω θεός).

30. "Not that he became two things, but he deigned to be made one thing out of the two [οὐ δύο γενόμενος, ἀλλ᾿ ἓν ἐκ τῶν δύο γενέσθαι ἀνασχόμενος]. . . . But not two sons: let us not give a false account of the blending [ἡ σύγκρασις]." See also *Or.* 29.19: "he was born as a single entity [εἷς]"; *Or.* 38.13: Christ is "one thing made out of two opposites [ἕν ἐκ δύο τῶν ἐναντίων], flesh and Spirit, of which the latter deifies and the former is deified"; *Ep.* 102.4: "We consider the Son of God, who was begotten of the Father and later [born] of the Virgin Mary, as a single entity [εἰς ἓν ἄγομεν],

and we do not name two sons. Rather, we worship one and the same [Son] in undivided Divinity and honor."

31. For example, *Or.* 38.13.

32. See, e.g., Eusebius, *Proof* 6.24 2; Apollinarius, *Frag.* 42, 109. Irenaeus also uses the phrase Christologically (*Haer.* 3.16.2), although it is not clear that he is a direct source for Eusebius and Apollinarius, as it is a fairly common Greek expression. Neither Basil nor Gregory of Nyssa use the phrase Christologically. See Beeley, "Early Christological Controversy," 393–94nn53–57 for further references and discussion.

33. The single-nature model frames the major exegetical section of the third and fourth *Theological Orations* (see esp. *Or.* 29.18–19 and 30.21), among other passages. For full discussion of the sources, see Beeley, "Gregory of Nazianzus," 99–111.

34. Hahn, *Bibliotek der Symbole*, §142; 153–54. In his Trinitarian doctrine Gregory also echoes the language of singularity that Origen advanced and that was replicated in the creed of Antioch 341: that there is "one God," "one Christ," and "one Holy Spirit." See *Or.* 25.15.

35. Egan, "Primal Cause."

36. See also *Or.* 30.21: the Son divinizes human nature not by grace but by his assumption of it.

37. Gregory gives a list of such examples in *Or.* 29.17.

38. Other statements of Gregory's exegetical method come in *Or.* 30.1, 2, and 34.10.

39. See Beeley, "Gregory of Nazianzus," 99–102 for further examples, and 111–16 for an account of why Gregory seems to oppose this method in other passages.

40. See also *Or.* 38.13: the child born of Mary is "God, together with what he has assumed"; and *Ep.* 101.17: Diodore is wrong to deny that the birth of Jesus is "the birth of God."

41. For a more detailed account of the council, with bibliographic references, see Beeley, *Gregory of Nazianzus*, 43–54.

42. The Greek text comes from Dossetti, *Il símbolo di Nicea e di Costantinopoli*, 244–50. I have rendered the creed here in a way that remains close to the Greek original, preserving the lengthy sentence structure exactly. The earliest witness to the text of the creed comes from the Council of Chalcedon in 451; yet, despite the gap of seventy years, there is currently little doubt that it is very close to the original, and possibly exact.

43. For further discussion, see Beeley, *Gregory of Nazianzus*, 46–53.

44. In the edict *Episcopis tradi*, from July 30: *Cod. Th.* 16.1.3.

45. Meredith, *Gregory of Nyssa*, 5–6.

46. The other stages being, first, Eunomius's *Apology*; second, Basil's *Against Eunomius*; and third, Eunomius's *Apology for the Apology*, which answered the objections of Basil.

47. Pottier, *Dieu et le Christ*, 59.

48. May, "Chronologie," 61, following the judgments of Lietzmann and Mühlenberg.

49. For example, Kelly, *Early Christian Doctrines*, 295–301; Grillmeier, *Christ in Christian Tradition* (1965), 278–91; rev. ed. (1975), 367–77; *Jesus der Christus* (1979), 435–47.

50. Quoting from Eunomius, *Apol.* 17.

51. Ramelli, "Origen's Anti-subordinationism," shows that Gregory knew both Eusebius's and Marcellus's exegesis of 1 Cor 15:28.

52. ὡς καθ' ἑνὸς καὶ τοῦ αὐτοῦ τὰς δύο κεῖσθαι φωνάς. On the use of ὡς plus the infinitive to limit an assertion, see LSJ s.v. B.II.3.

53. τὰς θεοπρεπεῖς ἐννοίας . . . διασώξει . . . φυλάσσων τῇ τε περὶ τὸ θεῖον καὶ τῇ περὶ τὸ ἀνθρώπινον ὑπολήψει τὸ πρόσφορον.

54. The Greek infers by contrast from Gregory's actual statement: it was not ἄλλος who suffered and ἕτερος who was honored, but (by implication) only one figure (ἄλλος) who experienced both things. *C.Eun.* 3.3.42.

55. See 3.59, referring to Basil, *C.Eun.* 2.577A.

56. διπλῆς γὰρ οὔσης καὶ ἀμφιβόλου τῆς ὑπολήψεως, εἴτε τὸ θεῖον εἴτε τὸ ἀνθρώπινον ἐν πάθει γέγονεν.

57. On Gregory's anti-Apollinarian argumentation, see Hubner, *Einheit des Leibes Christi*, 129–34.

58. Strangely, Gregory here denies teaching two *divine* sons, one who created the ages and another who was revealed through the flesh; see *Theoph.* 121.

59. On Gregory's idea of transformation, see Bouchet, "Le vocabulaire," 570–75.

60. εἰς δυϊκὴν διαφορὰν τὸ ἕν διασχίζειν.

61. ἑκάτερον ἰδιαξόντως ἐφ' ἑαυτοῦ ἀριθμῶν.

62. ἐν τοῖς ἰδίοις αὐτῆς ἰδιώμασιν.

63. See also *Theoph.* 126; *C.Eun.* 3.3.68.

64. See also *Antirrh.* 161.

65. Gregory's reference to 2 Cor 5:16, among other things, indicates the similarity of his position with Origen's notion of the transformation of Christ's flesh into a spiritual body. We should note, however, that Gregory speaks equally of the loss of Christ's "body" (*soma*), not only his "flesh" (*sarx*).

66. For an alternative reading of Gregory's idea of transformation, see Daley, "Divine Transcendence," 501.

67. As Bouchet notes, Gregory's appeal to Scripture in this passage is fairly gratuitous ("Le vocabulaire," 536).

68. See also *Cat.Or.* 16, 24.

69. See also *Cat.Or.* 27.

70. Or "in unmingled co-essentiality with God" (ἀκράτῳ τῇ τοῦ θεοῦ συνουσίᾳ).

71. σάρκινον ἰδιαζόντως ἐφ' ἑαυτόν; *Theoph.* 126.

72. οἰκεῖα καὶ κατὰ φύσιν εἶναι τῇ προαιωνίᾳ θεότητι.

73. On Christ's two conflicting wills in the passion narrative, see Canévet, *Grégoire de Nysse*, 163.

74. Gregory opposes Apollinarius's one-nature language as well (*Antirrh.* 147), which we saw Gregory Nazianzen was perfectly comfortable with.

75. See Mühlenberg, *Apollinaris von Laodicea*, 74. Apollinarius also accuses Gregory of denying Christ's personal preexistence and real unity (*Antirrh.* 174, 184).

CHAPTER 5. AUGUSTINE AND THE WEST

1. On Hilary's Christology, see esp. Weedman, *Trinitarian Theology of Hilary of Poitiers*, chap. 7.

2. Ibid., 169.

3. Ibid., 201.

4. Ambrose's polemical activity began in earnest after Emperor Gratian requested a statement of the Nicene faith following the Battle of Adrianople in 378. On Ambrose's theological work in the full context of his episcopate, see esp. Williams, *Ambrose of Milan*, and McLynn, *Ambrose of Milan*; on Ambrose's Christology in the context of his baptismal theology, see Smith, *Christian Grace*, chap. 6.

5. Faller, in Ambrose, *Inc.* ix–xi.

6. *eo quod biformis geminae que naturae unus sit, consors divinitatis et corporis.* See also Daley, "Giant's Twin Substances," 481; and Smith, *Christian Grace*, chap. 6.

7. *non divisus, sed unus, quia utrumque unus et unus in utroque, hoc est vel divinitate vel corpore.*

8. *idem aliter ex patre, aliter ex virgine.*

9. The justification of Christ's two births also plays against the Antiochenes for several writers.

10. *Idem enim patiebatur et non patiebatur, moriebatur et non moriebatur, sepeliebatur et non sepeliebatur, resurgebat et non resurgebat.*

11. On the language of assumption and indwelling, see also *Inc.* 3.22.

12. See the brief discussion in Hanson, *Search for the Christian Doctrine of God*, 673–75.

13. *opse igitur utrumque unus.*

14. For a similar judgment, see Smith, *Christian Grace*, 174.

15. Astonishingly, we still lack an adequate book-length study of Augustine's Christology. The most helpful recent treatments include Daley, "A Humble Mediator," and Williams, "Augustine's Christology."

16. Bavel, *Recherches*, and Drobner, *Person-Exegese*. A key text for marking this shift is Augustine's *Ep.* 137 to Volusianus, written around 411–412; e.g., §9: Christ "unites both natures in the unity of his person" (*in unitate personae copulans utramque naturam*). Also important in this regard is *C.Serm.Ar.* 9.7, where Augustine comments on the image of Christ as a twin-natured giant, from Ambrose's *Inc.* 7.77.

17. *deus apud patrem, homo apud nos.*

18. *ille homo erat, ut et deus esset.*

19. Literally, "according to [*secundum*] his participation in our existence."

20. *Etenim quod de illo clamat MISERERE MEI, tuum est, a te hoc accepit, propter te liberandum carne indutus est.* (English readers should note that the new *Works of Saint Augustine* translation of this entire passage, down through the rest of the section, is highly problematic.)

21. *homo et verbum unus homo, et verbum et homo unus Deus.*

22. *ideo enim petit quia exhibet.*

23. *homo in cruce; super caelos Deus.*

24. That Augustine envisions God as the single subject of this statement is clear from the fact that the psalm verse he is commenting on is addressed directly to God: "Be lifted up above the heavens, O God" (v. 6). God is therefore the subject of both claims.

25. *Deo Deus dicit: Miserere mei.*

26. *propterea in omnibus psalmis sic audiamus uoces capitis, ut audiamus et uoces corporis. noluit enim loqui separatim, quia noluit esse separatus.*

27. *loquitur in nobis, loquitur de nobis, loquitur per nos, quia et nos loquimur in illo et ideo verum loquimur, quia in illo loquimur.*

28. *Per carnem suam dominus duo genera factorum operatus est.*

29. See Williams, "Augustine's Christology," 177, for a similar observation.

30. *Nisi tamen idem ipse esset filius hominis propter formam serui quam accepit qui est filius dei propter dei formam in qua est.*

31. *scripturarum de Filio Dei.*

32. In a different metaphor, the incarnation is like human speech, which passes through the physical ears of the hearer while at the same time remaining as it was in the mind of the speaker (*Doctr.* 1.12).

33. Here Augustine's argument has affinities with both Eusebius's and Athanasius's views on Christ as the supreme theophany.

34. *per uiam quam strauit humanitate diuinitatis unigeniti sui, Trin.* 4.1.

35. *factus particeps mortalitatis nostrae fecit participes diuinitatis suae.*

36. From his priestly ordination in 393 through roughly 410, just before he began *The City of God*, a period that includes the *Confessions, Christian Doctrine*, and the early parts of *The Trinity*, which he completed in 419—thus spanning nearly his entire career.

37. *hoc totum et deus dicatur propter deum et homo propter hominem.*

38. *Verbo itaque dei ad unitatem personae copulatus, et quodam modo commixtus est homo.*

CHAPTER 6. CYRIL, LEO, AND CHALCEDON (451)

1. For example, Wickham, ed., *Cyril of Alexandria*, xi: "The patristic understanding of the Incarnation owes more to Cyril of Alexandria than to any other individual theologian"; see also Weinandy, "Cyril and the Mystery of the Incarnation," 23.

2. On Athanasius's influence on Cyril, see McGuckin, *Saint Cyril of Alexandria*, 176; McKinion, *Words, Imagery*, 17–18; Grillmeier, *Christ in Christian Tradition*, (1975), 414; and Kelly, *Early Christian Doctrines*, 318–19: "The clue to Cyril's own teaching is the realization that he was an Alexandrian, nurtured in the school of Athanasius and Didymus the Blind."

3. The complete florilegium is contained in ACO 1.1.2:54–59, 39–45. The texts are presented in the following order (with the number of lines in Schwartz's edition): Peter of Alexandria, *On Divination* (19 ll.); Athanasius, *Ar.* 3.3 (18 ll.); *Letter to Epictetus* (16 ll.); Julius of Rome, *Ep. Prosdoc.* (5 ll.); Felix of Rome, *Letter to Maximus* (5 ll.); Theophilus of Alexandria, *Paschal Letters* 5 and 6 (18 ll.); Gregory of Nazianzus, *Letter* 101 (31 ll.); Basil of Caesarea, *Spirit* 18 (4 ll.); Gregory of Nyssa, *Oration* 1, *On the Beatitudes*. (14 ll.). On the new practice of citing earlier "fathers" by name, and its background in the fourth century, see also Graumann, *Kirche der Väter*.

4. The *Oration to Augusta* (or *On Right Faith to Arcadia and Marina*) and the *Oration to Domina* (or *On Right Faith to Pulcheria and Eudocia*) were the second and third of three texts, *On Faith*, that Cyril sent to the imperial courts. The first text, the *Oration to Theodosius*, is a more direct doctrinal argument, supported by many biblical citations but no patristic references. The *Oration to Augusta* consists entirely of biblical excerpts; the *Oration to Domina* contains some dogmatic exposition, followed by a confession from the famous Apollinarian text that Cyril believed was written by Athanasius, which contains the pregnant statement that Christ is "one incarnate and worshipped nature of the Word of God" (ACO 1.1.5:10, 65.27). The *Oration to Domina* includes just two pages of excerpts from selected bishops in Greece, Antioch, and Alexandria, including Amphilochius of Iconium, John Chrysostom, and Theophilus of Alexandria, but neither Athanasius nor Gregory Nazianzen (ACO 1.1.5:11–18, 66–68), followed by more biblical quotations. On Cyril's

indebtedness to the fourth-century fathers in his works before the Nestorian controversy, see Boulnois, *Le paradoxe Trinitaire*, 659–74.

5. See also Chadwick, "Eucharist and Christology," 150–51; and Keating, *Appropriation of Divine Life*, 23–24.

6. See also *3Ep.Nest.* 4, 5, 11, 12 anathema 2.

7. For a more comprehensive account of these phrases across Cyril's career, see Beeley, "Cyril of Alexandria," 394n59.

8. See also *3Ep.Nest.* 4: the Word dwells in Christ (κατοίκησις, John 1:14) not by grace, as in the saints, but by being united "by nature" (κατὰ φύσιν), like the relation of one's soul to one's body; and *2Ep.Succ.* 3.

9. See also *Ep.* 1.12; *Exp.xii.cap.* 11, 14; *Schol.Inc.* 8; *Ep.* 45.4; *1Ep.Succ.* 5; *Un.Chr.* 376/78.

10. Helpfully summarized in Weinandy, "Cyril and the Mystery of the Incarnation," 36–37n35, with bibliography; see also Liébaert, *La doctrine christologique*, 197n2.

11. See also *Ep.Eulog.* 64: a union refers to the joining together (σύνοδος) of two or more different things, not of a single entity; *Ep.* 45.7.

12. ἐν ἰδιότητι τῇ κατὰ φύσιν ἑκατέρου.

13. See also *Exp.xii.cap.* 5, 17, 25; *Un.Chr.* 307/51.

14. εἰς ἑτερότητα καὶ ἰδικήν. See also *1Ep.Succ.* 6: Christ is "one and the same" Christ and Lord: both God and a human being, not two different beings (ἕτερος καὶ ἕτερος).

15. An exception comes in the late *Un.Chr.* 316/55: Christ, who is God by nature, "thought it good to be made human and in his own person to reveal our nature honored in the dignities of the divinity."

16. See also *Exp.xii.cap.* 27; *Un.Chr.* 378, 390/79, 84: on the "vast difference between God and human existence."

17. See also *Ep.* 1.4: if Christ is God, then Mary is Theotokos; *Ep.* 1.18: Christ is true God revealed to us in human form; *Exp.xii.cap.* 8. The point receives special emphasis in the late *Un.Chr.* 330–41, 358, 384/60–64, 71, 81.

18. See also *Ep.* 11.5 to Celestine: Nestorius fails to see that "all the orthodox bishops and laity throughout the world confess that Christ is God, and so the Virgin is Theotokos."

19. In the early works, see *Com.Jn.* 6.53; and esp. *Thes.* 120A–21C; 156A–B; 277D; 289A; 372B; 388D–89A; 396D; and Siddals, "Logic and Christology," 358–360.

20. In the face of further Antiochene objections that he will not allow the differing biblical statements to refer to different hypostases or persons, Cyril refers to the fourth anathema, repeats the argument of *Ep.* 44, and reemphasizes that the Eastern practice accords with his own (*Ep.Acac.* 15–20). In §15

Cyril notes approvingly that John of Antioch and company "maintain a difference of natures" while confessing that there is only one person in Christ; see also *Ep.Acac.Scyth.* 18–19; *2Ep.Succ.* 2–4.

21. For the former view, see Grillmeier, *Christ in Christian Tradition*, 312; Hanson, *Search for the Christian Doctrine of God*, 447–48; Young, *From Nicaea to Chalcedon*, 67–78; for the latter, see Grillmeier, *Christ in Christian Tradition*, 314–15; Hanson, *Search for the Christian Doctrine of God*, 448–49; Anatolios, *Athanasius*, 238–39nn134, 156.

22. See also Young, "Reconsideration," and Smith, "Suffering Impassibly."

23. See also *Ep.* 101.51: the Son himself must actually undergo human suffering and death in order to purify like by like.

24. Θεὸς παθητὸς κατὰ τῆς ἁμαρτίας.

25. σεσωμένοι τοῖς τοῦ ἀπαθοῦς πάθειν.

26. Θεὸν σταυρούμενον βλέπειν.

27. See also *C.Ar.* 2.55; 3.34; *Ep.Epict.* 6; and Anatolios, *Athanasius*, 144.

28. Anatolios, *Athanasius*, 144–52.

29. A similar perspective, no doubt coming from his initial study of Athanasius, can be seen in the early *Com.Jn.* 1.23: in Christ, Life suffered death in his own body, suffering nothing in his own nature (because he is life), although the sufferings are *said* to be his on account of his having become flesh; *Com.Jn.* 1.25: by "refusing to suffer anything contrary to his nature," he destroyed death; Christ suffered as a human being in order to save us as God. In a similarly Athanasian vein, Cyril argues from the beginning of his career that in the incarnation the Word underwent no change: see *Pasch.Hom.* 8, a passage that Chadwick ("Eucharist and Christology") takes as early evidence of anti-Antiochene argumentation; *Com.Jn.* 6.54; *Exp.xii.cap.* 5, 8, 16; *Ep.* 33.7; *Un.Chr.* 312–14, 398–400/53–54, 88.

30. Similar patterns can be seen in *1Ep.Succ.*, which begins with a solidly Gregorian confession of divine suffering in Christ, then adds the Athanasian qualification that he did not suffer in the nature of the Godhead (§§9–10); *Ep.Acac.*, which explains that Christ suffers as a human but not as God and the Word "has no share in death," as an interpretation of the two goats and two birds in Lev 16 (§§13, 16–19); *Schol.Inc.* 8; and *Ep.* 33.7; 39.9.

31. As Chadwick briefly observes, with reference to *Schol.Inc.* 8 ("Eucharist and Christology," 160).

32. At Ephesus he defends himself against the charge of confusing, mixing, or blending the natures in the incarnation: *Ep.* 33.7; 39.9; *Un.Chr.* 312–16/54–55. Cyril can be seen employing the term early on: in the *Pasch.Hom.* of 421 he speaks of the incomprehensible mixture (ἀνάκρασις) of the Word with flesh—though he is forced to abandon the terminology once the controversy

starts (§8). In *C.Nest.* Cyril admits his awareness of this earlier patristic usage of the term, and even tries to defend it: "Some of the holy Fathers used the term 'mixture' (κρᾶσις)" (1.3.33).

33. Chadwick, e.g., argues that Cyril's insistence on the suffering of the Word reflects an Apollinarian influence ("Eucharist and Christology," 158). The true source, we may now recognize, is not Apollinarius but Gregory, and certainly not Athanasius.

34. Wessel, *Cyril of Alexandria*, 215.

35. On the question of the *Tome*'s method of composition, see Wessel, *Leo the Great*, 210–11.

36. *aut deum . . . sine homine aut sine deo solum hominem credidisse.* In the same passage Leo comments further that the faith of the catholic church holds that Christ possesses "neither humanity without true divinity nor divinity without true humanity."

37. The fact that Leo regularly attached Nestorius to the name of Eutyches in works from 449 to at least 458 (Green, *Soteriology*, 202–6) shows the full extent to which he wanted to present himself as taking a balanced stance in the debates.

38. Leo quotes from the Roman (Apostles) Creed and then adds phrases from the Nicene Creed in the ensuing argument.

39. See also *Tome* 4: while still existing in the glory of the Father, the Son was "born in a new order, by a new birth" (*nouo ordine, noua natiuitate*).

40. *inpassibilis deus non dedignatus est homo esse passibilis.*

41. *agit enim utraque forma cum alterius communione quod proprium est, uerbo scilicet operante quod verbi est, et carne exequente quod carnis est.*

42. Leo rewrote the self-defense again in 458 as *Ep.* 165.

43. See Wessel, *Leo the Great*, 235: "The bond [in Christ] that Leo conceived of was not as deeply knit as the ontological connection that Augustine devised. Leo did not rule out, as Augustine had, that God and man, Christ and the church, were two distinct entities somehow connected in one discrete flesh."

44. The dubious condition of the minutes of this session, which made no doctrinal discussion of the *Tome*, shows the degree to which it functioned as a propaganda machine. See Price, "Narrative," 78.

45. The *Acts of Chalcedon* being our earliest witness to the Creed of Constantinople. The assembled bishops were so committed to the normative status of Nicaea and Constantinople (381), as established at Ephesus (431), that they initially refused the government's charge to draw up a new doctrinal statement in the second session of the council (Church Councils, *Acts* II.3–7).

46. On the Antiochene biases of Chalcedon and the adverse reaction to it by miaphysite churches, see esp. Frend, *Rise of the Monophysite Movement*.

47. Or "truly a human being [ἄνθρωπος]."

48. The same sense is reiterated in the second and third instances of the phrase "one and the same" later in the Definition. They could certainly be taken in a Nicene—that is, a single-subject—sense if the rest of the Definition and its political rationale had been different.

49. The controversial nature of the phrase can be seen in the fact that the emperor himself had to pressure the bishops to come to some agreement (Church Councils, *Acts* 2.198–99).

50. Church Councils, *Acts* 1.69.

51. Literally, "unconfusedly, unchangeably, undividedly, inseparably."

52. With Chadwick, "Chalcedonian Definition," 12; and de Halleux, "Actualité du néochalcédonisme," 52, against the recent argument of Price and Gaddis for the supposedly pro-Cyrilline nature of the committee (Church Councils, *Acts* 1.65–66; 2.188–89).

53. Early manuscripts of Athanasius's *Inc.*, for example, were preserved by Antiochenes; in Athanasius, *C.Gent.* and *Inc.*, trans. Thomson.

CHAPTER 7. POST-CHALCEDONIAN CHRISTOLOGY

1. On the modern misattribution of *enhypostasia* to Leontius, see Daley, "'A Richer Union.'"

2. A hypostasis admits of existence in itself (τὸν τοῦ καθ' ἑαυτὸ εἶναι); nature admits of the λόγος of existence but does not exist per se.

3. See also *Sol.Sever.* 1945A.

4. Athanasius does not use this particular term, but if he did, his thinking would run thus.

5. For the second definition, see also *Sol.Sever.* 1925C–28D.

6. According to the logicians, "partial things share in those that are common, and common things are predicated of things partially, and an individual has communion in the species according to nature, while common things have communion in partial things according to their naming," which is why we can call the part by the name of the whole.

7. See also *Sol.Sever.* 1945D: divine and human statements refer to the one hypostasis *and also* to the individual natures themselves (thus still resisting true cross-predication). In *C.Aphth.* 1320B, however, Leontius appears to allow for some cross-predication.

8. Leontius repeats the same procedure following his treatise *C.Aphth.*

9. Basil, *Ep.* 214.4; 236.6 (two times); 125. For these references to Leontius's sources I am indebted to Brian Daley's unpublished Greek edition of Leontius.

10. The list of authors, in the order presented and the number of quotations from each, includes Basil of Caesarea (four), Gregory of Nazianzus (three),

Proclus of Constantinople (one), Isidore the Ascetic (one), Justin Martyr (four), Irenaeus of Lyons (one), Hippolytus (one), Peter of Alexandria (one), Cyriacus of Paphos (one), Athanasius (three), Basil of Caesarea (two), Gregory Nazianzen (four), Gregory of Nyssa (five), Julius of Rome (one), Hilary of Poitiers (four), Ambrose (six), Amphilochius of Iconium (four), Gelasius of Caesarea in Palestine (two), Augustine (two), John of Constantinople (three), Ephrem the Syrian (one), Cyril of Jerusalem (one), Flavian of Antioch (two), Antiochus of Ptolemais (one), Proclus of Constantinople (two), Isidore of Pelusium (four), Cyril of Alexandria (eight), Paul of Emessa (two), and Cyril (fifteen). Several of the works quoted are spurious, including Pseudo-Basil, *C.Eun.* 4, and Pseudo-Athanasius, *C.Apol.*

11. Interrupted only by the two from Paul of Emessa, which are introduced here because Cyril replies to them.

12. Duchesne, *L'Église au VIᵉ siècle*, 210.

13. Of the council's fourteen anathemas, twelve are against Theodore, one against Theodoret, and one against Ibas. It is in the eleventh anathema of this council that the name of Origen appears for the first time in a list of those named heretics. Scholars still debate the authenticity of the charge.

14. See esp. *2Const.* 3 (vindicating the apostles and the traditions of the fathers), 4–5 (the unique truth-making quality of councils), 5 (proclaiming "the same faith" of Nicaea, Constantinople, Ephesus, and Chalcedon), 16 (quoting Augustine and other Africans in defense of its actions), 18 (resolving disputes over the interpretation of the fathers), and 24 ("Nothing that has been written by anyone ought to be accepted unless it has been shown conclusively that it is in accord with the true faith of the holy Fathers").

15. See also *Ambig.* 4, which similarly misreads Gregory's *Or.* 30.2.

16. The Leontine background of Maximus's expressions in these texts has been observed by Piret, *Le Christ et la Trinité*, 204.

17. Hence I concur with Thurnberg, *Microcosm and Mediator*, 48, against the recent argument by Barthellos, *Byzantine Christ*, 113.

18. "The incarnate Word guards without loss the properties of both natures" (*Opusc.* 73C).

19. On which see Daley, "Making a Human Will Divine."

20. For polemical reasons, Cyril generally omits Gregory's attention to Christ's full humanity, ignoring his emphasis on Christ's human soul in particular. The reason probably has to do with the legacy of Origen, for whom Jesus's human soul played such a controversial role.

21. Apart from Maximus's citation, there appears to be no other ancient witness to this text by Cyril. See also Doucet, "Dispute," 758n108.

22. "He lived in our midst a new kind of activity: the theandric."

23. Particularly in his anti-Apollinarian arguments in the later sections of *Ep.* 101.

24. See, e.g., Augustine, *Enchir.*

25. See also *Pyrrh.* 293C–D: Christ's two natures have nothing in common except their common hypostasis, as if the divine nature were not the unifying agent; also 341B: the "one" who acts in Christ is the hypostasis, which suggests that the Son is not divine (nature) as well.

26. On the idea that Christ exists "from and in" two natures, see also *Pyrrh.* 289B.

27. Here support is given from a lost (most likely spurious) text of Athanasius.

28. See Louth, *St. John Damascene*, 36–37. One of John's major sources was the *Doctrina Patrum*, an earlier collection that scholars believe may have been compiled by a member of Maximus's circle sometime between 660 and 685.

29. As Louth notes, the *Fount of Knowledge* provides "a recapitulation of Christian doctrine in its Chalcedonian form" (*St. John Damascene*, 37).

30. Louth, *St. John Damascene*, 144–46, 174.

31. The subtitle of chapter 1. Some manuscripts add "and on [God's or Christ's] care for us and for our salvation" (*Exp.Fid.*, ed. Kotter, 106).

32. On Maximus's use of this text, see Louth, *Maximus the Confessor*, 52.

33. ACO 4.2.187–95. In 428 or 429 Proclus preached against Nestorius (in his presence) in defense of the Theotokos; his *Tome* (*Ep.* 2) is directed against Theodore of Mopsuestia.

34. Occasional unitive statements include Cyril's phrase "one incarnate nature of the Word," which John is concerned not to forfeit (*Exp.Fid.* 51), and the statement following close behind that the mutual immanence of the two natures comes from the divine nature. Their rarity makes them the exception that proves the rule.

Bibliography

The bibliography contains only works cited in this book. Further studies of the period and the authors and events in question can be found in the standard histories and reference works.

ABBREVIATIONS

ACO   *Acta Conciliorum Oecumenicorum.* 1st series, 4 vols. Ed. Eduard Schwartz and Johannes Straub. Berlin: Walter de Gruyter, 1914–1982; 2nd series, 3 vols. Ed. Rudolf Riedlinger. Berlin: Walter de Gruyter, 1984–2008.

ACW   *Ancient Christian Writers.* 63 vols. New York: Paulist Press, 1946–.

ANF   *The Ante-Nicene Fathers: The Writings of the Fathers Down to A.D. 325.* 10 vols. Edinburgh, 1864. Reprint, Peabody, MA: Hendrickson, 1995.

CCG   *Corpus Christianorum Series Graeca.* 69 vols. Turnhout: Brepols, 1977–.

CCL   *Corpus Christianorum, Series Latina.* 173 vols. Turnhout: Brepols, 1954–.

CSEL   *Corpus Scriptorum Ecclesiasticorum Latinorum.* 97 vols. Vienna: C. Gerodi et al., 1866–.

FC   *The Fathers of the Church.* 122 vols. Washington, DC: Catholic University of America Press, 1947–.

GCS   *Die griechischen christlichen Schriftsteller der ersten drei Jahrhunderte.* 53 vols. Leipzig: J. C. Hinrichs, 1897–1969. New series, 14 vols. Berlin: Walter de Gruyter, 1995–.

LCL   *Loeb Classical Library.* 516 vols. London: Heinemann; and Cambridge, MA: Harvard University Press, 1912–.

LSJ   *A Greek-English Lexicon.* Comp. Henry George Liddell, Robert Scott, Henry Stuart Jones, with Roderick McKenzie. 9th ed. Oxford: Clarendon, 1940.

NPNF   *A Select Library of Nicene and Post-Nicene Fathers of the Christian Church.* Series 1–2, 14 vols. Edinburgh, 1886. Reprint, Peabody, MA: Hendrickson, 1995.

PG   *Patrologiae Cursus Completus Series Graeca.* 161 vols. Ed. J. P. Migne et al. Paris: Garnier, 1857–1912.

PL   *Patrologiae Cursus Completus Series Latina.* 221 vols. Ed. J. P. Migne et al.
        Paris: Garnier, 1844–1864.

SC   *Sources Chrétiennes.* 529 vols. Paris: Cerf, 1941–.

ANCIENT SOURCES

ALEXANDER OF ALEXANDRIA

He philarchos/ Letter to Alexander of Byzantium (Phil.). Ed. Hans-Georg Opitz,
    Athanasius Werke, 3.1:19–29. Berlin: Walter de Gruyter, 1934–. Trans. J. B. H.
    Hawkins. ANF 6:291–96.

AMBROSE OF MILAN

Concerning Virgins (Virg.). Ed. O. Faller. *Florilegium Patristicum* 31 (Bonn).
    Trans. H. de Romestin, E. de Romestin, and H. T. F. Duckwork. NPNF 10.

Exposition of the Gospel according to Luke (Exp.Lk.). Ed. Karl and Heinrich
    Schenkl. CSEL 32.4. Trans. Theodosia Tomkinson. Saint Ambrose of Milan,
    *Exposition of the Holy Gospel according to Saint Luke, with Fragments on the
    Prophecy of Isaias.* Etna, CA: Center for Traditionalist Orthodox Studies,
    1998.

Homily on Psalm 61 (In Ps. 61). Ed. M. Petschenig. CSEL 64.

Letters (Ep.). Books 1–6, ed. O. Faller. CSEL 82.1. Books 7–10 and *Epistulae extra
    collectionem,* ed. M. Zelzer. CSEL 82.2–3. Trans. M. M. Beyenka. FC 26.

On the Sacrament of the Incarnation of the Lord (Inc.). Ed. O. Faller. CSEL 79.
    Trans. Roy Deferrari. FC 44.

APOLLINARIUS OF LAODICEA

Detailed Confession of Faith/ἡ κατὰ μέρος πίστις (Conf.Faith). Ed. Hans
    Lietzmann, *Apollinaris von Laodicea und seine Schule.* Texte und
    Untersuchungen. Tübingen: Mohr, 1904: 167–85. Trans. Kelley McCarthy
    Spoerl, "A Study of the Κατὰ Μέρος Πίστις by Apollinarius of Laodicea."
    Diss: University of Toronto, 1991: 378–97.

Fragments (Frag.). Ed. Lietzmann, *Apollinaris:* 204–42. *Frag.* 9–10, 17–19, 22,
    25–26, 28, 38, 41–42, 45, 69–72, 74, 76, 85, 87, 89, 91, 93, 108–9, 117, 123–24,
    126–29 trans. Richard A. Norris Jr., *The Christological Controversy.* Sources of
    Early Christian Thought. Philadelphia: Fortress Press, 1980: 107–11.

Letter to Dionysius (Ep.Dion.). Ed. Lietzmann, *Apollinaris:* 256–62.

On the Faith and the Incarnation (Inc.). Ed. Lietzmann, *Apollinaris:* 194–203.

On the Union of the Body with the Divinity in Christ (Union). Ed. Lietzmann,
    Apollinaris: 185–93. Trans. Norris, *Christological Controversy,* 103–7.

ARISTOTLE

Categories (Cat.). Ed. Immanuel Bekker. Trans. Harold P. Cooker. LCL 325.

ARIUS

Confession of Faith of Arius and His Associates to Alexander of Alexandria (Urk.
  6). Ed. Opitz, *Athanasius Werke* 3.1:12–13. Trans. Williams, *Arius: Heresy and
  Tradition*. London: Darton, Longman and Todd, 1987: 270–71.

Letter of Arius to Eusebius of Nicomedia (Urk. 1). Ed. Opitz, *Athanasius Werke*
  3.1:1–3. Trans. Edward R. Hardy, *Christology of the Later Fathers*. Library of
  Christian Classics. Louisville, KY: Westminster, 1954: 329–31.

Letter to Constantine (Urk. 30). Ed. Opitz, *Athanasius Werke* 3.1:64–65. Trans.
  Rowan Williams. *Arius: Heresy and Tradition*. London: Darton, Longman and
  Todd, 1987: 278–79.

Thalia (*Thal.*). In Athanasius, *C.Ar.* 1.5; *Syn.* 15. Trans. Williams, *Arius*, 85,
  100–3. Cited by fragment number (*Frag.*) of M. L. West, "The Metre of
  Arius' *Thalia*," *Journal of Theological Studies* 33 (1982): 98–105.

ATHANASIUS OF ALEXANDRIA

Against the Pagans (*C.Gent.*). Athanasius of Alexandria, *Contra Gentes and De
  Incarnatione*. Ed. and trans. Robert W. Thomson. Oxford Early Christian
  Texts. Oxford: Clarendon, 1971.

Catholic Epistle (*Ep.Cath.*). Ed. Martin Tetz, "Ein enzyklisches Schreiben der
  Synode von Alexandrian (362)." *Zeitschrift für die neutestamentliche
  Wissenschaft* 79 (1988): 271–73.

Henos somatos (Urk. 4b). Ed. Opitz, *Athanasius Werke* 3.1:6–11. Trans. J. B. H.
  Hawkins. ANF 6:296–99.

Letter to Adelphius (*Ep.Adelph.*). PG 26.1071–84. Trans. Archibald Robertson.
  NPNF 4.575–78.

Letter to the Bishops of Egypt and Libya (*Ep.Episc.*). PG 25.537–94. Trans. M.
  Atkinson and Archibald Robertson. NPNF 2.4.222–35.

Letter to Epictetus (*Ep.Epict.*). PG 26.1049–70. Trans. Archibald Robertson.
  NPNF 4.570–74.

Letter to the Emperor Jovian (*Ep.Jov.*). PG 26.813–20. Trans. Archibald Robertson.
  NPNF 4.567–68.

Letter to Maximus (*Ep.Max.*). PG 26.1085–90. Trans. Archibald Robertson.
  NPNF 4.578–79.

Letters to Serapion concerning the Holy Spirit (*Ep.Serap.*). Ed. J. Lebon. SC 15.
  Trans. C. R. B. Shapland, *The Letters of Saint Athanasius Concerning the Holy
  Spirit*. London: Epworth, 1951.

On the Councils of Ariminum and Seleucia (*Syn.*). Ed. Opitz, *Athanasius
  Werke* 2.1:231–78. Trans. John Henry Newman and Archibald Robertson.
  NPNF 2.4.448–80.

On the Decrees of Nicaea (*Decr.*). Ed. Opitz, *Athanasius Werke* 2.1.1–45. Trans.
  John Henry Newman and Archibald Robertson. NPNF 2.4.150–72.

On the Incarnation (Inc.). Athanasius of Alexandria, *Contra Gentes and De Incarnatione*. Ed. and trans. Thomson. Oxford Early Christian Texts. Oxford: Clarendon, 1971.

On the Sayings of Dionysius (Dion.). Ed. Opitz, *Athanasius Werke* 2:1.46–67. Trans. Archibald Robertson. NPNF 2.4.173–87.

Orations against the Arians (C.Ar.). Ed. Karin Metzler and Kyriakos Savvidis, *Athanasius Werke* 1.1.2–3. Trans. John Henry Newman and Archibald Robertson. NPNF 2.4.303–447.

Tome to the Antiochenes (Tom.). PG 26.796. Trans. H. Ellershaw. NPNF 2.4.481–86.

AUGUSTINE OF HIPPO

Against the Arian Sermon (C.Serm.Ar.). PL 42.677–708. Trans. Roland Teske. Saint Augustine, *Arianism and Other Heresies*. Works of Saint Augustine 1.18. Hyde Park, NY: New City Press, 1995: 118–71.

Catechizing the Uninstructed (Catech.) Ed. I. Bauer. CCL 46. Trans. Raymond Canning. Augustine of Hippo, *Instructing Beginners in the Faith*. The Augustine Series 5. Hyde Park, NY: New City Press, 2006.

The City of God (Civ.Dei). Ed. E. Hoffmann. CSEL 40. Augustine, *The City of God*. Trans. Henry Bettenson. Hammondsworth: Penguin Books, 1972.

Christian Doctrine (Doctr.). Ed. W. M. Green. CSEL 32. Augustine, *Teaching Christianity: De Doctrina Christiana*. Trans. Edmund Hill. Works of Saint Augustine 1.11. Hyde Park, NY: New City Press, 1996.

Confessions (Conf.). Augustine, *Confessions*. Ed. James O'Donnell, vol. 1. Oxford: Clarendon, 1992. Augustine, *Confessions*. Trans. Henry Chadwick. Oxford World's Classics. Oxford: Oxford University Press, 1991.

Enchiridion on Faith, Hope, and Love (Enchir.) Ed. E. Evans. CCL 46. Trans. Bruce Harbert. Augustine of Hippo, *The Augustine Catechism*. Hyde Park, NY: New City Press, 1999.

Exposition of Psalm 56 (En.Ps. 56). Ed. Hanspeter Müller. CSEL 94. Augustine, *Expositions of the Psalms 51–72*. Trans. Maria Boulding. Works of Saint Augustine 3.17. New York: New City Press, 2001.

The Trinity (Trin.). Ed. J. Mountain. CCL 50, 50A. Augustine, *The Trinity*. Trans. Edmund Hill. Works of Saint Augustine 1.5. Hyde Park, NY: New City Press, 1991.

BASIL OF CAESAREA

Against Eunomius (C.Eun.). Ed. Bernard Sesboüé, Georges-Matthieu de Durand, and Louis Doutreleau. SC 299, 305. Trans. Mark Del Cogliano and Andrew Radde-Gallwitz. FC 122.

Letters (Ep.). Saint Basile, *Lettres*. 3 vols. Ed. Yves Courtonne. Collection
    Guillaume Budé. Paris: Les Belles Lettres, 1957–1966. Trans. Roy Defferrari.
    LCL 190, 215, 243, 270.
Sermons. PG 31.163–618, 1429–1514.

CHURCH COUNCILS

Acts of Chalcedon (451) (*Acts*). Ed. Eduard Schwartz. ACO 2. *Acts of the Council
    of Chalcedon*. 3 vols. Trans. Richard Price and Michael Gaddis. Translated
    Texts for Historians 45. Liverpool: Liverpool University Press, 2005.
Acts of the Second Council of Constantinople (553) (*2Const.*). Ed. Johannes Straub.
    ACO 4.1. Trans. Norman Tanner, *Decrees of the Ecumenical Councils*. 2 vols.
    London: Sheed and Ward, 1990: 107–22. Cited by section number in Straub/
    page number in Tanner.
Acts of the Third Council of Constantinople (680–81) (*3Const.*). Ed. Rudolf
    Riedinger. ACO 2.2.1–2. Trans. Tanner, *Decrees of the Ecumenical Councils*,
    124–30. Cited by page numbers in Riedinger/ Tanner.
Canons of Church Councils. *Die Kanones der wichtigsten altkirchlichen
    Concilien, nebst den Apostolischen Kanones*. Ed. Freidrich Lauchert. Freiburg:
    Mohr, 1896.
Definition of Chalcedon (451) (*Chalc.Def.*). ACO 2.1.2.126–30. Ed. Schwartz.
    Trans. Tanner, *Decrees of the Ecumenical Councils*, 83–87. Cited by page
    numbers in Schwartz/ Tanner.

CLEMENT OF ALEXANDRIA

Stromata (*Strom.*). Ed. Otto Stählen and Ludwig Früchtel. GCS 15, 17. Trans.
    William Wilson. ANF 2.299–567.

CYRIL OF ALEXANDRIA

Against Nestorius (*C.Nest.*). Ed. Schwartz. ACO 1.1.6.13–106. Trans. Philip
    Edward Pusey. St. Cyril of Alexandria, *Five Tomes against Nestorius: Scholia
    on the Incarnation, Christ Is One, Fragments against Diodore of Tarsus,
    Theodore of Mopsuestia, The Synousiasts*. Library of the Fathers of the Holy
    Catholic Church 47. Oxford: J. Parker, 1881.
Commentary on John (*Com.Jn.*). Ed. Pusey. Saint Cyril of Alexandria, *Sancti patris
    nostri Cyrilli Archiepiscopi Alexandrini In D. Joannis Evangelium: accedunt
    fragmenta varia necnon tractatus ad Tiberium diaconum duo*. 3 vols. Oxford:
    Clarendon Press, 1872. Trans. Pusey and Thomas Randell. Saint Cyril,
    Commentary on the Gospel according to St. John. 2 vols. Library of the Fathers
    of the Holy Catholic Church. London: Rivingtons, 1874–1885.
Explanation of the Twelve Chapters (*Exp.xii.cap.*). Ed. Schwartz. ACO 1.1.5.15–25.
    Trans. John A. McGuckin, *St. Cyril of Alexandria: The Christological*

Controversy: Its History, Theology, and Texts. Crestwood, NY: St. Vladimir's Seminary Press, 2004: 282–93.

First and *Second Letters to Succensus (Letters 45–46) (1Ep.Succ., 2Ep.Succ.)*. Cyril of Alexandria, *Select Letters*. Ed. and trans. Lionel Wickham. Oxford Early Christian Texts. Oxford: Clarendon, 1993: 70–93.

Letters (Ep.). Ed. Schwartz. ACO 1. Trans. John I. McEnerney. FC 76–77.

Letter to Acacius of Melitene (Letter 40) (Ep.Acac.). Cyril of Alexandria, *Select Letters*. Ed. and trans. Wickham, 34–61.

Letter to Acacius of Scythopolis (Letter 41) (Ep.Acac.Scyth.). Ed. Schwartz. ACO 1.1.4:46–47. Trans. McEnerney. FC 76.

Letter to Eulogius (Letter 44) (Ep.Eulog.). Ed. and trans. Wickham, 62–69.

Paschal Letters (Pasch.Hom.). Ed. W. H. Burns. Trans. Louis Arragon. Cyril of Alexandria, *Lettres Festale*. SC 372, 392, 434.

Scholia on the Incarnation of the Only Begotten (Schol.Inc.). Cyril of Alexandria, *Epistolae Tres Oecumenicae*. Ed. Pusey. Oxford: Oxford University Press, 1875. Trans. McGuckin, *Cyril of Alexandria*, 294–335.

Second and *Third Letters to Nestorius (Ep. 4 and 17) (2Ep.Nest., 3Ep.Nest.)*. Ed. and trans. Wickham, 2–33.

Thesaurus on the Holy and Consubstantial Trinity (Thes.). PG 75.9–656.

The Unity of Christ (Un.Chr.). Ed. G. M. de Durand. SC 97. Cyril of Alexandria, *The Unity of Christ*. Trans. John McGuckin. Crestwood, NY: St. Vladimir's Seminary Press, 1995. Cited by page numbers in Durand/McGuckin.

DAMASUS OF ROME

Exemplum synodi (Ex.Syn.). Ed. and trans. Lester L. Field, Jr. *On the Communion of Damasus and Meletius: Fourth-Century Synodal Formulae in the Codex Veronensis LX*. PIMS Studies and Texts 145. Toronto: Pontifical Institute of Mediaeval Studies, 2004.

Illut sane (Il. sane). Ed. and trans. Field, *On the Communion of Damasus*, 17–19.

Letters (Ep.). Ed. and trans. Glen Louis Thompson, "The Earliest Papal Correspondence." Diss: Columbia University, 1990: 278–372.

DIO CHRYSOSTOM

Orations (Or.). Ed. Hans von Arnim and Guy de Budé. Trans. J. W. Cohoon and H. Lamar Crosby. LCL 257, 339, 358, 376, 385.

DIODORE OF TARSUS

Commentary on the Psalms (Com.Ps.). Ed. Jean-Marie Olivier. CCG 6. Trans. Robert C. Hill. Diodore of Tarsus, *Commentary on Psalms 1–51*. Writings from the Greco-Roman World 9. Atlanta, GA: Society of Biblical Literature, 2005.

Fragments (Frag.). Ed. and trans. John Behr. *The Case against Diodore and Theodore: Texts and Their Contexts.* Oxford Early Christian Texts. Oxford: Oxford University Press, 2011.

EPIPHANIUS OF SALAMIS

Panarion (Panar.). Ed. Karl Holl. GCS 25, 31, 37. Epiphanius, *The Panarion of Epiphanius of Salamis.* 2 vols. Trans. Frank Williams. Leiden: Brill, 1987.

EUNOMIUS OF CYZICUS

Apology (Apol.). Eunomius, *The Extant Works.* Ed. and trans. Richard Paul Vaggione. Oxford Early Christian Texts. Oxford: Clarendon, 1987: 43–75.
Apology for the Apology (Apol.Apol.). Ed. and trans. Vaggione, 99–127.
Fragments (Frag.). Ed and trans. Vaggione, 176–79.

EUSEBIUS OF CAESAREA

Against Marcellus (C.Marcel.). Ed. Erich Klostermann and Günter Christian Hansen. GCS 4b.1–58.
Commentary on the Psalms (Com.Ps.). PG 23; 24.9–76.
Ecclesiastical History (H.E.). Ed. Schwartz. SC 31, 41, 51, 73. Eusebius of Caesarea, *The Ecclesiastical History and the Martyrs of Palestine.* 2 vols. Trans. Hugh Jackson Lawlor and John Ernest Leonard Oulton. London: SPCK, 1954.
Ecclesiastical Theology (E.Th.). Ed. Klostermann. GCS 4b.60–182.
In Praise of Constantine (L.C.). Ed. I. A. Heikel. GCS 7.193–259. Trans. Ernest Cushing Richardson. NPNF 2.1.581–610.
Letter to Euphration of Balanea (Urk. 3). Ed. Opitz. *Athanasius Werke* 3.1:4–6.
Letter to the People of Caesarea (Ep.Caes.). In Athanasius, *Decr.* 33.
Life of Constantine (V.Const.). Ed. Friedhelm Winkelman. Rev. ed. GCS 1.1. Eusebius, *Life of Constantine.* Trans. Averil Cameron and Stuart G. Hall. Oxford: Oxford University Press, 1999.
The Martyrs of Palestine (Mart.Pal.). Ed. Schwartz. GCS 9.2. Trans. Lawlor and Oulton, *Ecclesiastical History and Martyrs of Palestine.*
Preparation for the Gospel (Prep.). Ed. E. des Places, J. Sirinelli, G. Schroeder, G. Favrelle, O. Zink. SC 206, 215, 228, 262, 266, 292, 307, 338, 369. Eusebius of Caesarea, *Preparation for the Gospel.* Trans. Edwin Hamilton Gifford. Oxford: Clarendon, 1903.
Proof of the Gospel (Proof). Ed. Heikel. GCS 6. Eusebius of Caesarea, *The Proof of the Gospel: Being the* Demonstratio evangelica *of Eusebius of Caesarea.* 2 vols. Trans. W. J. Ferrar. Translations of Christian Literature Series 1. London: SPCK, 1920.

Prophetic Extracts (Ec.Proph.). Ed. T. Gaisford. *Eusebii Caesariensis Eclogae Ptopheticae.* Oxford: Oxford University Press, 1842. PG 22.1021–1262.

Theophany (Theoph.). Ed. Hugo Gressman. GCS 11.2. Eusebius of Caesarea, *On the Theophania or Divine Manifestation of Our Lord and Saviour Jesus Christ: A Syriac Version.* Ed. and trans. Samuel Lee. London: Society for the Publication of Oriental Texts, 1842.

GREGORY OF NAZIANZUS

Orations (Or.)

Or. 1–3. Ed. Jean Bernardi. SC 247. Trans. Charles Gordon Browne and James Edward Swallow. NPNF 2.7.203–29.

Or. 4–5. Ed. Bernardi. SC 309. Trans. Charles W. King, *Julian the Emperor, Containing Gregory Nazianzen's Two Invectives and Libanius' Monody with Julian's Extant Theosophical Works.* Bohn's Classical Library. London: George Bell and Sons, 1888: 1–121.

Or. 6–12. Ed. Marie-Ange Calvet-Sebasti. SC 405. *Or.* 6, 9–11 trans. Martha Vinson. FC 107. 3–35. *Or.* 8 trans. Brian E. Daley, *Gregory of Nazianzus.* Early Church Fathers. London: Routledge, 2006: 63–75. *Or.* 7–8, 12 trans. Browne and Swallow. NPNF 2.7.227–47.

Or. 13–19. Ed. Armand Benjamin Caillau. PG 35. *Or.* 13–15, 17, 19 trans. Vinson. FC 107. 36–106. *Or.* 14 trans. Daley. *Gregory of Nazianzus,* 75–97. *Or.* 16, 18 trans. Browne and Swallow. NPNF 2.7.247–69.

Or. 20–23. Ed. Justin Mossay and Guy Lafontaine. SC 270. *Or.* 20, 22–23 trans. Vinson. FC 107. 107–41. *Or.* 20 trans. Daley, *Gregory of Nazianzus,* 98–105. *Or.* 21 trans. Browne and Swallow. NPNF 2.7.269–84.

Or. 24–26. Ed. Mossay and Lafontaine. SC 284. Trans. Vinson. FC 107. 142–90. *Or.* 26 trans. Daley, *Gregory of Nazianzus,* 105–17.

Or. 27–31. Ed. Paul Gallay. SC 250. Trans. Browne and Swallow. NPNF 2.7.284–328; repr. with notes in Hardy, ed., *Christology of the Later Fathers,* 128–214. Trans. Frederick Williams (*Or.* 27) and Lionel Wickham (*Or.* 28–31), in Frederick W. Norris, *Faith Gives Fullness to Reasoning: The Five Theological Orations of Gregory Nazianzen.* Supplements to Vigiliae Christianae 13. Leiden: Brill, 1991; repr. with notes in St. Gregory of Nazianzus, *On God and Christ: The Five Theological Orations and Two Letters to Cledonius.* Popular Patristic Series. Crestwood, NY: St. Vladimir's Seminary Press, 2002.

Or. 32–37. Ed. Claudio Moreschini. SC 318. *Or.* 32, 35–36 trans. Vinson. FC 107. 191–229. *Or.* 33–34, 37 trans. Browne and Swallow. NPNF 2.7.328–45.

Or. 38–41. Ed. Moreschini. SC 358. Trans. Browne and Swallow. NPNF 2.7.345–85. *Or.* 38–39 trans. Daley, *Gregory of Nazianzus,* 117–38.

Or. 42–43. Ed. Bernardi. SC 384. *Or.* 42 trans. Daley. *Gregory of Nazianzus,*
138–54. *Or.* 42–43 trans. Browne and Swallow, NPNF 2.7.385–422.

Or. 44–45. Ed. Caillau. PG 36. *Or.* 44 trans. Vinson. FC 107. 230–38; Daley,
Gregory of Nazianzus, 154–61. *Or.* 45 trans. Browne and Swallow. NPNF
2.7.422–34.

Letters (Ep.)

Ed. Gallay. *Saint Grégoire de Nazianze, Lettres.* Collection des Universités de
France. 2 vols. Paris: Les Belles Lettres, 1964/1967. *Ep.* 101–102, 202 repr. SC
208. *Ep.* 1–2, 4–9, 12–13, 16–19, 21–22, 25–29, 37, 39–55, 58–60, 62–66, 77, 88,
91, 93, 101–102, 104–106, 115, 121–124, 126, 131, 135, 139–146, 151–154, 157,
163, 171, 183–186, 202 trans. Browne and Swallow. NPNF 2.7.437–82. Trans.
of *Ep.* 101–102, 202 repr. with notes in Hardy, ed., *Christology of the Later
Fathers,* 215–32.

Poems

De vita sua (Vita). Ed. Christoph Jungck. *Gregor von Nazianz, De Vita sua:
Einleitung, Text, Übersetzung, Kommentar.* Wissenschaftliche Kommentare zu
griechischen und lateinischen Schriftstellern. Heidelberg: C. Winter, 1974.
Trans. Denis Mollaise Meehan. FC 75. Trans. Caroline White. *Gregory of
Nazianzus, Autobiographical Poems.* Cambridge Medieval Classics 6.
Cambridge: Cambridge University Press, 1996.

GREGORY OF NYSSA

Against Eunomius (C.Eun.). Ed. Werner Jaeger, *Gregorii Nysseni Opera* 1–2.
Leiden: Brill, 1952. Trans. H. C. Ogle, H. A. Wilson, and M. Day. NPNF
2.5.33–248.

Catechetical Oration (Cat.Or.). Ed. Ekkehard Mühlenberg, *Gregorii Nysseni Opera*
3–4. Leiden: Brill, 1952. Trans. Cyril Richardson, in Hardy, ed., *Christology of
the Later Fathers,* 268–325.

Commentary on the Song of Songs (Com.Sg.). Ed. Hermann Langerbeck,
Gregorii Nysseni Opera 6. Gregory of Nyssa, *Commentary on the Song of
Songs.* Trans. Casimir McCambley. Brookline, MA: Hellenic College Press,
1987.

Letter to Theophilus of Alexandria (Theoph.). Ed. F. Mueller, *Gregorii Nysseni
Opera* 3.1. Leiden: Brill, 1958: 119–28.

Refutation (Antirrheticus) of Apollinarius (Antirrh.). Ed. Mueller, *Gregorii Nysseni
Opera* 3.1. Leiden: Brill, 1958: 127–233.

GREGORY THAUMATURGUS

Address of Thanksgiving to Origen (Addr.). Ed. Henri Crouzel. SC 148. Trans.
Michael Slusser. FC 98.91–126.

HILARY OF POITIERS

Against Valentinus and Ursacius (*Adv.Valent.Ursac.*). Ed. A. Feder. CSEL 65.

On the Councils (*Syn.*). PL 10.471–546. Trans. W. Sanday. NPNF 2.9.4–29.

The Trinity (*Trin.*). Ed. P. Smulders. SC 443, 448, 462. Trans. Stephen McKenna. FC 25.

IRENAEUS OF LYONS

Against the Heresies (*Haer.*). Ed. A. Rousseau, L. Doutreleau, B. Hemmerdinger, and C. Mercier. SC 100, 152, 153, 210, 211, 263, 264, 293, 294. Trans. A. Roberts and W. H. Rambaut. ANF 1.315–578.

JEROME

Against Rufinus (*C.Ruf.*). Ed. Pierre Lardet. SC 303. Trans. William Henry Fremantle. NPNF 2.3.482–541.

Commentary on Titus (*Com.Tit.*). PL 26.589–635. Trans. Thomas P. Scheck. *St. Jerome's Commentaries on Galatians, Titus, and Philemon.* South Bend, IN: University of Notre Dame Press, 2010.

Letters (*Ep.*). Ed. I. Hilberg. CSEL 54–56. Trans. F. A. Wright. LCL 262.

On Famous Men (*Vir.Ill.*). Ed. E. C. Richardson, *Hieronymus liber De viris inlustribus.* Leipzig: J. C. Hinrichs, 1896. Trans. Thomas Halton. FC 100.

JOHN OF DAMASCUS

Exposition of the Faith (*Exp.Fid.*). Ed. Bonifatius Kotter, *Die Schriften des Johannes von Damaskos* 2. Patristische Texte und Studien 12. Berlin: Walter de Gruyter, 1973. Trans. F. H. Chase. FC 37.

LEO OF ROME

Letters (*Ep.*). Ed. Schwartz. ACO 2.4. Trans. C. L. Feltoe. NPNF 2.12.

Sermons (*Serm.*). Ed. A. Chavasse. CCSL 138–138A. Trans. Jane Patricia Freeland and Agnes Josephine Conway. FC 93.

Tome to Flavian (*Ep. 28.*) (*Tome*). Ed. Schwartz. ACO 2.2.1.24–33. Trans. William Bright, *Select Sermons of St. Leo the Great on the Incarnation, with His Twenty-Eighth Epistle, Called the Tome,* 2nd ed. London: Masters, 1886: 109–23.

LEONTIUS OF BYZANTIUM

Against the Aphthartodocetists (*C.Aphth.*). PG 86.1.1315–53.

Against the Nestorians and Eutychians (*C.Nest.Eut.*). PG 86.1.1268–1314.

Solutions to the Arguments Proposed by Severus (*Sol.Sever.*). PG 86.2.1915–45.

MARCELLUS OF ANCYRA

Fragments (*Frag*). Markell von Ankyra, *Die Fragmente, Der Brief an Julius von Rom.* Ed. and trans. Markus Vinzent. Supplements to Vigiliae Christianae 39. Leiden: Brill, 1997.

MAXIMUS CONFESSOR

Ambigua ad Iohannem (*Ambig.* 6–71). PG 91.1061–1418. *Ambig.* 7 trans. Robert
  Wilken; 8, 42 trans. Paul Blowers. St Maximus the Confessor, *On the Cosmic
  Mystery of Jesus Christ.* Popular Patristics Series 25. Crestwood, NY: St.
  Vladimir's Seminary Press, 2003: 45–95. *Ambig.* 10, 41, 71 trans. Andrew
  Louth, *Maximus the Confessor.* Routledge Early Church Fathers. London:
  Routledge, 1996: 94–168.

Ambigua ad Thomam (*Ambig.* 1–5). Ed. Bart Janssens. CCG 48. *Ambig.* 1, 5 trans.
  Louth, *Maximus the Confessor,* 169–79.

Dialog with Pyrrhus (*Pyrrh.*). PG 91.288–353.

Opuscula (*Opusc*). PG 91.9–285. *Opuscule* 7 (the "Tome to Marinus") trans.
  Louth, *Maximus the Confessor,* 180–91.

Questions and Doubts (*Quaest.*). Ed. José Declerck. CCG 10. Trans. Despina D.
  Prassas, *St. Maximus the Confessor's Questions and Doubts.* DeKalb, IL:
  Northern Illinois University Press, 2010.

ORIGEN OF ALEXANDRIA

Against Celsus (*C.Cels.*). Ed. Marcel Borret. SC 132, 136, 147, 150, 227. Trans.
  Henry Chadwick, *Origen: Contra Celsum.* Cambridge: Cambridge University
  Press, 1965.

Commentary on Romans (*Com.Rom.*). Ed. Caroline P. Hammond Bammel. SC 532,
  539. Trans. Thomas Scheck. FC 103–4. Cited by section number in Hammond
  Bammel, which are different from those in Scheck.

Commentary on the Gospel of John (*Com.Jn.*). Ed. Cécile Blanc. SC 120, 157, 222,
  290, 385. Trans. Ronald E. Heine. FC 80, 89.

Commentary on the Gospel of Matthew (*Com.Mt.*). Ed. Erich Klostermann. GCS
  40.1–2. Books 1–2, 10–14 trans. John Patrick. ANF 10.413–512.

Commentary on the Song of Songs (*Com.Song*). Ed. Luc Brésard, Henri Crouzel,
  and Marcel Borret. SC 375–76. Trans. R. P. Lawson. Origen, *The Song of
  Songs: Commentary and Homilies.* ACW 26.

Dialog with Heraclides (*Heracl.*). Ed. Jean Scherer. SC 67. Trans. Robert J. Daly.
  ACW 54.

Exhortation to Martyrdom (*Ex.Mart.*). Ed. Paul Koetschau. GCS 2. Trans.
  Rowan A. Greer. Origen, *An Exhortation to Martyrdom, Prayer, and
  Selected Works.* Classics of Western Spirituality. New York: Paulist Press,
  1979:41–79.

First Principles (*Princ.*). Ed. Henri Crouzel and Manlio Simonetti. SC 252, 253,
  268, 269, 312. Origen, *On First Principles.* Trans. Henry Butterworth.
  Gloucester, MA: Peter Smith, 1973.

Fragments on the Psalms (*Frag.Ps.*). Ed. Carl Lommatzsch, *Origenes Opera Omnia*
  13. Berlin: Haude and Spener, 1831–1848.

Homilies on Genesis (Hom.Gen.). Ed. Louis Doutreleau. SC 7. Trans. Ronald E.
Heine. FC 71.

Homilies on Isaiah. Ed. Maria Ignazia Danieli. Origen, *Omelie su Isaia*. Rome:
Città nuova editrice, 1996.

Homilies on Jeremiah (Hom.Jer.). Ed. Pierre Nautin. SC 232, 238. Trans. John
Clark Smith. FC 97.

Homilies on 1 Kings (Hom.1Kg). Ed. Klostermann. GCS 3.

Homilies on Leviticus (Hom.Lev.). Ed. Borret. SC 286–87. Trans. Gary Wayne
Barkley. FC 83.

Homilies on Numbers (Hom.Num.). Ed. Doutreleau. SC 415, 442. Trans. Thomas
P. Scheck. Origen, *Homilies on Numbers*. Downers Grove, IL: IVP Academic,
2009.

Homilies on 1 Samuel (Hom.1Sam.). Ed. Pierre and Marie-Thérèse Nautin. SC 328.

Homily on the Witch of Endor (Hom.Endor). Ed. Simonetti, *La Maga di Endor:
Origene, Eustazio, Gregorio di Nissa*. Biblioteca Patristica 15. Florence:
Nardini, 1989. Trans. Rowan A. Greer and Margaret Mitchell, *The "Belly-
Myther of Endor": Interpretations of 1 Kingdoms 28 in the Early Church*. SBL
Writings from the Greco-Roman World 16. Atlanta: Society of Biblical
Literature, 2007.

On Prayer (Prayer). Ed. Koetschau. GCS 3.297–403. Trans. Greer, *Origen: An
Exhortation to Martyrdom, Prayer*, 81–170.

Philocalia (Phil.). Ed. Marguerite Harl and Éric Junod. SC 302, 226. Trans.
George Lewis, *The Philocalia of Origen*. Edinburgh: T&T Clark, 1911.

Scholia on Revelation (Schol.Apoc.). Ed. Constantin Diobouniotis and Adolf von
Harnack, *Der Scholien-Kommentar des Origenes zur Apokalypse Johannes, nebst
einim Stück aus Irenaeus, liber V, graece*. Texte und Untersuchungen 38.3.
Leipzig: J. C. Hinrichs, 1912.

PAMPHILUS OF CAESAREA

Apology for Origen (Apol.). Ed. René Amacker and Éric Junod. SC 464, 465.
Trans. Thomas P. Scheck. FC 120.

PHILO OF ALEXANDRIA

On the Giants (Giants). Philo of Alexandria, *The Contemplative Life, The Giants,
and Selections*. Ed. and trans. David Winston. Classics of Western Spirituality.
New York: Paulist Press, 1981.

PHILOSTORGIUS

Ecclesiastical History (H.E.). Ed. Joseph Bidez and Friedhelm Winkelmann. GCS
21. Sozomen, *The Ecclesiastical History of Sozomen: Comprising a History of
the Church from A.D. 324 to A.D. 440, Translated from the Greek with a Memoir*

of the Author. Also, *The Ecclesiastical History of Philostrogius, as Epitomized by Photius*. Trans. Edward Walford. London: H. G. Bohn, 1855.

PHOTIUS OF CONSTANTINOPLE

Bibliotheca (*Bibl.*). Ed. René Henry. Photius, *Biblioteque*. Paris: Belles Lettres, 1959–91.

PLATO

Phaedo (*Phaed.*). Ed. Martin von Schantz. Trans. Harold North Fowler. LCL 36.
Republic (*Rep.*). Ed. Martin Wohlrab. Trans. Paul Shorey. LCL 237, 276.
Sophist (*Soph.*). Ed. and trans. Harold North Fowler. LCL 123.
Symposium (*Symp.*). Ed. Schanz. Trans. W. R. M. Lamb. LCL 166.

PROCLUS OF CONSTANTINOPLE

Tome to the Armenians (*Tome*). Ed. Johannes Straub. ACO 4.2.187–95.

RUFINUS OF AQUILEIA

On the Falsification of Origen's Books (*Falsif.*) Ed. René Amacker and Éric Junod. SC 464–65.

SEXTUS EMPIRICUS

Outlines of Pyrrhonism (*Pyrr.*). Ed. Herman Mutschmann, *Sexti Empirici Opera* 1. Leipzig: Teubner, 1912. Trans. Julia Annas and Jonathan Barnes. Sextus Empiricus, *Outlines of Skepticism*. 2nd ed. Cambridge: Cambridge University Press, 2000.

SOCRATES

Ecclesiastical History (*H.E.*). PG 67.33–841. Trans. A. C. Zenos. NPNF 2.2.1–178.

SOZOMEN

Ecclesiastical History (*H.E.*). Ed. Joseph Bidez. SC 306, 418, 495. Trans. Chester D. Hartranft. NPNF 2.2.179–427.

TERTULLIAN

On the Flesh of Christ (*Flesh*). Ed. E. Kroymann. CSEL 70.189–250. Trans. P. Holmes. ANF 3.521–42.

THEODORET

Dialogs (*Eranistes*) (*Dial.*). Ed. Gerard H. Ettlinger. Theodoret, *Eranistes: Critical Text and Prolegomena*. Oxford: Clarendon Press, 1975. Trans. Blomfield Jackson. NPNF 2.3.160–449.

Ecclesiastical History (*H.E.*). Ed. Felix Scheidweiler. GCS 44. Trans. Jackson. NPNF 2.3.33–159.

History of Heresies (*Comp.Haer.*). PG 83.335–556.

THEODOSIAN CODE

Theodosian Code (*Cod.Th.*). Ed. Paul Krüger, Theodore Mommsen, and Paul Meyer, *Theodosiani Libri XVI cum Constitutionibus sirmondianis*. 3rd ed. 3 vols. Hildesheim: Weidmann, 2002–2005. Trans. Clyde Pharr, *The Theodosian Code and Novels*. New York: Greenwood, 1969.

MODERN SOURCES

Anatolios, Khaled. *Athanasius: The Coherence of His Thought*. Routledge Early Christian Monographs. London: Routledge, 1998.

Ayres, Lewis. *Nicaea and Its Legacy: An Approach to Fourth-Century Trinitarian Theology*. Oxford: Oxford University Press, 2006.

Bagnall, Roger, and Dominic Rathbone. *Egypt from Alexander to the Copts*. London: British Museum Press, 2004.

Bardy, Gustave. "Aux origines de l'ecole d'Alexandrie." *Recherches de science religieuse* 27 (1937): 65–90.

Barnes, Timothy D. *Athanasius and Constantius: Theology and Politics in the Constantinian Empire*. Cambridge, MA: Harvard University Press, 2001.

———. *Constantine and Eusebius*. Cambridge, MA: Harvard University Press, 1981.

Barthellos, Demetrios. *The Byzantine Christ: Person, Nature, and Will in the Christology of Saint Maximus the Confessor*. Oxford Early Christian Studies. Oxford: Oxford University Press, 2004.

Bavel, Tarsicius J. van. *Recherches sur la christologie de saint Augustin*. Fribourg: Éditions Universitaires, 1954.

Beeley, Christopher A. "Cyril of Alexandria and Gregory Nazianzen: Tradition and Complexity in Patristic Christology." *Journal of Early Christian Studies* 17.3 (2009): 381–419.

———. "The Early Christological Controversy: Apollinarius, Diodore, and Gregory Nazianzen." *Vigiliae Christianae* 65.2 (2011): 1–32.

———. "Eusebius Contra Marcellum: Anti-Modalist Doctrine and Orthodox Christology." *Zeitschrift für Antikes Christentum* 12.3 (2009): 433–52.

———. *Gregory of Nazianzus on the Trinity and Knowledge of God*. Oxford Studies in Historical Theology. New York: Oxford University Press, 2008.

———. "Gregory of Nazianzus on the Unity of Christ." In *In the Shadow of the Incarnation: Essays on Jesus Christ in the Early Church in Honor of Brian E. Daley, SJ*, ed. Peter Martens, 97–120. South Bend, IN: University of Notre Dame Press, 2008.

Behr, John. *The Nicene Faith*. 2 vols. The Formation of Christian Theology. Crestwood, NY: St. Vladimir's Seminary Press, 2004.

Berkhof, Hendrick. *Theologie des Eusebius*. Amsterdam: Uitgeversmaatschappij, Holland, 1939.

Böhm, Thomas. *Die Christologie des Arius: Dogmengeschichtliche Überlegungen unter besonderer Berücksichtigung der Hellenisierungsfrage*. St. Ottilien: EOS Verlag, 1991.

Bostock, Gerald. "Origen and the Pythagoreanism of Alexandria." *Origeniana Octava* (2003): 465–78.

———. "Quality and Corporeity." *Origeniana Secunda* (1980): 323–37.

Bouchet, J.-R. "Le vocabulaire de l'union et du rapport des natures chez saint Grégoire de Nysse." *Revue Thomiste* 68 (1968): 533–38.

Boulnois, Marie-Odile. *Le paradoxe Trinitaire chez Cyrille D'Alexandrie: Herméneutique, analyses philosophiques et argumentation théologique*. Collection des Études Augustiniennes, Série Antiquité 143. Paris: Institut d'Études Augustiniennes, 1994.

Brakke, David. "Athanasius." In *The Early Christian World*. 2 vols, ed. Philip F. Esler, 1102–27. London: Routledge, 2000.

———. *Athanasius and the Politics of Asceticism*. Oxford Early Christian Studies. Oxford: Clarendon, 1995.

Burckhardt, Jacob. *Die Zeit Constantins des Grossen*. 2nd ed. Leipzig: E. A. Seemann, 1880.

Canévet, Mariette. *Grégoire de Nysse et l'herméneutique biblique: Étude des rapports entre le langage et la connaissance de Dieu*. Paris: Études augustiniennes, 1983.

Carriker, Andrew James. *The Library of Eusebius of Caesarea*. Supplements to Vigiliae Christianae 67. Leiden and Boston: Brill, 2003.

Chadwick, Henry. "The Chalcedonian Definition." In *Actes du Concile de Chalcédoine: Sessions III–VI (La Définition de la Foi)*, ed. A. J. Festugière, 3–12. Cahiers d'Orientalisme 4 (Geneva, 1983).

———. "Eucharist and Christology." *Journal of Theological Studies* n.s. 2 (1951): 150–51.

Clark, Elizabeth A. *The Origenist Controversy: The Cultural Construction of an Early Christian Debate*. Princeton: Princeton University Press, 1992.

Connybeare, F. C., and St. George Stock. *A Grammar of Septuagint Greek*. Grand Rapids, MI: Zondervan, 1980.

Crouzel, Henri. *Origen*. Trans. A. S. Worall. San Francisco: Harper and Row, 1989.

———. *Théologie de l'Image de Dieu chez Origène*. Théologie 34. Paris: Aubier, 1956.

Daley, Brian E. "Divine Transcendence and Human Transformation: Gregory of Nyssa's Anti-Apollinarian Christology." *Modern Theology* 18.4 (2002): 497–506.

——. "The Giant's Twin Substances: Ambrose and the Christology of Augustine's *Contra sermonem Arianorum*." In *Augustine: Presbyter Factus Sum*, ed. Joseph Lienhard, Earl Muller, and Roland Teske, 477–96. Collectanea Augustiniana. New York: Peter Lang, 1993.

——. *God Visible: Patristic Christology Reconsidered*. The 2002 D'Arcy Lectures in the University of Oxford (forthcoming).

——. *The Hope of the Early Church: A Handbook of Patristic Eschatology*. Cambridge: Cambridge University Press, 1991.

——. "A Humble Mediator: The Distinctive Elements in Saint Augustine's Christology." *Word and Spirit* 9 (1987): 100–17.

——. "Making a Human Will Divine: Augustine and Maximus on Christ and Human Salvation." In *Orthodox Readings of Augustine*, ed. George E. Demacopoulos and Aristotle Papanikolaou, 101–26. Crestwood, NY: St. Vladimir's Seminary Press, 2008.

——. "'One Thing and Another': The Persons in God and the Person of Christ in Patristic Theology." *Pro Ecclesia* 15 (2006): 17–46.

——. "Origen's 'De Principiis': A Guide to the 'Principles' of Christian Scriptures Interpretation." In *Nova et Vetera: Patristic Studies in Honor of Thomas Patrick Halton*, ed. John Petruccione, 3–21. Washington, DC: Catholic University of America Press, 1998.

——. "'A Richer Union': Leontius of Byzantium and the Relationship of Human and Divine in Christ." *Studia Patristica* 24 (1993): 239–65.

Davis, Stephen J. *The Early Coptic Papacy: The Egyptian Church and Its Leadership in Late Antiquity*. The Popes of Egypt 1. Cairo and New York: American University in Cairo Press, 2004.

Dively Lauro, Elizabeth. "The Anthropological Context of Origen's Two Higher Senses of Scriptural Meaning." *Origeniana Octava* 1 (2003): 613–24.

Dorival, Gilles. "Les débuts du christianisme à Alexandrie." In *Alexandrie: Une mégapole cosmopolite: Actes du 9ème colloque de la Villa Kérylos à Beaulieu-sur-Mer les 2 & 3 Octobre 1998*, 157–74. Paris: Académie des Inscriptions et Belles-Lettres, 1999.

Dossetti, Giuseppe. *Il simbolo di Nicea e di Costantinopoli: Edizione critica*. Testi e ricerche di scienze religiose 2. Rome: Herder, 1967.

Doucet, Marcel. "Dispute de Maxime le Confesseur avec Pyrrhus. Introduction, texte critique, traducion et notes." Diss.: University of Montreal, 1972.

Drake Harold. *In Praise of Constantine: A Historical Study and New Translation of Eusebius' Tricennial Orations*. UC Publications in Classical Studies 15. Berkeley: University of California Press, 1976.

Drobner, Hubertus. *Person-Exegese und Christologie bei Augustinus: Zur Herkunft der Formel Una Persona*. Philosophia Patrum 8. Leiden: Brill, 1986.

Duchesne, Louis. *L'Église au VIe siècle*. Paris: Ancienne Librairie Fontemoing, 1925.

Edwards, Mark J. "Ammonius, Teacher of Origen." *Journal of Ecclesiastical History* 44 (1993): 169–81.

——. *Catholicity and Heresy in the Early Church*. Franham: Ashgate, 2009.

——. "First Council of Nicaea." In *The Cambridge History of Early Christianity*. Vol. 1: *Origins to Constantine*, ed. Margaret M. Mitchell and Frances M. Young, 552–67. Cambridge: Cambridge University Press, 2006.

——. *Origen against Plato*. Ashgate Studies in Philosophy and Theology in Late Antiquity. Aldershot: Ashgate, 2002.

Egan, John. "Primal Cause and Trinitarian *Perichoresis*: Saint Gregory the Theologian, *Oration* 31.14." *Greek Orthodox Theological Review* 39 (1994): 83–93.

Eger, Hans. "Kaiser und Kirche in der Geschichtstheologie Eusebius' von Cäsarea." *Zeitschrift für die Neutestamentliche Wissenschaft* 38 (1939): 97–115.

Field, Lester L. *On the Communion of Damasus and Meletius: Fourth-Century Synodal Formulae in the "Codex Veronensis LX."* PIMS Studies and Texts 145. Toronto: Pontifical Institute of Mediaeval Studies, 2004.

Frend, W. H. C. *The Rise of the Monophysite Movement: Chapters in the History of the Church in the Fifth and Sixth Centuries*. Cambridge: Cambridge University Press, 1972.

Fuks, Alexander. "Aspects of the Jewish Revolt." *Journal of Roman Studies* 51 (1961): 98–104.

Grafton, Anthony, and Megan Williams. *Christianity and the Transformation of the Book: Origen, Eusebius, and the Library of Caesarea*. Cambridge, MA: Harvard University Press, 2006.

Grant, Robert M. *Eusebius as Church Historian*. Oxford: Clarendon, 1980.

Graumann, Thomas. *Die Kirche der Väter: Vätertheologie und Väterbeweis in den Kirchen des Ostens bis zum Konzil von Ephesus (431)*. Beiträge zur historischen Theologie 118. Tübingen: Mohr Siebeck, 2002.

Green, Bernard. *The Soteriology of Leo the Great*. Oxford Theological Monographs. Oxford: Oxford University Press, 2008.

Greer, Rowan A. "The Antiochene Christology of Diodore of Tarsus." *Journal of Theological Studies* 17.2 (1966): 327–41.

Grillmeier, Aloys. *Christ in Christian Tradition*. Vol. 1: *From the Apostolic Age to Chalcedon (451)*. Trans. John Bowden. London: Mowbrays, 1965. 2nd rev. ed., 1975. New German ed., *Jesus der Christus im Glauben der Kirche*. Freiburg: Herder, 1979.

——. *Das Konzil von Chalkedon*. Würzburg: Echter-Verlag, 1962.

Haas, Christopher. *Alexandria in Late Antiquity*. Baltimore: Johns Hopkins University Press, 1997.

Hahn, August, ed. *Bibliothek der Symbole und Glaubensregeln der alten Kirche*. 3rd rev. ed. Hildesheim: Georg Olms, 1962.

Halleux, André de. "Actualité du néochalcédonisme." *Revue théologique de Louvain* 21 (1990): 32–54.

Hanson, R. P. C. "Did Origen Apply the Word Homoousios to the Son?" In *Epektasis: Mélanges patristiques offerts au Cardinal Jean Daniélou*, ed. Jacques Fontaine and Charles Kannengiesser, 293–304. Paris: Beauchesne, 1972.

——. *The Search for the Christian Doctrine of God: The Arian Controversy 318–381*. Edinburgh: T&T Clark, 1988.

——. *Tradition in the Early Church*. London: SCM, 1962.

Harl, Marguerite. *Origène et la fonction révélatrice du Verbe incarné*. Patristics Sobornensia 2. Paris: Éditions du Seuil, 1958.

Heil, Uta. "Athanasius als Apologet des Christentums: Einleitungsfragen zum Doppelwerk *Contra gentes/De incarnatione*." In *Three Greek Apologists: Origen, Eusebius, and Athanasius*, ed. Anders-Christian Jacobsen and Jörg Ulrich, 159–87. Early Christianity in the Context of Antiquity 3. Frankfurt: Peter Lang, 2007.

Heine, Ronald E. "Epinoiai." In *The Westminster Handbook to Origen*, ed. John Anthony McGuckin, 93–95. Louisville, KY: Westminster John Knox, 2004.

——. *Origen: Scholarship in the Service of the Church*. Christian Theology in Context. Oxford: Oxford University Press, 2010.

Hubner, Reinhard M. *Die Einheit des Leibes Christi bei Gregor von Nyssa*. Leiden: Brill, 1974.

Jacobsen, Anders-Christian. "Christology in the Homilies of Origen." *Origeniana Nona* (2009):637–52.

——. "Origen on the Human Body." *Origeniana Octava* (2003): 649–56.

Jakab, Attila. *Ecclesia alexandrina: Evolution sociale et institutionelle du christianisme alexandrin (IIe et IIIe siècles)*. Bern: Peter Lang, 2001.

Jasper, R. C. D., and G. J. Cumming. *Prayers of the Eucharist: Early and Reformed*. 3rd ed. Collegeville, MN: Liturgical Press, 1987.

Jensen, Robin. M. *Face to Face: Portraits of the Divine in Early Christianity*. Minneapolis, MN: Fortress, 2005.

Johnson, Maxwell E. *The Prayers of Sarapion of Thumis: A Literary, Liturgical, and Theological Analysis*. Orientalia Christiana Analecta 249. Rome: Pontificio Istituto Orientale, 1995.

Kannengiesser, Charles. "Christ/Christology." In *Westminster Handbook to Origen*, ed. John Anthony McGuckin, 25–26. Louisville, KY: Westminster John Knox Press, 2004.

Keating, Daniel. *The Appropriation of Divine Life in Cyril of Alexandria*. Oxford Theological Monographs. Oxford: Oxford University Press, 2004.

Kelber, Wilhelm. *Die Logoslehre: Von Heraclit bis Origenes*. Stuttgart: Verlag Urachhaus, 1958.

Kelly, J. N. D. *Early Christian Doctrines*. 3rd ed. San Francisco: HarperSanFrancisco, 1978.

Layton, Bentley. "The Significance of Basilides in Early Christian Thought." *Representations* 28 (1989): 135–51.

Liébaert, Jacques. *La doctrine christologique de saint Cyrille d'Alexandrie avant la querelle nestorienne*. Mémoires et travaux 58. Lille: Facultés catholiques, 1951.

Lienhard, Joseph T. *Contra Marcellum: Marcellus of Ancyra and Fourth-Century Theology*. Washington, DC: Catholic University of America Press, 1999.

Lieske, Alois. *Die Theologie der Logos-Mystik bei Origenes*. Münsterische Beiträge zur Theologie 22. Münster: Aschendorff, 1938.

Lightfoot, Joseph. "Eusebius of Caesarea." In *Dictionary of Christian Biography*, ed. William Smith and Henry Wace, vol. 2, 308–49. London: John Murray, 1880.

Löhr, Winrich. "Arius Reconsidered (Part 1)." *Zeitschrift für Antikes Christentum* 9 (2005): 524–60.

———. "Arius Reconsidered (Part 2)." *Zeitschrift für Antikes Christentum* 10 (2006): 121–57.

Lorenz, Rudolf. *Arius Iudaizans? Untersuchung zur dogmengeschichtliche Einordnung des Arius*. Forschungen zur Kirchen- und Dogmenschichte 31. Göttingen: Vandenhoeck und Ruprecht, 1980.

Louth, Andrew. *Maximus the Confessor*. The Early Church Fathers. London: Routledge, 1996.

———. *St. John Damascene: Tradition and Originality in Byzantine Theology*. Oxford Early Christian Studies. Oxford: Oxford University Press, 2002.

Lyman, Rebecca. "Arius and Arians." In *The Oxford Handbook of Early Christian Studies*, ed. Susan Ashbrook Harvey and David G. Hunter, 237–57. Oxford: Oxford University Press, 2008.

———. *Christology and Cosmology: Models of Divine Activity in Origen, Eusebius, and Athanasius*. Oxford Theological Monographs. Oxford: Clarendon, 1993.

———. "A Topography of Heresy: Mapping the Rhetorical Creation of Arianism." In *Arianism after Arius: Essays on the Development of the Fourth Century Trinitarian Conflicts*, ed. Michael Barnes and Daniel Williams, 45–62. Edinburgh: T&T Clark, 1993.

Mansi, J. D., ed. *Sacrorum Conciliorum Nova et Amplissima Collectio*. 31 vols. Florence: Expensis Antonii Zatta, 1759–1798.

May, Gerhard. "Die Chronologie des Lebens und der Werke des Gregor von Nyssa." In *Écriture et culture philosophique dans la pensée de Grégoire de Nysse*, ed. Marguerite Harl, 51–66. Leiden: Brill, 1971.

McGuckin, John A. "Life of Origen (ca. 185–255)." In *The Westminster Handbook to Origen*, ed. John Anthony McGuckin, 1–23. Louisville, KY: Westminster John Knox, 2004.

———. *Saint Cyril of Alexandria and the Christological Controversy: Its History, Theology, and Texts*. Supplements to Vigiliae Christianae 23. Leiden: Brill, 1994. Reprint Crestwood, NY: St. Vladimir's Seminary Press, 2004.

———. "The Scholarly Works of Origen." In *The Westminster Handbook to Origen*, ed. John Anthony McGuckin, 25–41. Louisville, KY: Westminster John Knox, 2004.

McKinion, Stephen. *Words, Imagery, and the Mystery of Christ: A Reconstruction of Cyril of Alexandria's Christology*. Supplements to Vigiliae Christianae 55. Leiden: Brill, 2000.

McLynn, Neil B. *Ambrose of Milan: Church and Court in a Christian Capital*. Transformation of the Classical Heritage 22. Berkeley: University of California Press, 1994.

Mélèze-Modrzejewski, Joseph. *The Jews of Egypt: From Ramses II to Emperor Hadrian*. Princeton, NJ: Princeton University Press, 1997.

Meredith, Anthony. *Gregory of Nyssa*. The Early Church Fathers. London: Routledge, 1999.

Mühlenberg, Ekkehard. *Apollinaris von Laodicea*. Forschungen zur Kirchen- und Dogmengeschichte 23. Göttingen: Vandenhoeck und Ruprecht, 1969.

Murray, Mary Charles. "Art and the Early Church." *Journal of Theological Studies* 28 (1977): 303–45.

Nautin, Pierre. *Lettres et Écrivains Chrétiens des IIe et IIIe siècles*. Patristica 2. Paris: Éditions du Cerf, 1961.

———. *Origène: Sa vie et son oeuvre*. Christianisme antique 1. Paris: Beauchesne, 1977.

Neuschäfer, Bernhard. *Origenes als Philologe*. Schweizerische Beiträge zur Altertumswissenschaft 18. Basel: Friedrich Reinhardt, 1987.

Newman, John Henry. *The Arians of the Fourth Century*. 3rd ed. London: E. Lumley, 1871.

O'Cleirigh, Padraig. "The Dualism of Origen." *Origeniana Quinta* (1992): 346–50.

Opitz, Hans-Georg. "Euseb von Caesarea als Theologe." *Zeitschrift für die Neutestamentliche Wissenschaft* 34 (1935): 1–19.

Parvis, Sara. *Marcellus of Ancyra and the Lost Years of the Arian Controversy, 325–345*. Oxford Early Christian Studies. Oxford: Oxford University Press, 2006.

———. "Τὰ τίνων ἄρα ῥήματα θεολογεῖ?: The Exegetical Relationship between Athanasius's *Orationes contra Arianos* I–III and Marcellus of Ancyra's *Contra Asterium*." In *The Reception and Interpretation of the Bible in Late Antiquity. Proceedings of the Montréal Colloquium in Honour of Charles Kannengiesser, 11–13 October 2006*, ed. L. DeTommaso and L. Turcescu. The Bible in Ancient Christianity 6. Leiden: Brill, 2008.

Pearson, "Earliest Christianity in Egypt: Some Observations." In *The Roots of Egyptian Christianity*, ed. Birger A. Pearson and James E. Goehring, 132–59. Studies in Antiquity and Christianity. Philadelphia: Fortress, 1986.

———. "Egypt." In *The Cambridge History of Christianity*. Vol. 1: *Origins to Constantine*, ed. Margaret M. Mitchell and Frances M. Young, 331–50. Cambridge: Cambridge University Press, 2006.

———. *Gnosticism and Christianity in Roman and Coptic Egypt*. Studies in Antiquity and Christianity. London: T&T Clark, 2004.

Pettersen, Alvyn. "A Reconsideration of the Date of the *Contra Gentes–De Incarnatione* of Athanasius of Alexandria." *Studia Patristica* 18 (1982): 1030–40.

Piret, Pierre. *Le Christ et la Trinité selon Maxime le Confesseur*. Théologie Historique 69. Paris: Beauchesne, 1983.

Pottier, Bernard. *Dieu et le Christ selon Grégoire de Nysse: Étude systématique du "Contre Eunome" avec traduction inédite des extraits d'Eunome*. Série Ouvertures 12. Namur: Culture et vérité, 1994.

Price, Richard M. "The Council of Chalcedon (451): A Narrative." In *Chalcedon in Context: Church Councils 400–700*, ed. Richard Price and Mary Whitby, 70–91. Translated Texts for Historians, Contexts 1. Liverpool: Liverpool University Press, 2009.

Radde-Gallwitz, Andrew. *Basil of Caesarea, Gregory of Nyssa, and the Transformation of Divine Simplicity*. Oxford Early Christian Studies. Oxford: Oxford University Press, 2009.

Ramelli, Ilaria. "Origen's Anti-subordinationism and Its Heritage in the Nicene and Cappadocian Line." *Vigilae Christianae* 65 (2011): 21–49.

Ramelli, Ilaria, and David Konstan. *Terms for Eternity: Aiônios and Aïdios in Classical and Christian Texts*. Piscataway, NJ: Gorgias, 2007.

Refoulé, François. "La christologie d'Évagre et l'origénisme." *Orientalia Christiana Periodica* 27 (1961): 221–66.

Richard, Marcel. "Saint Athanase et la psyhologie du Christ selon les Ariens." *Mélanges de science religieuse* 2 (1947): 5–54.

Ricken, Friedo. "Nikaia als Krisis des altchristlichen Platonismus." *Theologie und Philosophie* 44 (1969): 321–41.

Roberts, Colin H. *Manuscript, Society, and Belief in Early Christian Egypt*. The Schweich Lectures of the British Academy, 1977. London: Oxford University Press, 1979.

Rowe, Nigel J. *Origen's Doctrine of Subordination: A Study in Origen's Christology*. European University Studies 272. Bern: Peter Lang, 1987.

Runia, David T. "Origen and Hellenism." *Origeniana Octava* (2003): 43–47.

———. *Philo in Early Christian Literature: A Survey*. Compendium Rerum Iudaicarum ad Novum Testamentum 3.3. Minneapolis, MN: Fortress, 1993.

Schwartz, Eduard. *Kaiser Constantin und die christliche Kirche*. Leipzig: Tuebner, 1936.

Siddals, Ruth M. "Logic and Christology in Cyril of Alexandria." *Journal of Theological Studies* 38 (1987): 341–67.

Simonetti, Manlio. *La Crisi Ariana nel IV Secolo*. Studia Ephemeridis Augustinianum 11. Rome: Institutum Patristicum Augustinianum, 1975.

Smith, J. Warren. *Christian Grace and Pagan Virtue: The Theological Foundation of Ambrose's Ethics*. Oxford Studies in Historical Theology. New York: Oxford University Press, 2010.

———. "Suffering Impassibly: Christ's Passion in Cyril of Alexandria's Soteriology." *Pro Ecclesia* 11 (2002): 463–83.

Stead, Christopher. "The Word 'from nothing.'" *Journal of Theological Studies* 49 (1998): 671–84.

Strutwolf, Holger. *Die Trinitätstheologie und Christologie des Euseb von Caesarea: Eine dogmengeschichtliche Untersuchung seiner Platonismusrezeption und Wirkungsgeschichte*. Forschungen zur Kirchen- und Dogmengeschichte 72. Göttingen: Vandenhoeck and Ruprecht, 1999.

Telfer, William. "Episcopal Succession." *Journal of Ecclesial History* 3 (1952): 1–13.

Thunberg, Lars. *Microcosm and Mediator: The Theological Anthropology of Maximus the Confessor*. 2nd ed. Chicago: Open Court, 1995.

Trigg, Joseph W. *Origen*. The Early Church Fathers. London: Routledge, 1998.

Vaggione, Richard Paul. *Eunomius of Cyzicus and the Nicene Revolution*. Oxford Early Christian Studies. Oxford: Oxford University Press, 2000.

Van Dam, Raymond. *The Roman Revolution of Constantine*. New York: Cambridge University Press, 2007.

Van den Broek, Roelof. "Juden und Christen in Alexandrien im 2 und 3 Jahrhundert." In *Juden und Christen in der Antike*, ed. J. van Amersfoort and J. van Oort, 101–15. Kampen, Netherlands: J. H. Kok, 1990.

Van den Hoek, Annewies. "The 'Catechetical School' of Alexandrian Christianity and Its Philonic Heritage." *Harvard Theological Review* 90.1 (1997): 59–87.

——. "Origen's Role in Formulating Later Christological Language: The Case of ἀνάκρισις." In *Origeniana Septima* (1999): 39–50.

Vinzent, Markus. "Die Entstehung des 'Römischen Glaubensbekenntnisses.'" In *Tauffragen und Bekenntnis: Studien zur sogenannten "Traditio Apostolica," zu den "Interrogationes de fide" und zum "Römischen Glaubensbekenntnis,"* ed. Wolfram Kinzig, Christoph Markschies, and Markus Vinzent, 185–409. Arbeiten zur Kirchengeschichte 74. Berlin: Walter de Gruyter, 1999.

——. *Markell von Ankyra: Die Fragmente und der Brief an Julius von Rom.* Supplements to Vigilae Christianae 39. Leiden: Brill, 1997.

Vivian, Tim. *Saint Peter of Alexandria: Bishop and Martyr.* Studies in Antiquity and Christianity. Philadelphia: Fortress, 1988.

Wallace-Hadrill, David. *Eusebius of Caesarea.* London: A. R. Mowbray, 1960.

Weber, Anton. *APXH: Ein Beitrag zur Christologie des Eusebius von Cäsarea.* Munich: Verlag Neue Stadt, 1965.

Weedman, Mark. *The Trinitarian Theology of Hilary of Poitiers.* Supplements to Vigiliae Christianae 89. Leiden: Brill, 2007.

Weinandy, Thomas G. "Cyril and the Mystery of the Incarnation." In *The Theology of St. Cyril of Alexandria: A Critical Appreciation*, ed. Thomas G. Weinandy and Daniel A. Keating, 23–54. London: T&T Clark, 2003.

Wessel, Susan. *Cyril of Alexandria and the Nestorian Controversy: The Making of a Saint and a Heretic.* Oxford Early Christian Studies. Oxford: Oxford University Press, 2004.

——. *Leo the Great and the Spiritual Rebuilding of a Universal Rome.* Supplements to Vigiliae Christianae 93. Leiden: Brill, 2008.

Widdicombe, Peter. *The Fatherhood of God from Origen to Athanasius.* Oxford Theological Monographs. Oxford: Clarendon, 1994.

Wiles, Maurice F. *Archetypal Heresy: Arianism through the Centuries.* Oxford: Clarendon, 1996.

Williams, Daniel H. *Ambrose of Milan and the End of the Nicene-Arian Conflicts.* Oxford Early Christian Studies. Oxford: Oxford University Press, 1995.

Williams, Rowan. *Arius: Heresy and Tradition.* London: Darton, Longman and Todd, 1987.

——. "Augustine's Christology: Its Spirituality and Rhetoric." In *In the Shadow of the Incarnation: Essays on Jesus Christ in the Early Church in Honor of Brian E. Daley, SJ*, ed. Peter W. Martens, 176–89. South Bend, IN: University of Notre Dame Press, 2008.

——. "*Damnosa Haereditas*: Pamphilus' *Apology* and the Reputation of Origen." In *Logos: Festschrift für Luise Abramowski zum 8. Juli 1993*, ed. Hanns Christoff Brennecke, Ernst Ludwig Grasmück, and Christoph Markschies,

151–69. Beihefte zur Zeitschrift für die neutestamentliche Wissenschaft und die Kunde der älteren Kirche 67. Berlin: Walter De Gruyter, 1993.

———. "Origen between Orthodoxy and Heresy." *Origeniana Septima* (1999):3–14.

Young, Frances M. *From Nicaea to Chalcedon: A Guide to the Literature and Its Background*. Philadelphia: Fortress, 1993.

———. "Monotheism and Christology." In *The Cambridge History of Christianity*. Vol. 1: *Origins to Constantine*, ed. Margaret M. Mitchell and Frances M. Young, 452–70. Cambridge: Cambridge University Press, 2006.

———. "A Reconsideration of Alexandrian Christology." *Journal of Ecclesiastical History* 22 (1971): 103–14.

General Index

253–54; Eusebius of Caesarea's response
to, 58–59, 103–4
Proclus of Constantinople, 306
prosopon/πρόσωπον, 81–82, 141, 153–54,
176, 206, 282–83, 287, 291
Prosper of Aquitaine, 274
Protoctetus, Caesarean priest, 8
Protogenes, 123
psilanthropism, 54, 61–62, 87, 336
Pulcheria, 278
Pythagorean philosophy, 13

resurrection, 12, 53–54, 106, 114, 131, 196, 210,
239, 325, 337; of the body: spiritual, 15–17,
43. *See also* Jesus Christ
Rufinus of Aquileia, 50
rule of faith, the, 175, 188; Nicaea I and,
120; Origen on, 10–11, 13, 19, 22–23, 44,
51, 53, 114

Sabellius/Sabellianism, 63, 72, 84, 123, 142,
160, 162, 198
Saturninus, 99
Scripture: authority of, 5, 9–12, 15, 45, 49, 51,
56, 79, 116, 126, 140, 242, 256–58, 280;
Eusebius of Caesarea, 88–89; inspired by
the Holy Spirit, 61, 63, 89; multiple voices
in, 239–40; source of the knowledge of the
distinct existence of Father, Son, and Holy
Spirit, 20; source of knowledge of Christ,
18; theophanies in, 213, 228, 242, 246–48.
See also biblical interpretation
Septimius Severus, Emperor, 6
Septuagint, 4
Seth, 29
Sethians, 52
Severus of Antioch, 286, 299
Simeon the New Theologian, 183
Son of God, 13, 87, 203–4; adapts himself
toward creatures, 29–31; anointed eternally
with the Holy Spirit, 215; as *arche* of God,
18; chief title of Christ, 18–20, 79; not the
chief title of Christ, 128, 141–42, 203;
communicative principle of God, 19,
28–31, 228; created from nothing, 111, 121;
distinct existence of (*See* modalism,
arguments against); like the Father, 148,
173; like the Father according to the
Scriptures, 175; like the Father in all things,
90, 114, 149, 173; like the Father in being,

148–49, 160, 173; unlike the Father in
being, 173–175; God from God, 52, 72,
86–87, 121–22; as hypostasis, 20, 31, 69, 86,
115, 172, 204; incorporeal, 19–20, 27, 43,
73–74, 94, 127, 133, 136, 215, 218, 267–68,
317; ineffable, 7, 18, 33, 66, 72, 98;
immutable, 21, 94, 121, 182; inseparable
from God the Father, 19, 23–26, 34, 36, 53,
91, 114, 243, 269; invisible, 19, 31–32,
42–45, 73, 112, 127, 135, 188, 227, 274,
322–23; Life, 18–20, 28, 37, 39, 41, 80,
87–88, 120, 122, 208–9, 247, 346; Light, 18,
34, 66, 80, 94–95, 112, 120, 166, 190, 320;
Light from Light, 23–24, 28, 30–31, 72, 87,
115, 120–22, 147–50, 196, 322; not Light
from Light, 91; mediator between God and
creatures, 13, 30–31, 52, 70–71, 74, 88, 92,
114, 127, 129, 147–48, 203–4, 211, 218, 237,
245, 151–55, 273–74, 291, 305; medium of
prayer to God, 20, 22, 166–67, 190,
237–40; mystery of, 8–86; in the Old
Testament, 68, 191; oneness of, 18, 73, 80,
145, 159–60, 166, 227; only-begotten
(μονογενής), 17–18, 21, 23, 43, 66–67–
68, 72, 79–81, 84, 87–88, 90, 94–95, 110,
114, 121, 143, 167, 190, 226, 295, 297, 305;
revealer, 28–33, 37–38, 44–45, 68–74, 79,
84–89, 115, 130, 135–36, 147–48, 152, 167,
206, 226–28, 242–43, 247–48, 250–55, 299,
345; second to God the Father, 53, 66–68,
70–71, 110, 317, 319; simple, 21, 29, 321;
theos, 21, 23, 149, 319; "there was a time
when he was not," 90–91, 117, 121; there
never was a time when he was not, 24, 52;
true God from true God, 88, 121–22, 167,
196, 345; truly son, 20, 73, 120, 141, 150,
161, 226; Truth, 13, 18–19, 25–28, 37, 39,
41, 150, 168, 247, 254, 322; Way, 30, 39, 41,
247–48, 251, 324. *See also* God the Father;
Jesus Christ; suffering, divine; Wisdom of
God; Word of God
—born only once, divinely: Chalcedon,
282–84; Diodore, 182; Gregory of Nyssa,
207, 219, 221; Origen, 32, 39, 34, 5
—born twice, divinely and humanly:
Ambrose, 231; Apollinarius, 182;
Athanasius, 132–33; Augustine, 238,
243–44; Constantinople II, 295;
Constantinople III, 303; Cyril, 268–69;
Eusebius, 86; Gregory Nazianzen, 184,

190, 192, 339–40; Gregory of Nyssa, 213;
Hilary, 228; John of Damascus, 305; Leo
of Rome, 274, 347
—divinity of: Alexander, 115; Ambrose, 231,
234; Augustine, 236–40, 244–51, 254;
Caesarean creed, 120; Chalcedon, 282–84;
Constantinople I, 196–97; Constantinople
II, 295; Constantinople III, 303–4; Cyril of
Alexandria, 261–64, 266, 269–70; essential
divinity and existence, 21–22, 26; Eusebius
of Caesarea, 63, 65, 84; Hilary, 226–27;
John of Damascus, 305–6; Leo of Rome,
274; Maximus, 297–301; Nicaea I, 121–23;
Origen, 17–19, 21–22, 27–29
—exact image of the Father: Alexander, 114,
116; Athanasius, 129, 147–49, 336;
Dedication Creed of Antioch (341), 172;
Origen, 30
—generation of, 10, 23–27, 52–54, 66–68,
71–72, 79–80, 84, 86–93, 110–11, 114–16,
121–23, 142, 151, 154, 159, 196, 226–27, 231,
290, 320, 332–33; without division or
passion, 24; eternal, 10, 23, 26, 52, 67, 72,
86, 91, 110, 114, 116, 121, 123, 142, 172, 231,
320; by God's will, 25–26, 91, 111, 115–16,
151, 333; incorporeal, 23–25, 114, 122;
ineffable, 72, 89, 114; inseparable, 23–26,
53, 114, 122; out of the being of the Father,
122, 150–51, 161; transcendent, 23–27, 88,
92–93, 114, 320–21; unknowable, 24, 86; in
unity, 23–26
—image of God the Father: Alexander, 114,
116, 149; Athanasius, 129–32, 147–50, 159,
161; Dedication Creed of Antioch (341),
172; Eusebius of Caesarea, 70–71, 80, 88,
90, 95; Gregory Nazianzen, 204; Hilary,
227–28; Marcellus against, 141–43, 335;
Origen, 25, 29–32, 38, 40, 42–43, 52, 112,
139, 168, 206, 321–22
soul, 53; ascent beyond the body, 14–17, 43,
318; controversy over the nature of, 12;
freedom of, 53; human beings as, 15;
liberation of, 254; preexistence of, 54, 106,
323–25; a principle of faith, 11; source of
sin, 233; transmigration of, 54; union with
God, 316; weak, 228–29. See also Jesus
Christ, human mind/soul of
Stephen, martyr, 97
Stoic ethics, 13
subordinationism, 10, 106; Eusebius accused

of, 55; homoian, 173–75; Marcellus seeks to
avoid, 82; Origen accused of, 17, 54
suffering, affirmation of divine: Ambrose,
231–32; Augustine, 244; Cyril, 268–69;
Gregory Nazianzen, 187, 191–93, 266;
Leo, 274
suffering, denial of divine: Apollinarius, 179;
Athanasius, 133–35, 138–39, 156, 164–65,
168–69, 267; Diodore, 182; Eusebius of
Caesarea, 94; Gregory of Nyssa, 206–7,
209–11, 219–20; Hilary, 229; John of
Damascus, 308; Maximus, 296; Origen, 36,
41, 44–45

Tatian, 61
Terennius of Scythis, 198
Tertullian, 58, 225, 227
Theoctistus of Caesarea, 8
Theodore of Mopsuestia, 179–80, 209,
258–59, 283, 294
Theodoret of Cyrus, 61, 278, 294
Theodosius, Emperor, 179–80, 194–95, 198,
272; Theodosian settlement, 167, 212
Theodosius II, Emperor, 278
Theodotus the Cobbler, 61
Theognostus, 106, 158
theology/theologizing, 61–62, 64–65, 66,
68–69, 79, 83–86, 92, 184, 197, 205, 208.
See also economy
Theonas of Alexandria, 106
Theophilus of Alexandria, 200, 212
Three Chapters controversy, 294
Timothy of Alexandria, 198
Trinity, the, 27, 45, 52, 54, 100; Athanasius,
138–39, 159; Augustine, 241–43, 246–47,
255; and biblical theophanies, 246–48;
central mystery of the faith, 85, 142;
Chalcedon, 283, 286; versus Christology,
189; Cyril of Alexandria, 260; economic
only, 142; Father-Son language
theologically superior to Creator-creature,
174, 226; Gregory Nazianzen, 183, 296;
Gregory of Nyssa, 204, 210, 219–20;
Hilary, 226–27; Leontius of Byzantium,
290; Marcellus, 141–44; Maximus
Confessor, 295; monistic view of, 141–42;
mystery of, 85; "one of the Holy Trinity
was crucified in the flesh," 295; order
within, 89, 91; plurality within, 159–60;
principle of existence of all things, 90;

Scripture Index